King
of the
Mountain

King of the Mountain

The Nature of Political Leadership

ARNOLD M. LUDWIG

THE UNIVERSITY PRESS OF KENTUCKY

Publication of this volume was made possible in part by a grant
from the National Endowment for the Humanities.

Editorial and Sales Offices: The University Press of Kentucky
663 South Limestone Street, Lexington, Kentucky 40508<n>4008

06 05 04 03 02   5 4 3 2 1

Library of Congress Cataloging-in-Publication Data

Ludwig, Arnold M.
King of the mountain : the nature of political leadership / Arnold M. Ludwig.
   p. cm.
   ISBN 0-8131-2233-3 (cloth : alk. paper)
   1. Political leadership. 2. Political leadership—Psychological aspects.
3. Politicians—Psychology. I. Title.
JC330.3 .L83 2001
303.3'4—dc21

                                    2001007227

With appreciation
to Anne and Dan
&
to Lucinda and Gary
for enriching my life

Most play included some form
of wrestling and chasing, and games such as
"king of the mountain" and "follow the leader."

—G.B. Schaller, *The Mountain Gorilla*

CONTENTS

Illustrations

INTRODUCTION

> Initially I often had to wait for up to a half an hour, pretending to
> feed on foliage, before the gorillas gave in to their inquisitiveness and
> climbed trees surrounding me. Once their curiosity was satisfied,
> they would resume their usual activities, forgetting that I was there.
> This is what I had come to observe.
>
> —Dian Fossey, *Gorillas in the Mist*

In this book, I present the results of my eighteen-year investigation into why rulers want to rule and what, if anything, distinguishes them from other kinds of people.[1] As part of this investigation, I have examined many aspects of rulers and ruling that never have been studied before. My assorted findings have led me to develop a new theory about why people seek ultimate political power and tend to cling to it as long as possible.

As it happens, the timing of my project was fortunate since it gave me a chance to approach these issues from a *fin de siècle* perspective. The subjects for my study include all the primary rulers of all the independent countries in the world during what I call a "baker's century" (one hundred plus one years), from January 1, 1900, through December 31, 2000, which covers both the popular notion of and the actual time frame of the twentieth century. With this method of selection, I was able to identify 1,941 rulers from 199 countries.[2] The figure below gives the percentages of rulers within the different geographical regions. With a group this size, I was able to establish base rates for the first time ever for certain kinds of important information on rulers, such as how they came to power, how they lost power, and the dangers they faced.

Then, for a more probing analysis of the lives, character, careers, and mental health of rulers, I was able to do an in-depth study of a large sample on whom more extensive personal information was available.[3] The method I hit upon to do this was to capitalize on the work of experts who already had decided which world leaders were worthy enough to have biographical entries in the online *Encyclopaedia Britannica* or the *Encyclopedia Americana*, the two most authoritative reference sources.

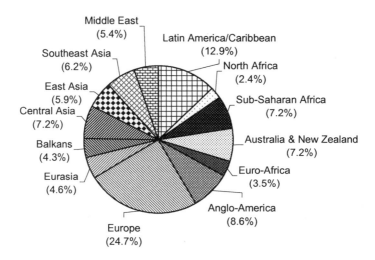

Worldwide Distribution of Twentieth-Century Rulers

Middle East (5.4%)
Latin America/Caribbean (12.9%)
Southeast Asia (6.2%)
North Africa (2.4%)
East Asia (5.9%)
Sub-Saharan Africa (7.2%)
Central Asia (7.2%)
Australia & New Zealand (7.2%)
Balkans (4.3%)
Euro-Africa (3.5%)
Eurasia (4.6%)
Anglo-America (8.6%)
Europe (24.7%)

Among those rulers with entries, I identified 377 who had sufficient other biographical information available about them to answer the many probing questions I had. This sample of rulers included virtually all the rulers in the world over the past century who had a major impact on their countries, as well as many who had not, and was the largest group of rulers ever assembled to be studied in depth.

During the course of my studies, I read over twelve hundred full-length biographies, treatises, theses, and political accounts about these rulers; consulted the historical dictionaries of various countries and regions; read the relevant topical biographies included in a series of books published by the Greenwood Press; gathered supplementary material from newspaper articles and magazines; surfed the Internet for interesting tidbits about leaders; and made full use of such online databases on rulers as are offered by the Library of Congress Area Handbooks, the Central Intelligence Agency publications, the World Ruler website, the Lexus-Nexus® Academic Universe, and various other informational sources. Aside from reviewing all the appropriate encyclopedia material, I also was fortunate to have access to perhaps the most comprehensive information source on rulers, Harris Lentz's two-volume work, *Heads of States and Governments: A Worldwide Encyclopedia*, which I supplemented with material from numerous *Europa* volumes and the *Political Handbook of the World*.[4]

In reporting my findings and observations, I wrestled with how technical to be. Since I was writing this book for general readers rather than specialists, I wanted the narrative to be sufficiently substantive, entertaining, and enlightening that it would not put them to sleep. The way I decided to resolve this dilemma was to sprinkle the main narrative with enough facts and figures to make my points but not enough to make it seem like a dull scientific treatise and to make liberal use of appendices and chapter notes. That way readers could have their pick. They could learn what they wanted to about rulers and ruling without delving too much into academic issues, or, if they wanted something more meaty to devour, they could pore over the detailed discussion about methodology and statistical results in the appendices.

At the outset, I need to set the record straight. Although this book is about political leaders, I do not pose as an expert on politics. To be sure, like most people who try to keep up with the news, I have opinions about politics, but I am not a political scientist, a sociologist, a historian, or a political correspondent. In fact, I have a general antipathy toward politicking and take pride in the fact that I never was elected to any office in my life. What I am is a psychiatrist who simply prefers to consider himself a student of human nature. In that capacity, my interest is in the actual people who govern and their relationship with their subjects rather than in forms of government and the mechanics of governance. So with that qualification about my abilities and interests, I trust I will be forgiven if I do not always describe political situations in the proper academic ways, which I prefer to believe gives me an advantage, and even more unorthodox, if I do not always look upon politics as a distinctly human activity.

1

WHY RULERS RULE

At first sight Yeroen's supremacy seemed to rest on unparalleled physical strength. Yeroen's bulk and his self-assured manners gave rise to the naive assumption that a chimpanzee community is governed by the law of the strongest. Yeroen looked much stronger than the second adult male, Luit. This false impression was created by the fact that in the years of his supremacy Yeroen's hair was constantly slightly on end—even when he wasn't actively displaying—and he walked in an exaggerat- edly slow and heavy manner. This habit of making the body look deceptively large and heavy is characteristic of the alpha male, as we saw again later when the other individuals filled this role. The fact of being in a position of power makes a male physically impressive, hence the assumption that he occupies the position that fits his appearance.
—Frans de Waal, *Chimpanzee Politics*

Why do people want to rule? You may think the reason is obvious—power, privilege, and perks—but it's not. Nor does it have anything to do with the more high-minded motives of patriotism, duty, and service. What I hope to show is that all of the usual reasons aspiring rulers give for seeking high office are simply rationalizations by them to do what they are socially and biologically driven to do. Just as the orgastic pleasures associated with sex ensure procreation and contribute to the preservation of the species— regardless of the reasons people give for copulating, such as doing it for love, intimacy, or fun—the rewards that come with ultimate power likewise serve as powerful motivators for would-be rulers to do Nature's bidding.

WHAT NEEDS TO BE EXPLAINED

During the course of my investigation into the lives and careers of 1,941 twentieth-century rulers, I uncovered a number of puzzling findings.

Certain of these findings seemed obvious, but few people had bothered before to ask what they might mean. Other findings seemed contradictory. Yet other findings were so startling that I found it hard to believe they had not been reported before. Any adequate theory about the nature of ruling needs to explain all of these findings. No theory to date does.

Here is what needs to be explained.

- *All nations have rulers.*[1] This fact is almost a truism. It is simply the way things are. Yet people should not take it for granted, since it is a remarkable happening. It represents a clear statement about the way societies work. Despite times of anarchy and the attempts of collective forms of government, such as troikas, juntas, councils, or assemblies, to diffuse executive power, one person usually emerges sooner or later to take charge of the country. Whether countries happen to be democracies or dictatorships, the people eventually want one person at the helm whom they can identify as their leader.
- *Essentially all the rulers of all the nations in the world during the past century have been men.* Despite the advances made by women during the last part of this past century, especially in democratic nations, males still dominate the global political scene. Even more telling, no woman rules as a dictator or wields absolute power. If a wily and persistent Eve could have tempted a rather dull-witted Adam to defy the Lord's instructions and eat the forbidden fruit, then surely more clever and resourceful women throughout the ages should have been able to circumvent male hegemony in society at large and displace them as rulers, despite being handicapped by the burden of child-bearing, a relative lack of strength, and the oppressive efforts of men to keep them in their place.
- *In many societies throughout the world, male rulers have a decided breeding advantage over other men, not only in their access to women but also in the size of the harems and the number of mistresses they keep.* Among the different kinds of rulers, a relationship seems to exist between the relative amount of authority they hold and the extent of their sexual promiscuity, which, in turn, has a direct bearing on the size of their brood. Monarchs and tyrants, for instance, who seem to look upon the fertilization of nubile women as one of their sacred duties, are much more fecund than leaders of emerging and established democracies, who exercise less power.
- *No identifiable form of intelligence, talent, genius, or even experi-*

ence seems necessary for ruling a country. Would-be rulers do not have to pass qualifying examinations in leadership or demonstrate competence in administration or show skill in diplomacy. They do not need to have good communication skills or even be popular with their subjects. While many leaders are imaginative, worldly, and intelligent, others are pedestrian, narrow-minded, and ignorant, which suggests that demonstrated ability or achievement has little to do with securing the highest office in the land.

• *Leaders need not be sane, rational, or even mentally competent to rule a country.* My results reveal high rates of alcoholism, drug use, depression, mania, and paranoia among certain kinds of rulers. Remarkably, over this past century, many rulers even have managed to keep power despite being floridly crazy or demented.

• *Although intellectual or academic credentials seem irrelevant for ruling, one of the time-honored ways individuals establish their qualifications for leadership is by showing physical prowess and courage in battle.* If a David can slay a Goliath, then he is worthy of being crowned a king. Being a fierce "warrior" is important for being a hero, and being a hero is important for being a ruler. Therefore, it is not surprising to find that in many regions of the world a military career is a prerequisite for becoming a ruler and, in those regions where it is not, being a lawyer, who uses words as weapons, is a popular profession.

• *Many leaders who come to power forcibly do not seem to learn from the mistakes of past rulers.* Nor are most really interested in consulting with their predecessors and potentially benefitting from their advice. This suggests there is something about ruling or the people who become rulers that fosters a kind of personal grandiosity that blinds them to political reality and lets them believe they will be able to accomplish in the future what ex-rulers were unable to do in the past.

• *In many instances, would-be rulers risk their lives to gain ultimate power and, once they have it, risk their lives to keep it.* Sometimes they cling to power so tenaciously that they even ignore warnings about their imminent death. These are not occasional happenings. As my results reveal, the mortality rate among all rulers worldwide due to assassination, execution, and suicide is astounding, making ruling the most dangerous professional activity known.

• *Throughout history, rulers who attain legendary status often tend to be those who have conquered other nations, won major wars, ex-*

panded their country's boundaries, founded new nations, forcibly trans-
formed their societies, and imposed their own beliefs on their subjects.
In short, they have killed, plundered, oppressed, and destroyed. Rarely
do rulers achieve greatness who have been ambassadors for peace,
kept the status quo, defended free speech, promoted independent
thinking, and avoided wars at all costs.

HUMANS ARE ANIMALS, TOO

While it is possible to come up with sociological, religious, or psychological theories for all of these observations, no credible explanation of
ruling can ignore the potential influences of biology—although almost
all past and current theories about leadership do! Missing from all explanations of political behavior to date is the simple fact that humans
are mammals who belong to the order of primates, the family of homi-
nids, the genus of homo, and the species of sapiens. As primates, they
share the characteristics of other higher primates and so can be expected
to act at times like monkeys and apes. Once you accept this reality, everything else about the process of becoming and being a ruler begins to
make sense.

By comparing the behaviors of individuals with those of their simian ancestors, I am not trying to disparage the political activity of humans—nor, for that matter, of other primates. I am only saying there is a
dimension of ruling that has not yet been adequately explored. People
may choose to ignore their animal heritage by interpreting their behavior as divinely inspired, socially purposeful, or even self-serving, all of
which they attribute to being human; but they masticate, defecate, mas-
turbate, fornicate, and procreate much as chimps and other apes do, so
they should have little cause to get upset if they learn that they act like
other primates when they politically agitate, debate, abdicate, placate,
and administrate, too.

As it happens, of all the fields of human endeavor, politics seems to
be the one most rooted in primitive primate behavior. The natural and
social sciences rely heavily on information-gathering, problem-solving,
and reasoning. The arts rely heavily on creative expression, intuition,
and the exercise of special skills. In contrast to the arts and sciences, which
require the use of mankind's highest mental faculties, located largely in
the neocortex, the most evolutionarily advanced part of the brain, the
striving for political power seems fueled more by secretions from man's
nether parts—his gonads and adrenal glands—as well as activity from

within the limbic system and hypothalamus, the most ancient parts of the brain, all of which deal with such instinctive responses as fight-or-flight, territoriality, aggression, sex, and survival.

By saying that potential neurophysiological and hormonal factors influence political activity, I am not suggesting that rulers do not rely heavily on their higher critical faculties as well, which certainly are necessary for managing the complexities of government and the formulation of economic and social politics. It is a matter of emphasis. In the arts and sciences, the creative and problem-solving activities of individuals seem to stem from the natural curiosity and exploratory activity often shown by our simian ancestors, which seem to be more evolutionarily advanced forms of mental activity than the expression of dominance, aggression, and territoriality, which are common to ruling but are likewise found in many lower forms of animal life. In the arts and the sciences, man's higher cognitive functions are put to use largely in the service of his curiosity about the world and himself, whereas in his striving for ultimate power they are put to use for the expression of the even more primitive instincts found in animal life forms antedating the existence of monkeys and apes.

There are other differences between the arts and sciences and politics to consider. Within the arts and the sciences, individuals give performances, produce works, or create actual products that bear their personal mark and become identified with them. In politics, aspiring leaders come to power through fulfilling certain social expectations and winning people over to them. Because they usually have no identifiable work product attributed exclusively to them other than their ability to get others to comply with their wishes, people's reaction to them often depends more on their personal biases, beliefs, and vested interests than on any critical appraisal of a specific body of work. Instead of depending on brilliance, breadth of knowledge, creative problem-solving, or special talents, which are necessary for achievement in the arts and sciences, many would-be rulers seem to rely more on cunning, courage, physical prowess, deception, and power tactics to ascend the social hierarchy and gain ultimate power. That is why becoming a ruler requires no special academic training, artistic skills, or even superior intellect. That is why charisma, oratory, manipulation, and intimidation are often more important than wisdom, special expertise, and administrative experience. Humans have evolved more sophisticated and civilized methods than other primates for awarding leaders power, such as election campaigns, constitutions, and rules for succession; but, when you strip away all the trappings, the different ways that aspirants for high office jockey for power over others and keep it seem remarkably similar at times to those of our simian kin. And in many instances, such as when potential rulers resort to assassinations, wholesale killings, or armed conflicts to gain power, the human methods seem even more primitive.

It is not my intention to review the vast literature on primate behavior. Most readers are already familiar with the importance of dominance hierarchies, the breeding advantages of the alpha male, the numerous challenges by other males to topple the reigning leader, the formation of alliances among chimps to reduce the power of the alpha male, and the responsibilities of the leader to his troupe. As such pioneers in the field of primatology as Jane Goodall, Dian Fossey, and Robert M. Sapolsky have shown,[2] the resemblances between how chimps, gorillas, and baboons establish dominance and how humans do are striking. In his trailblazing books, *Chimpanzee Politics* and *Peacemaking among Primates*, Frans de Waal[3] describes certain political behaviors in chimps that resemble those in humans. Certain animal purists criticized de Waal for "anthropomorphizing" the activities of chimps; that is, imputing human motives to their behaviors instead of interpreting them as unique to chimps. My approach, which mirrors his, may evoke a more negative reaction. I shall be interpreting the political activities of humans on the basis of behaviors observed in chimps, baboons, and gorillas, "simianizing" or "primatomorphizing" them, if you will. Now, that does not mean I do not see many kinds of political behaviors as unique to humans, with no obvious analogue in other primates. There are important differences. For instance, although humans and baboons may fight among themselves, dominate others, and keep harems, only humans have the ability to give pious excuses for what they do.

UNSEEN FORCES AT WORK

A Head for the Body Politic

As a result of my studies, I have come to the conclusion that the reason people want to rule is the same reason all societies want a ruler: *It is part of the natural order of things.* Just as every person needs a head, every society needs a leader. Just as any head with a brain will do for controlling the body, any leader will do for controlling the body politic. The existence of a leader is simply a matter of completeness. This may seem like a trivial observation on my part, but it is not. It has enormous implications. The compelling need for a leader, often *any* leader, is the only way to account for many of the rulers who have emerged during this past century. Just as the brain serves as a nerve center for integrating all the incoming messages from the physical body, the leader assumes executive control of the social body, with responsibility for coordinating the actions of its component parts. Not every brain lets the body function optimally. Likewise, there is no rule that a leader will carry out his social role wisely or well; he simply needs to do it. Except for rare periods of social anarchy or political chaos, there always will be a leader or, if not, a multi-headed ruling body until a suitable leader emerges, because the body politic cannot function independently on its own.

To demonstrate that my notion about the importance of a single leader serving as the head of a social body is not entirely fanciful, I cite the observation made by G.B. Schaller, who conducted the classical study on mountain gorillas, on the central role of the leader in the gorilla community.[4]

The focal point of each group is the leader, who is, without exception, the dominant silver-backed male. The entire daily routine—the time of rising, the direction and distance of travel, the location and duration

1.1: Silverback gorilla. Between the ages of nine and ten, adult males turn silver. Blackbacks have been reported to turn silver prematurely after assuming leadership. Photograph by Nancy Staley/WRPC AV Archives.

of rest periods, and finally the time of nest building—is largely determined by the leader. Every independent animal in the group, except occasionally subordinate males, appears to be constantly aware of the location and activity of the leader either directly or through the behavior of animals in his vicinity. Cues reflecting a changed pattern of activity are rapidly transmitted through the group and the subsequent behavior of the members is patterned after that of the leader. This response insures cohesiveness and co-ordination of action. The complete adherence of gorillas to one leader must be considered in all discussions of groups, for variations in behavior between groups tend to reflect individual idiosyncracies of the leader.

What G.B. Schaller observed with respect to the importance of a leader for mountain gorillas, I claim also applies for humans, although perhaps in less dramatic ways. From the vantage point of the social unit, it probably makes little difference if the leader is brilliant, fair, capricious, stupid, or insane, just as it makes little difference for the existence of a family unit if either parent has those qualities. That does not mean a social unit is as well off with a deficient head as with a competent one; it only means that a country can exist as a social unit with one or the other. What matters is that the country has an acknowledged leader to guide it and that he stays in charge until someone else replaces him. In such a political cauldron, you would expect to find a wide range of personality types among rulers having no single attribute in common except for their fervent desire to rule—a situation, as you will see, that corresponds to what actually exists. Although rulers drawn to certain kinds of rule share certain features, rulers in general come from all levels of society; represent every race, color, and creed; show the gamut of intelligence and imagination; and have almost every kind of quality.

The need for a single leader to be head of a social unit seems biologically and psychologically rooted in our being. It is part of the genetic blueprint that governs our lives. The drive to be the alpha male provides the basic impetus for the dominance hierarchy, which, with the apparent exception of the bonobos,[5] seems to govern most social interactions among higher primates. In humans, this need for a strong male leader becomes powerfully reinforced within the family unit. Born as helpless infants, people could not survive without their parents to nourish and protect them during their early years of dependency. Almost universally in ancient times but still common in most societies today, the traditional family unit represents a totalitarian state in microcosm, with each member of the family playing a distinctive role. The mother raises the children and runs the household. The children obey their parents, compete among themselves for their attention and love, and model their behavior after them. And the father serves as provider, protector, and ultimate authority.

In Roman times, for instance, the father, as *paterfamilias*, was the absolute ruler of his household.[6] His very word was law, and his actions did not need justification. Within the bounds of his household, he could do and say anything he wished. No law of the senate and people of Rome interfered with his absolute authority over his household. If any member of his family—from his wife through his sons and his daughters to his mother and other dependents—transgressed the bounds of what he regarded as decent conduct, he personally could have him or her killed. And he could act as arbitrarily as he was inclined, because Rome had structured its laws to ensure that the Roman family was above the law of all but the paterfamilias.

With man's notions of authority rooted in his relations to his parents and the role of the paterfamilias in the family, it is no wonder that, once he leaves his parents' household, he still should carry within him this need for an all-powerful, totalitarian parent and would fashion for himself a male god whose rule is absolute, arbitrary, and often whimsical, too. In fact, in most societies, God is portrayed as the Ultimate Alpha Male (i.e., "Thou shalt have no other God before me."), with even absolute kings and powerful despots claiming obeisance to Him. Just as it is not up to a child to fathom the father's intentions, it is not up to humans to fathom God-the-Father's intentions. They simply must do whatever the authority figure directs. Then, with a father as ruler of the family and a God-the-Father as ruler of the universe, it becomes inevitable that humans also should look to the ruler of their society to treat them in similar, paternalistic ways. So it seems that in essentially all of their major relationships with others—their relationship with their family, their relationship with society, and their relationship with God—most humans have been socially, psychologically, and biologically programmed with the need for a single dominant male figure to govern their communal lives. And this programming corresponds closely to how almost all anthropoid primate societies are run.

A Breeding Advantage for Rulers

With a social status comparable to that of the alpha male, human rulers during the past century seem to have shown a sexual prowess similar to what likely existed millions of years ago after early primates evolved and later when their Neanderthal ancestors roamed the land. From what we know about the mating behavior of other primates, especially chimpanzees, the alpha male has far greater access to females in estrus than any subordinate male. In fact, it is clear that Nature does not qualify as being an equal opportunity employer to get baboons, chimps, and gorillas to do its bidding. With respect to perpetuating the species, it clearly discriminates in favor of dominant males. For example, research studies with talapoin monkeys show that subordinate males do not experience a rise in their plasma testosterone levels when caged with sexually attractive females if the dominant male of the group is present. However, their plasma testosterone levels shoot up when the dominant male is absent.[7] Dominant males do not even have to bare their teeth to frighten potential competitors away from their females; their presence alone ensures that they will be the only ones with sexual access. As happened with Sir Lancelot and Lady Guinevere, when the leader goes away, subordinates get a chance to play.

If you can read any intent to Nature, which Charles Darwin implicitly gave us permission to do, you may assume that the breeding advantage reserved for alpha males among primates was to be for the general benefit of the species. Supposedly, the superior genes of the alpha males, which were associated with strength, ferocity, and perhaps cunning, would be passed down through the process of natural selection as part of a genetic upgrade and would thereby increase the chances of survival for the entire species. It is interesting that the mating patterns and sexual activities of the twentieth-century rulers seemed to mimic those of their early primate kin in certain remarkable ways. As the supposed thoroughbreds of the ruling world—with bloodlines selected for such royal traits as mediocrity, intellectual shallowness, self-indulgence and certain genetic aberrations—kings, sheiks, emperors, and assorted monarchs, especially those with more absolute powers, seem to have acted as the personal emissaries of Nature by producing impressive-sized broods. Among the other kinds of rulers, as I shortly will show, tyrants, as political parvenus who likewise aspire to royalty and sometimes crown themselves as emperor or heap even more exalted titles upon themselves, almost match the reproductive feats of true monarchs, but not quite.

What needs to be recognized in the case of these rulers is that it is not only the size of the brood that matters. Any ordinary brute male can sire umpteen children, although he may not have adequate resources to feed, house, and clothe them. What is so special about these particular rulers is that they have sexual access to multiple women, usually some of the most attractive ones in the land, and keep fertilizing them. From an evolutionary standpoint, this match-up between the most dominant man and the most beautiful women in the kingdom should produce a richer genetic mix of offspring than if they confined their activities to only one or two breeding partners. Through the process of natural selection, the "superior" progeny of the ruler (= having many of the ruler's traits) supposedly should have an evolutionary advantage over the "inferior" progeny (= having none of the ruler's traits). As a result, the superior progeny then theoretically should continue to provide comparable levels of topnotch leadership for society.

It is perhaps in the sexual practices of rulers that you find the construct of Nature, like all humans, also has clay feet, or can goof, so to speak. What could Nature have been thinking or not thinking (or the equivalent of thinking or not thinking in a construct that has no objective reality) when it gave those with ultimate power rather than those with ultimate wisdom the breeding advantage? With monarchs and tyrants having the largest broods and leaders of established democracies having the smallest, Nature was making a clear statement where it stood as far as the future evolution of humans went. It did not give a damn about the advancement of civilization and the fostering of wise, peace-loving rulers; being strong, ferocious, and perhaps cunning mattered more. Among our simian ancestors, these traits helped males establish dominance within the social hierarchy; and, among humans, they seem to help establish social dominance, too, especially in societies favoring more autocratic forms of rule.

What all of these observations suggest is that the only condition necessary for being a ruler is to be one. Throughout much of recorded history, the best way to become one was through military prowess or risking one's life. A conquering hero not only gave people a chance to share in his glory but also to partake in any booty confiscated from defeated tribes, city-states, or nations. The body politic really did not care about the hero's knowledge of economics, administrative skills, breadth of vision, or academic background. What mattered most was for him to show the basic attributes of the alpha male beneath a social veneer of civilized behavior. He should not kill, plunder, pillage, and rape for his own pleasure or benefit. If he wanted to be revered by the people, he had to do all these things for the greater glory of Rome or some other worthy cause.

With the growing trend toward democratic governments, rulers no longer need to establish their credentials for high office by being ferocious warriors or military heroes. Although the attributes associated with being an alpha male are still important for leadership, they can appear in less obvious ways. In democracies there are no outright physical battles to establish political dominance among contestants, but something meta-phorically equivalent still takes place during elections. It is therefore no accident that so much military terminology should be used to describe political "campaigns."[8] Opponents do "battle" and "face off" against each other in debates and speeches. They raise a "war chest" to support their campaign. They classify others as "doves or hawks." They do not bare their teeth or pound their chests or display their rears, but each candi-date presents himself as tougher and more qualified than the other. They try to maintain control over the "rank and file" and keep them from "breaking rank." With tough decisions, they "hold the line," "bite the bullet," or "stick to their guns." Their advisors offer them "briefings." They wage a "war of words," "attack" the positions of the other, or "ride roughshod" over the opposition. Opponents accuse them of doing an "about face" or being guilty of "appeasement." They call out the "big guns" or create a "task force" to deal with difficult matters and declare "wars" on poverty or drugs or crime. They resort to "dirty tricks," use "under-handed tactics," or "stonewall" the press. The loser "concedes defeat" to the victor after an election. And then victory celebrations are held. So although new democratic leaders do not actually take power by physical force, they engage in symbolic battles through their words. Perhaps that is why more lawyers than soldiers become leaders in democracies.

That does not mean it is not important for democratic leaders to be heroes. That would be an added bonus. Although many democratic lead-ers had shown courage in battle before coming to office, the vast major-ity of them were more politically handicapped than dictators by their relative lack of opportunities to do so. So they had to find other aggres-sive outlets to show that they had what it took to be rulers. As my results reveal, democrats were more likely than other types of rulers to have been active in competitive sports during their youths and early adult-hood, which at least gave them a chance to show their physical prowess on the playing field. And if they did not have a chance to defeat competi-tors in athletic contests or kill enemies in battle before being elected to high office, they sometimes could compensate for these deprivations once they became ruler and assumed the accompanying role of com-mander-in-chief of the armed services. As already noted, hardly any democratic leader could expect to achieve lasting fame and win the acclaim of his people unless he successfully tested his courage and resolve in battle, killed lots of people in wars, and assumed responsibility for others' lives.

Sometimes this expectation for showing physical prowess can tax the imagination of rulers who seek to gain some measure of lasting fame but are operating under unfair political constraints. How, for instance, can a ruler show his courage and daring if he is the president of a democracy but does not have any army to command? That is a real problem, but certain of our rulers have shown amazing resourcefulness and imagination in still finding opportunities to be manly—and oftentimes stupid, qualities that more often than not tend to be associated. José Figueres, president of Costa Rica (1953–58 and 1970–74), who abolished the army and gave women the right to vote, was such a ruler. Fortune smiled upon him one day when he learned that hijackers had forced a jet airliner to land in his country for refueling. He became so incensed that he rushed to the airport and, once there, burst from his car with a machine gun and began running toward the plane, only to be restrained by the guards.[9] What he hoped to achieve by charging the plane like a madman other than to get himself and all the hostages killed is hard to fathom. But this question never was raised by the media who were present and able to witness his "heroic" act.

An Endless Supply of Would-be Rulers

My results establish that ruling is a very dangerous activity. How then does Nature ensure that there always will be an endless supply of potential leaders despite the risks involved or the hopelessness of the political situation? In some countries, no sooner does one leader depose or kill another than another would-be leader topples him. Even when the political situation is chaotic or doomed to failure, someone is always ready to step in.

The reason that would-be leaders are always ready to try their hand at ruling seems to be because they have little other choice. Just as when a man physically confronts another, causing the other man to become physiologically primed for fight or flight, any vacuum in leadership seems to unleash powerful social and biological forces within potential candidates to ensure that any power void will not exist for too long. The absence of a leader, even the weakening of one already in power, fuels whatever glowing embers of ambition were present in potential prospects, inciting them to vie for ultimate power themselves. The tendency for this response seems coded in their genes and represents a latent archetypal response in much the same way as male chimps and baboons must challenge the existing leader whenever they sense they have the slightest chance to win—and often even when they do not. Someone has to fill the vacant role of ruler or supplant a perceived-to-be weakened leader.

Studies on primates show that social events themselves can change their physical appearance along with producing increases in plasma testosterone and androgen levels, which generally correspond with the amount of aggression and ferocity they then display. For instance, while silverback male gorillas usually change their coloration between nine or ten years old, they have been observed to turn silver prematurely upon becoming a leader. With olive baboons in the wild, when the dominance hierarchy is stable and all subordinates know their relative place, the top-ranked males are not especially aggressive and have relatively normal levels of testosterone. However, during periods of social instability, as when the alpha male is wounded, the top-ranked males in the dominance hierarchy become very aggressive, and their testosterone levels peak. It is as if the event itself reflexively triggers a physiological response in them that prepares them to do battle and begin vying for the top-ranked position.[10]

One feature common to all aspirants for high office is that, once they gain a scent of real power, the more obsessed by it they become, even if they had never consciously had this ambition before. The chance to acquire ultimate power begins to relieve any doubts they may have had beforehand about their qualifications to rule. From the way prospective rulers catch fire with ambition, it seems that some as-yet-undiscovered chemical—perhaps a human analogue of catnip—gets released in their brains and begins to affect their judgment. Even the subordinate males, who had never seriously indulged in fantasies about ruling, begin to get grandiose twinges about what remarkable things they could do if only they were in charge.

Because of the metamorphosis that occurs in people when they become potential candidates for ultimate power, an endless supply of understudies is always available in the wings, ready to come onstage to assume the part of leader and already equipped with scripts that have been written in their genes and edited by their cultures, even when their reason tells them they would be foolhardy to do so. It is as if they experience a kind of "state-dependent learning" whereby what they know while in a rational state of mind, such as the dangers of being a ruler, gets rationalized away when they become suffused with ambition, perhaps because different neurophysiological states underlie these different frames of mind.[11] Once they begin to believe that they have a legitimate chance to become the alpha male (and often even when they do not), they readily drop most of the reservations they may have had beforehand about their suitability for the role or the reality of the dangers involved and begin vying for the position, doing what they are socially, psychologically, and, most important, biologically primed to do.

This rationalization process is evident in the following letter from Abubakar Tafawa Balewa, who was to become the first federal prime minister of Nigeria, to a British official he regarded as a friend, asking for advice about whether to run for prime minister.

> I am forced to write to you on my personal problems. I am now think-ing very much about my future. The climate of Lagos is not suitable to my health and I am never happy here though I find the work most interesting. . . . There is much talk now about a Prime Minister for Nigeria after the Constitutional Conference and my name is being freely suggested as one. Now I do not like to be Prime Minister under the present arrangements and I also do not like to continue with my stay in Lagos. I am very tired of politics and I am seriously thinking of retiring quietly at the end of this year . . . and take up my Education work again. I have been discussing this matter with my colleagues for some time but they do not seem to appreciate my difficulties. Some of them even say to my face that only death can free me from Lagos! No British Administra-tor knows more about us in the North than you do and so I come to you for guidance in helping me to solve my personal difficulties.[12]

In his letter Abubakar clearly states that he does not want to be prime minister, that he does not want to stay in Lagos, that death awaits him if he stays in the capital, and that he is tired of politics and wants to retire quietly and take up his beloved teaching again. All that adds up to a seem-ingly clear message that he wants out of politics. In response, Sir Bryan replied there could only be one Abubakar, that his experience could not be matched, and that Nigeria's survival depended on a realistic approach, which only he could give. So what happens? Abubakar immediately drops all of his objections and goes on to become prime minister, not because of the convincing arguments of his friend but simply because his friend told him what he wanted to hear—and, in my opinion, knew what he was going to hear, since that was why he wrote that particular friend in the first place. So what happens next? As he had ominously suggested in his letter, he only would be able to leave Lagos in a coffin. That happened when he was killed in a military coup.

In other instances, individuals end up becoming rulers not because they deliberately set out to do so but because they happen to be advanta-geously positioned to be selected at opportune times. Take Imre Nagy's situation.[13] As a former premier who had been forced out of office by the Russians for his independent attitude, a reluctant Nagy was pressed into service again by the anti-Soviets during the October 1956 Hungarian Revolution. The revolutionaries needed a respected statesman to repre-sent them, and Nagy admirably filled the bill of sacrificial lamb. Although he knew failure could spell his death sentence, he let himself be elected premier, giving himself all kinds of patriotic reasons for doing so. Then, after the Soviet troops invaded Hungary, as many predicted they would, he took sanctuary in the Yugoslav embassy. Inexplicably, he then left the embassy, after which he was arrested and eventually tried. Then what he sensed would happen before he accepted the nomination actually came about. Convicted for his treachery, he was summarily sentenced and ex-ecuted. The story, though, presumably had a satisfactory ending for all concerned except for the martyred Nagy. Hungary's supreme court post-humously rehabilitated him in 1989, which, I suppose it figured, would gladden his grieving family and make up for his death.

The point is that, whenever there is a void in leadership, candidates like Nagy or Abubakar always will be ready to step in. The reason is once the hypothalamus of male primates becomes activated and stimulates their testicles to manufacture testosterone and other androgens, which increase their sexual libido, aggressiveness, and competitiveness, they are inducted into the struggle for dominance and lose all sense of perspec-tive and rationality. At that point, unbeknownst to them, they assume a role on behalf of their species that they are genetically programmed to play, regardless of the rationalizations they give for their decisions.

Then, once they finally secure ultimate power, a further transforma-tion takes place in them. In some instances, their personal appearance and manner change dramatically. Like the alpha male monkeys and apes that move about in a more upright, slow-and-sure manner, making their bodies seem larger than they are so that they can appear more ferocious and formidable to subordinates (see photo 1.2), human leaders, in re-sponse to their newly acquired power, often begin to strut about in full military regalia, with their puffed-out chests weighted down by medals attesting to their physical prowess, bravery, and masculinity. They also begin to hold forth, pontificate, and bark out orders with new authority. While the communications of rulers show no clear equivalent in their simian relatives, dominant male gorillas, baboons, and chimps do have recourse to a large repertoire of vocalizations, including hoots, pant-

1.2: Two male chimpanzees of roughly the same size demonstrate rank by creating an illusory size difference; the dominant walks upright with raised hair, the subordinate bows and pant-grunts. Courtesy of Frans de Waal.

grunts, whimpers, waa-barks, roars, lip smacks, and screeches, which likewise can rouse their cohorts to respond. The nonverbal message implicit in the dress, demeanor, and speech of these rulers is captured by the following ditty: "Roses are Red and Violets are Blue, You Think You're Special, But I'm Better Than You!"

Aside from this change in their general demeanor, an even more profound change takes place within alpha male primates once they become the leader of their community. Previously they may have been feisty malcontents and started fights with all potential competitors, but now they begin to act as social stabilizers, assuming responsibility for the defense and welfare of their community and, in many instances, acting as "peacemakers" as well.[14] Alpha males have been known to stop a fight simply by raising an eyebrow or taking a single step forward. With all of their hair erect, dominant chimpanzees can break up fights by moving between two combatants until they stop screaming, scattering them with a charging display, or literally prying locked fighters apart with both hands. As leaders, they now interfere more on the basis of how best to restore peace than on how best to keep friends.[15] This dramatic alteration in their actions makes sense when you consider that, in their new social roles as leader, they now begin to look upon their subordinates as extensions of themselves. So when serious conflicts or disturbances exist, the ruler, as head, feels compelled to restore peace within the social body as a whole.

A similar transformation in attitude and behavior often takes place in human rulers. After seizing power, those challengers who previously had been socially disruptive, rebellious, and antagonistic toward existing authorities now become passionate about preserving peace at all costs, even to the point of imposing martial law and stifling all dissension. Paradoxically, the common practice of social oppression by dictators appears to be integral to their biologically programmed peacemaker role. As leader, they are obligated to keep peace within their nation, even if that involves imprisoning and killing lots of people to do so.

Other changes also take place. Just as male gorillas, chimps, and baboons seem to swell in size and become more confident after they achieve the alpha status, rulers, once in power, also begin to show a personal expansiveness and grandiosity that comes from being the foremost person in their land. As an expression of the intoxicating effects of their social role, they typically come to believe that they are smarter than their predecessors and can handle any personal threats that come their way. So typically they often fail to heed advisors who do not tell them what they want to hear and they ignore all lessons from the past. Then after problems arise, instead of bailing out of office while they can, they have trouble fathoming the seriousness of their situation and the inevitability of their downfall. As rulers, they feel compelled to rule, even when their authority no longer exists. How else, for example, can you explain the behavior of a Tsar Nicholas during the long period before his execution, when conservatives already were trying to depose him in the hope of saving the monarchy? Even the murder of Rasputin failed to dispel his illusions about his divine right to rule. He not only ignored this ominous warning but those more urgent ones by highly placed persons, including members of his own family, and hung onto power until it was too late for all the Romanovs.

In his play, *Julius Caesar*, William Shakespeare brilliantly captures the mind-set of so many rulers who end up being executed, assassinated, or deposed despite clear warnings of these imminent events. At least two times before his assassination, the soothsayers warned Caesar to beware of the Ides of March. On the night before he was to go to the senate, where the planned assassination was to take place, his wife, Calpurnia, had a premonitory nightmare in which she cried out three times, "They murder Caesar!" and pleaded with him not to go to the senate. After scoffing at his wife's dream, in which she saw blood running from his statue like a fountain with a hundred spouts, Caesar asked his servant what the augurs had to say and was told that he should not set forth to the senate. Spurning these warnings, he preferred to listen to the conspirator Decius's clever interpretation of Calpurnia's dream, which was that the bleeding statue signified Caesar's great bounty in which so many smiling Romans bathed, because that was what he wanted to believe. Then, even more amazing, he carried an unopened scroll describing the plot to kill him on his way to the Senate, which his friend, Artemidorus, had placed in his hand beforehand and pleaded with him to read. Even with all those warnings, he was still surprised to be betrayed by his colleagues, who inflicted twenty-three stab wounds before he slumped to the floor in the senate chamber, uttering his famous last words of "Et tu, Brute? Then fall, Caesar!"

When you read this play, you cannot help but wonder whether Caesar could have avoided assassination if the message of the soothsayers had not been so obscure and his wife's dream had not been so symbolic. But from studying the behavior of many rulers throughout the world, I have become convinced that, even if Shakespeare could have had Caesar stop to read the warning scroll beforehand, it would not have made any difference in the outcome. Intoxicated by his power and almost divine status, Caesar likely believed he was so beloved by the people and so respected by his colleagues and so favored by the gods that no danger could befall him in the sacrosanct senate chambers. It took Brutus's betrayal to sober him up to the reality of his predicament, but by then he was only a moment of consciousness away from being dead.

THE PRIMATE MODEL OF RULING (WITH A SPECIAL EMPHASIS ON CHIMPS, GORILLAS, AND BABOONS)

All of these observations about humans politics can be explained readily on the basis of a primate model of ruling that was patterned after that of our simian ancestors and perpetuated throughout the process of evolution, from Australopithecus to homo habilis, to homo erectus, and finally to homo sapiens. All the emphasis on rulers being great warriors, hunters, heroes, and conquerors; the common tendency to send monarchs to military academies for their training; and the large number of rulers who have been generals or leaders of paramilitary groups before-hand seem to be derivative expressions of a primate model of ruling that accords paramount social status to the dominant alpha male. This model favors males, is implemented by males, is preserved by males, and makes the most important functions of rulers ones that males seem well-suited to fill. Of course, there have been many exceptions. But in almost all of those instances when women reigned, as I will later show, they largely operated within rather than outside this model. Either they were expected to act like alpha males, being tough with adversaries and "kicking butt" if need be, or they took on the identities of their martyred male kin, or, in the case of past queens who had the authority to rule as autocrats, they were obliged to forfeit much of their power to prime ministers or chancellors, who always were men.

As I review the current state of political affairs, I sometimes wonder if the trial-and-error struggles of natural selection led the social structure of primates down the wrong evolutionary path. There is no logical necessity for a model of leadership to be based primarily on physical prowess, ferocity, and brute strength. It potentially could have been similar to the model for bees, in which the queen is supreme, with all other bees serving as her warriors or drones. It could have favored ant-like creatures with seeming telepathic powers, who could have influenced others within the colony to act in the best interests of all through thought messages instead of force. Or instead of there continuing to be two distinct sexes, Nature could have had them evolve into one, creating only true hermaphrodites who reproduced through impregnating themselves. That way, at least two potential sources of conflict could have been eliminated—the battle between men over women and the battle between men and women over everything else—because then they would have to compete only with themselves for access to their own bodies. And they also would not have to search too far for pleasure.

At a less fanciful level, taking the basic physical attributes and mental capacities of higher primates as givens, the process of natural selection could have tried the daring experiment of favoring menopausal females, who no longer had the responsibilities of child-rearing, as rulers instead of priapic men, dedicated to proving their manhood. That way, instead of a society in which potentially the dumbest, strongest, or most ferocious primate could be in charge, the most empathetic, the most caring, and the most nurturing could be, assuming these traits to be more feminine in nature.

But perhaps I am doing the process of natural selection an injustice.

Perhaps in its typically blind, stumbling, haphazard way it sensed if it let a model of ruling flourish in which humans were not always competing, jockeying for power, and killing each other, it would be mocking its own credo of the survival of the fittest, fouling the process of evolution, and upsetting the entire balance of nature. Besides, if the survival of the species is the ultimate criterion for judging evolutionary success, as many Darwinians might claim, then Nature must have been doing something right, so to speak, in awarding leadership within primate societies to dominant alpha males. Even with all the death and destruction caused by male rulers over the ages, the world population has soared from about 500 million in 1600 A.D. to more than 6 billion people at last count and continues to grow at a rate of about 2 percent every year.[16] In fact, the survival of the human species has been so successful that it is now threatening to wipe out many other forms of life. This impressive growth in population may not be my own criterion for evolutionary success, but, then again, Nature, like God, acts in mysterious ways and may not care a whit about my personal opinion.

Undoubtedly, some readers may object that my thesis, which emphasizes the primate basis for ruling, does not give sufficient due to the more ennobling and humane motives of many leaders, such as the desire for a just and free society. Actually, the notion that humans are capable of engaging in distinctive forms of political activity not found in their simian relatives is perfectly compatible with my thesis. As more evolutionarily advanced creatures who are capable of being influenced by historical, religious, and cultural factors, humans do bring certain unique features into the political arena, which I shall comment on in the last chapter. However, what needs to be emphasized is, just because humans display certain political activities without any analogues in other primates, that does not mean evolutionary forces are not at work. Up until now, these forces have been relatively ignored in almost all discussions of ruling. This is equivalent to someone trying to explain the nature of the family without any appreciation for the biological influences on the roles males and females play.

These, then, are some of my observations about the nature of ruling. In the chapters that follow, I present evidence to support my theory and pursue its ramifications. In the process, I examine many aspects about ruling and rulers that never have been looked at before. Naturally, the test of any theory depends on how convincingly it explains existing phenomena, how well it accommodates exceptions, and how useful it is in predicting the future. I plan to show that my theory meets this test well.

2

IT'S A MAN'S WORLD

What if only primate males have political prowess? Could there ever
be a woman president; should we even allow it? What if females are
evolutionarily so constructed as to be able to do nothing except rear
babies? As I traced the history of ideas about baboons, . . . there was
no mistaking its compelling message: males were the building blocks
and the cement of the group. The male-dominance hierarchy . . . was
what gave the group its social structure.

—Shirley C. Strum,
Almost Human: A Journey into the World of Baboons

While being intelligent, competent, well-educated, and emotionally stable
does not bar you from holding high office, you also can be the ruler of a
nation if you have never read a book, do not know how to make a budget, still count with your fingers, take delight in murdering and tortur-
ing people, stay zonked out on drugs or alcohol during cabinet meetings,
pay more attention to the imaginary voices in your head than to your
advisors, or, simply put, are ignorant, demented, or crazy. With notable
exceptions, the one thing you cannot be as a ruler is a woman.

Naturally, many people will immediately counter this statement with
a ready list of well-known women rulers, such as Indira Gandhi, Margaret Thatcher, Benazir Bhutto, or Golda Meir, who serve as inspirations
for schoolgirls that they, too, like little boys, someday can become the
chief executive of their country. But consider this fact. Over the entire
twentieth century, only 27 of the 1,941 rulers from all the independent
countries all over the world have been women.[1] That is only 1.4 percent!
You then have to temper your interpretation of this statistic with the fact
that almost half of these women rulers gained power only because of the
infectious charisma that came from being "widows-of-Him" or "daughters-of-Him"—the "Him" being their martyred or revered husbands or

fathers—and because of a desire to carry on their mission. When you subtract these widows-of-Him and daughters-of-Him from the total list of women rulers (because their qualifications for high office seem due more to the people's admiration for the dead husband or father than to their own popular appeal), you are left with about three-quarters of 1 percent—0.78 percent to be exact—who became leaders not as stand-ins for the dead but as standalones for their living selves. In other words, *the odds against a women gaining ultimate power on her own merits are well over a hundred to one.*

Among this remainder of independent women rulers, you have Lidia Gueiler of Bolivia, Ertha Pascal-Troillot of Haiti, Maria Lourdes Pintasilgo of Portugal, Reneta Indzhova of Bulgaria, and Kim Campbell of Canada, who really were interim, acting, caretaker, or short-time chief executives (Helen Clark of New Zealand and Vaira Vike-Freiberga of Latvia were elected shortly before the end of 1999), most spending less that one year in office and one even less than one week, hardly enough time to order their personalized stationery and redecorate their offices before they disappeared into political oblivion.

The only women rulers left are Golda Meir of Israel (known to be "as tough as nails"), Margaret Thatcher of England (dubbed "the Iron Maiden"), Tansu Ciller of Turkey (noted for her "smile of steel" and depicted in political cartoons as someone, like Brutus, who would stab you in the back), Mary Eugenia Charles of Dominica (called the "Iron Lady

2.1: Margaret Thatcher, the "Iron Maiden," holding her own with other world leaders at the G7 Economic Summit. Courtesy Ronald Reagan Library.

of the Caribbean"), Gro Harlem Brutland of Norway (a former physician with a mind as sharp as a scalpel), Jenny Shipley of New Zealand (described by opponents as a "perfumed bulldozer"), and the Empress Tz'u-hsi (the "iron-willed" former concubine who wielded absolute power within China for years, first as co-regent for her son and then as regent for her docile adopted nephew). But when you take into account the sometimes metalliferous descriptions of these women as *brassy*, having *iron* wills, flashing *steel* smiles, being a *bulldozer*, or acting tough as *nails*, which, to their male adversaries, means that they are "ball-breakers" or, to their supporters, means that they have "balls"—the highest compliment you can pay a woman—and the suspicion that Empress Tz'u-hsi, alias the dragon lady because she was as devious and cunning as a man, had a dangling appendage as well, you are left with no one to give a ringing endorsement for femininity as a valued attribute for becoming a ruler.

Independent Women vs. Daughters-of-Him vs. Widows-of-Him

Unfortunately, because of the small number of women rulers within each of these three groups, statistical comparisons among them are not feasible. However, some general observations and impressions are. In contrasting the lives, personal characteristics, and accomplishments of these three types of female leaders, you would be hard-pressed to detect any appreciable differences between two of these groups—those women who came to power through their own maneuvers and the daughters of deceased or martyred rulers—nor, for that matter, between both of these women groups and their democratic male colleagues, except for the women usually being better educated and more qualified for holding high office. They probably would have to be in order to be considered as potential rulers by their political parties and the constituencies that elected them.

   Among those women who came to power on their own merits, Golda Meir, Tansu Ciller, Gro Harlem Brutland, and Jenny Shipley were effective and dynamic as speakers; and Margaret Thatcher, though serious, snappish, and dry, had no trouble holding her own during parliamentary debates. Except for Waiseru Zauditu (1916–28), the daughter of King Menelek II who was chosen to be empress of Ethiopia but who let her second cousin, Haile Selassie, become regent and run the government in her stead because it was unseemly for a woman to rule in her own right,

2.2: Benazir Bhutto—a "daughter-of-Him"—in front of a picture of her father exhorting his countrymen. © Corbis/Francoise de Mulder.

the daughters-of-Him were equally effective. Benazir Bhutto of Pakistan, Chandrika Kumaratunge of Sri Lanka, Hasina Wajed of Bangladesh were all forceful orators, and Indira Gandhi of India, perhaps the most charismatic of these women, achieved great international stature.

The majority of these independent women and daughters-of-Him likewise seemed to be every bit as driven, tough, calculating, manipulative, and courageous as any of their male colleagues. Though none of them fought in battle or won medals for their valor, as did many would-be male leaders, most seemed just as willing to risk their lives and personal freedom for their political convictions. In 1945, Golda Meir initiated a five-day hunger strike to get the British to let a shipload of Jews migrate to Palestine. Indira Gandhi was jailed in 1942 by the British for about nine months for her political activities. She also remained undaunted by several assassination attempts on her life once she became ruler. Benazir Bhutto risked her life in challenging General Zia, who had been responsible for sentencing her father to death, and spent about five years in jail or detention for her political activities. Hasina Wajed, the daughter of Mujibur Rahman, became prime minister of Bangladesh after defeating Khaleda Zia, the wife of the prior ruler, Ziaur Rahman, who was later murdered himself. Before her rise to power, she and other members of her family had been held captive briefly in 1971 after taking part in an uprising during the war for liberation. Then, in 1975, after the assassination of her parents and three brothers by military officers, she spent six years in exile before returning home to oppose military rule and take up the cause of human rights. Because of her political activities, she was frequently placed under house arrest.

Compared to both those women who came to power independently and those who were daughters-of-Him, the widows-of-Him appeared to be an entirely different breed of ruler on the political scene, largely because they had no administrative experience or even knowledge about running a government. Mostly, these women were less educated than their husbands and, except for Janet Jagan of Guyana (who worked alongside her husband during his rise to power) and Isabel Peron of Argentina (who had been a figurehead vice president under her husband), had little personal involvement in politics before assuming office. Instead, portraying themselves as devoted wives and mothers, they had largely satisfied their desires for power and fame vicariously through their husbands and seemed to be reasonably content in their domestic roles. Mireya Moscoso, for example, was a former secretary and homemaker. And Sirimavo Bandaranaike of Ceylon studied home economics and domestic science at school so that she could better fulfill her roles as wife and mother.

With their "sunny" dispositions, "serene" outlooks, "sincere" manners, and seeming "lack of vanity," these "widows-of-Him" gave the impression of being nice people, which should have made them unsuitable for the world of realpolitik, with all of its intrigues, scheming, and dangers. Certainly, Machiavelli would not have approved of them, and probably few of their contemporary male leaders of the caudillo mold looked upon them as worthy adversaries. If these women hoped to win the respect of these implacable, overbearing men, they would have done well to have shown the brazen confidence of a Margaret Thatcher who, when told by Tito that politics should be left to men and that women belonged at home, lashed back, "I am politics!" causing Tito to shake his head in admiration.

Without any special qualifications to fall back on, the widows-of-Him understandably compensated for their lack of political know-how and their general ignorance about the world by committing themselves to their deceased husband's policies, or what influential party members (who often hoped to be able to manipulate them) told them those policies were. Unable to tout their own political expertise and experience,

2.3: Corazon Aquino—a "wife-of-Him"—poses before a group of nuns. She adopted the unique political strategy of professing "sincerity." © Corbis/Catherine Karnow.

they instead tended to exploit their nurturing image to gain the voters' confidence.

The few snippets below show how much some of them even were able to make a political virtue out of necessity by capitalizing on their relationship to their dead spouse.

   •   Corazon Aquino, a former housewife and the mother of five, was drafted by the united opposition to run against Ferdinand Marcos after the assassination of her husband, Benigno, whose policies she promised to follow. During a hotly contested presidential campaign, she tried to reassure the Philippine voters about her qualifications for the presidency by claiming, "The only thing I can really offer the Filipino people is my sincerity," while Marcos apparently took the position that sincerity belonged in the home, not in the capital. After the election, Marcos claimed a landslide victory, and Aquino claimed widespread voting fraud. Since the United States let it be known that it was time for Marcos to go, the military sided with Aquino. So Marcos, along with his wife, Imelda, and a plane full of loot, hightailed it out of the country. But once Aquino took office, she began catching lots of flak for her controversial economic policies as well as for the alleged corruption of her administration. Although she completed her term, the steady erosion of her popular support made it apparent that Aquino's noble experiment of introducing sincerity in government had failed.

• Violeta Barrios de Chamorro studied to be a secretary but dropped out of school to get married and raise a family. After her husband, Pedro, owner of the newspaper, *La Prensa*, and a popular candidate for president, was assassinated, she served a stint as an appointed member of the military junta that ran the country. After the subsequent revolution, she reluctantly decided to run for the presidency of Nicaragua in response to the glowing editorials about her that began appearing in the influential newspaper she now owned. What finally convinced her to overcome any misgivings she had about entering the political fray was getting the go-ahead from two infallible authorities, "God and my dead husband." Unpretentious, plainspoken, and considerate, she tried to leave her own distinctive mark on her country by adopting two pet projects, one having to do with changing the color of the uniform of the national police from tan to light blue and the other with changing the color of the Nicaraguan flag.

• In what had been dubbed a "race between two corpses" and an election that offered voters a chance to "break with the past," Mireya Moscoso, the widow of Arnulfo Arias, Panama's three-time former president and dictator (who died in exile after being deposed), beat out Martin Torrijos, the son of Gen. Omar Torrijos, the former dictator of Panama who had helped depose her husband. Although her political opponents accused Moscoso, a former secretary, of being poorly educated and likely to be easily manipulated, she angrily countered with, "My biggest University was that of Dr. Arias. He adapted me to him completely: he told me how I was going to wear my hair, how I was going to talk." Statements such as these supposedly reassured the populace that she was competent and able to act independently. She then went on to quash any lingering doubts about her qualifications by claiming, "I can wear pants just like the men in this country."[2]

• Isabel Perón who, as vice president, assumed the presidency of Argentina after her husband, Juan Perón, died, relied on her Svengali-like mentor, José López Rega, for guidance. So that Isabel might capitalize on the popularity of her predecessor, Rega had her lie on top of Eva Peron's coffin to absorb the spiritual essence from her corpse while he burned candles and muttered incantations. He also wrote her speeches, getting her to shout, sometimes midway through a sentence, "We feel it! We feel it! Evita is present!" Then, while she was speaking, he often mouthed her words to give them greater import, claiming he was serving as an intermediary for Juan Perón, who was communicating with his widow from the grave.

All told, it appears that, despite their seeming lack of political experience, poor education, and meager knowledge about the world, these widows-of-Him, including those with their grandmotherly bake-a-cake and eat-some-soup images, fared as well or as poorly as most of the men who preceded or followed them in high office. What attests even more to their being the equal of their male counterparts is that several had administrations that were just as corrupt.

In a fair and just world, these observations about the three categories of women rulers would argue for the inclusion of many more women among the world leaders, since even the least qualified of them appears capable of doing anything a male ruler can do. But human logic and human practice need not coincide. Even during the entire year 2000 A.D., the last year of a century during which women made unprecedented gains in their voting rights, not a single woman came to ultimate power anywhere in the world. Although Tarja Halonen was elected as president of Finland on March 1, 2000, a new constitution went into effect simultaneously that made her role only ceremonial and shifted most of the executive power to Parliament. Of course, there are various social, religious, or political explanations for the paucity of women who have held positions of ultimate power during the twentieth century, but, as I hope to show in later chapters, only the primate model of ruling also takes into account a number of other crucial facts.

This blanket prejudice against female rulers goes back to antiquity. Even when queens ascended to the throne by hereditary succession, they had to confront similar biases about their temperamental, intellectual, and moral unfitness to rule. One common way they chose to counter these biases, as did almost all of the modern day widows-of-Him and daughters-of-Him, was to argue that, while they had the body of a woman, they possessed the spirit or mind of their departed male kin. Queen Elizabeth I, for example, invited comparisons between her headstrong father, Henry VIII, who had beheaded her mother, and herself: "I know I have the body of a weak and feeble woman," she told her troops, while dressed in a silver breastplate and white gown, "but I have the heart and stomach of a king, and a king of England, too." To emphasize her fitness to rule, her tutor wrote, "Her mind has no womanly weakness, her perseverance is equal to that of a man, and her memory long keeps what it quickly picks up." Then, to assuage the doubts of those who advanced more "reasoned" arguments against women rulers, dealing with their innate unsuitability to rule, apologists for the queen devised the ingenious theory of "the king's two bodies," which held that, when she assumed the throne, her whole being was altered. Once her mortal flesh, which was subject to all the imperfections of womanhood, became wedded to the immortal body politic, which was timeless and perfect, all her female shortcomings were eliminated. Therefore, as a result of this transformation in her being, her gender no longer posed a danger to the glory and welfare of the nation.[3]

Granted, male rulers are a hard act to follow. Some have created new countries, overturned existing orders, and transformed societies, accomplishments so far denied to any women. But as the price for these wondrous feats, they also have managed to kill more people through wars and disastrous social policies than a wrathful Jehovah ever smote during His Great Flood or His destruction of the wicked cities of Sodom and Gomorrah, being collectively responsible during this past century for over 200 million deaths[4] and at least another billion casualties when you include all the wounded and suffering.[5] That's an average of over 2 million deaths and 10 million casualties a year, an almost impossible goal for women to match—but, as they say in sports, records are made to be broken.

So the old adage that it's a man's world is true, at least as far as ruling the world goes, but that does not necessarily make it a better world. Although there is an inkling that women have made some gains in political leadership in the last half of this past century, especially in parliamentary governments, without having to draw on the posthumous charisma of their dead husbands and fathers, their numbers are minuscule, and none has yet gained absolute power. Nor are any promising female Saddam Husseins or Idi Amins, capable of rousing the wrath and indignation of the free world, on the immediate horizon. Though this situation bespeaks of rank social discrimination and certainly needs to be remedied, it offers one unexpected consolation (the only one as far as I can tell if you happen to be a writer): it lets you use the terms "he" or "man" with impunity instead of the politically correct but stylistically awful "he or she" or "men or women." Like Ivory soap, the maleness of rulers as a group is literally 99 44/100 percent pure. So even if you wanted to portray women as chartered members of this elite club, you would be misrepresenting the global situation if you did.

My comments so far should not be interpreted as a polemic against the sexual inequities existing in politics or necessarily as a plea for more women as rulers (although I personally would like to see that). Rather, my intention is simply to establish the startling fact about the paucity of women rulers, which not only serves to justify the greater amount of attention I will be devoting to male rulers but also says something important about what ruling others is all about. However, if certain female readers happen to believe that this exclusion of women is unfair (as I do), I urge them to withhold judgment until they have read my entire book. I would not be surprised if they then should decide, for a different reason than Groucho Marx, that if they are ever invited to join that exclusive club of male rulers, they just might not want to become a member.

Being a woman may be a drawback for becoming a ruler, but being a man is no guarantee that you will become one. Even if you have the right genitalia, the odds of making it to the top of the heap are slim, much worse odds than winning a lottery jackpot. But common sense and experience suggest that it takes more to become a ruler than chance alone (although you can find myriad examples of people who seem like they could not have become rulers any other way). Just as scientific discovery favors the prepared mind, it seems reasonable to suppose that fortune favors those aspirants for certain kinds of rule who possess certain distinctive personal characteristics. However, nobody yet has identified what these particular characteristics are, if any. In this book, I try to remedy this lack.

Different Ways of Dominating Others

As soon as you try to characterize rulers, you are obliged to clarify what kinds of rulers you are talking about.[6] A rose by any other name may still be a rose, but some have thorns and others do not, and they come in different colors. The same applies to rulers. Rulers who are dictators are likely to be of a different nature than those who are democrats. Then, among the dictators, you find monarchs, tyrants, visionaries, and authoritarians who are separate subtypes despite their superficial resemblances. The same holds for leaders of emerging democracies and those of established ones. Although much overlap exists among these different types—for example, visionaries also may have authoritarian or despotic tendencies; monarchs may act at times like tyrants or visionaries; authoritarians may prepare their countries for democracy; transitional democrats may seem like visionaries; and established democrats, under certain circumstances, may act as authoritarians—you usually can fit any ruler, albeit sometimes with a Procrustean shoehorn, into one or another category by emphasizing his main characteristics. Admittedly, this classification is artificial; but, as I hope to show, it represents a useful way of bringing order to the current conceptual chaos about ruler types.

At this point, a brief description of each of these types seems necessary to make sure we are talking about the same kinds of creatures (see chart 2.1 for summary). Later, I will be fleshing out these descriptions with the results from numerous statistical analyses to show how certain kinds of people are drawn to certain kinds of rule and how these certain kinds of rule reciprocally shape their characters.

Supreme Monarchs

In a monarchy, supreme authority is vested in the sovereign, who is the permanent head of state. This authority usually comes from kinship with a reigning family or, when state religions exist, from consecration by the church. When *monarchs* get their authority to rule from God, they naturally cannot be held accountable for their actions by any earthly authority such as a parliament or court of law. As executive agents for a divine power, many also are the possessors of supernatural powers such as the healing touch, omniscience, or the capacity for prophetic dreams. Whether kings, emperors, or sheikhs really accept these questionable notions is hard to say, but it is likely that most of them do, since they have been indoctrinated to believe in their specialness from an early age and are not likely to object to being infallible. Since the very basis for their authority is predicated on their divine right to rule or their kinship with a revered, semi-divine figure like a prophet or folk hero, they need to keep fostering among their people the belief in their specialness. Therefore, when doubts about their qualifications arise, they need to put them immediately to rest. This is not always easy to do, especially if rulers cannot show a Hapsburg lip and jaw (known as mandibular prognathism syndrome) or a Hessian strain of hemophilia or another genetic aberration as proof of their superior blue-blooded lineage. But even without access to advanced scientific methods for blood typing, many of these monarchs have found even more foolproof ways for establishing their royal credentials.

Ibn Saud, for example, hired an Egyptian religious sheikh by the name of Muhammad Tammimi to fabricate a family tree that proved him to be a direct descendent of the Prophet so that he could gain acceptance from his people after he had defeated three of the more established families who ruled what is now Saudi Arabia. In an amazing feat of genealogical legerdemain that likely spanned over sixty generations, even without access to Internet search engines, Tammimi did this persuasively enough to convince Saud that Allah had entrusted him with the mission of uniting the kingdom to make the Arabs once again a great power and the champions of Islam. Later, King Farouk of Egypt also hired the same family-tree maker to construct a suitable religious lineage for himself. Again, the scholar, in another virtuoso performance, presumably found enough unsuspected kin to fill in the many generational gaps between his current patron and Fatima, daughter of the Prophet.

Despite the questionable kinship of King Ibn Saud and King Farouk with the Prophet, no scientific evidence exists to date to show that absolute monarchs with phony genealogies are any worse as rulers than those with legitimate ones. They are probably all equally bad. So maybe the authenticity of their lineage does not matter. Also, the counterfeiting of quasi-divine credentials or, put in less accusatory terms, the loose documentation of them, is a time-honored practice among many rulers throughout history. To the credit of these particular kings, they were not as presumptuous as certain other rulers in my study who bypassed genealogy entirely by proclaiming themselves to be God or at least to be intimate confidantes of Him.

Tyrants and Despots

Since *tyrants* have no hereditary, institutional, or legal basis for their authority, they rule by personal power, which usually requires the use of force. Unable to justify their cruelty and oppression on the basis of divine inspiration, as can monarchs (or for the sake of history, as can visionaries; or for the good of society, as can authoritarians), they often compensate for this deficiency by not even bothering to offer a rationale and punishing anyone who asks for one. Because of the tenuousness of their positions, they usually need to secure the backing of the military and so have to placate its leaders with special favors. Unlike other dictators bent on implementing a particular political ideology, preserving the monarchy, or maintaining social order; tyrants seem driven primarily by greed and the prerogatives of power (although many of them counter this notion with the argument that, since they *are* their country, whatever benefits them also benefits their country).

There is no more fitting prototype for a tyrant than Francois Duvalier, also known as "Papa Doc," who unleashed the Tonton Macoutes ("Bogeymen"), a private force of hooligans, to murder suspected foes of the regime and terrorize the population of Haiti.[7] During the early part of his fourteen-year "papadocracy," Duvalier set a target for his government of killing three hundred men a year. But being an extremely ambitious person, he kept raising the bar for himself, so in time he was sometimes able to match his original quota in a single month. However, this dubious achievement was marred by his cheating, because toward the end of his rule he stopped exempting women and children as victims.

Not all of Duvalier's despotic actions involved the torture, exploitation, and repression of his subjects. With a stretch of the imagination, you might be able to construe certain of his actions as being motivated by a concern for the spiritual needs of his people—or, at least, that seems to be what he told himself. For instance, he revised the Lord's Prayer so it would have special relevance for them. Instead of uttering the traditional "Now I lay me down to sleep" each night before they went to bed, they now could repeat, "Our Doc, who art in the National Palace for life,/Hallowed be thy name/By generations present and future,/Thy will be done/In Port-au-Prince and in the provinces...."[8]

Later in his reign, he also believed he was instilling a greater national pride in his subjects when he courageously opposed the United States. Incensed that American newspapers were insulting his nation when they accurately reported that thousands of Haitians were near starvation because of a drought, he retaliated by refusing to accept any desperately needed American aid shipments for his people. These assorted interventions on his part led one of his people to offer this qualified praise: "Duvalier has performed an economic miracle. He has taught us to live without money . . . to eat without food . . . and to live without life."

Authoritarians

Authoritarianism refers to a political system that concentrates power in the hands of one ruler who is not directly responsible to the people or existing bodies of law. Unlike totalitarian governments with visionary leaders, authoritarian governments do not operate under an all-pervasive ideology and often suffer some pluralism in society. The primary purpose of *authoritarians* is to preserve law and order, maintain social stability, and keep the machinery of government running. Authoritarians come in several varieties: as leaders of military coups, as appointees by military juntas, as caudillos or nationalistic strongmen, or as successful governmental bureaucrats, sometimes known as *apparatchiks*.[9] In general, authoritarians value discipline, duty, obedience, tradition, and respect for authority far more than personal freedom, innovation, democracy, and debate. Social order supersedes individual rights. The dogma of the organization—the party, the military, the government, the church—overrides freedom of expression.

Unlike tyrants, who act in their own selfish interests, authoritarians often act in accord with what they believe are their country's best interests. They also may show compassion for the people, but in a remote, paternalistic way. Apparatchiks, more so than military rulers, often come to power through their knowledge of official rules, regulations, and protocol; their mastery of the nuts and bolts of government; their efficiency and proficiency in executing the orders of their superiors; and their ability to cite chapter and verse verbatim from the operating manual to support any ideological position. Because of their remarkable capacity to adapt to the changing orthodoxies of their organization or party, they usually are reluctant to venture opinions of their own. But by knowing what makes the machinery of government run, they in effect come to run the government.

Some understandably may wonder how seemingly mediocre people like these ever get to be rulers and, once rulers, how they ever accomplish anything of note. Janos Kadar, premier of Hungary (1956–58, 1961–65) and first secretary (1956–88) of Hungary's Communist Party, is a good example of an authoritarian who shows how potentially powerful an apparatchik can be. So lacking in personal magnetism that his colleagues yawned in his presence, so conventional and conservative that even a keeper of the faith seemed radical in comparison, so deficient in oratorical abilities that his listeners nodded and clapped in dutiful respect at the wrong times, so cautious in his decisions that it often was hard to tell what he had decided, and so unoriginal that his most quotable and notable observation was "He who is not against us is with us," he had all the valued attributes of a successful bureaucrat. These attributes had let him steadily advance within the party hierarchy in such barely noticeable increments that he threatened neither his coworkers nor his superiors until they suddenly discovered that their former colleague or underling had now become their boss.

But those drawn to more dynamic leaders should not underestimate Kadar's effectiveness. With his cautious, terrapin style of leadership, he was able to accomplish what someone with far more panache never could have done. For instance, when Imre Nagy, his more charismatic predecessor, pledged during the Hungarian Revolution to remove all Soviet troops from the country and to liberalize the Communist regime, he almost invited the harsh Soviet reprisal that followed and his own trial and death sentence as well. Under Soviet auspices, Kadar, whose credentials as a loyal party member were unquestioned, then formed a new government and, to the admiration of the Soviet invaders, quashed any remaining pockets of rebellion. Once the Soviets saw how firmly Kadar dealt with troublemakers within his own country and how his foreign policy mirrored Moscow's lead, they withdrew their troops and began interfering less and less in the internal affairs of Hungary. While the Soviets began turning their attention to other trouble spots, Kadar methodically worked at raising the standard of living for Hungarians, improving their cultural life, and allowing more freedom of expression. By being viewed by the Soviets as a dedicated Communist who supported their hegemony over Hungary, he was able to accomplish far more than his more independent, outspoken, and rebellious predecessor ever could.

A story circulating around Hungary at the time of the Soviet reprisal about Kadar's response to the chairman of a committee investigating his ideological position illustrates the mind-set of an apparatchik in all of its devious simplicity.

> "Now, Comrade Kadar, perhaps you could tell us your opinion."
> "Thank you, Comrade Chairman. Well, Marx once wrote . . ."
> "Yes, Comrade Kadar, we know what Marx wrote. It's your opinion we want."
> "Of course, of course, Comrade Chairman. Well, according to Lenin . . ."
> "Please, Comrade Kadar, please; your own thoughts please."
> "Oh, very well, Comrade Chairman, of course comrade, but before I state my own opinion I should like to make very clear in advance that I do not agree with it."[10]

Visionaries (Social Engineers)

When I use the term *visionary*, I am not referring to a ruler who anticipates future political happenings or proposes political initiatives well ahead of his time. I am using this term in a more restricted sense, referring to those rulers who not only have a grand vision for society but who also autocratically try to reshape society to conform to their vision. A visionary is a playwright, director, and producer, as well as a ticket agent, all rolled into one. Unlike a tyrant, who will rob his people of their possessions, a visionary wants only to confiscate their hearts and souls. Among the different kinds of rulers, he is far more ambitious for his people than those who promise them only health, wealth, and happiness. He offers them the prospects of a meaningful existence and an eternal afterlife as actors in his grand production. The devotees won't get top billing or even be mentioned as a part of the cast, but they will at least have the satisfaction of knowing they played an integral part in the national drama that included all their fellow citizens, too. If they happen to have a bit of stage fright or simply do not like the show being produced, the visionary, with all the resources of a totalitarian state at his disposal, can help them overcome their hesitancy to go onstage by exposing them to state-run personality cults, indoctrination programs, torture, imprisonment, and even death. There is no room for pluralism, deviationism, or individuality in a totalitarian society; the dreams of the visionary are more than sufficient for all. "I am your dreams," Kemal Atatürk told his countrymen, expressing the sentiments of all visionaries, and then informed them about what he had dreamed for them.

The Italians looked upon Benito Mussolini as a visionary during his early years in power, when he was praised around the world as a genius for transforming Italy into a fascist state. Pope Pius referred to him as "a man sent by Providence" to deliver Italy from the heresies of liberalism. Others hailed him as a "divine Caesar." Using the press, radio, education, and films for propaganda about fascism, Mussolini portrayed himself as an infallible "Duce" who could solve all the problems of society. For a while, he did what he said he would. He got the trains to run on time. He built monumental architectural structures in the imperial style. He brought more efficiency to government. He curbed organized crime by arresting Mafia members. It did not seem to matter to the masses that Mussolini took away their personal freedom, abolished parliamentary government, weakened the trade unions, controlled the media, and imposed censorship in the arts. They accepted the necessity of supplanting their long-cherished notions of "liberty, equality, and fraternity" with the fascist slogan of "believe, obey, and fight" as a small price to pay to recapture the glories of ancient Rome. "War is to the man what maternity is to the woman," Mussolini perceptively proclaimed—meaning a woman's job is to raise children so that they later can be slaughtered in battle by men—and his countrymen rushed off to war intoxicated with the prospect of creating a modern Roman Empire.

But there was one fatal flaw in fascism: it made no allowance for failure. Mussolini's dream became a living nightmare for the people once they awoke to the realization that so many more of them were dying in battle than the Allies, which, according to the prevailing propaganda, was not supposed to happen, since fascism held that the strong (= Axis powers) were invincible against the weak (= Allied powers). That realization held certain practical implications for them. It meant that, if war continued, they might not be around to enjoy the restoration of glories past.[11] That obviously was carrying ideology too far.

Transitional Democrats or Rulers of Emerging Democracies

As leaders of emerging democracies, *transitional* rulers guide their countries during the shift from colonial rule to independence, from an absolute monarchy to parliamentary rule, or from a longstanding dictatorship to a free society. Aside from laying the groundwork for the nation's domestic and foreign policies, they are instrumental in introducing new constitutions setting limits on the ruler's power and extending the personal freedoms of the people. While the visionary creates a totalitarian society conforming to his own utopian vision, the transitional ruler serves more as midwife during his country's birthing experience for bringing common notions of democracy into being. As the proclaimed father of his nation or as the liberator of his country or as the shepherd guiding his flock to freedom, the transitional ruler often gains a revered status seldom found among the leaders of more established democracies. Because neither he nor the people may have had any past experience with democracy, he oftentimes rules his fledgling nation like an over-concerned father, worrying that his grown children are not yet ready to assume adult responsibilities, while his subjects sometimes act like rebellious adolescents periodically compelling him to impose limits on them. With his paternalistic attitude, the transitional leader often functions in the role of an autocrat or "presidential monarch" during this initial period of democracy, although he continues to operate within the context of a constitutional democracy.

Typical of a transitional ruler is his propensity to evoke radically different responses from different segments of the population during his struggles for independence or liberation. To many people, he is the devil incarnate; to others, a saint or savior. For those who want to keep their powers, prerogatives, or territories, he is a sadistic, psychopathic murderer; for others who want to take these powers, prerogatives, or territories away, he is a hero and a liberator. Jomo Kenyatta is a case in point. Blamed for engineering the bloody Mau-Mau uprising against the white colonists, the British governor before Kenya's independence called Kenyatta a leader into "darkness and death," and Elspeth Huxley compared him to Hitler. In contrast, the blacks saw Kenyatta as their savior who would restore their homeland to them. After independence, the same white colonists, now fearful of a bloodbath from black vengeance, looked upon Kenyatta as a stabilizing force who would unify Kenyans on the basis of their national identity rather than along racial lines, which he actually managed to do over the course of his three terms in office.[12]

Robert Mugabe, who was to become the first prime minister (1980–87) of the reconstituted state of Zimbabwe, evoked similar responses. As a joint leader, with Nkomo, of the Patriotic Front of Zimbabwe, whose guerrillas operated against the Rhodesian government from bases in neighboring counties, he was a hero to his people and a sadistic killer and unscrupulous terrorist to the whites. After being elected prime minister of his newly independent country, he was hailed throughout the world for being a great statesman and peacemaker for his efforts to reassure the remaining white farmers and businessmen that their skills were important for the economy and they would have a substantial representation in parliament—not that the representation would mean much, since Mugabe mostly acted autocratically without consulting parliament, but it was a nice gesture nonetheless. At least in this fledgling democracy, Mugabe treated both whites and blacks equally. Neither group had much say in running the government.

Examples of this sort are commonplace. Michael Collins in Ireland, Nelson Mandela in South Africa, and Jawaharlal Nehru in India, among others, were passionately hated by their enemies and passionately loved by their supporters during their struggles for freedom and then were perceived more realistically by all concerned once independence was achieved. Among transitionals, terrorists and liberators are opposite sides of the same coin. Then after the differences between the perceived oppressors and the perceived insurgents are settled, another transformation in perception takes place: they often tend to be perceived as peacemakers, or at least as pragmatic statesmen.

Democrats or Leaders of Established Democracies

In using the term "democrats," I am referring to leaders of established democracies and not to members of a particular political party. What distinguishes the functions of *established democrats* from those of transitional democrats is simply the length of time the democracy has been in existence. But this is not an insignificant distinction. Starting democracy anew or renewing it after a long period of dictatorship or foreign domination, transitional democrats are less bound by precedent in the exercise of their power than leaders of established democracies in which constitutional checks and balances on executive power have long been in place. Because of these limits to their authority, leaders of established democracies usually have more trouble acting on their own initiative than rulers of other forms of government. As a result, to implement their policies, they have to rely more on negotiation and compromise with political opponents or even with members of their own party. Persuasion, wheeling and dealing, and the forming of coalitions are perhaps more important for democratic leaders in parliamentary governments than in republics with strong presidential systems.

Despite these constraints on their executive authority, many leaders of nations with a long tradition of democracy do manage to wield great power by taking full advantage of the prerogatives of their office. However, no matter how great their power, rulers of established democracies seldom have as much as they would like. Franklin D. Roosevelt, for instance, who transformed the social fabric of the United States and brandished more power during the past century than almost any other democratic leader, lamented: "The Treasury is so ingrained in its practices that I find it is almost impossible to get the action and results I want. But the Treasury is not to be compared with the State Department. You should go through the experience of trying to get any changes in the thinking, policy, and action of the career diplomats and then you'd know what a real problem was. But the Treasury and the State Department put together are nothing compared with the Navy. The admirals are really something to cope with—and I should know. To change anything in the Navy is like punching a feather bed."[13] President Harry S Truman, his successor, expressed his own exasperation in running a democracy when he voiced sympathy for General Eisenhower, who would succeed him in office. "He'll sit here and he'll say 'Do this! Do that!'" Truman observed. "*And nothing will happen.* Poor Ike—it won't be a bit like the Army."[14] Remarkably, this commiseration came from the man who had unleashed the atom bomb, intervened when the Communist North invaded South Korea in 1950, unconstitutionally seized the steel industry in 1952 to avoid a strike and maintain production, and, in an even more daring and controversial action, fired Gen. Douglas MacArthur for insubordination. Nevertheless, this sense of executive impotency is common in democratic leaders. They never could imagine Papa Doc Duvalier or Joseph Stalin or Benito Mussolini or even a Janos Kadar having to go through the indignity of trying to convince subordinates to back their decisions or suffer the frustration of not having their underlings carry out their orders immediately.

Chart 2.1 Selected Features of Different Rulers

Supreme Monarchs

- Consecrated by Church or authority by kinship to esteemed figure
- Absolute rule or strong constitutional powers
- Rule for life
- Endowed with special powers such as healing touch, infallibility

Tyrants

- Authority to rule based on military backing
- Decrees and edicts, implemented by force
- Commonly display cruelty, greed, corruption
- No ideological basis for governing

Visionaries

- Totalitarian rule
- Promotion of a particular political ideology
- Social engineering
- No fixed term in office

Authoritarians

- Dictatorship established to preserve social stability
- Emphasis on law, order, and tradition
- Bureaucratic rule common with emphasis on regulations
- No fixed term in office

Transitionals

- Rule country after liberation or independence
- Introduction of constitutional democracy with fixed terms in office
- Usually show autocratic tendencies
- Many have special status as "Father of Nation"

Democrats

- Elected to a limited term in office within an established democracy
- Executive powers defined by constitution
- Balance of power with judicial and legislative bodies
- Greater emphasis on negotiation and compromise

THE SURREALISTIC LANDSCAPE

No rulers operate in a political vacuum. Since I make no pretensions to being a political scientist, I have no intention of describing in an authoritative way the differences among the various parliamentary and presidential forms of democracy or among the various kinds of dictatorship. Besides, that really is irrelevant for my study. What I do want to share are certain personal impressions I have gathered from my struggles to make sense of the different systems of government in various nations around the world, which often do not conform to what students learn in Political Science 101 about how they should function or even who should be in charge. The reason that most of what they learn in class is useless is that it does not take one critical fact into account: *people run these governments*, and most of them did not take Political Science 101, so they are not hampered by knowing how they should act. This leaves them with the prerogative of acting in any way they damn well choose or can get away with. That frequently makes for some bizarre variations in certain forms of government.

Because there are so many exceptions to every rule about governments, I need to offer several general caveats to set the stage for much of the discussion to follow. Most of these caveats are self-evident, but they need to stated for the record.

Caveat #1: Words Don't Always Mean What They Say

The first caveat is that labels given to governments do not always reflect what these governments actually are about. This is especially so for the term *democracy*. Just as all institutions and organizations claim to strive for "excellence," no matter how inferior or unimaginative they are, even the most brutal and despotic rulers, with few exceptions, like to refer to their governments as "democratic," not only because of the cachet of the word but because they actually believe it (and they would probably affirm their commitment to excellence, too). Pol Pot, who created one of the most repressive regimes in history, renamed Cambodia "Democratic Kampuchea." Hafiz al-Assad of Syria claimed to have had a constitutional democracy even though the constitution gave him absolute powers in political, legislative, administrative, and military matters and the country fostered a one-party presidential system. As proof of the democratic process in action, he ordered a public referendum in 1971, which gave him a 99.2 percent approval rating as president. Buoyed by these results, he ordered another referendum in 1978, which gave him a 99.6

percent approval rating, and another one in 1985, which gave him a 99.9 percent approval rating.[15] Rumor had it that in the latest referendum he garnered a 104.3 percent rating, but, at the last minute, his minister of finance, who was a mathematical whiz, convinced him not to release the results since that left the opposition with only 5.7 percent of the total vote—too small a percentage to be credible.[16]

Declaring parliamentary government a failure in Nepal, King Mahendra insisted that his country needed a democratic political system consistent with its traditions. In 1962, he instituted a new constitution, establishing a partyless system of "panchayats," or councils—an ingenious, multi-tiered, pyramidal structure that progressed from village, town, and district councils to the National Parliament. With this "democratic" system, the people had a chance to voice their concerns to their elected councils at every level of government. Since the king was at the top of the pyramid, he continued to rule in autocratic fashion, not accountable to anyone, accepting the recommendations of the parliament that he agreed with and discarding those he didn't, and generally doing whatever he wanted.

In communist Russia, because members of the Politboro could vote, usually to give approval to the initiatives of the Central Committee, former Soviet leaders claimed to have a democratic society that truly expressed the will of the people. As long as some segment of the populace can vote, rulers claim to be democratically elected even if the outcome of the election is guaranteed because they were the only candidate or because the election was rigged. In some countries, dictators even boast of their commitment to democracy because they force people to exercise their constitutional right to vote for them, while jailing those who do not. In many supposedly democratic countries, the landed oligarchy, as in Argentina; or the *genro*, as in Japan; or the outgoing president, as sometimes has happened in Colombia or Uruguay; or the ruling party, as in Mexico (especially in the past), traditionally selected the candidate for president or prime minister whom the general electorate was almost certain to elect.

Lest we believe that "voting," which many people automatically equate with democracy, distinguishes us from our simian ancestors, we may be humbled to learn that a similar activity exists among bands of Hamadryas baboons. But in this case, it involves a form of decision-making among leaders of bands rather than the selection of a particular leader. For instance, when several bands are gathered together on a cliff, the leader of a departing band may "notify" (by first standing on outstretched arms and legs, as stiff as a sawhorse, and then advancing a few yards) the other leaders to come along. In response to this notification, a leader of another band either may accept this invitation by joining the procession or refuse it by abruptly lowering his head to his chest so that he no longer can see what is happening, indicating he will not budge from that spot for at least two minutes. By his refusal "to see," the leader registers his *no* vote, and his followers remain put.[17] This constant give and take among baboon leaders does not seem so different from what transpires among parliamentary leaders of different political parties who are trying to reach a consensus about what direction to take on certain controversial issues. Male baboon leaders do not raise their arms to signify "Aye" or "Nay," but their communications may be as effective and sometimes more so in negotiating differences among themselves as in most legislative bodies(see photo 2.4).

With all these different usages of the word "democracy," I am not about to risk the censure of political scientists by defining what it really should mean. Rather, I only want to say how I will be using it in this book. By democracy, I mean a form of government in which enfran-

2.4: A vote against the direction proposed by another member of a band of baboons. The male on the right abruptly lowers his head as another signals him in passing. Kummer, Hans; *In Quest of the Sacred Baboon.* 1995 Princeton University Press. Reprinted by permission of Princeton University Press.

chised citizens have the right to elect leaders and make political decisions either directly or through their elected representatives, while also having certain constitutional rights such as freedom of speech or freedom of worship. This designation holds for one-party, two-party, or multi-party systems of government. I am aware also of the many imperfections in most of the democracies around the world, even those that have served as models for newly emerging democracies. Some of the main problems have had to do with a disenfranchised citizenry or a poorly informed rural one unable to participate intelligently in the political decision-making process. It is also important to remember that even in ancient Greece, the cradle of democracy, women and slaves had no political rights; and, since the whole citizen body formed the legislature, no political parties existed. So what many refer to as "democracy" today differs greatly from what existed before, and the word conveys different meanings to different people.[18]

Caveat #2: Constitutions Are Only Words Written on Paper

This leads me to the second caveat, which is that people should not assume that the existence of a constitution ensures democracy or necessarily guarantees human rights. A constitution is simply a formal document that spells out the governance of the country and the supposed rights of the citizenry. Constitutions can grant more freedom or can, in fact, take it away. They can be operational or can exist mainly for show. They can indelibly fix the rights and privileges of the populace, not allowing for amendments and change, or they can accommodate slow, coral-like accretions or radical changes over time. Most important, constitutions can be written so that rulers either are compelled to follow them both in letter and spirit or can simply interpret them as they see fit.

Over the past century, a number of monarchs, still yearning for the halcyon days of absolute rule, looked upon their nations' constitutions as necessary evils, designed to mollify the ungodly agitators among their subjects who lacked respect for the traditional prerogatives of the throne. For instance, Abdul-Hamid II, sultan of the Ottoman Empire from 1876 to 1909, who inherited the constitution introduced by his father, looked upon it as "a dangerous and unsafe instrument." Though he kept it for window dressing, he ignored it entirely because "it is only by force that one can move people with whose protection God has entrusted me."[19] Alexander I, the Serbo-Croatian (1921–29) and later Yugoslavian king (1929–34), created and scrapped constitutions at whim. During his reign, he launched three coups, dissolved parliament twelve times, and, although he had sworn to uphold the 1921 constitution when he took office, abolished it in 1929 and then introduced a new constitution in 1931 that gave his royal dictatorship a legal basis. He was in the process of changing the constitution again in 1932 when he was assassinated by an agent of Croatian separatists.

"Constitutional rule," then, is simply another catchy term, like democracy, that has a favorable cachet. However, it does not ensure that it won't be used to curtail personal freedoms, like making Islam, Judiasm, the Church of England, or Catholicism a state religion; legislating morality; or keeping women subservient to men. It does not guarantee that a ruler won't be able to exert dictatorial powers, like appointing cronies to the legislature, removing noncompliant officials from office, or merely suspending or rewriting the constitution whenever he sees fit. For example, Hitler never abolished the Weimar Constitution, but he was able to amend it so that it let him do whatever he wished. Joseph Stalin took great pride in the 1936 constitution bearing his name, which, along with the Rules of the Communist Party of the Soviet Union, served as the formal framework of government for many years. Mao Zedong likewise encouraged constitutional rule. With these three dictators (who were responsible for more deaths and suffering during the twentieth century than most of the other leaders combined) being staunch advocates of constitutional rule, their subjects likely yearned for the less-confusing, halcyon days of plain, old-fashioned repression, when they had known exactly what was what.

Caveat #3: Bad Can Be Good, and Good Can Be Bad

The third caveat (which I hope won't get me into trouble) is that democracies are not always good, and dictatorships are not always bad. Even in supposedly "true" democracies, social injustices and inequities happen. For example, in democratic South Africa, under *apartheid*, blacks could not vote or hold land; in democratic Israel, the extent of participation by Arab citizens in the running of the government is limited by law; and, in the United States, women did not win the right to vote until 1920, and blacks did not gain full civil rights until the latter half of this past century. Conversely, benevolent dictators have brought peace, stability, economic prosperity, and even greater freedom to countries, or have kept political anarchy from arising. Under Mikhail Gorbachev, the people of the Soviet Union experienced an unprecedented amount of personal freedom. Through military rule, Atatürk was able to lay the groundwork for democracy and a secular state in Turkey. President Lee of Singapore was able to raise the standard of living of his people and create an economic boom while maintaining law and order. And Josip Broz Tito was able to unite Yugoslavia under one central government and, within limits, keep the Serbs, Croats, Bosnians, and other ethnic groups from slaughtering each other.

Caveat #4: Legal Rulers Aren't Always the Real Rulers

The fourth caveat is that the designated leader of a country is not always the person with the most political clout. There are both *de jure* leaders and *de facto* rulers. Sometimes those operating behind the scenes without official titles are much more powerful than those who are ostensibly the leaders. For example, after President Trujillo of the Dominican Republic finished his term in office, he simply appointed puppet presidents to do his bidding. General Noriega never held public office but ran Panama behind a puppet president. Much like Caesar Augustus, who gave up his formal power to assume an even greater personal authority known as *imperium majus*, which he used mainly to deal with crises or other matters of his choosing, Mao Zedong and later his former lieutenant, Deng Xiaoping, ruled China as absolute dictators without the burden of having to perform the official duties associated with certain formal titles. In a similar fashion, Muammar Qadaffi appointed himself spiritual head of Libya and supposedly disassociated himself from any official political title while he continued to run the country. Jozef Pilsudski, marshal of the Polish army, became dictator of Poland for ninety-eight days, after which he turned his authority over to the Constituent Seym, which then, in turn, appointed him chief of state and made him responsible to it, ensuring that he kept his immense power for the rest of his life without having any official duties to perform. Though he was the spiritual leader of Iran, the Ayatollah Khomeini was the de facto ruler of the country whose decisions superseded those of the nominal heads of state. So, recognizing the reality of the situation, when I use the term *ruler* or *leader* in my study, I am referring only to the most powerful person in the country, the de facto ruler or the leader with the greatest executive clout, the one with no administrative superior, and not necessarily the official who had the most power on paper by law.[20]

Caveat #5: All Rules Have Exceptions, and All Exceptions Have Rules

The fifth and last caveat about the different kinds of government is that there are exceptions made for every rule and rules made for every exception. Many constitutional monarchies tend to revert to their dictatorial heritage not unlike domestic pigs reverting to wild boars when released from their pens. Certain monarchs even give up their positions to gain an advantage. King Norodom Sihanouk of Cambodia, for instance, once abdicated his throne to his father so that he could wield more power as the leader of a major political party and then as prime minister. Some prime ministers in governments where monarchs have immense executive powers, such as Eleutherios Venizelos of Greece (1910–15, 1917, 1924, 1928–30) or Aleksandur Stamboliyski of Bulgaria (1919–23), take advantage of the ineptness or indifference of the ruler in power to function as a *de facto* dictator.

When the lines of executive authority are not clear between presidents and prime ministers in parliamentary governments, ambitious leaders often will create or exploit every opportunity, legal loophole, or constitutional ambiguity to accumulate as much power as they can within the context of their particular form of government. Some monarchs who previously had immense authority, such as King Carlos of Spain, are instrumental in fostering democracy for their nations. Some leaders of democratic countries act as dictators or autocrats in times of crisis or war. Some military juntas depose leaders who threaten democracy, and then rule dictatorially until free elections can be held. When democracies sometimes resemble dictatorships and dictatorships sometimes serve to preserve freedom, you sometimes have trouble telling one kind of government from another. This situation reminds me at times of the proverbial story of the communist who declares to the capitalist, "The problem with capitalism is it's dog eat dog. But with communism, it's the other way around."

What all these different caveats about governments add up to is that, in the world of politics, almost anything goes. As disorienting as this realization may be, this situation need not be discouraging. Despite the different kinds of rulers and the different kinds of government, conditions are not as chaotic as they at first seem. When you survey the entire surrealistic landscape of politics from a certain perspective, you find a remarkable consistency in the behavior of rulers worldwide, with all categories of rulers having both common and differing features. But there is more. Once would-be rulers enter the political fray, a powerful logic, usually unknown to them and at variance with their stated intentions, begins to govern their drive for power and their clinging to it as long as they can. Although they may believe that their choices are deliberate, they actually get caught up in the momentum of an inexorable process, which makes it hard for them to pursue any other course. In accord with my theory of ruling, natural forces will ensure that they soon will desire to do what they unknowingly are obliged to do.

3

THE PERKS OF POWER

The Ultimate selective force that drives the male chimpanzee to vigorous and aggressive attempts to better his status should be the maximizing of his own reproductive potential at the expense of his competitors. . . . As we have seen, an alpha male chimpanzee can sometimes monopolize a female at the height of estrus and sometimes maintain exclusive mating rights over more than one female. And even if he is not all powerful, he can still gain an edge over rivals by achieving the highest number of matings in the promiscuous situation.

—Jane Goodall, *The Chimpanzees of Gombe*

Would-be rulers give many highfaluting reasons for seeking high office—to restore democracy, to return power to the people, to unite the country, to overthrow tyranny, to improve the economy, to get rid of corruption in government, and so on—which they may or may not believe and which may or may not be true. But if my thesis about the evolutionary basis of ruling is correct—that unseen natural forces are at work within them to motivate them to vie for ultimate power—then whatever selfish or selfless reasons aspiring leaders give for their ambitions are irrelevant. What is relevant is that they come up with a compelling reason for themselves to engage in the struggle for dominance. That way, Nature can ensure a constant supply of potential leaders to compete for the position of alpha male. But sometimes the adversity and suffering they encounter may lessen their zeal. In that event, unless the dubious prospects of a glorious martyrdom or a measure of immortality or the making of history can override these deterrents, they may need more tangible rewards to spur them on. As it happens, Nature has powerful rewards at its disposal to keep their desire for ultimate power alive. It offers aspiring rulers the chance to gain certain incredible perquisites should they ever manage to rise to the top.

According to my thesis, the prerogatives of rulers should parallel those available to the alpha-male leaders within communities of monkeys and apes. But naturally, because rulers are even higher-order primates, these perks likely should have a distinctly human flavor. In chart 3.1 below, I extrapolate from the known advantages for alpha-male primates to comparable advantages for human rulers. Since alpha males within chimpanzee and baboon societies have sexual access to more females than subordinate males do and keep their own harems, too, human rulers throughout the world likewise should. Since alpha males copulate with many more females than subordinate males do, which gives them a greater breeding advantage, human rulers also should sire larger broods than their social inferiors. By virtue of their superior strength and status, alpha males have the first crack at scarce food supplies. They also can bully their way into any protective shelters. Among human rulers, a similar situation should exist for all material benefits. From the standpoint of social survival, this makes good sense. Just as the body preferentially shunts blood flow to the brain at the expense of less vital organs in times of medical emergencies, the social body provides for the favored treatment of its head so that it can continue to provide leadership for the community as a whole. In times of crisis, leaders should be expected to have ready access to the finest foods and the best quarters. During normal times, if they are in office long enough, they should have no difficulty accumulating sufficient wealth to buy and own almost anything they want. And last, since alpha males command deference from their subordinates, human rulers also should, especially when they get a chance to play at being God.

Chart 3.1 Predicted Advantages for Human Rulers Based On Those for Alpha Male Primates within a Dominance Hierarchy

Monkeys and Apes	*Humans*
• Sexual access to more females ➡	*• More extramarital affairs or polygamy*
• More offspring ➡	*• More offspring*
• Greater access to food and shelter ➡	*• Opportunities for greater wealth*
• Deference by subordinate males ➡	*• Deference and respect by subjects*

These predicted advantages need to be tempered by certain realities. Unlike various simian communities in which alpha males operate primarily within the autocratic framework of a dominance hierarchy, human societies have evolved many different forms of government to curb the potential powers of rulers. Because of these great disparities in power among rulers, human rulers with absolute power, whose status most resembles that of alpha males in the wild, should be expected to command the greatest privileges and perquisites. In contrast, those rulers whose powers are watered down by democratic constitutional constraints, the separation of powers, checks and balances in government, and fixed terms of office should command the fewest privileges and perquisites, sometimes no more than those available to other influential citizens. Let's examine my findings to learn if these expectations hold true.

THE PREDICTED ADVANTAGES OF RULERS

Pleasures of the Flesh

Aside from the "highs" associated with certain drugs, sexual orgasm represents one of the most exquisite pleasures available to man. Men who pride themselves on their virility not only seek to have sex as often as possible but also with as many women as they can. Presumably, the handsomest and sexiest of these men should be able to attract and seduce the most beautiful women. If they are not especially handsome or sexy, then another effective love potion is power, which serves as an alternative aphrodisiac for many women and prompts them to submit to their sexual advances. If men are not handsome, sexy, or powerful, then too bad for them. They sadly must settle for whatever they get.

From the many photographs of the male rulers I have examined, only a small minority qualify as handsome and hardly any seem sexy, although I probably do not have the proper hormones or inclinations to judge objectively. So, for the vast majority of rulers, their seductive or coercive appeal for women has to rest mostly on their prominence and power. Although it is not possible to compare the sexual prowess of rulers with that of their subjects worldwide, mainly because no reliable global base rates for philandering among the different populations exist, the next best alternative is to do so among the rulers themselves. Also, because substantial differences exist among the different kinds of rulers in the average ages at which they assume high office—for example, the average age for monarchs is thirty-two; for tyrants, forty-two; for visionaries, forty-seven; for authoritarians, fifty-one; for transitionals, fifty-one; and for democrats, fifty-six, suggesting that rulers with relatively more concentrated powers begin exercising them at a younger age than do those with less concentrated powers. It seemed unfair to compare the sexual scruples and antics of thirty-two-year-old monarchs, for instance, with fifty-six-year-old democrats (although the results indicate that some of these old goats could fare quite well). Therefore, the way I chose to compensate for these disparities in age was to extend my observations to the known sexual behavior of rulers over their entire married adult lives rather than confine them only to the period of their rule. This meant that any substantial differences among these rulers in their sexual activities could be linked both to the kind of power they were drawn to and eventually wielded.

If a connection exists between the relative amount of power rulers possess and the extent of their copulatory activity, then, on the basis of the discussion so far, rulers with the least curbs on their powers—namely, monarchs and tyrants—should engage in more philandering over the course of their married lives than those with the most curbs on their power—namely, leaders of established democracies. Visionaries, whose powers are often totalitarian, should have sexual prerogatives comparable to monarchs and tyrants, but that expectation needs to be tempered by the reality that many of them sublimate so much of their energies into their political missions and so may forgo opportunities for sexual emissions. Because authoritarians include a grab-bag of military dictators, autocratic caudillos, and party apparatchiks, who may be responsible to juntas, power cliques, or central committees, and because transitionals possess powers that range from autocratic to democratic, their sexual prerogatives should fall somewhere between these power extremes.

For the purpose of these comparisons, I decided to lump together all lawfully wedded monogamous rulers who had extramarital sexual affairs with polygamous ones who kept two or more wives in harems (or what I call "semenaries") and, as often happened, many concubines as well. What all these men had in common was that they had sexual access to more than one female partner whenever they chose, a less judgmental way of saying that they were sexually promiscuous. Polygamy may serve certain important social and religious functions in certain nations, but I suspect that the practice originally got started for other reasons. Knowing how much gonadal influences can affect men's judgment, I am inclined to believe that whatever noble or practical reasons men in various societies give to support this practice really represent sanctimonious excuses for them to indulge their carnal urges without community censure. That way, they not only can have their cake and eat it, too, so to speak, but they can eat as many cakes as they want while virtuously claiming to be dieting.

According to the latest Kinsey Institute report, which reviewed the results of six different major studies over a forty-year period, an estimated 37 percent of married men in the United States had at least one extramarital affair during their lifetimes,[1] a rate that is below the estimates in certain more controversial studies. Comparable statistics were not available for other geographical regions throughout the world. Within my entire sample of married rulers, at least 57 percent were sexually promiscuous, a rate substantially above that noted by the Kinsey Institute. Figure 3.1 below with the percentages of sexual profligacy (e.g., marital infidelity, promiscuity, and/or polygamy) among the different kinds of married male rulers is telling. I originally wanted to show these results with a pie chart but then realized that a bar graph was symbolically more appropriate.

Figure 3.1: Sexual Profligacy among Married Male Rulers

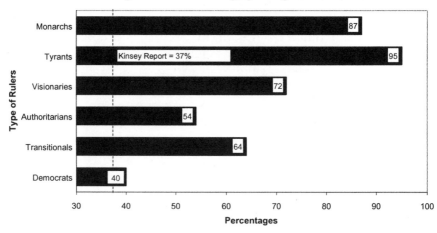

Legend: Note that monarchs and tyrants, who wield the greatest power, show the greatest sexual promiscuity, infidelity, or polygamy among rulers; and transitionals and democrats, who wield the least power, show the least.

As predicted, the results generally support the existence of a relationship between the inherent powers of a ruler as measured by the presence or absence of social curbs on his authority and the extent of his sexual profligacy. Leaders of established democracies, who serve fixed terms in office and have the most legal restraints on their authority, are the least sexually profligate among the different rulers, although by some standards a 40 percent rate is still impressive. But all judgments are relative. At the other end of the power spectrum are tyrants (95 percent) and monarchs (87 percent), whose display of sexual prowess makes democrats and all the other rulers seem like eunuchs. In fact, marital infidelity and/or polygamy is so universal among them that it may as well be considered a character trait.

Making judgments about infidelity:

Now, the first question to be asked about such highly personal information of this sort is how accurate it is. The answer is that it is as accurate as detailed biographical material can be and certainly more accurate than if you were foolhardy enough to interview these rulers face to face to gain concealed information about their sometimes sordid, private lives. So how did I arrive at these figures? My method was straightforward. When the available material on a ruler did not let me reach a conclusion about his fidelity, I did not; and when the material did let me reach a conclusion, I did. I also took the liberty of assuming that all suspected cases of infidelity were infidelity. Granting leeway for an occasional error, my clinical experience over the years has taught me that if you assume the worst after hearing rumors about the sexual shenanigans of males, you will be right in 90 percent of the cases, and despite their denials, the remaining 10 percent will be lying. This means that if there were rumors about a leader having mistresses or sexual affairs, or, as was the case for Prime Minister Tardieu of France, who was seen going into restaurants or to political events and even state dinners with a variety of beautiful women while his wife sat at home, or if a ruler was seen to disappear into the bedroom at a party with the wife of a guest and emerge disheveled and with his fly undone a half-hour later, or if a ruler had a reputation for being a womanizer, my bias was to assume that he probably had had extramarital sexual relations. Still, since I was not present in the bedrooms of these rulers (or wherever else they indulged themselves) to catch them in *flagrante delicto*, I suppose it is possible that they sequestered themselves in private quarters with these women only to gossip or share their existential *angst* with them, but I doubt it. On the contrary, given the tendency of many political leaders to hide their transgressions, I suspect that my percentages are on the low side despite my admitted bias to accept suggestive evidence as reality.

Harems, polygamy, and concubines:

While the prior figures on the percentages of married rulers who were sexually profligate are dramatic, they cannot capture just how important

3.1: Hamadryas male baboons with large harems sun themselves in the morning. Kummer, Hans; *In Quest of the Sacred Baboon*. © 1995 Princeton University Press. Reprinted by permission of Princeton University Press.

a role sex has played in their lives, as evidenced by the amazing numbers of women that many of these rulers serviced. A past king of Benin had somewhere between six hundred and four thousand wives. The likely reason for this large discrepancy in numbers was not due to the inability of his court chroniclers to count but because of his generous practice of giving wives away to those who had rendered him service, so the numbers were always changing.[2] Another reason for the marked differences in the numbers of spouses attributed to kings often has to do with confusion over how to categorize their many concubines, maids-of-honor, and serving-maids, along with the female slaves belonging to their wives— any of whom the ruler may enlist to perform wifely duties in bed. In order to impose some restraint on their king and encourage him to practice moderation, the Ashanti legislated a limit of 3,333 wives. While none of my sample matched the feat of King Mtessa of Uganda in the nineteenth century, who reputedly had about seven thousand wives, the twentieth-century rulers were hardly sexual slouches. However, simply because these rulers managed to institutionalize and legitimize the wildest sexual fantasies of many men throughout the world does not necessarily mean we automatically should impute licentious motives to their behavior. In their own eyes, at least, their motives often were noble and pure. Some even viewed their philandering as their religious or civic duty. Here are some of the justifications that polygamist rulers gave for their harems.

• Although Emperor Bokassa of the Central African Republic had a meager seventeen wives, he compensated for his relative deprivation with countless mistresses and *filles de joie*. With a special weakness for twelve-year-olds and blonds, he philosophized to a visitor one day, "I liked women, and I had many of them. There is an Iranian proverb to which I subscribe completely, which says, 'If God didn't like beautiful women, he would not have created them.'" [3]

• Sobhuza II of Swaziland accumulated at least seventy wives for the avowed purpose of binding the nation together by tying all important families to his own clan, the Dlamini, which composed about one-quarter of the population. As an added inducement to become his wife, he made each girl a mother of the nation and, because of his scrupulous desire to be fair, ranked them by seniority in order of their marriage to him. [4]

• Prince Sihanouk of Cambodia defended his rabbit-like behavior with at least six consorts and numerous mistresses to Western audiences with the argument, said with a knowing wink, that it was better to have had a private life marked by "excess" than to have been a pederast or impotent. However, by royal standards, Sihanouk was a pale comparison to his predecessors. His great-grandfather Norodom I kept a stable of women that numbered in the hundreds, and Monivong, Sihanouk's immediate predecessor, reportedly had sixty wives and who knows how many mistresses. Fortunately for these rulers, Cambodians have never been troubled by royal polygamy spiced up a bit with concubines and mistresses. As the source of all power within the kingdom, the monarch was supposed to ensure his succession and show his virility as a metaphor for the mystic forces he alone controlled and potentially could use to secure the strength and prosperity of the kingdom. [5] Cambodia has been blessed by having no dearth of dedicated rulers who were willing to display their virility on behalf of their nation.

• When asked why he had so many wives, King Chulalongkorn of Sri Lanka said that he could not wound the feelings of the princes and nobles who were kind enough to present him with their beautiful and fascinating daughters. But there were practical reasons for his having an estimated thirty-six to eighty-four wives. [6] By making sure that women throughout the kingdom shared his bedroom, he could ensure that the various ethnic groups throughout the country had equal representation. This was his creative version of democracy in action.[7]

Dictators' delights:

Not all rulers invoke the divine right of kingship to satisfy the erotic demands of their venerable bodies. Rulers in general have a tendency to believe they are entitled to these pleasures. Trujillo, the longtime dictator of the Dominican Republic who prided himself on being a devoted family man and a practicing Catholic, lighting a votive candle every morning to the image of the Dominican Republic's patron saint, the Virgin of Altagracia, sat as sole judge during his own version of a beauty contest held twice a week in his office at the palace. From a group of about thirty eligible young "hopefuls," Trujillo, with the practiced eye of a horse breeder and the lust of a satyr, selected his choices for the week. Mostly, he went to bed with each chosen woman once or twice, but he kept a few favorites longer. Then after he lost interest in them, as he inevitably did, he encouraged them to marry or sometimes arranged for their marriages himself. He also generously provided for the children he fathered and even legitimatized some.[8]

In certain ways, Trujillo's selection methods, though adequate for their purpose, were not as exotic as those of Chairman Mao's, but then Trujillo did not have access to Mao's collection of erotica and pornography, the finest in the entire Republic of China, to fire his imagination when it became stuck in a rut. Among Mao's works, *The Golden Lotus* was the greatest, since it described the sexual proclivities of Chinese upper-class society in the twelfth century in such explicit detail that the puritanical English translators had to transform page after page of it into Latin to disguise it contents from readers—although they could have done that easier if they had not translated it at all.[9] Mao especially liked his collection of hand-colored "pillow books" that had foldout picture guides to sexual practices. Armed with this information, Mao was never at a loss to explore new avenues of carnal pleasure. One of his favorite joys was to indulge in water sports in his heated indoor pool in which flocks of naked women, procured for him by his henchmen, seductively gamboled about.

In this age of modern travel, rulers need no longer be constrained by distance in seeking sexual fodder for their needs. Perez Jiminez, dictator of Venezuela, used his business partner as a minister of sexual affairs to procure women for him. At his inaugural party, he had two hundred beautiful women flown in from the mainland to his estate for a three-day orgy.[10] In more recent times, the sultan of Brunei, presumed to be the richest man in Asia, decided to westernize his tastes. A former Miss USA claimed she and a bevy of other women were misled by the sultan's offer of a twenty-five-thousand-dollar-a-week consultant fee and were kidnapped instead for 32 days and forced to do morally repulsive acts in his 1,788-room palace in Brunei. What was the Sultan's response to this charge? He waved it off with the claim of diplomatic immunity.[11]

Idi Amin also had a great appreciation of women, but he had bad luck in his choice of wives. Though he married five times, keeping several wives at any given time; had an estimated harem of over thirty mistresses; and had sex with countless other women throughout Uganda, he divorced his first three wives (and reputedly had one of them killed) because of their alleged affairs with lovers, immoral ingrates as they were. Idi Amin presumably was devastated by these betrayals, which for a while soured his attitudes toward women,[12] but in time his emotional wounds healed and he once again was able to relate to them as he normally had before.

But not all wounds in a ruler's love life are emotional. Sometimes they are physical. Cipriano Castro, who had twenty-two mistresses, proudly carried a bullet in him from being shot by his jealous wife. Atatürk, the founder of modern Turkey and a saint-like symbol for many of his countrymen, who was promiscuous all his life with women, perhaps best sums up the prevailing attitude of all these rulers. Asked once what qualities he admired most in a woman, he replied, "Availability."[13]

Democrats can be philanderers, too:

What needs emphasis is that not all nations are shocked by the sexual transgressions of their rulers, and not all rulers are embarrassed about them. In many instances, the leader's sexual exploits reflect on his manliness and, therefore, his qualifications and ability to rule. For instance, in France, a Catholic nation, the attitude toward unfaithful rulers seems in certain instances to be an amused but tolerant attitude of "What else can you expect from men?" Joseph Caillaux, the French premier whose opposition to World War I later led to his imprisonment for treason in 1920, divorced his wife after having an extramarital affair. Then after he remarried, he showed no compunction about exhibiting his mistresses in public and even bragged during parliamentary debates of his successes with women.[14]

Later, Francois Mitterand, the president of France, seemed to have had even less inhibitions about his indiscretions than did Monsieur Caillaux. He openly kept two families, spending weekdays and New Year's with his wife and his sons, and weekends and Christmas with his mistress and their daughter. He also managed to find time in his crowded schedule to have other sexual affairs.[15]

But perhaps the best example of sexual aplomb I have come across involves the leader of a Latin American nation. President Jose Remon Cantera of Panama, a well-known philanderer, was once caught in a compromising act with a woman and photographed without his being aware of it. Later the photographer tried to blackmail him after showing him the pictures. Remon examined the incriminating evidence with approval, then placed an order with the photographer for several copies.[16]

Given the libidinous predilections of world leaders, it is intriguing to note all the hoopla about the sexual escapades of Bill Clinton, the last of the twentieth-century U.S. presidents, who simply seemed to be carrying on the hallowed tradition set by his many predecessors. Of the eighteen presidents of the United States who ruled from 1900 through 2000, at least eight (45 percent) have had sexual affairs while married, and, as far as I am concerned, the complete story is not in on two others. Warren G. Harding, perhaps the most incompetent of these presidents, whose only qualification for office, according to a close associate, was that "he looked like a president," had an affinity for scandal not only while alive but also when dead. While he was alive, his administration was wracked with the Teapot Dome scandal and corruption in the Veteran's Bureau and the Office of the Alien Property Custodian. After he died, Nan Britton wrote a best-selling book, *The President's Daughter,* in which she revealed she had an illegitimate daughter by him. I suspect that the nervous breakdown in 1913 of his fashionable wife, Florence, whom he fondly referred to as "Duchess," had something to do with his philandering, since he also had a long extramarital affair with Carrie Phillips and who knows how many others.[17] Lady Bird Johnson dismissed a report of her husband's infidelity as "only a little fly on the wedding cake" but neglected to mention what that did to her appetite. When Ellen Louise Axson, Woodrow Wilson's wife, first heard rumors about her husband's affair with Mary Allen Hulbert Peck, she invited her competition to the White House and began treating her as a friend. Sometime later, like Mrs. Florence Harding, she, too, apparently suffered a nervous "breakdown,"[18] which appeared to be a common affliction among First Ladies. Then there was Dwight D. Eisenhower, commander of the U.S. Army during World War II, thirty-fourth president of the United States (1953–61), husband to Mamie, and a congenial and trustworthy man, who had a love affair with his driver, Kay Summersby, during the war.

But on a fine technicality he may not have, since Kay, coming to the defense of the man she loved—the heroic symbol of Western military might—"defended" him by reporting that, on the one occasion when they tried to have sex, he was impotent.[19]

A problem of this sort never bothered John Fitzgerald Kennedy despite his bad back and Addison's disease, conditions that would have rendered most ordinary men flaccid. During the brief Camelot years of his rule, Kennedy found time for numerous, almost compulsive sexual conquests. Women, whose names he often forgot, came late at night and left early in the morning. Jackie seemingly tolerated his philandering, even though he assured friends she did not suspect. Whenever he had a twinge in his crotch and even sometimes when he did not, he left reason and obligation behind and sometimes showed exceptionally poor judgment, like during his year-long affair with Judith Campbell Exner, a close friend to Mafia figures Sam Giancana and John Roselli, who were involved in the CIA plots to assassinate Fidel Castro. Only after FBI director J. Edgar Hoover confronted Kennedy about the inadvisability of his trysts with a Mafia mol did Exner's clandestine visits to the White House stop.[20]

Perhaps the most egregious flaunting of conventional morality took place by the greatest of the twentieth-century American presidents, Franklin Delano Roosevelt. Aside from an affair with his wife's personal social secretary, Lucy Mercer, as well as sexual encounters with many other women over the years, this moral exemplar who inspired an entire nation with his televised fireside chats set an amazing example that few past or future presidents are ever likely to match. He arranged for Missy LeHand, his mistress and private secretary for many years, to sleep in the room next door to his in the executive mansion.[21]

What about the leaders of Canada? Again, of the nine male prime ministers on whom I could gather adequate information, four had or were rumored to have had extramarital affairs, yielding almost the same percentage as American presidents (44 percent).[22] Brian Mulroney's marriage to the daughter of a psychiatrist was on the verge of collapse because of his heavy drinking and his many alleged affairs until he took the pledge to forgo both. In 1945, L.B. Pearson was rumored to have had an affair with a woman he had met in London. There was gossip that Wilfrid Laurier had an affair with Emilie Lavergne. Pierre Trudeau was noted to have had a "close relationship" with a woman during the trying times when his wife, Margaret Sinclair, was having many international affairs and writing two books of personal revelations about their life together, all of which was very humiliating to him.

Of course, some may argue that affairs of the sort found in the United States and Canada are not as likely to be found in more "civilized" nations such as Great Britain, with established traditions of decency and decorum. No proper and honorable gentleman who honors his word would be expected to cheat on his wife. So much for fantasy. By my calculations, about the same percentage of twentieth-century English prime ministers—excluding Arthur Balfour and Edward Heath, who never married, and, naturally, Margaret Thatcher—have likely been as unfaithful as have American presidents and Canadian leaders. The only difference I have found is that the biographical information available on British prime ministers is so much more discreet, making judgments about their sexual transgressions less absolute. Except for David Lloyd-George, who was called the "Goat" for his well-known sexual prowess, biographers of such PMs as Henry Campbell-Bannerman, Henry Asquith, Harold Wilson, Anthony Eden, John Major, and Winston Churchill allude to rumors of infidelity with secretaries, confidantes, or unnamed women instead of stating outright that their subject cheated in his marriage or had a mistress. I suppose this is what is known as tact, but it also may reflect a certain cattiness on the part of certain British writers, who seem artful in suggesting something immoral without actually saying it.

Some reasons for sexual continence:
By focusing so far only on the sexual excesses of rulers, I do not want to give the impression that all of them are servants to their groins. Nestled among these leaders, of whom 95 percent were heterosexual and 1 percent bisexual, were a small percentage, 4 percent, whose sexual activity was so discreet that no record of it exists. It is not that these leaders decided to forgo sex out of a deep spiritual conviction, as did Morarji Desai, prime minister of India from 1977 to 1979, who, like Mahatma Gandhi, took the vow of celibacy but, in his case, only after having five children and probably being too old to perform. There were several reasons for their supposed sexual abstinence. Both Edward Heath, prime minister of Britain from 1970 to 1974, and McKenzie King, prime minister of Canada for three terms,[23] may well have been struggling with homosexual longings. Whatever the cause of their relative sexual inactivity, they apparently were able to sublimate their urges by becoming master debaters. Both Ngo Dinh Diem, president of South Vietnam from 1954 to 1963, who took a vow of chastity as a young man after a woman he loved became a nun, and his adversary, Ho Chi Minh, president of North Vietnam from 1945 to 1969, offset the righteousness of the other by suppressing their sexual urges as part of a general pattern of asceticism. Then,

of course, there were more practical reasons for forgoing sex. According to an unsubstantiated source, Richard B. Bennett, prime minister of Canada from 1930 to 1935, supposedly avoided women because of his "phimosis," otherwise known as a tight foreskin, which caused him painful erections.[24] In the case of Adolph Hitler, the reason for his aberrant or absent sex life is still the subject of debate.[25]

Non-monogamous sexual activity on an international scale:

Aside from these seemingly abstinent leaders, the information presented so far suggests that most rulers, and some types more than others, are sexually profligate or, stated less moralistically, avoid exclusive attachments to one spouse. The question now is whether this tendency is confined only to rulers of certain nations or whether it is worldwide. My findings reveal that the sexual practices of rulers vary widely in different parts of the globe, with the highest percentages of philandering occurring in Latin America and North and Sub-Saharan Africa and the lowest in Euro-Africa. Why a region like Euro-Africa, which includes the former white-run South Africa, the Transvaal, the Orange Free State, and Rhodesia, where rulers show the most sexual continence among all the continents, should be the bulwark for monogamy and the mainstay of marital morality is a mystery. While you can speculate that this may be due to the sexually repressive religious upbringing of the male leaders or the prudery of available women, the only hard and remarkable fact you can be sure about is that all of the white-dominated governments constituting what was once Euro-Africa no longer exist. Is it remotely possible, then, that the extinction of these particular national entities could have been prevented if these rulers had devoted less time to dealing with the state of affairs within their country and more time, much like other leaders around the world, to being unfaithful to their wives, which they then could have justified as affairs of state?

Figure 3.2 below shows that about half of the sample of 377 twentieth-century rulers in Anglo-America (United States and Canada), Europe, Eurasia, the Balkans, and Central and East Asia; between 70 and 80 percent in the Mideast, Latin-America, and Sub-Saharan Africa; and 100 percent in North Africa have indulged in sex with other women outside of a monogamous relationship. But, remarkably, a couple of regions exist in the world in which rulers show a rare semblance of sexual restraint. Only 28 percent of prime ministers in Australia and New Zealand and 17 percent of leaders in Euro-Africa showed evidence of infidelity.

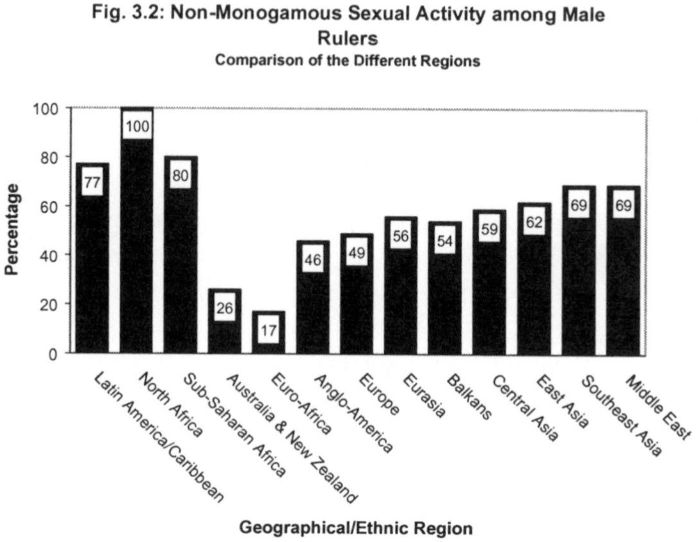

Fig. 3.2: Non-Monogamous Sexual Activity among Male Rulers
Comparison of the Different Regions

Geographical/Ethnic Region

Legend: Note the extremely high rates of non-monogamous sexual activity within North Africa, Sub-Saharan Africa, and Latin America and the extremely low rates within Australia/New Zealand and Euro-Africa.

An Abundance of Offspring

Before becoming too judgmental about the philandering of rulers, we need to consider the possibility that, although they knowingly are pursuing their own pleasures, they *unknowingly* may be doing Nature's bidding. As the number-one man in their nation, which arguably makes them superior in all attributes to all other men, they may be responding to some biological pressure to disseminate their seeds widely to strengthen the gene pool. And in case they consciously feel no obligation to the improvement of the human species, which they most likely do not, Nature helps out by making this activity highly enjoyable for them. This selective breeding by rulers might suit mankind's purpose well if all of these number-one men were of the caliber of a Winston Churchill, Charles de Gaulle, Franklin Roosevelt, or Nelson Mandela. But what if most of the copulating rulers were like Idi Amin, Joseph Stalin, Francois Duvalier, and Adolph Hitler? Instead of contributing to the perpetuation of the species, which would be the biological reason for giving them unlimited access to so many women, these villains might reverse the entire evolutionary process by producing offspring with a greater tendency to act like brutes.

Let's learn what the results say about the wisdom or stupidity of Nature.

Counting children:

Recording the actual number of children of rulers should be a relatively simple task, and for the most part it is. But certain snags occur. The problem is that some of these rulers fornicate so much with so many women that they have trouble keeping track of all their children, and, even when they do, they may decide to recognize some officially and deny the paternity of others. Also, within certain countries like Saudi Arabia, official biographies often make note of only the number of sons, since daughters do not matter. Despite these limitations, it is possible to get reasonable estimates if in some cases you do not mind being off plus or minus twenty-five to fifty children!

How do the reproductive capacities of these different categories of rulers compare? Naturally, because of all the methodological difficulties mentioned above, the following figures represent *gross estimates rather than precise values*, but they nonetheless get the basic message across mainly because the differences are so dramatic. The results indicated that two categories of rulers begot far more offspring than the rest of the rulers combined. Monarchs, who traditionally have been programmed to act as human sperm banks to ensure hereditary succession, had an average of thirty children each,[27] and tyrants had an average of twenty-eight. Democrats in contrast had a puny average of three. The average number of children for the other types of rulers ranged between three and four. These results are roughly consistent with the findings for sexual profligacy. Simply put, rulers with the most power, who can freely sample any woman they wish, produce the largest number of offspring.

Within my sample of rulers, the estimated number of children ranged from none for several rulers to over 500 for Sobhuza II of Swaziland, who shared triple-digit honors with Jean-Bédel Bokassa with at least 200, King Ibn Saud with about 168, and Juan Vicente Gómez with over 100, though he legitimatized only 7. On the next tier of fecund rulers, the double-digiters included Chulalongkorn with at least seventy-seven, Idi Amin with at least thirty-four, and Yüan Shih-K'ai with at least thirty, and then those with more modest broods, such as Paul Kruger with sixteen; Norodom Sihanouk and Alhaji Shehu Shagari with at least fifteen; Sergio Osmeña with about thirteen; and Mao Zedong, Reza Khan, and Moise Tshombe with at least ten.

Naturally, when fecund rulers sire double-digit or triple-digit broods, they may find their ingenuity taxed when they wish to establish mean-

3.2: Bokassa posing with seven of his "hundreds" of children, although he officially recognized only thirty. AFP Photo/Pierre Guillaud.

ingful relationships with their own children on occasion or even want to remember their names. Some have been fairly resourceful in meeting this challenge. For instance, Jean-Bédel Bokassa, the self-styled emperor of his Central African Empire whose children numbered in the hundreds (although he recognized only thirty officially), as any proud father, liked to be photographed each year surrounded by his growing brood of children. On other occasions during the year, when he was not too preoccupied with affairs of state, he enjoyed having them sit down around him while he regaled them with the history and legends of his people. So that he could maintain a special relationship with each of his many children, he devised a clever system of naming them. He named seven daughters Marie after their grandmother, Marie Yokowa; he named four sons Jean—Jean-Bertrand, Jean-Legrand, Jean-Serge, and Jean-Ives—after himself; and he used other clever memory joggers for his other children.[26] That way the likelihood of his using the wrong names for his children and hurting their feelings was greatly reduced.

Despite his busy schedule (which, I suspect, mostly involved trying to service his many wives), King Mongkut of Siam, who had 76 children by 36 wives (or 362 children by 84 wives, depending on which source you believe), was supposedly fond of his children and tried to see them regularly. Whether he ever mastered all their names is unknown, but he definitely tried to maintain meaningful contact with them by occasionally having them troop in during his midday meal and position themselves around his chair according to their age and rank. Presumably he found it heartwarming to have his entire brood nearby, and he sometimes showed his pleasure by giving them bites of any dishes he liked. Then, after the meal, he would dismiss them until the next occasion when he again could spend more quality time with them.[27]

Wealth and Creature Comforts

One of the basic tenets of ruling is that, if rulers remain in office for at least several years without getting killed, they need not ever worry again about financial security. Just as alpha-male primates have greater access to food and shelter and other material benefits that improve their chances of survival, rulers likewise have greater access to more creature comforts than do ordinary citizens. With rare exceptions, there have been no such creatures as pauper ex-kings, prime ministers, presidents, or sheikhs during the twentieth century. No ex-ruler has had to spend his nights at the Salvation Army, get food stamps, or apply for unemployment benefits. Somehow or other, if they have not already made plans to continue living luxuriously after their rule, then bunches of influential people are ready to come to their rescue with lucrative offers of honorary board positions or book offers or foundation chairmanships or senior law partnerships or other sinecures that capitalize on the ex-ruler's know-how and connections or enhance the prestige of their firm or simply give them a chance to brag to their own wives and mistresses about having an ex-ruler beholden to them. Even when no generous benefactor shows up, ex-rulers are charter members of the worldwide club of rulers, which looks after its own. As members of this club, they can expect the country hosting their exile to vote them a generous stipend if they are broke, since no self-respecting ruler wants to be responsible for a guest ex-ruler losing face by having to take handouts or, even worse, work, especially when he wants to set an example for generosity for other rulers to follow in case he ever has need of them.

God helps those who help themselves:

Many world leaders often find themselves in Oscar Wilde's dilemma of being able to resist anything but temptation. But when you consider their fragile hold on power, it is easy to appreciate why they often are more attracted to booty and graft than to duty and statecraft. Often feeling unappreciated and underpaid, many rulers reward themselves for their perceived sacrifices on behalf of their country with treasures that would sink a fleet of pirate galleons. Corruption and graft are especially rampant among rulers with autocratic powers.

As figure 3.3 below shows, the results generally conformed to predictions. Although tyrants towered above all other rulers in their cupidity, greed, and avarice (100 percent), high percentages of monarchs (26 percent), visionaries (32 percent), and authoritarians (19 percent) likewise helped themselves to whatever they wanted and were known to run corrupt regimes. These percentages should be regarded as minimums, since you have to take into account that the fiscal excesses of many of these rulers went undetected or never were defined as illegal. In contrast, only 4 percent of transitionals and 4 percent of democrats—those rulers with the most constraints on their power—gained reputations for being corrupt.

Fig. 3.3: Graft and Corruption among Male Rulers

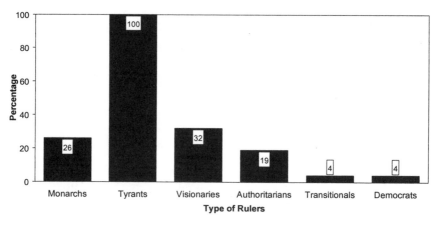

Legend: Note the higher rates of graft among all four groups of dictators, especially tyrants.

To an extent, these disparities in corruption and scandal among the rulers make a kind of perverse sense. Among the different kinds of rulers, tyrants are in the most precarious position for providing financially for their family's future, since any government established after they are forced from office will likely be more interested in retiring them from life than in giving them retirement benefits for life. So from the perspective of enlightened self-interest, they feel justified in taking advantage of whatever financial opportunities their privileged position entitles them to.

In contrast, monarchs need not be as avaricious as tyrants, since their royal predecessors probably had plundered the wealth of the nation already and left vast landholdings and riches to them. Besides, in most absolute monarchies, the line between public funds and the privy purse is blurred, so monarchs can feel free to avail themselves of whatever money they need.

Visionaries usually are so busy implementing their ideologies and trying to secure their place in history that they often cannot be troubled by all the extortion, graft, and stealing going on around them by their more practical-minded, devoted subordinates. However, about one-third of them do manage to put aside their ideological beliefs long enough to earn reputations for being corrupt. It is not that the people begrudge their esteemed leaders their material excesses. They expect their leaders to be able to indulge themselves. What they seem to resent far more is that their families, friends, and political cronies likewise exploit their insider positions for their own financial gain.

Authoritarians, with their propensity for law and order, often seem uncomfortable living too lavishly, but about one-fifth of them manage to overcome their inhibitions to avail themselves of extra funds.

I suspect the reason that relatively so few democrats in comparison to dictators are involved in graft, corruption, or financial scandal is not because they are less greedy than their more autocratic colleagues but because they have less direct access to the state coffers. And they also are the ones most likely to be held accountable, because they do not control the legal system.

Here are some examples of what I mean by corruption—real CORRUPTION, not the piddling kind of influence peddling, cheating on travel vouchers, padding deductions on income tax returns, practicing nepotism, accepting illegal gifts, taking vacations at taxpayers' expense, or tending to personal business on government time you find among many of the more honest rulers. When greedy rulers set out to better their financial positions, they do it on so grand a scale that they put even such robber barons as J.D. Rockefeller, Andrew Carnegie, and J.P. Morgan to shame.

Jean-Bédel Bokassa, sometimes called Popa Bok, not because of his paternal demeanor but because of his resemblance to another father figure in Haiti, had a knack for flimflammery that was the envy of many of his fellow African rulers. A vain man who loved pomp and circumstance, he had himself crowned emperor in a ceremony that cost over $200 million and effectively bankrupted the Central African Republic. Dressed in his military-style jacket, which he had to have reinforced to keep it from sagging under the weight of all the medals spread over the front, he could be quite charming and witty at times during dinner parties, although his hosts were apt to become anxious because of rumors about his cannibalism when he eyed them hungrily throughout the evening. An entrepreneur *par excellence*, he cornered monopolies on his country's ivory, coffee, diamond, and insecticide trade; and he also built the largest industrial complex at his palace, where government employees made records, bricks, furniture, and school uniforms, which he generously sold tax-free to the state. Ever resourceful, he saw opportunities for graft everywhere. For instance, when President Charles de Gaulle gave him a present of a DC-4, he sold the plane to Air Afrique. After the airline repaired it, he seized it on some pretext when it landed on a nearby airfield and then rented it to the state for his own use on official trips.[28]

More than three hundred criminal and civil cases were brought against Ferdinand Marcos and his wife, Imelda, who were accused of stealing up to $10 billion in gold bullion from the Philippine Central Bank and shipping it to vaults in Switzerland during their twenty-year rule. Incensed by what he saw as the casting of unjust aspersions on his good character, Ferdinand Marcos insisted he had discovered Yamashita's treasure before becoming president in 1966, and that was the basis of his immense wealth. But though no one but the Marcoses themselves found that story credible, many people regarded them with fond amusement, especially Imelda, a former beauty queen, because of her flamboyance and extravagances. Spending lavishly, she seldom bothered to examine the racks of clothes, shelves of books, and unauthenticated paintings and antiques she bought. But there were several items she seemed to collect more than others. She owned five hundred brassieres, even a bullet-proof one; vats of perfume; and more than a thousand pairs of shoes. Sometimes, on shopping trips, the Marcoses stayed at their townhouse on Fifth Avenue in New York, tastefully furnished, they believed, so as to impress even the most stylish and discriminating members of American high society. On the walls hung priceless paintings, including Picassos and Van Goghs, and next to them hung oversized photographs of the Marcoses and President and Mrs. Ronald Reagan, which had been enlarged and then painted over with oils![29]

President Suharto not only brought prosperity to Indonesia over much of his thirty-one-year reign but to himself and his family as well. In 1989 the Suhartos' assets were estimated to total about $30 billion, ranking them among the world's dozen richest families. The formula for financial success was simple. Like any devoted father, Suharto wanted his children to have certain advantages, so his government gave them exclusive licenses and concessions when they entered business that turned them into multimillionaires almost overnight despite their ignorance about business practices. Not only did they become part owners of essential industries throughout the country, but foreign companies sought them out as business partners so they could have favored access to government contracts and outlets for their products in Indonesia.

Suharto's 1995 decision to sponsor the building of a national car by a company owned by his youngest son, Hutomo, in association with Kia Motors of South Korea, typifies the kind of graft and corruption that took place. The car, called the Timor—which would end up causing the company and government more trouble than the rebellious island off-shore—was able to be sold for thousands of dollars per car less than its competitors, since it was exempted from paying duties on imported Korean parts. To get the company off to a good start, the Finance Ministry declared that all governmental agencies would now be required to add Timors to their fleets. The government then ordered a consortium of Indonesian banks to offer almost $700 million in start-up loans to the company, which seemingly was a no-risk venture. The company took the money, built thousands of cars, and then, along with its Korean partner, Kia Motors, accomplished the incredible feat of going bankrupt.[30]

In many ways, this feat bore a remarkable resemblance to what happened to Sanjay Gandhi, Indira Gandhi's son and heir apparent until his fatal accident, who likewise undertook to build a people's car for his country, named the Maruti. A common joke soon began spreading around India that the car would solve its gasoline and unemployment problems. Why? Because the engine would not accept any gas, and it would take fifteen Indians to push every Maruti.[31]

As with his appetite for women, Trujillo's hunger for treasure and material possessions was ravenous. After he acquired the sugar industry, he owned a half-million acres of improved land and vast amounts of unimproved land. At that time, the income of the Trujillo family was estimated to equal the combined national expenditures for education, public health, labor, social security, and public works. His factories employed about sixty thousand people. A rough estimate of his holdings at the time in the Dominican Republic and abroad was about $500 million, not adjusted for inflation and with a substantial portion invested in foreign bank accounts.[32]

Other rulers gained their fortunes in other ways. President Marcos Perez Jimenez of Venezuela (1953–58), for instance, an introverted, dull, and modest man but with a love for showy uniforms and sexual orgies, began a vast program of public works, including the construction of highways, hotels, office buildings, factories, and dams, financed by income from oil royalties. As reward for his initiative, he and his associates got a commission from every project. After being forced out of office in a coup, Perez Jiminez fled to the United States, reportedly taking with him a fortune estimated to be over $250 million.[33]

Then, of course, there was Mobutu Sese Seko, who renamed himself Mobutu Sese Seko Kuku Ngebendu wa za Bangathe, which officially means, "The all-powerful warrior who, because of his endurance and will to win, goes from conquest to conquest leaving fire in his wake." Mobutu plundered the profits from his country's enormous mineral wealth and plunged it into virtual bankruptcy. During his reign as president of Zaire, corruption was so rampant at every level of society that a new name, "kleptocracy," was coined to describe a vast patronage system in which persons at every level of government showed a mania for stealing. A member of his family described how Mobutu's close associates and cronies made their own millions by ripping the old man off. "Mobutu would ask one of us to go to the bank and take out a million. We'd go to an intermediary and tell him to get five million; he would go to the bank with Mobutu's authority, and take out ten. Mobutu got one, and we took the other nine."[34]

Interestingly, many of these rulers tended to be shocked and offended when accused of graft and corruption, regarding their activities not only as sound business practices but also their just due. The Reza Shah of Iran, for instance, staunchly claimed he never sought personal benefits at the cost of the public, yet when he abdicated in 1941 he owned two thousand villages, and a quarter million of his subjects worked for him on his land.[35]

Reverence and Deference[36]

All these perquisites of power so far are minor compared to the prospect of achieving an almost godlike status and gaining a measure of immortality. This is something neither wealth nor achievement nor any other human activity can buy. It potentially comes with the position of being a ruler, especially one with absolute power. In many instances, rulers may receive the kind of worship and obedience accorded a living god. Some gain this reverence and deference by the heroic roles they played in their nation's struggles. Others gain it by indoctrinating their people to believe they possess extraordinary abilities and powers.

This practice by rulers of transforming themselves into gods or attributing superhuman status to themselves has a hallowed tradition dating back to antiquity. All of the ancient pharaohs and kings promulgated the belief in their divinity to ensure the obedience and veneration of their subjects. Supposedly a direct descendent of the goddess Venus, Julius Caesar was declared to be a god in ancient Rome. His adopted son, Octavius, alias Caesar Augustus, later billed himself as the son of a god and upon his death was elevated by the Roman senate to full god status, too. Alexander the Great, whom the Pythian priestess declared to be invincible, was touted as the son of Zeus and deified for his accomplishments. And in more modern times, many absolute rulers, whether of royal blood or not, foster notions of this sort. If they do not tout themselves as being divine, then they are apt to claim being descended from somebody semidivine or extraordinary, such as the prophet Mohammad.

Throughout all history, titles loom large as a way of signifying a ruler's exalted status. This tradition holds for twentieth-century leaders as well. Among Abdul-Hamid II's titles, for instance, were Sultan of Sultans, Commander of the Faithful, Lord of Two Continents and of Two Seas, Guardian of the Holy Cities. Fidel Castro liked to be referred to as *el Jefe*, the maximum leader. Hafiz al-Assad of Syria was called the eternal leader. Nkrumah, who compared himself to Christ as Messiah, was called "Osagyefo," the redeemer, and "Messiah of Africa." Sobhuza II's titles ranged from "Powerful Creature" to "Eater of the Gourd, Lion, and Male Elephant." After his pilgrimage to Mecca, Ahmadu Ahidjo was designated "El Hadj" according to a well-known Islamic custom, so his full title now became, "His Excellency El Hadj Ahmadu Ahidjo, President of the Federal Republic of Cameroon, Father of the Nation, Pioneer of Negritude, Prophet of Pan Africanism, Defender of African Dignity." And Idi Amin, who sometimes argued that he was the last "King of Scotland," wanted supplicants to refer to him as "His Excellency President for Life Field Marshal Al Hadj Doctor Idi Amin Dada, VC, DSO, MC, Lord of All the Beasts of the Earth and Fishes of the Sea and Conqueror of the British Empire in Africa in General and Uganda in Particular" so that, by the time they finished addressing him, their short audience with him was over.

While impressive, grandiose titles only help to inflate the ruler's ego in the here and now. They are of no benefit to him when he is dead. If he hopes to gain some measure of immortality among his people for his godly, eternal status, then he must ensure that his living name becomes emblazoned on as many nonliving objects as possible. In this regard, Trujillo was a master.

A guided tour:

Let's construct a scenario for Trujillo, the longtime dictator of the Dominican Republic, to show how a ruler may go about hyping himself. One day a neighboring dictator, whose own people blame him for oppressing them, visits Trujillo to learn why his people seem to love and revere him so. Being a good host, Trujillo gives his guest a personal tour of his capital city so that he can see all of his accomplishments for himself. Bedecked in a uniform with a chestful of medals, Trujillo has his chauffeur drive him and his distinguished visitor in a black stretch bullet-proof limousine around the capital city, once named Santa Domingo by Columbus but now renamed Ciudad Trujillo, located in Trujillo Province next to the adjoining province of Trujillo Valdez, named in memory of his father. As his visitor travels along Trujillo Avenue past the Trujillo Memorial Park, he notices neon signs blinking "God and Trujillo" and advertisements for the lottery beckoning with double entendred slyness, "Be rid of poverty, and Trujillo forever."

Everywhere, statues of Trujillo and bronze plaques commemorating him as benefactor or liberator dot the tropical landscape. Off in the distance, Trujillo proudly points out Trujillo Peak, which is the highest mountain in the West Indies, and invites his guest, if he would like, to board the navy frigate, named—guess what—*Presidente Trujillo*. Then, on the ride back to the executive mansion, he instructs his driver to take a detour past the insane asylum (one of the few institutions he permits not to be named after him) to show him that he is loved even by the mental patients and, as proof, points to the sign on the door, which cryptically reads, "Everything we owe to Trujillo," never bothering to wonder why the patient who was crafty enough to write the sign was locked up and the people who read it without laughing were not.

Although I admit to minor embellishments, the gist of the above account is true—true enough that Jesus Galindez, from whose dissertation, the "Trujillo Era," portions of this description were borrowed, probably would have wished in retrospect that he had chosen a different thesis.[37] He unfortunately did not know that dictators have no sense of humor, especially when they are the butt of ridicule. After Trujillo learned of this sacrilege, he had Galindez abducted from New York, flown to the Dominican Republic, and then brought to him. For the crime of being disrespectful—not for being dishonest or inaccurate—Trujillo ordered his henchmen to strip Galindez, slowly lower him into a vat of boiling water, and then feed his body to sharks.[38]

What I have described so far is known as a personality cult. The main purpose of a government-sponsored personality cult is to get the people to believe that their ruler has extraordinary, even divine-like qualities so that they will follow his lead or be too scared to rebel. There probably is another reason as well. Like ordinary persons, rulers want the public to think well of them. So when they get a chance to influence the attitudes of their people toward them, they naturally want them to believe that they are as wonderful as they imagine themselves to be. After the people begin to repeat what they were programmed to say, the leaders often forget that they were the ones who programmed them to say it in the first place, and then, like writers who write their own blurbs for a book jacket, they become converts to their own hype.

That rulers can come to believe their own hype about themselves seems undeniable. How else, for example, can you explain the reaction of Nicolae Ceausescu, former president of Romania, who from his balcony used to address audiences trucked in for these occasions and trained to cheer on cue and join in on the prerecorded applause?[39] Then, in almost tearful gratitude for these warm, enthusiastic receptions, he would reward his audiences with multiple encores, sometimes lasting longer than five hours, as people below began shifting restlessly from foot to foot, unbearably needing to pee or already having done so. But this is not uncommon. You find variants of these bizarre situations with other rulers again and again. Being ruler, they expect to elicit deference, submission, and awe in their subjects. If their subjects won't confer a godhead upon them, then they bestow it upon themselves.

Kim Il-sung is a good example of a ruler who had perfected the personality cult to an art.[40,41] His adopted alias of "Il-sung," which means "becoming the sun," signified to his people that he had become the bright lodestar for Korea, the Twice Hero or Hero of Labor of the Republic. Official biographies proclaimed that, in the dark days of the nation when the midday sun and full moon had lost their luster, he came forth to place the destiny of the nation on his shoulders. Indoctrination programs about his exploits began in nursery school and continued throughout high school. Kim Il-sung University in Pyongyang even had departments specializing in Kim Il-sung: the Department of Kim Il-sung's Revolutionary History and the Department of Kim Il-sung's Works. Newspapers printed his words in bold type or red letters, just as many Christian Bibles quote the words of Christ. According to the myths fabricated about him, he had turned sand into rice to ward off starvation, had crossed rivers on a leaflet, and had taken part in a hundred thousand battles over a fifteen-year period (more than twenty battles a day), although he never engaged in real combat during the days of Japanese colonial rule. As constant reminders to his people of his exalted status, he saturated the country with countless plaster busts and statues of himself, had his subjects wear badges with his picture, insisted that they hang portraits of him in their households, and made his birthday the most important national holiday. Then after he died the North Korean authorities mummified his body and laid it in a coffin at a memorial palace under the pretext that he was "immortal and imperishable." Say what you will about the absurdity of these measures, but they brought him as close to being a god in an atheistic nation as an ordinary mortal can get.

If my predictions about the prerogatives of alpha males hold true, you should expect to find personality cults most common among rulers with the most power. This prediction is borne out. Dictators as a group rely on personality cults far more than democratic leaders. Almost all

3.3: Thousands of North Koreans hold up colored cards to form a picture of Kim Il Sung at a massive stadium rally in Pyongyang. AP/Wide World Photos.

visionaries relied on personality cults to facilitate their attempts at social engineering and the ideological indoctrination of the populace. About the same proportion of monarchs used elaborate, state-sponsored ceremonies and rituals and institutionalized oaths of allegiance and assorted activities that were designed to enhance their sense of majesty and their divine right to rule. Those tyrants and authoritarians who resorted to personality cults did so mainly to lend weight to their pronouncements for the purpose of social control. But as the percentages show, personality cults were not limited to dictatorships. In emerging democracies, about one-fifth of all rulers deliberately encouraged their people to perceive them as the venerated fathers or liberators of their nations and played on their special status to perpetuate themselves in office. While deliberate personality cults were relatively uncommon among leaders of established democracies, probably because strong opposition parties existed that kept pointing out that the "emperor had no clothes" (I am not referring now to his sexual exploits!), some rulers did employ them during times of national crisis or war, mostly to rally the people to carry out their agenda.

Among the dictators in my sample, 88 percent of visionaries, 83 percent of monarchs, 52 percent of tyrants, and 38 percent of authoritarians deliberately fostered personality cults, while, among the democratic leaders, 21 percent of transitionals and 6 percent of established democrats made use of them to some degree. Aside from the glorification of rulers, personality cults serve a very practical function; they help keep rulers in power. The results of my study revealed that those who used personality cults to manipulate the minds of their subjects kept their power much longer than those who did not, an average of eighteen years compared to seven years.

The next logical question is what impact the kind of rule had on how long rulers were in office. The answer is a lot. In all dictatorships, this same relationship with personality cults held. Those who relied on these cults averaged twenty years in power, while those who did not averaged ten years. Although their time in office was naturally less, democratic leaders likewise showed similar results. Democratic leaders who made concerted efforts to glorify themselves averaged eleven years in power, while those who did not averaged six years.

One other matter needs emphasis. While the vast majority of democratic leaders may not rely on formal personality cults, it is well to remember that one of their most important functions is to manipulate the minds and behaviors of their people to gain greater social cohesion. That is one of the main functions of leadership. In democratic nations, leaders often strengthen their authority to rule by consulting public relations firms or advertising agencies to help them present a more appealing public image. All this suggests that there is a gradation from full-blown government-sponsored personality cults to image-making by public relations firms, such as the Camelot myth associated with the Kennedy administration, to the constant self-promotional activities by many political rulers.

Is the Prize Worth It?

What the findings in this chapter reveal is that every one of the predictions about the prerogatives and perquisites of rulers, based on the advantages for alpha-male primates, is borne out. Although all rulers have access to these different rewards, those with the most power are the most likely to be the most sexually promiscuous, sire the largest number of offspring, avail themselves of the greatest material benefits, and deliberately try to inspire the most awe, deference, and submission in their subjects by various methods. These are incredible perks, and, for many rulers, the equivalent of heaven on earth along with a touch of immortality thrown in.

Now comes the question of whether the potential price would-be rulers must pay to gain these fabulous perks is worth the personal cost. If my thesis is correct, this question should be moot. Would-be rulers should be willing to pay almost any price because their decisions would not governed by reason or prudence; they mainly would be determined by biological necessity. Once they are inducted into the struggle for ultimate power, natural evolutionary forces operating beyond their awareness should compel them to continue on their quest regardless of the perils involved. Many individuals even should be willing to undergo great privations and risk almost certain death rather than forgo their pursuit of ultimate power or relinquish it after they have gained it. Let's now examine the extent to which these expectations hold true.

A Dangerous Game

The fact that as many as five angry adult males can be intimidated by one determined individual, quite on his own, is another example of the importance of psychological factors in chimpanzee dominance interactions. It implies also that the lone male who dares to face such opposition is either stupid (cannot imagine the possible consequences) or has rather a large share of boldness—a quality that perhaps comes close to courage.

—Jane Goodall, *The Chimpanzees of Gombe*

King of the Mountain is a game played in some form or another by children throughout the world. The game tests strength, stamina, and cunning. The game requires a hill of rocks, sand, dirt, or ice with room at the top for only one child who is the king. Since all the other children also want to be king, they do everything possible to dislodge the current occupant from his lofty perch. They may try to do this by physical force—grabbing at the king's ankles, tugging at his arms, and trying to wrestle him down—or they may adopt different tactics and strategies to relax his guard or lure him off. They may challenge him one at a time or charge up the hill all together and attack him from all sides. Sometimes they get so frustrated and upset that they lose their tempers and get violent. But even when they form alliances among themselves to overthrow the king, they know that only one of them can become the new king. Then once the new king has made it to the top, he must defend himself against all the other children, who now want to topple him.

Just as certain games played by youngsters, such as "mommies and daddies" and "follow the leader," may prepare them for roles that they later play as adults, the game of King of the Mountain seems to serve a similar social function. What is so remarkable about the game is that it metaphorically depicts the struggle for ultimate power within society at

large, suggesting that children worldwide may have been biologically programmed to scrimmage well in advance for their later contests for social
supremacy. The observation that this game also happens to be one of the
favorite games played by young mountain gorillas lends support to this
notion.

When you compare the adult version of this game, known as "politics," with the child version, you find many similar features.

• Contestants do not need any special knowledge or qualifications.
All they need to do is to enter the fray.
• Although female participation is grudgingly tolerated, males are
the major competitors.
• Unlike other kinds of contests in which candidates who are caught
cheating are disqualified, nobody gets too upset or surprised when
players lie, cheat, and deceive. Chicanery and deception are expected,
and anything that works goes.
• So that large numbers of players keep competing and do not get
discouraged because they lack intelligence, wisdom, or ability, the
game allows for automatic adjustments to be made, which continually scale down the requirements for success so that anybody with
enough persistence, animal cunning, or luck can win. The absence of
any minimum requirements ensures there always will be a winner.
• The only major difference between the adult and child versions
of the game is that in the adult version participants do not know
they are playing a game and in the child version they do.

In figure 4.1 below, I list some of the obstacles, impediments, and
hardships would-be rulers can expect to encounter as they engage in this
real-life game. For instance, during their climb up the mountain, they
are likely to risk torture, imprisonment, exile, and death when they try to
displace the reigning leader. Then, if victorious, they will have little time
to rest on their laurels before facing a barrage of other crises such as
public riots, uprisings, assassination attempts, mental breakdowns, coups,
imprisonment, banishment, or execution. And even if their tenure in
office goes smoothly, they will need to be ever alert to the threat of adversaries trying to unseat them, much as they themselves had done with
their predecessors.

By listing all these hazards, I do not mean to imply this is the typical
scenario for all rulers. Certainly, among democratic rulers, these perils exist
but are not as common. But as I soon will show, these dangers are so wide-

spread among rulers as a whole and so frequent with certain kinds of rulers and so inevitable in certain parts of the world, that you almost have to regard them as characteristic features of ruling and the absence of them as aberrations.

KING OF THE MOUNTAIN
A Game That Portrays the Struggle for Social Dominance

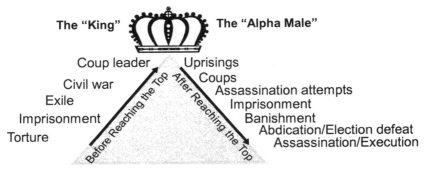

Fig. 4.1: This figure depicts the major obstacles, hardships, and dangers that would-be rulers face as they aspire to ultimate power, and the personal dangers that await them after they successfully manage to reach high office.

With this typical scenario, you are obliged to ask why any rational person should want to participate in a deadly activity of this sort. Although there are perquisites and privileges accorded to the alpha male at the top of the social dominance hierarchy, the game does not seem to offer the unsuccessful participants much fun. It is an all-or-nothing situation for them. It also is not safe. Perhaps the best outcome most candidates can expect is the humiliation of defeat. The remainder often encounter pain, suffering, and death at some point in their quest.

Why then do so many candidates stay engaged in the struggle for social dominance, especially when the odds for success seem so low and the potential rewards are often so long in coming? From my study of the personalities and careers of these rulers, I have come to the conclusion that the reason most men continue their pursuit of ultimate power has little to do with the nature of their ideological convictions, whether they be nationalistic, religious, political, or pragmatic. Would-be rulers court danger as a way to prove their manhood and establish their dominance over others. Additionally, existing within all societies is an unwritten code that bestows honor on those who risk death for the sake of some worthy cause. Many military leaders often aspire to no greater personal glory than the chance to "die with their boots on" or to "go down in flames" during battle with the enemy. The struggle for political supremacy, despite all of its personal risks, gives potential rulers a chance to test their courage and not be found wanting. It is the process of vying for ultimate power more than the end result of gaining it that keeps them in the game, win or lose. And the basic reason they continually need to be testing their manhood, at least according to my thesis, is for the same sociobiological reason that restive, subordinate baboons, gorillas, and chimps feel compelled to challenge, topple, and replace the reigning alpha male whenever an opportunity to do so presents itself: they do so because their genes dictate they must. Although it is hard to know the exact biological mechanism underlying this drive, like so many other aggressive male behaviors, it probably has to do with the amount of androgens or related hormones circulating within certain areas of their brains, which induces them to override their normal instincts for self-preservation to fulfill a broader social function.

These, then, are some of the unwritten rules of the game and the supposed reasons would-be rulers play it. Now I would like to introduce some of the players who became winners, describe some of the risks they took, and examine how they managed to exploit many of their hardships for their own political advantage.

BEFORE REACHING THE TOP

A University behind Bars

Because only one ruler at a time can exercise ultimate power, those who want it have to wrest it away from those who have it. Since those who have ultimate power usually do not want to give it up unless they are forced to, they have to keep any potential usurpers from overthrowing them. The surest way for them to stop usurpers in their tracks is to kill them. But this practical solution is not always politically feasible. Killing troublemakers may make martyrs out of them, invite more rebellion, and rankle human rights agencies that, they believe, are always meddling in other nations' affairs. So rulers may be obliged to resort to other options.

While many reigning rulers have murdered malcontents within their countries, fortunately all of the rulers being overthrown by the subjects in my study thought better of it. If they had not, these subjects would not have become rulers, and I would have had to select other ones to study who had been spared the death sentence. Instead, these reigning rulers, many of whom are likewise subjects in my study because they themselves had not been killed by their predecessors, usually opted for the next-best option, which was to imprison these troublemakers.

You would expect that going to jail would be an awful ordeal for aspiring rulers. And mostly it was. Aside from interrupting their personal careers, which had been dedicated to making life hell for those in power, they stood to lose their personal freedom and be separated from all their fellow conspirators. Some even might miss their spouses and children, whom they hardly saw anyway but did not like giving up the option of doing so. Then once inside prison, they would have to endure hardships, humiliations, and cruelties that would make it hard for them to keep their personal dignity. These ordeals usually were awful enough to dissuade most ordinary, sensible people from pursuing their political activities. But those would-be rulers who eventually were successful in their quest for ultimate power were not ordinary, sensible people. These ordeals only served to harden their resolve.

Living in a modern democracy such as in England, America, Canada, or Australia gives you a distorted notion about the legal difficulties of rulers around the world. For instance, over 20 percent of the 1,941 rulers in the world during the past century (and 39 percent within the smaller sample of more notable rulers) were arrested and imprisoned for their political activities sometime before they were able to assume high office (See figure 4.2). Imagine, more than one aspiring ruler in five spent time behind bars before gaining ultimate power! Visionaries (68 percent), authoritarians (65 percent), and transitionals (55 percent) were most likely to be imprisoned, averaging fifteen months, twelve months, and twenty-three months in jail, respectively. The amount of time in jail for transitional rulers is inflated, naturally, by Nelson Mandela's twenty-seven-year imprisonment, which set the all-time record for time served among all rulers. Next came tyrants (36 percent), who averaged about two months in jail. Leaders of established democracies (24 percent) and monarchs (19 percent) were the least likely to be arrested, averaging four months and less than one month in jail. The reasons for these arrests ranged from participating in political protests to belonging to outlawed political parties, distributing political leaflets, publishing critical articles about the regime, or partaking in strikes, uprisings, or coups.

The way these rulers eventually came to power determined why certain groups of rulers were arrested more than others. Among all the would-be rulers, visionaries, transitionals, and authoritarians (especially military strongmen) were obliged to operate in the open to win supporters for their cause, and so tended to be the most noticeable. Tyrants were more likely to ingratiate themselves with the powers-that-be and mask their intentions before launching their coups, and so were less apt to be conspicuous. And prospective leaders of established democracies and aspiring monarchs, who were mostly committed to preserving their form of government, represented the least immediate threat to those in power. In other words, those would-be rulers who openly sought the most sweeping social changes—namely, the visionaries and transitionals—were among the most likely to be identified by the regime in power as dangerous rabble-rousers who needed to be locked up. Those who were not threatening to overthrow the existing social order—namely, monarchs and democrats—were relatively more free to pursue their aims.

Fig. 4.2: Percentage of Rulers Arrested before Gaining Power

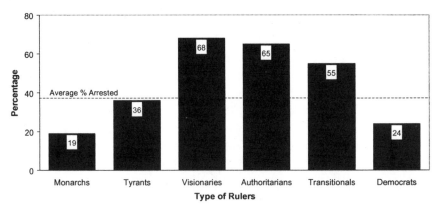

Legend: Note that those who were the most socially disruptive, namely, visionaries and transitionals, were most likely to be arrested during their rise to power; and those who were the least socially disruptive, namely monarchs and democrats, were least likely.

A sabbatical of sorts:
If someone happened to be one of the would-be rulers with a high likelihood of being arrested, he would be well advised to keep his bags packed and be ready on a moment's notice to take a forced sabbatical in jail at

government expense. There probably are people who believe that all politicians should be given the opportunity to spend an extended time in prison, but that would be a short-sighted policy, since, as it turns out, imprisonment often improves the political prospects for those who aspire to become rulers. Even more to the point, in many instances prison actually comes to serve as an institute of higher learning for many political activists and revolutionaries who want to further the formal education they failed to complete. While there, they gain better educations and training experiences in politics than they ever could have gotten at any premier university. If they can endure the torture, solitary confinement, humiliations, and privations while in prison, and treat them as part of the initiation rites for becoming a ruler, like hazing at a fraternity, they will have a big advantage over all of their fellow competitors. They may not earn a formal degree in prison, but they will gain something even more valuable. They will command the admiration of the people for defying the powers that be, showing the courage of their convictions, and living to tell their story. For many of their future followers, those are all of the qualifications necessary for being a ruler.

A time for learning and reflection:

One potential benefit of prison is that it gives would-be rulers a chance to become well-grounded in political ideology. For instance, it was at Doftana prison, which the Romanian police described as a "communist university," where Nicolae Ceausescu became thoroughly indoctrinated in Marxism-Leninism and learned the argot and nonsequiturs that he later spouted in his deadly speeches. The same held true for Tito during his seven years in jail, and for Joseph Stalin during his seven and one half years' imprisonment. In prison, the communists enforced their own discipline, kept themselves apart from other prisoners, and led a harsh monastic existence, spending much of their curriculum time mastering all the "socialist" dogma and the arguments against capitalism.

Say what you will negative about prison, but it is an equal opportunity institution, showing no discrimination at all in its admission policies for *political dissidents*. Anyone who meets the minimal requirements of committing a political offense qualifies for admission, regardless of race, religion, or creed. And once enrolled in prison, proselytizers do everything possible to make sure the efforts new initiates expend on their studies during their time there will prove to be successful and rewarding. They have no entrance exams or scholastic aptitude tests to pass. They do not have to cram for midterms or finals. They do not have to worry about flunking. With seemingly infinite time to spend, they can go over and over the same material, memorizing it even if they do not understand it—which probably is better anyway, since understanding prompts questions, and questions can be the enemy of faith.

Prison also is a perfect setting for working out their political ideology and sharpening their persuasive skills on a captive audience. As a kind of think tank, the setting is ideal for scholarly activity. When the inmates are not being tortured or going crazy in solitary confinement, they have plenty of time to read and write and plot and scheme, as the examples below show.

- During Hitler's five-month stay in prison, where he was coddled by sympathetic jailers, he enjoyed all sorts of special privileges. He could receive visitors at all hours, who often brought him delicacies and treats. He also was allowed to select Rudolf Hess as a companion to share his spacious, sunny cell and serve as his secretary while he completed his infamous book, *Mein Kampf* (My Struggle).
- Vladimir Lenin enjoyed the chance prison offered for scholarly pursuits and began work there on his important treatise, *The Development of Capitalism in Russia*.
- While in prison, Patrice Lumumba finished writing *Le Congo, terre d'avenir, est-il menacé?*—a book about Belgian colonial policy that he never got published, probably because the CIA made sure he did not.
- Nelson Mandela read many biographies and developed his political philosophy while imprisoned on Robben Island. During his years there, he was able to further his education by being exposed to the arguments of the "communist" and "nationalist" wings of the ANC, and between both of these groups and the "Africanists" of the Pan-African Congress and later the Black Consciousness Movement.[1]
- U Nu of Burma wrote two novels and several plays while he was in jail.
- Leon Blum used his incarceration by the Nazis to write his memoirs and reflections on politics.
- After a failed coup attempt, Fidel Castro spent his time in prison reading revolutionary material and planning another coup.
- During the ten years Robert Mugabe spent in a Rhodesian prison for "subversive speech," he acquired a law degree by correspondence courses and even managed to lead a coup in 1974 to become leader of the Zimbabwe African National Union.

Despite all these political advantages of prison, I suspect that few if

4.1: Nelson Mandela cell at Maximum Security Prison, Robben Island, Capetown, S.A. Photograph by Robert Kraus.

any of these graduates would have voiced their regrets years later, as many individuals do about their college years, that they should have taken more advantage of all the educational opportunities there.

A haven for making new friends:

Aside from its potential academic advantages, prison is also a great place for networking. These would-be rulers get a chance to meet hooligans, criminals, degenerates, killers, and political activists from all walks of life who can have a dubious broadening influence on them. For instance, during their struggles for independence from Great Britain, the Irish were fond of referring to the British jails and internment camps in Ireland and England as Republican University, with its many constituent colleges. These were great places to forge close bonds with fellow convicts; meet new terrorists who were experts in making bombs, plastic explosive devices, and other ingenious weapons of destruction; and exchange strategies for assassinations and raids with them, all on a collegial basis. There often is nothing like having a common adversary to serve as a basis for becoming close friends. The more mutual hatred someone can share with another person toward some outside authority, the closer these two individuals will feel toward each other. Later, after these would-be rulers are released or escape from prison, they will command the allegiance of a brotherhood of former inmates for life, provided none of those former inmates are seeking ultimate power, too. If they are, then once the would-be ruler has the advantage, he may have to send his competitors back to jail for some additional postgraduate education.

The spiritual and psychological benefits of being locked up:
Aside from these practical benefits of being imprisoned, there are intangible ones as well. After their ordeal in prison, many aspiring rulers look upon it as having been an enriching experience, contributing to their personal growth and maturity. And in certain instances, they were able to gain more spirituality there than they ever could have realized from going to church. Here are some examples.

- The first time Nehru was arrested for his protests about British rule in India, he was delighted, since he considered it an indication that he had earned the respect of his politically active father, who likewise was in jail at the time.
- Anwar Sadat believed he had been reborn and purged of evil by his sufferings in Cell 54.[2]
- Menachim Begin claimed profound relief when he was arrested by the communists in Poland because he was in despair at the time and had a need to suffer. In his autobiography, *White Nights*, Begin wrote that the constant attempts to brainwash him during his eight-year incarceration and his failure to crack under the constant interrogation strengthened him emotionally for dealing with the political challenges ahead.[3]
- Ahmed Ben Bella of Algeria claimed that his six-year stay in prison matured him as a person.[4]
- Mujibur Rahman, who was to become the first prime minister and later president of Bangladesh, credited his prior ten years of imprisonment with hardening his heart and spirit and preparing him to rule.[5]

The symbolic aspects of imprisonment:
For the aspiring leader, yet another advantage of going to prison is that it marks him as a hero and gives him more eclat with his followers. While in prison, he can serve as an inspirational symbol for his people even if the authorities muffle and shackle him and try to keep him out of sight.

- During his long years of imprisonment, Nelson Mandela was a powerful symbol of resistance against the apartheid policies of the South African government.

- Instead of crushing the trade union, Solidarity, the Polish government only strengthened it by arresting Lech Walesa more than a dozen times and putting him under house arrest for nearly a year.
- Jomo Kenyatta's nine years in prison crystallized Kenya's bid for independence.
- Jozef Pilsudski was proclaimed as the savior of Polish independence after his imprisonment by the Germans in World War I.
- Kenneth Kaunda became a national hero after his imprisonment by the British because of his struggles to gain independence for Zambia.
- In 1955 Agostinho Neto, who already was becoming famous as an Angolan poet, was arrested by the secret police and sentenced to eighteen months in prison but then was released because of the clamor raised by the international community. When he was arrested again in 1960, his supporters staged a mass protest rally. The violent response of the authorities to the rally led to the government's collapse and Neto's eventual rise to power.

With so much precedent to draw from, most rulers should have figured out long since that jailing their political opponents could backfire and lead to their own downfall. Perhaps it was a bit of hubris on their part to believe that, if they jailed these aspiring leaders once, they always could do so again if the need arose. How could they respect or fear someone they had arrested and now had under their power? But where they went wrong in their calculations was in underestimating the resolve and resourcefulness of their captives. Those who eventually win the game of King of the Mountain learn to use their captivity to their advantage rather than be crushed by it.

A Home away from Home

As an alternative to jail, authorities also have the option of banishing their political nemeses. Out of sight, out of mind, so the saying goes. By forcing their opponents to leave the country, besieged leaders not only deprive the opposition of an inspirational symbol to rally around but show their frugality by saving the cost of paying for their upkeep in prison, while at the same time relieving overcrowding there as well. Ordinarily, you would think that exiling troublemakers would be an excellent way for rulers to teach adversaries about the inadvisability of attacking their regime. When I use the term "exile," I am not referring to the glamorous and exciting kind of exile many people imagine from novels and movies about expatriate writers, artists, and dissidents who sit around in cafés in Paris or Rio de Janeiro and have heated discussions about the futility of life; the meaninglessness of existence; the irrelevance of all current political systems, philosophy, and art; and other emotionally uplifting topics. By beginning their lives anew on foreign soil, these would-be rulers usually have to endure all sorts of privations. They often lack adequate funds, accepted professional credentials for earning a living, the support of their former friends and colleagues, and proficiency in the language of the host country. With all of these handicaps, you might suppose that these would-be rulers would be so busy simply trying to

In my sample of rulers, 15 percent spent from several months to many years in exile before gaining ultimate power. The exile usually came about because they were forced to leave the country; voluntarily left to protest the existing government; left to avoid impending arrest; left for strategic purposes; or, as in the case of Gen. Charles de Gaulle, who went to England to become the leader of the Free French during World War II, left for a combination of these reasons. No sooner did these would-be rulers get settled in their host countries than they began plotting ways to overthrow the government in power and planning for their eventual return. For example, the Ayatollah Khomeini, who had been banished by the Shah of Iran for speaking out against his reforms, spent his fifteen years in exile in France successfully plotting the overthrow of the shah. Then there is the case of Syngman Rhee, first president of the Republic of Korea (South Korea) from 1948 to 1960, who was the all-time leader for years spent in exile. Rhee spent forty years of his life in both voluntary and forced exile before he took power and then again after he forfeited it. To add to his ordeal, he also was imprisoned for seven years, tortured, and placed in solitary confinement for opposing Japanese rule of Korea.

Among the different kinds of rulers, visionaries (36 percent) and transitionals (26 percent) were most likely to spend time in exile, followed next by authoritarians (22 percent) and tyrants (17 percent), and last by monarchs (14 percent) and democrats (6 percent). This is roughly the same ordering of rulers as existed for the likelihood of imprisonment, suggesting that the reasons for these differences are the same. Governments in power tend to view visionaries and transitionals as much greater threats than they do aspiring democrats and monarchs, and tyrants and authoritarians (especially apparatchiks) usually do not make their intentions known until it is too late for the existing ruler to intervene.

eke out a living and survive that they would not have any time left to cause trouble for the rulers who banished them. But the rulers-in-charge miscalculated with the would-be rulers in my study. Instead of the ban-ishers ridding themselves forever of those they banished, as you reason-ably might expect to happen, the banished, like pesky nits in their hair, kept driving them crazy by organizing protests or launching coups against them from afar.

Imprisonment, exile, or both:
Since the reasons for imprisonment and exile are so similar, you would expect that the likelihood of would-be rulers being subjected to one or the other or both would be substantially higher than for either impris-onment or exile alone. And that naturally is so. What is remarkable about these particular findings is not only the ordering of percentages for the different types of rulers but also the actual magnitude of the percentages for certain types. Imagine, roughly two out of every three transitionals or visionaries and roughly one out of every two authoritarians or ty-rants experienced these hardships at some point in their political careers before actually coming to power. These telling statistics show how great the ambition, dedication, or zeal of these would-be leaders must have been for them to have endured these various traumas as they made their way along the path toward ultimate power.

As figure 4.3 below shows, the prospects for would-be rulers being jailed or banished vary widely throughout the world. For example, roughly three-fourths of all aspiring rulers undergo these hardships in North Africa sometime before assuming power; about one-half do so in Latin-America, Sub-Saharan Africa, the Balkans, Asia, and the Middle East; about one-fourth do so in Europe and Eurasia; and less than one-tenth do so in Euro-Africa, Anglo-America, and Australia/New Zealand. Obviously, racial, ethnic, cultural, and geographical factors contribute to the dramatic differences in these forms of punishment in the different regions throughout the world, but perhaps the one influence that cuts through all the other factors happens to be the form of government ex-

Among all the rulers worldwide, 21 percent spent time in prison or in exile, and 4 percent spent time in both.[6] Within the smaller sample, transitionals (65 percent) and visionaries (60 percent) were the most likely types of rulers to spend time in one or the other or in both, with authoritarians (48 percent) and tyrants (41 percent) the next most likely and democrats (21 percent) and monarchs (17 percent) the least.

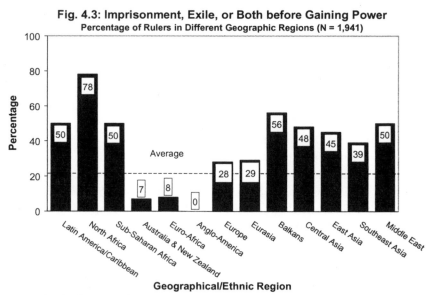

Fig. 4.3: Imprisonment, Exile, or Both before Gaining Power
Percentage of Rulers in Different Geographic Regions (N = 1,941)

Legend: The figure within each bar represent the percentage of rulers within the geographical region who were jailed or exiled or both.

isting at the time. Persons seeking power in countries with strict constitutional safeguards for personal freedom and due process will be less likely to be arrested for political offenses or be banished from the country than in nations that do not have these safeguards. It would seem, then, that, if someone wanted to rule a country without risking imprisonment or banishment, he would be wise to engage in political activities only in established democracies. Otherwise, his chances of making it to high office without first undergoing the ordeal of prison, exile, or both are not much better than a coin flip in most regions around the world, and are negligible in North Africa.

Potentially Lethal Political Activities

King of the Mountain would be a much more genteel game if, after a reasonable time at the top, the reigning ruler told the person impatiently waiting for his chance to rule, "Now it's your turn," and then graciously retired to become a respected elder statesman. The Swiss form of government, which has a council of ministers with a yearly rotation of them as president, comes closest to that civilized way of playing the game except for the fact that the reigning president has hardly any executive power, since it mostly resides within the twenty-six independent cantons. That is why the outgoing presidents can be so accommodating to the incoming ones: it is much easier to give up power if you do not really have any. And that is the crux of the problem. Rulers with true executive power do not want to give it up unless they are required to do so because of fixed constitutional limits for their terms in office or because they cannot command a parliamentary majority.

Since most autocratic rulers will not give up their power voluntarily, others who really want it have to wrest it forcibly away from them. This is a real measure of how much they want to rule, because, once they openly commit themselves to toppling the regime in power, they risk being killed in battle or being executed if they are caught.

Despite the risks, an endless supply of participants court danger in their efforts to rid their nations of foreign rule, unify their countries, or simply overthrow existing governments no matter how benign or malignant they are. Accounts of guerrilla warfare, bloody battles, prison escapes, torture, and suffering are commonplace for would-be rulers. For instance, Mao Zedong's six-thousand-mile trek to Northern China to escape Chiang's pursuing army, known as the Long March of 1934–35, has become legendary. Many other aspiring rulers have endured comparable hardships during their quest for ultimate power. Nothing short of death could deter them from pursuing their goal.

> Among all of the twentieth-century world rulers, 23 percent risked their lives in coups, revolutions, uprisings, civil wars, wars of liberation, sabotage campaigns, terrorism, or successionist movements before gaining high office. Often cited for their daring in these engagements, they then capitalized on their reputations as heroes in their bids for ultimate power. Among the four kinds of autocratic leaders, tyrants (73 percent), visionaries (68 percent), and authoritarians (55 percent) were the most likely rulers to secure power this way, and monarchs (31 percent) were the least likely (see figure 4.4 below).
>
> Not surprisingly, trying to become a democratic leader is a lot safer than trying to become a dictator. Nonetheless, almost one-third of transitional democrats (30 percent), still a substantial percentage, risked their lives beforehand in civil wars or wars of independence. Only the leaders of established democracies (6 percent) had a relatively risk-free time in pursuing high office. That was because they did not have to overthrow the existing leader, since the form of government ensured free elections and fixed terms in office.

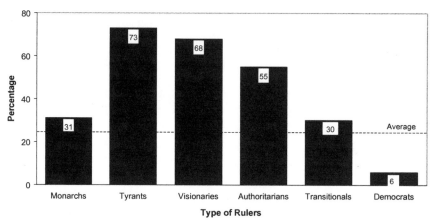

Figure 4.4: Participation in Coups, Civil Wars, or Paramilitary Activity

Legend: Note that, except for monarchs, transitionals, and democrats, whose rule was based on tradition or law, most of the remaining rulers gained high office by resorting to force.

Anything Goes

When individuals are willing to court danger and risk death during their quest for ultimate power, you should not be surprised to discover that they likewise may resort to deception and other treacherous means to gain their ends. For many aspiring rulers, all that matters is political survival. Moral expediency is the basic law of the political jungle. To emerge victorious, they will do whatever it takes.

In order to gauge the extent to which aspiring rulers placed a higher premium on political practicality than on personal scruples, I have tried to gauge the likelihood of them betraying their prior benefactors. Presumably, only extremely ambitious, unprincipled persons would be disposed to turn against those individuals who had helped them advance in their political careers. Since virtue should be its own reward, would-be rulers who turn against past benefactors should be deserving of moral censure. At the very least, in a fair and just world, they should not expect to benefit politically from their treachery.

"Nonsense," Machiavelli—the patron sinner for many aspiring rulers—would say. In the world of politics, gratitude is not the best attitude. Rather, it represents a foolish sentiment. In *The Prince*, he states, "A wise lord cannot, nor ought he to, keep faith when such observance may be turned against him, and when the reasons that caused him to pledge it exist no longer. If men were entirely good this precept would not hold, but because they are bad, and will not keep faith with you, you too are not bound to observe it with them." In other words, if rulers want to gain and retain power, they need not be bound by loyalty. As it happens, my results clearly show that Machiavelli's observation was correct.

Mentors, sponsors, patrons, or colleagues played key roles in helping 36 percent of the rulers in my sample rise to power. If a key measure of political success is how long a ruler retains power, then we should be able to tell whether continued loyalty to these persons resulted in a shorter or longer term in office. A comparison between all rulers who remained loyal to their mentors (58 percent) and those who did not (42 percent) revealed that the loyalists spent an average of eight years in office, while the betrayers, who became political enemies, bitter adversaries, or even murderers of their former patrons, spent an average of fourteen years, almost twice as long!

Among the four kinds of dictators, the percentages of those betraying their mentors or patrons varied widely. Tyrants (100 percent) and monarchs (86 percent) were the most likely to turn against their mentors, and authoritarians (52 percent) and visionaries (27 percent) were the least likely. When you confine the analyses to only these four kinds of dictators, ignoring the two kinds of democrats, a substantial difference still exists with respect to their time in office, with the loyalists spending an average of twelve years and the betrayers eighteen years.

Among the two kinds of democratic rulers, almost one-half of all transitionals and one-fourth of leaders of established democracies betrayed influential people who previously had served as their mentors or benefactors. As with the dictators, betrayal often turned out to be a good career move. The democratic rulers who betrayed their former benefactors averaged 6.4 years in office, while those who remained loyal to them averaged 5.7 years.

Here are some instances of betrayal by dictators.

• As prime minister of Pakistan, Bhutto appointed General Zia, a little-known military officer at the time, as chief of the army staff in 1976 because he felt he was completely trustworthy. About one year later Zia overthrew his benefactor and hung him on the charge of murdering a political opponent.

• Appointed supreme military commander by his cousin, President David Dacko, Eddine Ahmed Bokassa soon overthrew him and declared himself president of the newly independent Central African Republic.

• Hafiz al-Assad engaged in a protracted power struggle against Salah al-Jadid, the effective leader of Syria and Assad's political mentor, until finally Assad arrested Jadid and other members of the government in November 1970 and assumed absolute power.

• Slobodan Milosevic entered politics in 1984 as a protégé of Ivan Stambolic, head of the League of Communists of Serbia (LCS), and took over as head of the local Communist Party organization in Belgrade later that year. Within three years, capitalizing on his growing popularity, he ousted his former mentor from his position and, two years later, prompted the national assembly to replace Stambolic as president of Yugoslavia and elect him.

• Idi Amin was one of the few Ugandan soldiers elevated to officer rank before Ugandan independence in 1962, and he became closely associated with the new nation's prime minister and president, Milton Obote, who appointed him chief of the army and air force (1966–70). When he began suspecting that he was losing favor with Obote, Amin overthrew his former patron.

• Abdul Hamid, sultan of the Ottoman Empire, nourished a special hatred against a benefactor who had supported him before he ascended to the throne. But banishing and imprisoning that man on a trumped-up charge of murder was not satisfaction enough for Abdul Hamid. He ordered him to be strangled and then had his body dug up and decapitated to make sure that the man was dead.

It would be comforting to believe that only dictators were ingrates, but the results reveal that democrats were opportunistic, too. Here are a few examples.

• French Prime Minister Edouard Herriot invited his former pupil, Edouard Daladier, to join his government and offered him his first cabinet post. Later, Daladier emerged as Herriot's major rival and enemy within the party.

• Lazaro Cardenas, former president of Mexico (1934–40), overthrew President Plutarco Elias Calles, his former benefactor.

• Fidel Ramos rebelled against his cousin, Ferdinand Marcos, president of the Philippines, who had been his first mentor.

The message of these assorted findings is clear. A large portion of

aspiring and reigning rulers—dictators and democratic leaders alike—
are quite willing to betray their former mentors, patrons, sponsors, or
benefactors. One reason for this practice may be personal: many individuals aspiring to alpha-male status simply do not like being beholden
to anybody. Another reason may be practical: when past benefactors no
longer are in a position to benefit them politically, then they no longer
qualify as benefactors. Yet another reason may be political: when former
mentors and patrons stand in their way or occupy the position they want,
then they become redefined as enemies.

ON THE WAY DOWN

Beaucoup de Coups

> Over the past century, about one-fourth of all the rulers around the world
> have had to deal at some point during their reign with coup attempts,
> insurrections, or civil wars, which were aimed at overthrowing them. In a
> telling statistic, of those rulers who came to power through coups, over 50
> percent were themselves either deposed or killed by new leaders.
>
> Within the sample of twentieth-century rulers, 50 percent of the mon-
> archs, 82 percent of tyrants, 44 percent of visionaries, 39 percent of
> authoritarians, 36 percent of transitionals, and 10 percent of established
> democratic leaders have had at least one coup launched against them dur-
> ing their terms in office.

Since coups d'etat figure so prominently in world politics, especially in
certain Latin-American, Middle Eastern, and African countries, where
they represent the surest and most direct routes to power, it seems appropriate to make some general observations about them. Ordinarily
the reigning ruler should hold a tactical advantage during any attempt
by a usurper to unseat him, especially if he retains control of the military. However, when you study the ways insurgents gain power and the
ways reigning rulers manage to lose it, you cannot help but wonder
whether Nature has leveled the playing field for aspirants striving for
ultimate power by "dumbing down" all those playing the adult version
of King of the Mountain. The result is a kind of natural handicapping
process for challengers, which often evens the odds. Because rulers tend
to believe themselves to be far cleverer than they are, they are apt to make
stupid miscalculations. And because challengers begin to believe in their

own invincibility, they often take stupid risks. Intellectual brilliance, careful strategic planning, and wisdom are not the prized qualities of caudillos, strongmen, or military heroes who often take greater pride in their animal cunning, daring, and sexual exploits. Sometimes the rulers and their challengers become so preoccupied with displaying their manhood during these struggles that they seem to forget what they were fighting about.

Leveling the odds:

In such a high-stakes game, where many human lives are at risk, you would think that coup leaders would not act until they designed a foolproof plan they could carry out with a high likelihood of success. Although that happens at times, the more likely scenario is that their plans are seriously flawed. Still, like the players in a casino poker game, the coup leaders have a chance of winning because of a run of luck or mistakes by the dealer. Admittedly, in what follows, I have taken literary license in describing what transpires during run-of-the-mill coups, but not much. In fact, the more you read about how various coup leaders are defeated and rulers are deposed, the more these accounts seem like bad

4.2: Two coalition partners engage in a charging display, which makes them appear larger and more ferocious than they are. Chimps may form coalitions to overthrow a reigning alpha male. Photograph by Hugo van Lawick, courtesy of the Jane Goodall Institute.

fiction. Here are some instances of losing and winning participants in struggles whose outcome seemed a tossup at times.

With the profits he made from his novel *Day of the Jackal*, Frederick Forsyth funded an attempt to overthrow Macias Nguema of Equatorial Guinea, who was responsible for murdering over fifty thousand people and conducting a reign of terror. Unfortunately, the coup attempt failed miserably, presumably because of the incompetence of its leaders. As a result, Forsyth lost about seventy-five thousand dollars on this venture. To his credit, he was resourceful enough to use the material from the coup attempt as the basis for another book, *Dogs of War*, which later was made into a movie that paid him an incredible return on his original investment.[7] Nguema, shaken by the coup, responded by dismissing or executing all of his competent government workers and administrators and replacing them one by one with sycophants and thugs. Eventually only relatives and members of his own clan held positions of authority, relieving him of his worries about being overthrown. So what happened? He aided in his own overthrow by violating his own credo: "Don't trust anybody!" His nephew led a coup that toppled him in 1979 and sentenced him to death shortly afterward.

Then there were the nine disorganized, ill-equipped, poorly funded coups directed toward the overthrow of François Duvalier, whose regime served as inspiration for Graham Greene's novel and later movie *The Comedians.* The incompetence of the conspirators was so great that some suspected Duvalier of funding the coups himself. But from what I know of Duvalier's erratic ways, this prospect seems unlikely because had he actually been responsible, he somehow would have found a way to topple himself.

Sometimes the bumbling and slapstick happenings during these coups are so comical that you are reminded of the Keystone Cops. Anwar Sadat, for example, got excluded from the coup he had planned for years with Nasser because he had been at a movie with his family and did not know when the coup was supposed to begin.[8] When he got Nasser's note that the coup had started, he could not get through the cordon of soldiers for a long while to join his co-conspirators because he did not know the code word. Eventually one of the officers recognized him and he was able to get through and take his place among the revolutionaries, but only after the coup was a *fait accompli.*

Here is another instance of both a reigning ruler and his challenger seemingly trying their best to lose. Although many credited Fidel Castro with brilliance for eventually overthrowing Batista with his badly outmanned force of 800 guerrillas, some years earlier Castro had led about 160 men in a suicidal attack on the military barracks in Santiago de Cuba in the hope of sparking a popular uprising. His scheme backfired completely, and most of his men were killed. The results were even more disastrous than President Kennedy's later but similar fiasco when he invaded the Bay of Pigs. You might think Castro would have learned from this debacle, especially after spending a year in prison. But no. He then launched another invasion with a revolutionary group of eighty-one men, called the 26th of July Movement, and promptly got almost all of them killed before retreating to the mountains to continue his fight against the Batista regime.

What about Batista's role in this scenario? His first mistake was to let Castro and his brother out of prison when he had them in his clutches after they served only one year of a fifteen-year sentence. His next mistake was in not tracking Castro and his handful of men down after Castro's second failed invasion, when Batista held the clear advantage. And his worst error was in not taking better care of his demoralized and poorly fed professional army of thirty thousand men, the backbone of any self-respecting, people-oppressing despot, and preparing them to deal with the tactics of a small contingent of radical revolutionaries. So if Castro is a genius as a revolutionary, then Batista deserves credit as the mastermind who made him one.[9]

Standard operating procedure:
Now let's say that despite their bumbling, certain coup leaders actually manage to gain power. Ordinarily, you would think that once they exploited the mistakes contributing to the downfall of their predecessor, they should be less likely to repeat them. But remarkably, once in power themselves, many of these new leaders begin committing the same mistakes again, making it seem that they are following the same unknown manual for wielding power, along with its appendix on how to forfeit it, too.

With some exceptions and variations, most of the rulers in my sample who came to power through coups adopted the same self-defeating practices to preserve their authority. With monotonous regularity, they kept following the same flawed script regardless of the geographical region, the society, or the literacy of the populace. It did not make any difference if the coup occurred in a backward third-world country or in a more sophisticated and advanced one. Nor did it make any difference if the leader was brilliant or stupid. The rules for running a country after a coup were roughly the same. I suspect that largely was why over half of these coup leaders were later deposed or killed.

Typically, the first thing most successful coup leaders did after toppling the reigning ruler was to proclaim their contradictory commitment to restoring liberty and freedom for the people and establishing law and order in society. In Chile, for example, the junta that brought Pinochet to power spoke of *democratic restoration*. Edict 5 and Decree Law 1 claimed it was the moral duty of the military to oust the government that fell into flagrant illegitimacy by destroying the national unity and violating human rights. The duration of the military government, the new regime declared, would last only as long as it took to restore justice, social stability, and pride in national identity.[10] In other words, it would last as long as possible.

Typically, to preserve a facade of democracy and constitutional government, the new leaders pledged new elections. If they honored their pledge, they usually arranged to run against token opposition. Then, after their inevitable victory at the polls, which they took as a mandate to rule, they went about the task of consolidating their power. Because of constitutional limits on their term in office, they either got their handpicked legislature to pass a special statute permitting a one-time reelection every time they chose to run, held a plebiscite to make an exception for their reelection, or got a compliant judiciary to interpret the constitution to allow reelections under special circumstances. If the leaders prided themselves on being law-abiding citizens who adhered to their constitutions, they might honor the limits on their term in office, but only after arranging for a handpicked successor to win.

Juan Vicente Gomez, for example, ruled Venezuela for twenty-seven years either as president or through puppet presidents. Noriega controlled Panama as Commander of the Armed Forces while another duly elected person served as president. And Trujillo, during his thirty-one year rule as ruler of the Dominican Republic, held absolute power either directly or indirectly through numerous puppets, including his brother Hector.[11] One of his puppets, Jacinto Peynado, held office in a cramped, sweltering suite of one room, with a drowsy guard outside, while Trujillo, who officially no longer held power, gave instructions to the top military and police officials, drafted legislation, and conducted diplomacy from a sumptuous suite of air-conditioned offices nearby. Trujillo often acted without the knowledge of the State Department, which officially reported to President Peynado, who, I suspect, spent most of his time behind his desk using copies of the constitution that spelled out his executive powers to make paper airplanes that would not fly.

At some point during the rule of these coup leaders or their lackeys, an economic crisis often would arise and trigger public protests. In response to the supposed "dangers to freedom" by these protestors, the rulers either would declare martial law or issue restrictive decrees, edicts, and regulations granting themselves extraordinary powers. Then, after quashing the troublemakers, they would begin tending to their own and their family's needs. Operating mostly without legal constraints and with unlimited access to the state coffers, they would begin accumulating personal fortunes and sending money to foreign bank accounts. When journalists or political factions began protesting about corruption in government, they reacted by imposing censorship on the media and locking up these political agitators in jail, under the guise of preserving social stability. Within this typical, admittedly oversimplified, scenario, it usually was only a matter of time before new challengers would emerge and attempt to unseat them. And once any of these challengers were successful, the whole cycle would begin again.

Launching self-coups:
Let's say that the reigning leaders managed to put down the insurgents and eliminate any immediate threat to their rule. What then? Surely, the rulers now should be able to relax their guard and not have to worry for a while about the possibility of being toppled. That would be a reasonable expectation if even more formidable enemies were not waiting in the wings—themselves! After their triumph, these rulers, metaphorically speaking, seemed to launch coups against themselves with their self-defeating decisions. Whether their shortsightedness was due to poor judgement, a blinding grandiosity, or an instinctive natural drive to give the dissidents cause for hope is hard to say. The net result for many was the destabilization of their regime.

Take the case of Shah Mohammed Reza Pahlavi, who overthrew Mossaddeq with the aid of the C.I.A. after being overthrown himself by Mossaddeq several years before. During his reign, the Shah managed to push through a westernizing reform program, called the White Revolution, that changed the infrastructure of Iranian society. This ambitious program promoted the enfranchisement of women, increased industrialization, put a greater emphasis on higher education, improved transportation, and undertook the modernizing of society. Changes of this nature and on this scale, naturally, provoked resentment from the more conservative members of society, but that was easily contained by the Shah's secret police, SAVAK, feared by the entire population for its ruthlessness and brutality. Where the Shah really went wrong was in not fully appreciating the special sensitivities of his own people. For a man who believed he was protected and chosen by Allah to rule the country and who desperately wanted to be loved and admired by his people, he showed remarkable ignorance about the potential effects of certain seemingly "minor" changes that violated Muslim tradition. One of these "minor" changes was to replace the Islamic calender around which all Islamic business, spiritual, and cultural activities revolved with an Imperial calender that marked time from the earliest Iranian kingship.

Once he had shifted the emphasis of the country from a more theological to a more regal one, it would have been reasonable to suppose he would make an effort to let his beloved people believe they were part of this new social order. Wrong. To commemorate the 2,500th anniversary of the Iranian kingship, he held an immense celebration in Persepolis at an estimated cost of $300 million, to which he invited every head of state in the world but excluded the Iranians themselves. In a single stroke he managed to alienate and offend the people throughout his entire country although most would have boycotted the event even if they had been invited, mainly because they feared reprisals by more fundamentalist members of society. Nonetheless, they interpreted the lack of an invitation as a personal social snub.

Mistakes of this sort perhaps are excusable on the basis of his arrogance and ignorance, but what was completely unforgivable for a ruler of an Islamic country was not to have known that he could not undertake to make wholesale changes in his society without making some concessions to the clerics by giving them the impression that they were part of the power structure and that their opinions mattered. That omission was bad enough. What really incited the Islamic clergy and the Ayatollah Khomeini in particular against the Shah were his land reform program, which threatened to reduce the size of their religious estates, and his intention to emancipate women, which they believed undermined the fundamental rights of all fundamentalist men to be shahs within their own homes.

The Shah then compounded his goof by the way he dealt with Khomeini. When Khomeini began condemning the Shah for his satanic acts, the Shah committed the ultimate mistake of imprisoning him for a year, thereby ensuring that he would become a national hero, and then later, after anti-government riots, letting him go into exile, thereby ensuring that he could keep hatching plots to dethrone him. Years later, when the riots and protests became worse, many wondered why the Shah had not ordered his powerful military to squelch the revolutionaries. The Shah nobly answered, "I can never fire on my own people,"[12] at a time when his ambassadors were querying foreign governments on the acceptable number of Iranians he could kill and jail to keep power without having other leaders denounce him and withdraw their support for his regime. However, by the time he was ready to act, he already had sealed his fate.[13]

A publicist for the enemy:

"Close your eyes. Now whatever you do, do not think of a purple elephant." Unless you are obstreperous, you *cannot not* think of one. That is because the way your mind works is first to picture the thing it is not supposed to before it tries to substitute some other object in its place.

Now let's suppose I hypnotize you and tell you that you won't be able to see me when I awaken you. As I count backwards from five to one, you gradually open your eyes, and on the count of one you are fully awake.

I ask, "How are you feeling?"

You answer, "Fine," while searching the room to locate the source of my voice, although I am sitting only a few feet away.

I say, "Look at me."

You seem puzzled, and your glance ricochets about and takes in the easy chair, the sofa, the picture on the wall, and the window, everything but me.

I say, "I'm sitting right in front of you."

You look confused, and insist, "No, you're not."

Am I truly invisible because of my post-hypnotic suggestion of a negative hallucination? No. The reason you cannot see me is because to comply with my suggestion, you must look everywhere about the room except at me, and when your eyes move toward me, they quickly dart away whenever they catch sight of the outline of my body. The paradox is that in order for you not to see me, you have to be hyperaware of my presence.

So given these psychological laws, you would think that rulers should be very wary of violating them with their tactics when they tell their people what they can and cannot think since that might cause the people to become even more aware of what is prohibited. Take for instance Marcos Perez Jiminez, president of Venezuela from 1953 to 1958. Members of the opposition party, Acción Democrática, objected to his practice of accepting commissions on his vast program of public works, which included building highways, office buildings, hotels, and dams. Jiminez, intensely angered by the criticism from his opposition, not only arrested, tortured, and exiled its members, but went to the extreme of banning automobile license plates in Caracas that had the letters AD, the abbreviation for Acción Democrática; the serial letters on the plates jumped from AC to AE and on down the alphabet.[14] As a result, the absurd absence of these letters became a free advertisement for the party's existence.

Let's take another bizarre example, which is so comical it is hard to believe.[15] In 1956, while Juan Perón was in exile, the Aramburu regime began an intensive campaign to blot out any trace of the former dictator and Evita. Newspapers could not use his name and could only refer to Perón by the code words of "Fugitive-Tyrant." The words "Peronism," "Peronist," "*justicialismo*" and the abbreviation "PP" (for Peronist Party) became illegal. Nobody could sing or play the Peronist anthem, "Los muchachos Peronistas." No photographs of Perón or Eva could be shown. All public works, towns, streets, buildings, and monuments that once referred to them were renamed. Teachers were required to cross out all references to them in school textbooks. The Aramburu regime ordered the presidential residence razed and the Eva Perón Foundation closed.

As the *pièce de résistance* of the regime's attempt to extirpate ex-President "Fugitive-Tyrant" (the new designation for "Perón") from the national consciousness, it undertook the delicate mission of disposing of Eva "Fugitive-Tyrant's" embalmed body, which the people had begun to look upon as that of a saint. The problem was that wherever the new regime decided to house the body, people immediately went on pilgrimages to see it. Worried that the "Fugitive-Tyrantists" might kidnap the body and use it as a rallying symbol against the government, the regime selected one of its most trusted men to carry out a highly sensitive mission. In the dark of night, the chief of the Army Information Service and an elite corp of officers, armed to the hilt with submachine guns, entered the building where the cadaver was kept, placed it in a wooden box, and hauled it off in a flatbed truck to a marine base in the city, where it stayed until it could be better concealed. So what happened? Now that the people no longer knew where the body was, its hiding place became the main topic of speculation throughout the country, generating more positive sympathy for their former leader than he ever could have generated on his own.

Voting themselves out of office:
How rulers of nations, with their networks of spies and various intelligence agencies, can so totally misread the feelings of their people toward them can be amazing. Either their advisors only tell them what they want to hear or their vanity and grandiosity blinds them to the reality of the

situation. Even when they have a firm grip on power, they keep finding new and ingenious ways of undermining themselves. One of these ways is to foolishly test their popularity during a scheduled election when they have no pressing need to do so, thereby handing their opponents the means for unseating them.

Here are some examples.

- U Ne Win, the military leader of Burma (now Myanmar), made Burma into a one-party state and got himself elected president in 1974.[16] Resigning the presidency in 1981, he subsequently kept the post of chairman of his party, which still let him effectively control the government. In late 1987, widespread anti-government rioting broke out in the major cities, prompting Ne Win to resign his position but remain the paramount leader. Protests and demonstrations grew. The Law and Order Restoration Council declared martial law. Many thousands of people were killed during the army crackdown. Because of the worldwide outcry, the military government felt it needed to make some concessions to keep the foreign aid flowing in. Confident that it now was in sufficient control of the country, it decided to allow free elections. The situation seemed right. From what the governmental officials could gather, the people seemed grateful that peace and order had been restored and that their leader was in firm control.

Since Ne Win's lucky number was nine, he set the date for the elections on the fourth Sunday of the fifth month (4 + 5) of 1990, May 27 (2 + 7). Aung San Suu Kyi, the popular opposition leader, ran against Sein Linn, one of Ne Win's most hated henchmen. To the great shock of the regime's pundits, the opposition had an overwhelming victory, winning 392 out 485 seats in the assembly. Obviously, something was seriously amiss. The government responded by placing Aung San Suu Kyi under house arrest, putting many elected members of the opposition in prison, and declaring the results of the election invalid. Although Aung San Suu Kyi was to win the Nobel Peace Prize in October of 1991 for her courageous efforts, the Ne Win government was not about to chance a popular election again.

- About a week before a commission of inquiry was to release a critical report on his role in the disastrous Moroccan War of 1921, King Alfonso XIII of Spain allowed Gen. Miguel Primo de Rivera to rescue him from potential humiliation with a coup d'etat in 1923. After the general fell from power in 1930, the king tried various ways to bring about a return to a constitutional monarchy without the risk of elections. Reassured that the sentiments of the people were to retain the monarchy, he eventually agreed to hold elections. This led to a landslide victory for members of the anti-monarchist opposition, who immediately demanded the king's abdication. After the army withdrew its support, Alfonso was forced to leave Spain, but he managed to salvage his pride by refusing to abdicate. He was still king, although he now had no country to rule.[17]

• After he overthrew Salvador Allende, General Pinochet instituted a number of economic initiatives that reduced the rate of inflation and led to an economic boom from 1976 to 1979. Emboldened by these accomplishments, he held a plebiscite, in which 75 percent of the electorate approved his policies.[18] In 1981, Pinochet agreed to a new constitution that increased his personal power and let him run for another eight-year term as president. So sure was he of his accomplishments and the admiration of his people that he agreed to abide by a national referendum on whether he should continue on as president at the end of this long term. In the plebiscite held in October 1988, 55 percent of the electorate voted "no" and 43 percent voted "yes" for his continuation as president. And so Pinochet was forced to vacate his office and later face serious criminal charges.

• Kenneth Kaunda, who led Zambia to independence in 1964 and served as that nation's president until 1991, was a revered leader during much of his rule. To ensure his continued election as president, he introduced a new constitution in 1973 that legitimized one-party rule for his country. Just to make sure that no one questioned his authority, he assumed emergency powers in 1976 but then had his policies endorsed by the populace by receiving an overwhelming majority of the votes in one-candidate elections in 1978 and 1983. With the eventual deterioration in the economy, public dissatisfaction began to grow, giving rise to new leaders who began to challenge his monopoly on power. Unable to believe that his countrymen would ever vote for anyone other than the person who served as the midwife in the birth of their nation—namely, him—Kaunda had little hesitancy in legalizing the opposition parties in 1990 and setting the date for free multiparty elections in 1991. As should be anticipated by now, Kaunda and the members of his party who were up for election were defeated in a landslide.[19]

The moral of all these examples is simply that if a ruler wants to hold on to power, he should not be too surprised if he loses it when he gives others a chance to take it away from him. If he wants to create the impression of having free elections in his country while still wielding absolute power, then he would do well to learn by Rafael Leonidas Trujillo's example.[20] Faced with the necessity of forming a credible opposition party to create a democratic facade in the Dominican Republic after it had declared war against the Axis Powers in 1942, Trujillo's advisors had a dilemma. Until that time, only one party existed, the Dominican Party, and Trujillo was its head. Finally, in a moment of genius, someone came up with a brilliant idea. A new Trujillista Party would be formed. To make it a serious contender in the upcoming national elections, a number of key members of the Dominican Party applied for membership, which triggered a frantic rush for everybody to join both parties to ensure that they would be on the winning side. Now that a viable opposition party existed, the press began reporting the claims and counterclaims of both parties. The only problem was that it was hard to tell these two parties apart, since the main topic of both parties involved testimonials about Trujillo.

As the weeks progressed, the suspense mounted because the people were not sure who the opposition party's candidate would be. Finally, the long-awaited moment had come. The leadership of the Trujillista Party had named its candidate. He would be none other than Generalisimo Dr. Rafael L. Trujillo Molina, benefactor of the country. The delegates were jubilant. There was no question now that they would win. But members of the Dominican Party, on learning about this action, were taken aback. The opposition was not playing fair. It had usurped their own candidate. They should have had first dibs. Apparently, after a series of heated conferences between the leaders of the opposition parties, a compromise was reached. Both parties would endorse Trujillo as their candidate. It was a wonderful and rational solution. This way there would be no losers. Both parties would win. And even more important, the biggest winners of all would be the people of the Dominican Republic, who would have an opportunity to be led by their benefactor again. All that remained was for the people to cast their votes.

On election day, the people waited with bated breath for the official tally of their ballots. Then the moment everybody hoped for finally came. The results were now official. In this day and age of controversy and division, the Dominican people had showed their solidarity and cohesiveness. They had re-elected their president unanimously.

Unplanned Extended "Vacations"

> Overall, 14 percent of worldwide rulers and 17 percent of the smaller sample went into exile after their rule. Tyrants were the most likely to be exiled, either hightailing it out of the country before they could be jailed or sentenced to exile or imprisonment. The next most affected group was the monarchs, who often moved their entire entourage with them to a friendly country and then went through the motions of holding court there with their carry-along crew. Unlike tyrants and monarchs, if authoritarians happened to be short-sighted apparatchiks or military strongmen who valued their duty over booty, they were likely to leave office not much wealthier than before and so probably found living in exile much harder. More so than any of these other dictators, visionaries resisted leaving their country of their own volition, perhaps because they saw their country as an extension of themselves. That probably accounts for why only 12 percent of them went into exile. See figure 4.5 for actual percentages.

Let's say an aspiring ruler has finally managed to gain power and remained in office for somewhere between several hours, as happened with some leaders in my study, to sixty-eight years, as happened with Emperor Franz Joseph of Austria, and it now comes time for him to leave high office either because the law says his term is over, he no longer commands a parliamentary majority, or others force him out. What is the likelihood of his being able to accept the inevitable and then graciously retire to his "modest" thousands-of-acres estate or oceanfront villa, where he can watch his grandchildren romp about, play golf with his cronies, sleep as late as he wants, hire someone to write his memoirs, and enjoy the remainder of his days as a respected elder statesman of his country? The answer is that it depends on what kind of regime he ran. If he happened to have been a dictator, his chances are not too good, especially if his successor does not happen to be one of his admirers. If his successor hates his guts and regards him as too much of a threat, he will try to find some way to silence him forever. If he is less vindictive, he will realize that it may be in his best interests to banish his predecessor from the country instead of jailing or killing him, hoping to set a good example for anyone who may topple him. Although the new leader knows that the former one robbed the treasury and bought property abroad and stashed away lots of money in foreign banks to provide adequately for his forced retirement, he may not want to prosecute him for his foresight if he cannot confiscate his money. The reason is because he probably plans to do the same as long as his predecessor left behind enough monetary scraps and dribblings for him.

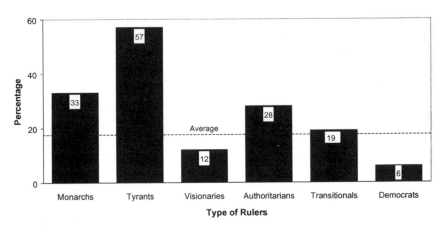

Fig 4.5: Exile or Banishment after Serving in High Office

Legend: The upright bars represent the percentage of different types of rulers who were forced to go into exile at some time after they had initially gained ultimate power.

A Worthless Postgraduate Education

As already noted, many aspiring rulers on their way to high office get waylaid in jail, where they manage to spend their time networking with fellow conspirators, working out their political strategies, hardening their spirits, and gaining their credentials for leadership. While this can be an invaluable experience for these would-be rulers during their quest for ultimate power, prison offers them nothing of value after they have reached their ambitious goal. It only highlights their failure. They had their chance, but they flubbed it. Now it is comeuppance time. As fallen rulers, they deserve whatever punishment they get. It is a fitting penalty for losing power. Now it is time for new contestants to enter the game. Discredited and disgraced, the former rulers no longer are eligible to play. Even if they could, they now carry the formidable handicap of being losers. Moreover, while in prison, they are rendered impotent to act. All they have control over are their memories. So now, these defeated leaders while away their time during their postgraduate imprisonment conjuring up excuses for all their supposed abuses in office, second-guessing themselves about how they could have avoided being overthrown, and dreaming up revenge against all their enemies.

Within the sample of rulers, 13 percent spent time in jail at some point after they became leaders of their nations, usually when they lost all power but sometimes between their terms in office. Authoritarians and tyrants (26 percent and 24 percent, respectively) were the most likely of the rulers to be jailed, followed next by visionaries, monarchs, and transitional democrats (12 percent to 15 percent), and last by leaders of established democracies (6 percent). Most often, the leaders spent time in jail or under house arrest after having been overthrown, but sometimes as the outcome of a later judicial inquiry.

On the losing side:
One common reason for rulers being jailed is that they happened to end up as losers in nasty wars in which the victors or their own people were not very forgiving.

- Luang Phibunsongkhram, premier of Thailand, was arrested and imprisoned for at least five months during his trial as a war criminal but was released after the court dropped the charges.
- Karl Donitz, charged with and convicted in 1946 at the Nuremburg trials of participating in war crimes, was sentenced to ten years in prison.
- Konoe Fumimaro, prime minister of Japan, after spending six days in jail as an accused war criminal, committed suicide rather than bear the humiliation of a public trial.
- Kurt von Schuschnigg, chancellor of Austria from 1934 to 1938, was imprisoned as a traitor by the Nazis after they came to power.
- Vidkun Quisling, the Benedict Arnold of Norway, was convicted for treason and then executed by his countrymen after World War II.
- Tojo Hideki, premier of Japan, was arrested and convicted as a war criminal after World War II and then eventually executed.
- In 1944, Philippe Petain, ruler of Vichy France, was convicted of treason and sentenced to death under the rule of Charles de Gaulle, his former protégé, whom Petain previously had sentenced to death in absentia for failing to accept the surrender of France.

Whatever the reasons given for jailing a former ruler, one consideration is paramount: from the perspective of a new ruler, a former ruler is dangerous on the loose. Not only is there the possibility that the opposition will rally around him, but, having once tasted ultimate power, he never can be trusted not to seek it out again.

Assassination Attempts

If at first you don't succeed, then try again:

> If we use the actual percentages of assassination attempts during the twentieth century as base rates, then if the ruler is a tyrant, there is a 77 percent chance that somebody will try to kill him, a 61 percent chance if he is a monarch, a 56 percent chance if he is a visionary, and a 46 percent chance if he is an authoritarian. Nor does being a democratic leader protect him from danger. If he is the leader of an emerging democracy, he has a 51 percent chance of being shot at or attacked, and he has a 19 percent chance if he is the leader of an established democracy.

Because there are likely to be people in the country who do not have the patience to plan a coup or who simply believe that the country needs new leadership, the current ruler had better be prepared to be shot at or blown up or poisoned at some point during his reign. Then, if he manages to survive one assassination attempt, he cannot assume that he will be safe from being attacked again during his remaining time in office. There are some determined people out there who still will want to get rid of him. Within my sample, rulers averaged almost one assassination attempt each, but certain individual rulers seemed to have more than their fair share of attempts. For example, King Hussein of Jordan survived at least seven assassination attempts, Mussolini four, Hitler at least two, Noriega three, Sukarno four, Ben Bella three, Brezhnev five, Muammar Qadaffi two, Yassir Arafat an estimated forty, and Saddam Hussein at least seven, one in which he escaped from the United States strafing of his palace. Without question, Fidel Castro takes the prize for having had the greatest number of assassination attempts made on his life. Estimates of the number range from 8 unsuccessful CIA attempts in the early 1960s, the official figure noted by U.S. lawmakers; to over two dozen, as noted by Castro himself; to over 612 during the 1959 to 1993 period, according to Div. Gen. Fabián Escalante, former head of Cuban State Security. Knowledge about the bizarre and persistent efforts of the Central Intelligence

Agency to kill Castro came to light mainly through the forced release of the 1967 *Inspector General's Report on Plots to Assassinate Fidel Castro.*[21]

Instant heroes:

As mentioned before, it usually is not the dangers leaders face that distinguish them from ordinary folks but how they manage to exploit them to their political advantage. As it happens, assassination attempts are the stuff of legends. They have the potential for creating instant heroes, and most leaders instinctively know that.

• Teddy Roosevelt perhaps takes the prize for his poise under fire. He was leaving his car to make a speech when John Schrank shot him in the chest. He first coughed into his hand to see if there was blood and, finding none, figured the wound was not fatal. He ordered his assassin brought to him and asked him why he shot him. He then defied the doctor's orders by telling the driver to go to the hall, saying, "I will make this speech or die. It is one thing or the other." The bullet had entered his right lung, but its velocity was spent by passing through his overcoat, a spectacle case, and the folded manuscript of his speech, which he held up to show the audience when he began speaking.[22] Only after he finished did he seek out medical attention.

• After an assassin's shot missed Nasser while he was speaking to an audience of workers, he stayed calm and continued, "my life is yours, my blood a sacrifice to Egypt. . . . I speak to you with God's help. . . . Nasser's life is your property." His listeners were so impressed by his calmness and bravery that he became an instant folk hero in their eyes.[23]

• Georges Clemenceau, a former premier of France, was shot by an anarchist, but that did not keep him from returning to work ten days later with the bullet lodged in his ribs. Naturally, the public was kept abreast of his day-to-day medical status.[24]

• Though not as dramatic, Ronald Reagan also managed to keep his cool under fire. In 1981 he was shot in the chest by John Hinckley, whose presumed motive was to impress actress Jodie Foster—and that reason probably was no more irrational than those that other assassins gave. All during his ride to the hospital, Reagan supposedly told jokes to his attendants and even tried to reassure them. Once in the hospital, when he was asked if he hurt, he supposedly replied in W.C. Fields fashion, "Only when I laugh." When the doctors were

4.3: Immediate aftermath of the assassination attempt on President Ronald Reagan. Courtesy Ronald Reagan Library.

about to operate, he was said to have remarked with mock concern, "I hope you're all Republicans."

Having survived an assassination attempt becomes a badge of honor for rulers. It is the presidential equivalent of receiving a Purple Heart for valor in battle. It not only gains the sympathy of their countrymen but contributes to the myth of their invincibility. Some rulers even manufacture assassination attempts as a way of generating political capital. Francois Mitterand, for instance, was accused of staging a mock attempt on his life to bolster his image during what has become known as the Observatory Affair. His parliamentary immunity was stripped so that he could stand trial for this deception, but, for complex reasons, he never was tried.

Just as impressive as these anecdotal cases of *sang froid* under duress are the many instances of rulers' continuing in their duties despite past attempts on their lives, sometimes even disregarding the warnings of their security chiefs. But when that happens, poor judgment sometimes gets confused with courage. Indira Gandhi, for instance, refused to get rid of the Sikhs among her "faithful" guard even though she knew that the Sikh population hated her for the killings at the Golden Temple in

Amritsar. The result was that she was murdered by two of them. Rajiv, her son, did not seem to learn from his mother's and his own past experience. Perhaps believing in his own invincibility after having survived at least two failed assassination attempts, he abandoned the heavy security precautions and also managed to get himself killed.

A sense of invulnerability:
The question is why do so many leaders who already have been exposed to a failed assassination attempt continue to take inordinate risks despite the warnings of their security advisors or, even more to the point, do not switch to a less dangerous activity like writing memoirs about their past deeds or how they were unjustly criticized for their actions.

There are several possible explanations for this cavalier and almost idiotic disregard of potential danger. You could say that these rulers were risk-takers because of their willingness to put their lives on the line. But that still begs the issue of why risk-takers cannot be smarter about their actions. Julius Caesar, the prototype of the great ruler, was a brilliant man, but in the end he acted like a dunce by ignoring all the warnings about his planned assassination. The only way to make sense of their denial is to blame it on a sense of grandiosity that lets them believe they are immune to death because some nebulous protective force is looking after them. Every time they successfully escape an assassin's bullet, they become even more convinced of their invulnerability. Getting killed is what happens to ordinary mortals. Of course, many rulers do become paranoid and take preposterous precautions against getting killed, but even then they often show a defiant sense of egotism that lets them believe they can outwit all conspirators and enemies. Rationally, they know they can be killed, but emotionally they do not really believe it.

Listen to Saddam Hussein, who has managed so far to elude not only countless assassination attempts within his own country but also the efforts of the United States, Britain, Israel, and probably Iran as well to put him out of commission. "I am far cleverer than they are. I know they are conspiring to kill me long before they actually start planning to do it."[25] That is a remarkable claim. It means that anybody charged by Hussein with conspiring against him has no defense against this accusation, since Hussein would know what that person was going to think long before he thought it. It also means that, like Stalin, Hussein survived because he regarded almost everybody as an enemy and so made sure that nobody would be in a position to harm him.

You get glimpses of this grandiose sense of invulnerability when you examine the ways that many of these leaders responded to past dangers.

• Among his many weird beliefs, Samuel Doe of Liberia publicly proclaimed, "No bullet can touch me, no knife can scratch me," and his belief held true through thirty-six failed coup attempts until at the relatively young age of forty he was killed, receiving the same special treatment he had made famous of having his eyes poked out, being castrated, and having his hands crushed and his legs amputated.[26]

• When Sukarno emerged unscathed after his first assassination attempt in 1957, he capitalized on the popular belief that he was destined to rule Indonesia. The myth of his invulnerability grew when he survived the strafing of the presidential palace by an air force jet in 1960; when he emerged unhurt in 1962 after hand grenades were thrown at the presidential car; and again, in 1962, when an assassin missed him at almost point-blank range. Through it all, he understandably clung to the belief, "The heavens preserved me for the nation,"[27] and he was right, at least until the heavens let him be overthrown in 1966.

• Hitler also was so convinced in his destiny to transform Germany that he believed almost until the end of his days, "Providence will intervene to save me." In fact, after the failed assassination attempt by General Stauffenberg on July 20, 1944, when Hitler sustained only minor injuries after the bomb exploded, the first thing he told Mussolini, who happened to believe in his own invincibility, too—not Hitler's—was, "Duce, this is proof that I am under the protection of Providence."[28] Hitler probably believed it, although he was irreligious and had only the vaguest idea of what he meant by Providence.

Different ways of getting killed:

Assassination attempts are one matter, actual assassinations are another. But as long as we are counting actual assassinations, we may as well include statistics for executions, because sometimes it is hard to tell the difference between them. Unlike assassination, execution tends to be a more formal procedure, usually a sentence imposed by a judicial or executive body; but this is not always so, since vigilante justice can happen, as in the case of Ceaucescu and his wife or Mussolini and his mistress. Although I prefer to believe that some higher morality is involved, the more common way of designating war criminals is to have the victors document unjustifiable killings by the losers. Hidecki Tojo, prime minister of Japan during World War II, who accepted full responsibility for the Japanese atrocities toward the Allied prisoners and casualties from the Bataan death march, offered this perspective: "I do not believe that makes me a war criminal. There is a difference between leading a nation in a war which it believes right and just, and being a war criminal. . . . But again, that is for the victorious nation to decide."[29] His distinction between criminal actions taken in a right and just war and those taken in a wrong and unjust one seems dubious, although he is probably correct in saying that historically the victorious nation has the prerogative of making these moral distinctions.

Because it is often difficult to make clear distinctions between being assassinated, being executed after a coup, being murdered while in custody of captors, or "committing suicide" while rebellious troops storm the presidential palace, I have decided to lump all these lethal conditions together under the rubric of death by violent means. If rulers receive summary justice after a coup or are executed after a formal trial in which the verdict is known beforehand or if they have been assassinated before they reach trial, they have been killed prematurely either way.

The results of my study reveal that 12 percent of all of the deceased twentieth-century rulers died a violent death (assassination = 7 percent, execution = 4 percent, suicide = 1 percent) at the hands of others or by their own hand at some point after reaching high office. (See figure 4.6 below) Within the sample of 377 rulers, the overall death rate by assassination, execution, and suicide was even higher, 18 percent. This probably reflected the greater renown and notoriety of the rulers in this sample. Just think, an almost one-in-five chance of dying a violent death simply because you held high office. Among the different kinds of rulers, 29 percent of transitionals, 28 percent of authoritarians, 25 percent of tyrants, 21 percent of monarchs, and 20 percent of visionaries died by assassination, execution, or suicide. As might be expected, these rates were lowest for leaders of established democracies (11 percent).

While different interpretations of these statistics are possible, you would be hard put to argue with the conclusion that *being a ruler is one of the most lethal activities known to mankind.* To my knowledge, there is not another profession pursued over an average ten-year period that is even close in potential dangerousness. The only nonprofessional activity I am aware of that has a comparable mortality rate is playing Russian roulette with a five-chamber gun about once a year.

Fig. 4.6: Causes of Death for All Twentieth-Century Rulers
Includes Only Rulers Who Died (N = 1,124)

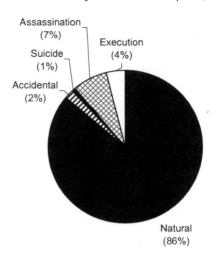

Assassination
(7%)

Execution
(4%)

Suicide
(1%)

Accidental
(2%)

Natural
(86%)

Since the chances of being killed vary depending on what kind of ruler an individual is, his chances of living to a ripe old age must, too. Monarchs, tyrants, and authoritarians had the shortest life spans, sixty-three, sixty-six, and sixty-nine years, respectively. Visionaries and transitionals were next with an average longevity of about seventy-one years. Among the different kinds of rulers, leaders of established democracies lived the longest, with an average life span of seventy-five years.

THE ODDS AGAINST SUCCESS

So far I have described the obstacles and hurdles participants face in trying to scale the mountain of political success, first during the climb up and then once they manage to reach the top. Now we are in a position to answer the fundamental question of what the actual odds are of winning at this sociobiological game—or at least breaking even with your reputation, pride, or life intact when you finally leave the political casino. From the findings on the sample of 377 rulers in the chart below, we can get a pretty good idea of the odds of leaving high office as a "winner" or a "loser," depending upon which kind of ruler you happen to be. (See Method and Statistics for comparable information on end-of-rule for the entire worldwide group of rulers.)

For these analyses, "good outcomes" represent completing one's constitutional term in office without an option to run again, voluntarily resigning from office for reasons of health, simply not wanting to deal with the hassle anymore, or dying naturally from disease or old age or by accident while in office. Under these circumstances, the ruler would qualify as a "winner." The ruler may not have done a good job or been enlightened or been liked during his rule, but that is irrelevant to the game. The point is that, during his reign, nobody managed to best him, and he left high office either with his head held high or his head still on his neck.

In contrast, "bad outcomes" represent being deposed, being forcibly removed from office by an oversight junta or central committee, being forced to abdicate, being stripped of power by a conquering country after having lost a war, committing suicide while in office, being assassinated, or simply losing the election after running for office again. Though

Percentages of Good and Bad Outcomes of Rule
(Rulers Not Still in Office)

	Monarch	Tyrant	Visionary	Authoritarian	Transitional	Democrat
Good Outcomes						
Natural Death in Office	41	15	48	21	16	9
Completed Term	0	0	5	4	5	11
Resignation (Voluntary)	0	0	4	3	18	25
Totals	*41*	*15*	*57*	*28*	*39*	*45*
Bad Outcomes						
Abdication	21	0	4	3	0	0
Suicide	0	0	9	0	0	1
Assassinated/Executed	12	15	4	13	18	6
Elected out of Office	0	10	5	13	23	45
Removal by Junta/Council	0	0	0	16	0	0
Deposed by Coup	23	50	17	15	16	2
Lost War/Overthrown	3	10	4	12	4	1
Totals	*59*	*85*	*43*	*72*	*61*	*55*

the ruler successfully may have managed to get to the top of the mountain (which was something everyone in this study managed to do), he still would qualify as a "loser" if any of these bad things happened to him.

Choosing Your Own Poison

If you are the kind of person who relies on actuarial tables and base-rate statistics to make important decisions, you now have a chance to decide if you want to become a certain kind of ruler based on the likelihood for certain kinds of outcomes for a large sample of twentieth-century rulers. Overall, my findings reveal that there is a certain truth to such sayings as "You reap what you sow" or "What goes around comes around." Tyrants, by far, are most likely to suffer a bad outcome, with half of them being deposed, one-fifth being ousted after having lost a war or being voted out of office, and another 15 percent being assassinated or executed. That is a whopping 85 percent chance of leaving office in disgrace or in a casket. Next come authoritarians, with almost a three-in-four chance of experiencing a bad outcome—almost 60 percent being forced to leave office in disgrace or defeat and another 13 percent being assassinated or executed. Interestingly, monarchs have about the same likelihood of experiencing a bad outcome as transitional democrats and established democrats, perhaps because they are protected somewhat by the mystique of royalty and the tradition of monarchy in their countries. Yet with almost one-half of them being forced out of office through coups, forced abdications, or defeat in war and another 12 percent being killed by their enemies, you can hardly call the outcome of their rule favorable, although a substantial portion of them are apt to die natural deaths in office. Interestingly, visionaries are the least likely among all the dictators to leave office in defeat or humiliation; but over one-quarter did, which was not a ringing endorsement from the populace that it appreciated all of the social engineering and brainwashing it was exposed to.

These statistics so far apply only to those rulers who qualify as dictators, so it is comforting to learn that most of them end up getting their comeuppance. What about the leaders of democratic nations, who in comparison to dictators are more likely to be seen as humane, wholesome, and good? Unfortunately, transitional democratic leaders, often revered as fathers or liberators of their nations, do not always end their days in high office feeling appreciated and loved by their people. Aside from a substantial portion of them being deposed, almost one-fourth of them are thanklessly voted out of office sometime later after giving their people the right to vote. Also, perhaps because they represent a threat to certain factions within their countries and do not have the dictatorial powers to enforce their rule, almost one-fifth of them—actually 18 percent, the highest percentage among all the rulers—end their reigns being assassinated or executed.

Of all the ruler types, you should expect that leaders of established democracies should be least likely to end their rule under adverse circumstances. To a certain extent, this is true, but the odds depend on how you measure bad outcomes. In terms of the most dire outcomes, such as being assassinated or forcibly overthrown, there is no question that established democratic rulers fare best among the different kinds of rulers. However, because most presidential and parliamentary forms of government give their leaders a chance to run again for at least one more consecutive term in office or to hold power as long as they can keep a majority in parliament, most democratic leaders do not resign voluntarily while they are still winners. As a result, almost one-half of them unsuccessfully run for office again or lose their majority support in parliament and eventually their party leadership as well, causing them to end their political careers on a sour note of defeat.

Turnover Rates

These, then, are the actual odds for a twentieth-century ruler for leaving high office as a "winner" or a "loser." As the results suggest, the odds strongly favor leaving office as a loser for most kinds of rule. From the situation with many stable democracies, such as in Great Britain, Sweden, Canada, or the United States, this conclusion may not seem believable; but you need only turn to other nations around the world to correct your impression. Although I shall be mentioning the different rulers by name in these selected countries, their actual names are irrelevant. Rather, it is the sequence of rulers, the length of their terms in office, and the way they gain and lose power that show just how unstable political power is and how likely rulers are to lose it. As my thesis suggests, this very high turnover rate in leadership paradoxically helps to explain why people persist in pursuing ultimate power even when the odds in favor of leaving high office as a winner are poor. The easier it is for the current leader to lose power, the greater the opportunity of aspiring rulers to gain it.

Bolivia will serve as an example of what transpired in a Latin American country. Over the course of the past century, it has had thirty-seven rulers, fifteen of whom were either assassinated or deposed. Starting in

1899, Jose Manuel Pando, then Eliodor Villazon, and then Ismael Montes completed consecutive terms as president without problems, which brings us to 1917. So far, so good. But now comes an extended period of governmental instability. G. Jose Gutierrez Guerra served as the ruler from 1917 to 1920 before he was deposed. Juan Batista Saavedra, his successor, completed a full term in office from 1920 to 1925. He was followed by Hernando Siles, who was deposed after four years, with Carlos Blanco Galindo finishing out the term. Then three rulers in succession, Salamanca, Tejada, and Toro, serving about four years, one year, and one year, were deposed, deposed, and deposed. After two years, German Busch died in office in 1939, with Carlos Quintannilla finishing out the term. Enrique Penaranda was elected to office but was deposed after four years. His successor, Gualberto Villaroel, was assassinated after three years, with Nester Guillen and Tomas Monje Gutiérrez spending less that one year each to complete the term in office. Then when Gutiérrez ran for office, he lost to Enrique Herzog, who spent two years in office before resigning. Mamerto Urriolagoitia then took over the helm and completed the term in office in 1951. That only covers about half of the entire century, but it is enough for you to get the idea, especially since the second half was much the same.

Now let's look at Nigeria, an African nation, to learn the political situation since it was granted independence from Great Britain in 1960. Abubaker Tafawa Balewa served as the country's powerful first prime minister until 1966, when he was assassinated in a coup. Johnson Aguiyi-Ironsi, his successor, was the head man for less than a year before he, too, was assassinated. Then came Yakubu Gowon, who ruled the country for nine years before he was deposed. His successor, Murtala Ramat Mohammed, remained in power for less than one year before he was assassinated in 1976. Olusegun Obasanjo then ruled until 1979, when he took the amazing step of stepping down of his own volition. Alhaji Shehu Shagari then took over the helm until 1983, when he was deposed. His deposer, Mohammed Buhari, was himself deposed in 1985 by Ernest Shonekan, who was himself deposed in less than one year. Ibrahim Babangida held power until 1993 and then resigned. Sani Abacha then took over, but in 1998 died a hero's death in office, likely poisoned from the juice he drank while carousing with three prostitutes with the aid of Viagra.[30] Next enter Gen. Abdulsalam Abubaker, the leader of a military junta who oversaw the government until free elections could be held in 1999. Now guess who won by an overwhelming majority of the small minority of citizens who cast their vote in an election marred by claims of widespread election fraud and ballot stuffing—Olusegun Obasanjo. As the only prior ruler who had stepped down on his own initiative to make way for free elections, he apparently has decided to play Russian roulette again. The odds of his completing a full term in office this time without something bad happening to him do not seem good, especially in a country that has been under military rule for twenty-eight of thirty-eight years since independence, has had eleven leaders, four of whom were assassinated and four of whom were deposed, and already has been through three failed attempts at democracy. I hope I am wrong, but we shall have to wait and see.

Last, let's examine a truly democratic nation like France, which over the past century has featured both a strong presidential system and a strong parliamentary system, depending upon what kind of republic existed at the time. There is no need to mention the names of all the rulers or the lengths of time they were in office. For our purposes, a summary of the leadership situation will do. The pertinent facts are these: Over the course of the past century, there have been fifty-one presidents or prime ministers who held the chief executive power. Except for the handful of rulers who were in office for five or more years, such as Francois Mitterand for fourteen, Charles de Gaulle for thirteen, Giscard d'Estaing for seven, Georges Clemenceau for six, and Ariste Briand for a total of about five years during his eleven appointments as premier of France, the remainder were in office for several months to four years; and, of these rulers, thirty-five served for one year or less. This impressive turnover rate was largely due to shifting alliances, coalition collapses, and election defeats, which led to the unseating of forty leaders. Of the fifty rulers before the current officeholder, only five (10 percent) voluntarily chose to complete their term in office or to resign on their own initiative and avoid ending their political careers as losers.

This high turnover rate of rulers is not so uncommon in democratic governments, especially in parliamentary systems. What is so intriguing in looking at national leadership in this way is that this high turnover rate in leadership in many parliamentary systems is not so different from what exists in many dictatorships except for the severity of the consequences when power is lost. In more autocratic systems, one of the favorite ways to get rid of leaders is to overthrow them and then imprison them, exile them, or execute them when necessary to ensure that they won't hold power again. In more democratic systems, there is no need to resort to these drastic means. The political system allows for the replacement of leaders at regularly scheduled elections or through formation of new coalitions and power blocs. In other words, there are formal and legal ways to topple an incumbent leader or beat out a competitor—although, as sometimes happens, as in Italy or Germany during World War II, there are no guarantees against democracies giving way to dictatorships.

Just in case all of these prior references to coups and coalitions and power blocs and shifting allegiances and high turnover rates in leadership in either dictatorial or democratic governments should seem to be describing a distinctly human activity, listen to the following description of the political life of a community of baboons by Robert M. Sapolsky, who spent more that twenty years studying them in the wild:

> The wonderfully cooperative junta that had overthrown Saul lasted all of a morning before it disintegrated into factionalism and both metaphorical and literal backbiting. All hell broke loose for months afterward. Joshua, Menasseh, Levi, Nebuchanezzar, Daniel, and Benjamin were clearly the upper-ranking cohort now. . . . But they didn't have a clue where they stood with respect to each other. Ranks flip-flopped daily. Levi would beat Daniel in a fight and supplant him a dozen emphatic times that subsequent afternoon, but by the next day, the direction of dominance would be reversed. Over the course of months, Menasseh might turn out to be dominant to Nebuchanezzar, but he'd be winning only 51 percent of the interactions, instead of the 95 percent you'd see in more stable times. Chaos reigned. Everyone was scheming, spending hours forming coalitional partnerships that would collapse within minutes of their first test. Nearly 40 percent of the time, when it did collapse, the erstwhile partner would wind up on the other side. The number of fights went through the roof, as did the rate of injuries."[31]

A Summing Up

What these assorted results show is that countless individuals will experience great privations, endure terrible suffering, and even risk death to compete for the position of leader. In most instances, they do so long before they have an opportunity to sample or exploit many of the extraordinary perks available to rulers, suggesting that underlying whatever rationales they offer for their actions, a compelling urge fuels their quest. All of these findings are consistent with my thesis that the urge to become "king of the mountain" is what drives these rulers to brave the various dangers, an urge that is likewise found in our simian ancestors when they strive to overthrow the alpha male. Although other interpretations of these findings are possible, none, in my opinion, explains as well why would-be rulers are so driven to court danger, endure so many privations, and even risk their lives to get to the top.

Earlier I have observed that under the right circumstances almost any kind of person can become a ruler. However, that does not mean that almost anybody can fulfill the particular requirements of certain kinds of leadership roles. What we now need to explore is what kinds of individuals tend to be drawn to what kinds of rule and, conversely, for what kinds of individuals each of the different kinds of rule tends to be selective.

REARING RULERS

The dominance drive to gain superior social status is little in evidence during the early months of life, becomes common during childhood, and is a conspicuous and highly important chimpanzee characteristic during adolescence and maturity. As soon as two unacquainted individuals who are well grown are brought together they proceed to settle their social status by looking one another appraisingly, by trial of physical prowess and courage, or by a combination of the two. Bluffing, and physical struggles in which teeth, hands, and feet are effectively used are common. But often they either give place to, or are supplemented by, what looks like a contest of wills, in which self confidence, initiative, resourcefulness, and persistence seem to be highly important.

—R.M. Yerkes, *Chimpanzees: A Laboratory Colony*

Because they act godlike at times and inspire awe, it is sometimes hard to picture rulers of nations as once having suckled at their mothers' breasts and having been helpless and dependent as children. Yet they obviously had, although you would have trouble proving it. With notable exceptions, that is because so little biographical information is available about their early lives, and what little information exists comes from self-serving memoirs, which never reveal their failings, or from state-sponsored propaganda materials, which portray them as exceptional children who were never helpless, scared, or wayward. There are many reasons information about their childhood is so unreliable and sparse, but the biggest one is that the leaders themselves do not want it known. Rafael Trujillo, for instance, fabricated his personal biography because of his shame at being part black and part Haitian. He claimed he was descended from a Spanish military family on his father's side and French nobility on his mother's. To add emphasis to his claim, he powdered his face to whiten it during public appearances.[1] Although biographers and scholars have managed to ferret out important but spotty details about the early lives of Stalin and Hitler, these rulers likewise were so touchy about their childhoods that they gagged, imprisoned, or eliminated anybody who had access to that information. In Ho Chi Minh's case, his biographer noted, "Everything known about Ho's life prior to 1941 is fragmentary, controversial and approximate."[2]

This practice of distorting information about their pasts is not confined to dictators. Yassir Arafat, for example, deliberately blurred facts about his personal history because he believed a symbol should be mythic. He once said he was not born until he became Abu Ammar, his nom de guerre, which means "the Building Father."[3] Eamon de Valera, a prime minister of Ireland, likely fabricated important details about his background to cover up his illegitimate birth. And Lyndon Johnson, who was listed in the San Marcos yearbook as a member of the Sophistry Club, described as "Master of the gentle art of spoofing the general public" and given the name of "Bull" because of his boasting and tall tales, removed pages from hundreds of copies of his college yearbook that gave clues to his years there.[4]

LYNDON JOHNSON

As he looks to us on the campus every day.
From far away, and we sincerely trust he is going back.
Sophistry Club. Master of the gentle art of spoofing the general public.

From the way leaders gloss over their childhoods, you may wonder if their pasts are marked by an endless series of those stock baby photos that mortify teenagers when their mothers show them to oth-

5.1: 1928 write up on Lyndon Johnson in *The Pedagog Yearbook* of Southwest Teachers College in San Marcos. Note the adjoining derogatory picture. Courtesy of the Lyndon Baines Johnson Library.

ers—photos of them lying on their backs, stark naked and bloat-bellied, with one pudgy hand reaching upward to distract the viewer from their other hand that is resting on their miniature genitalia and contributing to their toothless grins. But what are all those embarrassing events that they see as the equivalents to these photos? Perhaps some of their sensitivity about their pasts comes from shame over their humble origins or their uneducated, superstitious parents or their own immaturity or their once-helpless dependency, which others might ridicule. Perhaps some of it comes from their poor grades at school or their less-than-genius IQ scores or their own ignorance of the world that reveals them to be less than brilliant. Perhaps some of it comes from not wanting others to know about their adolescent excesses or stupidities. These are reasons enough for many leaders to censor information about their childhood. However, I suspect there is one reason that overrides all others. From my delving into the lives and character of all these rulers, I have come to the conclusion that the main reason for the blanket of secrecy many toss over their pasts is their fear that others will discover their very *ordinariness*.

Because of their ordinariness as children, adolescents, or even young men and women, most rulers are unable to concoct a convincing Joseph Campbell myth about their childhood. If they had their way, they would like others to believe that a cosmological event of Star-of-Bethlehem moment—perhaps a dazzling display of the northern lights in the night sky at the equator—proclaimed their entry into the world. Or as in many hero legends, they would have had their mothers put them in a reed basket daubed with pitch before setting them adrift in a river to save them from an evil tyrant, only to be discovered on the riverbank later by a wise shepherd who then raised them under humble circumstances. As a baby and later as a child, they naturally would have shown extraordinary strength or precociousness, presaging their future greatness. Then after a period of obscurity, they would have emerged from adolescence with a growing awareness of their predestined mission, which was to take vengeance on the ruler who had deprived them of their birthright, harmed their families, and oppressed their people.

Another variation of this childhood myth is to make a virtue of certain social handicaps. Many leaders, especially populists and demagogues, consider it to their advantage to play up their humble origins and the adversity they endured as youngsters to show the people that they are one of them and not one of the intellectuals who sneer at them or the elitists who supposedly are oppressing them. With this story-line, they ennoble poverty and large families and hard-working, uneducated parents and peasant superstitiousness and ignorance, although many of these leaders happen to come from comfortable, middle-class homes and are reasonably well educated.

But having peasant roots often is not a good enough background. Adopting a Lincolnesque tale of advancing from a log cabin to the White House or a Horatio Alger myth of going from rags to riches, they tell how they overcame one adversity after another to get where they are, convincing their audiences that their dreams of success also can come true or, even better, can be vicariously experienced through them. Using reverse snobbery, they make their lives mythic by rising above the social forces and circumstances that oppress most people. And if they have an opportunity to do so, they try to muzzle any family members or acquaintances from their past who might offer embarrassing revelations or explode their myths, like reporting that they had been caught cheating in school or used drugs or been arrested for rape, as actually happened with certain of our leaders.

Despite the relative dearth of information about their pasts, I believe it is possible to piece together reasonably coherent pictures about their backgrounds and personal attributes as children from the sketchy information available about them in scholarly treatises and reliable biographical sources. To do so, I shall have to adopt biographical techniques analogous to those of paleontologists who reconstruct facsimiles of our simian ancestors from assorted fragments of bone. This approach is not suitable for describing all the nuances in personality existing among our rulers as children, adolescents, and youths; but it is perfectly suitable for depicting their main characteristics. Naturally, this approach lends itself to stereotyping, but that may not be too great a disadvantage if it happens that certain of these characterizations fit most of the rulers well.

REPRESENTATIVE RULERS

Monarchs

Kings, sheikhs, sultans, emperors, and other regal rulers, including Faud, Farouk I, Carol II, Leopold II, Nicholas II, Ferdinand, and Hussein:
Farouk I, who was king of Egypt from 1936 to 1952, will serve as our prototype of an absolute monarch.[5] Born in Cairo, Egypt, the future king grew up in palatial splendor, with nursemaids and servants devoted to making all of his infantile wishes come true. As the only son of his parents, King Faud I and Queen Nazri, and with only two half-sisters, he was the natural heir to the throne. Although his mother was not of royal stock, she was as close to it as she could get due to the foresight of her father, a mercenary officer and hero who had married the daughter of the prime minister, a man with enormous personal stature because

of all the time he had spent in the royal presence. Bored by her life in her husband's harem, she turned all her attention on her precious son, whom she kept with her, dressing him as a girl and frittering away the time curling his hair and filling his head with her vacuous musings. Sometimes longing to escape from her seeming house arrest in the harem, and especially angry with her husband for monitoring her calls and keeping her in purdah, she periodically would fake nervous breakdowns so that she could be sent to different European spas for cures.

But most sympathies in the palace were reserved for Farouk's father for having to endure such an impossible woman. King Faud, a scrupulous and immaculate man who rummaged about and searched the palace for any dirt or dust that the servants had missed and sprayed cologne wherever he imagined an unsavory odor and who took his military responsibilities seriously, parading in front of a large mirror each morning in full military regalia, had to put up with her irrational tirades and peculiarities. Even worse, because of her complaints about him, his wife's brother shot him three times. Because one of bullets lodged in his throat, he had periodic laryngeal spasms, which made him bark and yelp when he spoke. I imagine that this must have been embarrassing for him if one of the purebred royal dogs began howling or growling in response. But he had little need to worry, since no one seemed to notice. The reason was that if anyone was untactful enough to give even the faintest hint of witnessing his weird behavior, that person would lose royal favor immediately and be stricken from the palace guest list.

Despite this tension between his parents, little Faroukie, as I shall call him, lived a happy and carefree existence. He was pampered, prettified, doted on, fawned on, and indulged by his mother and the other women in the harem. As the object of all this attention, he already was preparing for his later role as king, when his subjects and ministers would deem his every utterance profound. Little Faroukie was an adorable, charming, confident, and even-tempered child, occasionally given to rages when he didn't get his way. He also liked to throw things. One of his favorite games was to smash rare vases or to grab his pet kitten by the tail and toss it around the room. As he grew older, he also loved to play practical jokes, the more embarrassing to people the better. However, nobody could take his pranks or deceptions personally, since he was too self-centered to even regard those he tricked as real persons who had sensitivities and were capable of taking offense.

Faroukie's personality and behavior as a child mirrored that of other royal heirs, most of whom were oldest sons. Though neither especially outgoing nor reclusive, monarchs as youths were the least likely among the different types of rulers to be rebellious and were among the most likely to have temper outbursts. Trained from birth to rule and appear regal, they also happened to be among the least likely of the rulers to have shown any clear signs of leadership. What little leadership ability they showed as children was simply by virtue of their position as rulers-to-be.

As a child, William II, who was to become German emperor and king of Prussia from 1888 to the end of World War I in 1918, for instance, brooked no contradictions from his playmates, always insisting on commanding the toy armies and, whatever the outcome of their imaginary battles, always claiming victory, even if he had no soldiers left.

In contrast, Carol II of Romania (1930–40), who likewise had a passion for soldiering and rules, seemed to have had some legitimate leadership ability when young. Even at an early age he would practice ruling those around him, especially his younger siblings, by tyrannically issuing all sorts of laws, proscriptions, and decrees. One of his favorite games was to set up a customhouse in the corridor near where the other children were playing with their toys and charge them a toll every time they wanted to pass. When the other children decided to start a tennis club, he immediately took the lead and on his own drafted a book of rules for everyone to follow.[6]

At the appropriate age, Faroukie's parents secured a private tutor for him, since attending school with children of lesser rank would be unseemly for a future ruler. To prepare him for wisely ruling his kingdom, his tutor taught him about his divine right to rule and his genealogical connections with the Prophet Muhammad, one of the few topics, I suspect, that did not bore him. Also, as a keeper of the faith, Faroukie was supposed to be well-versed in the Koran, but, rather than study it on his own, his tutor recited passages of it to him, often when Faroukie was dozing or planning his next pranks. Nor was he diligent about his homework assignments or given to any form of creative expression, since he hated to read, never wrote a letter, and had no appreciation for art or poetry. Other than perpetrating obnoxious pranks, the only activities he enjoyed were taking pornographic pictures, collecting antique weapons, and riding in racing cars. After years of going through the motions of learning, he was finally ready at the age of fifteen to cap off his education for becoming an enlightened ruler by enrolling in the Royal Military Academy at Woolrich in England as an extramural student. As testimony to his military prowess, he was awarded a perfunctory certificate of attendance after a year despite flunking many of the exams. Later, as a gesture of admiration for his achievements, King George VI appointed him an honorary general in the British army. This legitimatized his future role as a fledgling Mideast Napoleon when he proudly inspected his troops on horse in the 1948 Arab-Israeli War before sending them off to be slaughtered.

5.2: A future leader in training. The baby gorilla is beating his chest. Courtesy of the Zoological Society of San Diego.

Faroukie's educational experience was not unusual for monarchs. Almost two-thirds of the monarchs had the equivalent of only an elementary school education, being mostly taught by tutors, as was the case with Faroukie, and a small percentage (3 percent) was completely illiterate. Being the least educated among all the different types of rulers, the vast majority of young monarchs (69 percent), not surprisingly, also received failing to average grades. The kind of training sought after by most royal heirs was military school, often prestigious schools like the British Military Academy at Sandhurst in England, where after several months they received an official seal of approval that testified to their newfound expertise in quashing rebellions and fighting wars. Still, none of these twentieth-century monarchs astounded their professors with their brilliance or later proved to be great military tacticians. Mostly, they responded as did Nicholas II, the last Russian emperor, who after finishing his military studies never again showed the slightest interest in anything intellectual; or as King Leopold II of Belgium and also sovereign of the Congo, presciently called the "little tyrant" by his father, who showed no interest in any of his studies except for geography. What they usually found academically to be most useful for their rule were the camaraderie and debaucheries with other officers and holding their own in drinking competitions with them.

Of course, this characterization of monarchs as academic dunces does some an injustice. For instance, King Ferdinand, ruler of Bulgaria from 1908 to 1918, not only knew five languages but was a skilled ornithologist as well. A passive and ineffectual leader in affairs of state, Ferdinand was extraordinary in other non-kingly ways. As a competent naturalist, he gave descriptions of the flora and fauna of Brazil and Northwest Africa that were included in scientific textbooks, and many species discovered by him were classified under the name of "ferdinandi." He collected gems and minerals and designed jewelry. He was an expert on snakes, plants, and butterflies. He could repair any auto and would test new locomotives in person. He was well read, an afficionado of the arts, and a competent painter as well. Unfortunately, the great tragedy of his reign was that he never put any of his brilliance or talent to use as king.[7]

When Farouk was only sixteen his father died (out of respect for his becoming king, it is only fitting that I now drop the diminutive ending of his name), but his subjects were confident that he was well prepared for taking over the helm of the nation, despite the appointment of a three-man regency council to help him rule until he was eighteen. After all, he had shown great cleverness in his childhood pranks, and he had received some military training in England. Once he gained his maturity, he adopted a novel administrative style that confounded many of his ministers: he avoided them if he felt they knew more than he, which meant he avoided them a lot. If they somehow managed to corner him to get a decision, he compensated for his ignorance by impatiently responding to all their comments and queries with his patented, "I know, I know," and so closed his mind to all new sources of information.

Although monarchs (24 percent) were more apt than tyrants (9 percent) but less apt than visionaries (36 percent) to have dabbled in art or music as children, they were singularly lacking in any special talents or abilities. Only 6 percent of them showed any signs of precocity or of being gifted, compared to 11 percent for the entire sample of rulers. Even more incriminating, most had no desire to broaden their knowledge or showed no curiosity about the world. This was reflected directly in their singular disinterest in reading, making them (17 percent) and tyrants (13 percent) the least well read by far among all of the rulers.

Even in organized athletics, few monarchs-to-be were willing to compete, as was the case with King Hussein of Jordan, who was told when he went off to school that it would be unseemly for him to lose to anybody of a lower social rank or, for that matter, to anybody at all. As with Faroukie, the interests of monarchs lay mostly with riding horses, hunting, racing sports cars, philandering, or dallying in other trivial pursuits. Perhaps none of this is surprising. If in truth they ruled by divine right, then they had nothing more to learn by reading. They likewise had no need to prove themselves by displaying more conventional forms of scholastic achievement. When whatever they decree becomes law, then even ignorance becomes brilliance.

As princes, these future monarchs had little need to prove themselves socially. Compared to the other kinds of rulers, they (14 percent) were about as likely to be insecure or timid as children. Although they tended to be more even-tempered (52 percent) and conforming (70 percent) than other rulers, they (18 percent), along with tyrants (10 percent), were the least likely to be outgoing or sociable with other children. The likely reason for their keeping a distance was that they were raised in relative isolation from other children, not only because their parents feared that most of their companions were not good enough for them but also because of the concern that familiarity could breed contempt.

Along with visionaries (36 percent) and transitionals (34 percent), monarchs (31 percent) were more likely than other ruler types to experience the death of either a mother or father before the age of fourteen They also were about twice as likely (22 percent) as other rulers to be very close with their mothers, as was Faroukie before he became king and learned about his mother's affair. However, this transformation of closeness at an early age into later alienation was far from rare. As happened with Faroukie, a sizeable minority (21 percent) of heirs apparent or budding monarchs developed stormy relationships with their mothers as teens or young adults—not as high a percentage as tyrants (36 percent) or visionaries (32 percent), but substantially higher than transitionals, democrats, and authoritarians (2 to 7 percent). Queen Marie had this to say in her diary about her son, Prince Carol, while her husband was dying: "I am martyred between my love for my son and my sense of duty toward the country. I have lost all belief in Carol. . . . He is fundamentally immoral. He does not see the fundamental difference between right and wrong, honor and dishonor, truth and lies, fair play and foul. He has repudiated all the old beliefs, the old gods, the old laws. I, his mother, alas, have found him a weakling."[8]

Statements of this sort seem more suited to the relationships between princes and their fathers. Along with tyrants (40 percent) and visionaries (50 percent), fledgling monarchs (41 percent) were alienated from their fathers, more than twice the percentage for any of the other ruler groups. Aside from their fathers usually being remote, forbidding figures during their childhoods, crown princes had certain inherent stresses in their relationships with their king-fathers. In many instances, these fathers could not become too endeared to their sons, whom they knew were waiting for them to die, and the sons could not be too loving toward their fathers, who stood in their way to the throne. Also, when two people are born with the divine right to rule, peaceful coexistence between them may be hard to achieve. For example, Amanullah, ruler of Afghanistan from 1919 to 1929, was a member of the Young Afghans, a revolutionary group that had plotted to kill his father. And Leopold II of Belgium, with a face disfigured by an enormous nose that made him look like a bird, and a personality warped by sullenness, was not a favorite of either parent. His mother was embarrassed by his appearance, and his father detested his personality, so between the two of them, there was not much left of him to like. In fact, he had such a remote relationship with his father that he had to make appointments to see him.[9] Faroukie's relationship with his father never had been this bad, but it was not especially close either.

But to Farouk's credit, he did know how to delegate authority. He let his ministers rule while he tended to his own interests and intervened only in important matters of state that were close to his heart. For example, one of his first official acts after becoming king was to sever all relations with his mother, banish her from the kingdom, and confiscate all her property after he learned that she was having an affair with his old teacher. This kind of behavior was not befitting a Muslim woman, let alone a supposedly pure and chaste mother. She responded to her son's harsh treatment by becoming a Christian, which I suspect she now thought excused her behavior.

Rulers are expected to grow in office. This certainly proved to be so for the now "King" Farouk, whose gluttony helped him to grow to over

5.3: King Farouk of Egypt. Staples of the royal diet consisted of a few tablespoons of caviar, lobster thermidor, slabs of roast lamb, about a cubic meter of trifle, a pound of chocolate, and a magnum of champagne. AP/Wide World Photos.

330 pounds. With the reputation of a playboy, he soon became renowned throughout the world for his womanizing, partying, and extravagances. But this seemingly decadent lifestyle was mitigated by his avoiding all alcoholic beverages except for a daily magnum (= 1.5 liters) of champagne and his praying daily, which made him devoutly religious, although he never read the Koran. He also always comported himself with regal dignity except for when he playfully threw bread balls at the people seated at nearby tables in restaurants, oblivious to the reactions of others.[10]

But who could condemn Farouk for these innocent moments of relaxation after laboring so hard day and night on behalf of his people? With a staff of three hundred people working for him at the palace, he had more than enough to do to keep them amused with his good-natured antics. Then, to keep physically fit, he liked to exercise by sitting on a bench in his garden and watching his lady companions walk. His daily routine apparently was so full that he never had time to read a newspaper, write a letter, or listen to music, which he never did anyway even when he had plenty of time. Nor did he take much time at night for rest and repose. He kept three telephones at his bedside and often called people in the middle of the night to play cards with him, talk about some new amusements, or keep him company while he sped around the city in a new sports car. But Farouk never complained about his weighty duties. As a deeply committed ruler, he would do whatever was necessary for the welfare of his people and in the interests of his country as long as he had nothing more pleasurable to do.

Authoritarians

Military rulers, caudillos, apparatchiks, and appointed leaders, including Pinochet, Rhee, and Ulbricht:

Political authoritarians come in all shapes, sizes, and colors, ranging from military dictators and strongmen to apparatchiks and party bureaucrats. Common to all authoritarians is a commitment to keeping law and order and preserving social stability. The differences among them stem mainly from their administrative styles and the kinds of government in which they operate. Though technically dictators, many authoritarians are selfless leaders who seem dedicated to the welfare of their countries and, unlike tyrants, although they may enjoy their prerogatives, do not necessarily exploit their power for personal gain. In most instances, military leaders come to power as heads of juntas and rule under states of emergency or revised constitutions that grant them extraordinary executive powers. Political strongmen or caudillos often head their own parties and, once in office, consolidate their power and engage in one-party, one-person rule. In contrast, apparatchiks or party bureaucrats, who do not project the romantic image of a swashbuckling caudillo or a strong military leader, mostly come to power through maneuvering their way to the top within the political bureaucracy, usually within a mono-ideological system such as communism or Marxism-socialism. Although they supposedly are responsible to a central committee or a broader politboro or assembly with the power to appoint them and remove them, many maneuver to gain supreme power themselves, which then lets them appoint and remove the people to whom they would ordinarily be responsible. One of the characteristics that distinguishes apparatchiks from visionaries is that the former follow the official party ideology while the latter promulgate an ideology of their own.

Augusto Pinochet, who led the bloody military coup that toppled the Marxist government of President Salvadore Allende of Chile in 1973[11] and, according to his backers, probably kept all of North, Central, and South America from falling to communism and, according to his detractors, practiced genocide and assorted crimes against mankind, will serve as our prototype of an authoritarian. Born into a lower-middle-class Catholic family of modest means, he was the first of six children and his mother's favorite. Except for taking on the burdens and responsibilities of an eldest child, he apparently experienced an uneventful childhood, serving as an occasional confidante for his mother and as a surrogate parent to his younger siblings while his father worked away from home as a customs officer and a salesman.

Though serious and reserved as a child, Augusto was always affable and accommodating. At school, he was respectful to teachers, behaved

---

Authoritarians come mostly from lower- to middle-class families with poor to modest means. Their parents are predominantly Catholic (52 percent) and have large families (average of 5.3 children). Perhaps because of the family size, they are more likely to be later than first-born males. Most were properly dutiful and respectful toward their parents, being far less likely than other kinds of dictators to become alienated from their mothers (7 percent) or antagonistic toward their fathers (11 percent). Although they were the least likely (12 percent) to lose a parent before the age of fourteen, they were the most likely of the ruler groups, along with tyrants (both 64 percent), to have parents with broken marriages.

well, and tended to his lessons, characteristics usually more valued by the school authorities and parents than intellectual curiosity and inquisitiveness. Despite being a hardworking and conscientious student, he was turned down twice by the National Military Academy because of his poor grades and a failing mark in English. Persistent as ever, he was finally accepted at the age of sixteen for the four-year officers' training course. A poor to average student, he compensated for his academic deficiencies by his devotion to duty, his love of discipline, his loyalty to his superiors,

The majority of authoritarians were obedient and conforming as children, about the same percentage as were leaders of emerging and established democracies. Being serious and sober-minded youngsters, they tended to be courteous to adults and respectful to their teachers, which often more than compensated for a wrong response. What they lacked in loveableness and sociability as children, they more than made up for by being even-tempered and levelheaded. Helping at home with family chores or working at odd jobs during their teens, they had little time to engage in competitive sports or cultivate any creative interests.

General Pinochet's choice of a military career as a route to becoming a ruler was the most popular choice for all authoritarians (52 percent), with law being the second-most-common career (10 percent). Surprisingly, but not so when you think about it, of all the rulers, authoritarians were least apt to show leadership abilities as children, because the usual ways youths show superiority over others are not suitable for advancing within a military organization or political bureaucracy. In an organizational setting, loyalty and dedication may be more valued than academic achievement or originality.

Pinochet's persistence at his studies despite his academic deficiencies was also consistent with the authoritarian tendency for conformity and serous-mindedness during childhood. Along with leaders of established democracies (3 percent), authoritarians (2 percent) were the least likely to drop out or fail out of school, while tyrants (35 percent), visionaries (35 percent), and monarchs (31 percent) were the most likely. As a group, authoritarians tended to be better-educated and get better grades than the other kinds of dictators, but they did not do as well as leaders of established democracies. This does not reflect as much on the general intelligence of these other dictators as on the lower value they place on formal schooling and academic performance, which they see as irrelevant for their own careers.

Despite the warning by parents and educators about the importance of good grades, figure 5.1 below clearly shows that, except for authoritarians, those who eventually go on to garner the most absolute power tend to perform the least well in school. Apparently, would-be rulers need good grades to get ahead in their careers only if they cannot accede to power by hereditary succession, charisma, or force.

Fig 5.1: Grades in School

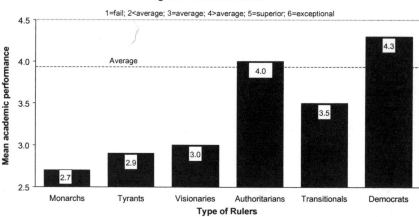

and his enthusiastic embracing of the spit-and-polish drills. Although he graduated fifth from the bottom of his class, he was perfectly suited for the military, where he could do well enough to advance steadily up the ranks but not well enough to arouse suspicion or threaten anyone. It was a perfect match. Being competent and plodding instead of brilliant and quirky, respectful and obedient instead of cheeky and questioning, and persevering and dedicated instead of lackadaisical and self-centered, he had all the attributes of a born commander. Perhaps his greatest asset was his remarkable ability to let everyone feel superior to him, so no one begrudged him his successes. Consistent with his military personality, he also held little respect for democracy. Debate was inefficient, compromise was surrender, and dissent was anarchy. "I'm a soldier," he said. "For me, what is white is white, and what is black is black," and there was no more to be said—except that he probably must have been color-blind.

General Pinochet's background was not so different from that of many apparatchiks. Walter Ulbricht, for instance, who was a German Communist leader and head of the post–World War II German Democratic Republic, or East Germany, and became the most hated man in Germany after he erected the Berlin Wall, likewise came from a lower-social-class background.[12] Both of his parents were members of the Socialist Democratic Party and very politically involved. Often, Walter and his siblings would help their father distribute political leaflets and listen to the lively political discussions that took place at their small, squalid apartment. At school, his classmates thought he was stupid because he never said much, but his intelligence was masked by his timidity and touchiness. This impression he gave would later serve him well as a budding apparatchik, since most party members were suspicious of intellectuals. Although diligent and well-behaved at school, he reinforced others' opinions of his dullness by his mediocre grades. Nonetheless, he did show an inkling of initiative by reading and mastering Engels, Lenin, and Marx as a teenager, which saved him the trouble of ever having to absorb any new ideas again.

After eight years of school, he left and became apprenticed to a cabinetmaker. At that time he also joined the Workers' Gymnastic Association and became more involved in sports and physical fitness. After the war he entered the new German Communist Party (KPD). By now a skilled bureaucrat and organizer, with the enviable ability to justify any decision by quoting from the masters, he was elected to the party's central committee in 1923. Since no one could match his knowledge of the inner workings of the party, he maneuvered his way into the leadership position. It was not that he challenged anyone outright for that position; he simply immobilized all potential rivals by his command of details and his procedural knowhow. His potential challengers might get frustrated and infuriated with him, but they could not argue with party regulations, principles, precedents, and dogma already in existence.

Aspects of Ulbricht's experience are found among other apparatchiks. Wladyslaw Gomulka, for example, who served as First Secretary of the Central Committee of the Polish Communist Party from 1956 to 1970, trained as a locksmith after completing primary school and then joined the youth Socialist movement when he was sixteen. As the son of a peasant, Klement Gottwald, who was to become president of Czechoslovakia (1948–53), had to work on a farm from the age of nine, and the little education he received was self-taught. When he was twelve, he trained to become an apprentice carpenter and cabinetmaker, and by the age of sixteen he had become a socialist. The stories of many of the Communist leaders are much the same. As cabinetmakers, lock-

Although authoritarians tend to be serious-minded and dedicated as children, they are not especially gifted. Syngman Rhee, first president of the Republic of Korea (South Korea), from 1948 to 1960, was only one of a relatively small group of authoritarians who showed certain extraordinary abilities as a child. By age seven, he had memorized several introductory books on Chinese and Korean history. While 12 percent of the sample of rulers showed special talents or abilities as children, authoritarians, tyrants, and monarchs had only about half that percentage, while visionaries, who were the most gifted group, had almost twice that percentage. Most often, being gifted took the form of an impressive or photographic memory and, far less often, some special musical ability or writing skill.

Actually, the overall percentage of precociousness among all rulers was unimpressive, especially when you compare them to other kinds of professionals. In a past study, for instance, I found that 25 percent of famous creative artists and 22 percent of notable scientists were gifted as children, a rate roughly twice that for rulers as a whole and over four times that for authoritarians. They had a much wider range of talents as well. The reason that few child prodigies end up as rulers may have more to do with their being too threatening to the powers-that-be than with their being too smart to end up in politics. Or it may be for both reasons. Since authoritarians as a group showed little inclination to excel in their studies and showed no special abilities as children—although they appeared like geniuses compared to monarchs—the skills they relied on to gain ultimate power were obviously of a different nature than those they would have needed to be successful in the arts or sciences or any academic profession, for that matter.

smiths, carpenters, farmers, or common laborers, they consolidated their identity with the workers or peasants and then dedicated themselves to the communist cause. Then after joining the party, they gave their undivided loyalty to it, much as Ulbricht did; and through their plodding, persistence, scheming, and bureaucratic skills; which compensate for their lack of any specialized knowledge about economics, diplomacy, jurisprudence, or even world history; they eventually gain ultimate power. Imagination, daring, and academic brilliance had little relevance for advancing within a highly bureaucratic system, although the agricultural or engineering backgrounds of several of the later leaders in the Soviet Union did seem to stand them in good stead. But for the most part, apparatchiks needed no special training. God (or, for the Communists, the "Apparatus," "Party," or even "History") was not in the details, as some have claimed. God created the details and then rearranged them to befuddle humans so that they would turn to Him for the answers. Most of the apparatchiks, being atheists, had no need to turn to God. But when one of them claimed to know where these details belonged and how to make sense of them and even added some of his own, then that person seemed destined for political leadership.

Tyrants

Oppressors, despots, and corrupt rulers, including Bokassa, Torrijos, Hussein, and Jean-Claude Duvalier:
Eddine Ahmed Bokassa, self-styled emperor of the Central African Republic, has many of the features of the typical tyrant.[13] Although information about his past is sparse, it seems reasonable to assume that his traumatic childhood must have warped his psyche. His father, who was the local headsman of his tribe, was jailed and then beaten to death by company officials when Bokassa was six years old after he freed some villagers who had rebelled against the French company that relied on forced labor. Bokassa's mother was so distraught by her husband's death that she committed suicide, leaving her son to be cared for by relatives.

When Bokassa reached secondary school, the priest at the mission advised him to join the army after his graduation, since he did not have an "aptitude for study," a gentle way of telling him he was not bright enough to succeed at anything else. So at the age of nineteen, Bokassa joined the French army. Showing the proper respect and obedience to his white superiors, he was identified as a soldier with considerable leadership potential. During World War II, he won several medals for bravery and finally earned the rank of captain. At the invitation of his cousin, President David Dacko, Bokassa then left the French army to become commander-in-chief of the newly formed military for the Central African Republic. Several years later, in gratitude for being entrusted with this enormous authority, he used it to overthrow his benefactor and declare himself president.

Manuel Noriega, the Panamanian military leader (1983–89), who, for the years of his command, was the actual power behind the civilian president, likewise had a stormy childhood.[14] His mother, who had been a cook and waitress, died a couple of days after he was born, and his father abandoned him when he was five. He was raised as an orphan by a relative and grew up in poverty, selling newspapers on the streets to earn a few pennies and hustling for other money and handouts. Because

Bokassa's troubles at school were typical of tyrants. Paralleling the abysmal scholastic performance of monarchs, 9 percent either were illiterate or had no formal education, and 35 percent had poor to failing grades. Despite their lack of academic interest or achievement, they were not necessarily the worst-behaved students. About half of them were reasonably conforming as children, not as high a percentage as for monarchs but over twice the rate for visionaries.

he was small for his age, other children picked on him, but, by the time he became a teenager, they left him alone once they learned he carried a small pistol. Surrounded by foreign sailors and prostitutes, he became street smart and had a real gift for words. Surprisingly, he finished high school and did reasonably well, but then he dropped out of college to work.

After some further studies, Noriega joined the national guard as a common soldier but with a commission of second lieutenant. Capt. Omar Torrijos apparently saw promise in him and became his patron despite Noriega's failing to be promoted after three years in the national guard and finishing 147th out of a class of 161 in a jungle operations course sponsored by the United States. Torrijos even intervened on his behalf with the police when he was arrested for beating up and raping a streetwalker. Torrijos did not mind Noriega's youthful excesses so much, but what he could not tolerate was not being listened to. After telling Noriega to be more careful, Torrijos angrily confined Noriega in his quarters for thirty days when he continued to drink heavily and get in fights. But Torrijos apparently saw some hidden quality of greatness in Noriega and took him under his wing again. Then, when Noriega remained loyal to him during an attempted coup, Torrijos commended himself for being such a good judge of character. Despite all of Noriega's seeming failings, he was a man who could be thoroughly trusted. In gratitude for his loyalty, Torrijos promoted him to lieutenant colonel and chief of military intelligence. Noriega then used this position to catapult himself into power after his benefactor died in a plane crash, which some suspect Noriega engineered.

Like Bokassa and Noriega, Saddam Hussein also had a difficult childhood. His father had died before he was born, and his mother essentially abandoned him to be raised by his uncle. After the children started picking on him mercilessly for having no father, he began carrying an iron bar to protect himself against their attacks. Lacking any friends among the village boys, he took to engaging in solitary activities. According to

Tyrants mostly were raised in small towns and villages and came from poor, lower- to lower-middle-class backgrounds. As children, they tended to be the least outgoing of all the ruler groups. They also were most likely to be short-tempered and moody—perhaps with good reason, given their stormy childhoods. Twenty-six percent of their fathers died before these would-be tyrants reached the age of fourteen, the highest percentage among the different kinds of rulers, as did 17 percent of their mothers. But even for those whose parents lived on, their relationships with them were not especially close. More than any other group of rulers, tyrants (36 percent) were most likely to be antagonistic toward their mothers and, as with monarchs and visionaries, hostile toward their fathers as well. Among all the rulers, tyrants also were the least likely to show any exceptional leadership ability as youths. Hardly any tyrants (6 percent) showed any signs of precocity or special abilities or, for that matter, as with monarchs, any desire to broaden their knowledge about life or the world through reading. Though reasonably healthy as youngsters, they apparently had little time or inclination to participate in team sports, either because they had to work or because they dropped out of school.

one source, one of his favorite amusements was to heat the bar he carried for protection over a fire and then stab an animal in the stomach as it passed by.[15] With practice he became so good at this that he could rip the animal open and almost split it in half with one stroke.

But these diversions never kept him from taking his education seriously. Although he reputedly still did not know how to spell his name by the age of ten, he persisted in class anyway and gained a certain measure of popularity by amusing his classmates with practical jokes. After graduating from primary school, he enrolled in high school at age eighteen although he had little interest in academics. Still committed to furthering his education, he then went to Cairo Law School and continued his studies at Baghdad Law College after the Ba'thists took power in Iraq in 1963, but he never finished his law degree. Even this did not deter him from his educational pursuits. Nine years later he showed up in the dean's office with a pistol and four bodyguards to get his certificate. Four years later, still recognizing the importance of an education for getting ahead in the world, he ordered the school to award him a master of arts degree. Now he had so many advanced degrees and diplomas that some might conclude he was overqualified for his office.

As was the case with Saddam Hussein, enlisting in the military appeared to be a wise choice for many would-be tyrants who mostly did not have the necessary academic smarts to succeed in other professions. Fifty-nine percent of them took the military route to ultimate power, the highest percentage among all the rulers. Some examples follow.

- The military was a godsend for Idi Amin, whose parents separated when he was an infant, and a devil-send for the people of Uganda. Sent to a missionary school, he barely completed six grades and was hardly able to speak English. Because of his skimpy education, his virtual illiteracy, his large size, and his Nubian origins, he was an ideal recruit for the British army, since the British believed that uneducated Nubians would make obedient soldiers and good fighters.
- Juan Vicente Gómez, who was to become dictator of Venezuela, learned to read only as an adult, if he learned at all. But this did not stop him from becoming a wealthy cattle rustler in Colombia and then using his money as leverage to rise rapidly to the rank of field commander in the private army of Cipriano Castro, a local caudillo, and then, when a suitable opportunity arose, to overthrow him.
- Samuel K. Doe, who was to become president of Liberia, claimed to have graduated summa cum laude from college, although he had dropped out of the eleventh grade to join the army at the age of eighteen. He rose to the rank of master sergeant but then appointed himself general after having successfully launched a coup against President William R. Tolbert.
- Fulgencio Batista, who was to become dictator of Cuba, also found the military to be a convenient route to ultimate power. In the army, he was able to learn shorthand and typing, which he then somehow used to his advantage in advancing in rank and influence, along with his participation in two coups.
- Yuan Shih-K'ai, first president of the Republic of China, from 1912 to 1916, wisely decided on an army career once he became convinced that he would not be able to get the three degrees necessary for a civil service career because his debauching did not allow him enough time to study for them.

Again, as noted with the authoritarians, the military offered an opportunity for all these academic misfits to achieve ultimate power eventually in their countries, not necessarily through any special genius but through their craftiness and daring, usually backed up by force.

Even though, as a group, tyrants are more apt to be illiterate or poorly educated and get poorer grades than most of the other kinds of rulers, not all tyrants are stupid, ignorant, and uneducated. Nestled among them are a sizable number who have gone to college, law school, and even medical school, as the figure below shows. For instance, Arnulfo Arias, three times president of Panama, had the finest academic training, receiving his bachelor's degree from the University of Chicago, his medical training at Harvard Medical School, and a residency in surgery at Boston City Hospital. Francois Duvalier graduated in 1934 from the University of Haiti School of Medicine, where he served as a hospital staff physician until 1943, when he became prominently active in the U.S.-sponsored anti-yaws campaign. He actually made some important clinical contributions to the treatment of this awful disease. Samuel Doe earned his bachelor of arts degree, graduating summa cum laude. Ngo Diem graduated at the top of his class at the School for Law and Administration. William Tubman of Liberia received a law degree and was admitted to the bar. And Ferdinand Marcos scored so high on the bar examination, receiving a 98.01, that he was suspected by the school authorities of cheating. The authorities soon dropped their suspicions when they heard him recite long passages of legal texts from memory. What these examples show is that tyrants do not need to be poorly educated to be cruel and greedy. A sizable minority of them actually are well-educated, intelligent louts (see figure 5.2).

Junior tyrants: Not all tyrants have to struggle to get to the top. Some have had their ways greased for them by their fathers, succeeding to absolute rule by virtue of their birth much as a crown prince might in a monarchy. When this happens, they also seem to become as indolent and decadent as do many youthful members of the royalty. Jean-Claude Duvalier, known as "Baby Doc," is a case in point.[16] A well-mannered, friendly but spoiled child who evolved into a good-humored, slothful hedonist as a teenager, Jean-Claude easily could have dropped out of high school after failing all his classes without detriment to his career, but he cared too much about his education to take the easy way out. So he complained to his mother, who not only made sure that her son was passed but that he was admitted to the University of Haiti Law School as well. To ensure his success, she also came up with the clever idea of special tutoring for Jean-Claude with somebody else taking notes while he slept. Unfortunately, his father's untimely death when Jean-Claude was only nineteen forced him to curtail his education and his naps. Realizing that he still had a lot to learn, he let his mother rule the country with the

Fig. 5.2: Educational Status of Tyrants

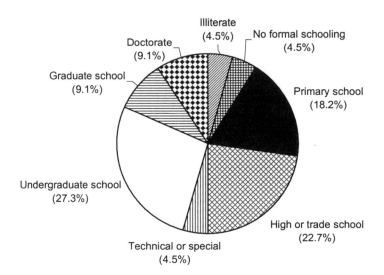

able assistance of the Tonton Macoutes while he prepared himself further for leadership by continuing to race sports cars, hunt, listen to music, party, womanize, and partake in assorted depravities.

However, not all promising candidates for high office get a chance to follow in their father's footsteps even when their credentials are outstanding. This turned out to be so for Ramfis Trujillo, whom his doting father had been grooming to succeed him.[17] Despite being pampered and spoiled as a child, Ramfis showed every sign of being a worthy successor to his father. What other petite tyrants could boast of his achievements? At nine years of age he earned the rank of brigadier general. Because of public criticism from some uninformed quarters that he might have been awarded this rank at too early an age (perhaps the age of sixteen or seventeen might have convinced skeptics that his rank was well deserved) and the potential demoralizing effect on many career officers to be outranked and ordered about by a mere child, Ramfis, a sensitive child, voluntarily decided at the age of fourteen to give up his commission and start his military career anew from the ground up, without currying favors from anyone. The magnanimity of his announcement caused much rejoicing throughout the country. This laudatory act proved that he had all the qualities necessary to be a responsible leader, someone whom the Dominican youths could emulate. Aware that the whole country was now pulling for him, Ramfis began applying himself to his studies and, as a result of his initiative and dedication, began rising rapidly through the ranks entirely on his own merits, this time without any unjust criticism that his advancement had anything to do with his name.

Not all of Ramfis's superiors, though, were impressed by his military genius, especially those who lived outside the country and were not directly subject to his father's authority. When Ramfis was denied a diploma from Fort Leavenworth, his father responded angrily to this insult by immediately promoting him to the rank of full general, naming him Chief of the Combined Chiefs of Staff and ordering home thirty Dominican cadets taking courses in the United States. The Congress of the Dominican Republic then retaliated further against the United States by passing a resolution terminating the Military Assistance treaty that had assured the country a continuing influx of American dollars. Admittedly, this was a drastic measure but one the congress felt necessary to take as a matter of national pride and principle. In the meanwhile, Ramfis, now a highly decorated general at the age of twenty-three, also managed to acquire a doctorate in law despite his extracurricular activities of racing sports cars and speedboats, cavorting with women, and indulging in orgies.

As it happens, there is a disheartening ending to this story. Despite his many achievements, Ramfis proved to be a big disappointment to his father, not because of his innocent youthful shenanigans, which his dad understood well, but because he showed no real interest in political affairs and public life. That was a shame, for he had the potential makings of a great tyrant, as exemplified by his claim, "The more I know of men, the more I love dogs."

Visionaries

Social engineers, utopian socialists, and mass murderers, including Sukarno, Atatürk, Castro, plus the Infamous Five:
Two features distinguish a visionary from a tyrant: a visionary has an idealistic rationale for oppressing and killing people, and a tyrant does not. A visionary wants people to conform to his utopian vision for society, and a tyrant simply wants people to obey him. These differences are more than superficial. The fact that one kind of leader operates within the framework of a social model and another kind has more self-centered, hedonic concerns suggests that these leaders differ in other personal ways as well. When differences exist between different kinds of leaders as adults, then these differences should be rooted in their childhood, too.

Sukarno, who formulated a "Guided Democracy" for Indonesia, a confused *mélange à trois* of capitalism, socialism, and Indonesian ideals that let him rule an unmanageable country through controlled chaos, will serve as a prototype of a visionary leader.[18] Born of a mixed ethnic marriage between a Balinese mother and a poor Javanese schoolteacher, Sukarno was brought up with mixed religious beliefs, combining Hinduism, Buddhism, and Islam with the tenets of traditional Javanese animism. Perhaps it was his exposure to these diverse belief systems that let him unify the many political, ethnic, and cultural divisions that made up Indonesia after its independence.

Separated often from his parents, Sukarno spent much time during his childhood with his grandmother, who believed he was a saint with supernatural powers and made him lick the bodies of sick villagers to cure them of their maladies. These supposed powers, though, did not keep him from becoming seriously ill from malaria and dysentery when he was older, but fortunately his grandmother was not around then to have her faith in him shaken. Although he spoke with respect and affection of his father, he was not especially close to him. The younger of two children, Sukarno was a precocious child with a photographic memory and a remarkable facility for languages. After receiving a Western-style education at the village school where his father taught, he went to live with a prominent civic and religious leader who treated him as a protégé and foster son while Sukarno attended a Dutch high school. In that household Sukarno was introduced to prominent political thinkers of Indonesia and learned a lot about politics. Sukarno wrote that he became the tail of his benefactor. "Wherever he went I followed . . . and I just sat and observed."

While in school, he mastered Javanese, Sudanese, Balinese, Indonesian, Arabic, Dutch, German, French, English, and Japanese. Instead of showing his usual stubbornness and feistiness, he became quiet and withdrawn in response to the racial remarks and taunts by the Dutch Colonial children. Mostly keeping to himself, he became an omnivorous reader, studying various political theories and philosophies, including the works of Thomas Jefferson, Rousseau, Immanuel Kant, and other leaders of Western thought. Later, after he went on to earn a civil engineering degree at the University of Technology at Bandung, he broke with his mentor because he was not radical enough for Sukarno's tastes (although he did marry his daughter and make her his first wife) and probably because he did not like the idea of playing second fiddle to anyone.

Sukarno was a model of conformity during his teens compared to other rulers. Nasser, whose mother died when he was eight years old, also spent much time away from home with his relatives, especially when his father was transferred to another job. A shy but extremely sensitive child, he could turn ferocious toward anyone who made even the faintest suggestion of an insult. In his teens, Nasser already showed considerable leadership ability, with his talent for organizing others and his outspokenness and impudence toward the British authorities, which earned him the admiration of his schoolmates. At school, he was a rebel and troublemaker, seldom attending classes because of his political activities. During these years, though, he read copiously, especially about the lives of great leaders such as Mahatma Gandhi, Julius Caesar, and Alexander the Great. He also joined the drama society and played the role of Julius Caesar. Eager to enter the military academy, he reapplied one year after his original application was turned down, and he was finally accepted. Years later, with three fellow officers, one being Anwar el-Sadat, he formed a secret revolutionary group, the Free Officers, whose purpose was to oust the British and remove the Egyptian royal family from power.

At the age of seven, Mustafa Kemal, later known as Atatürk, likewise had his education interrupted by his father's death. Headstrong and independent as a student, he rebelled against the traditional Turkish clothes of wide pants and a cummerbund, as well as the half-kneeling sitting at the Muslim school. He also rebelled against his barely literate mother, who wanted him to become a cleric or a businessman, drawn instead to the glamor and discipline of a military career. To keep peace with her obstinate son, his mother relented but only after conveniently having had a dream in which she was told that he would be successful if she let him become a soldier.

Fidel Castro exemplifies certain features found in many visionaries during their childhoods.[19] Highly competitive, he would do almost anything to win. Once he bet a fellow student five dollars that he could run his bike into a wall and not get hurt. He then crashed head-on into some columns and hurt himself so badly that he needed to be hospitalized for several days. He showed this same passion in sports. When he first learned to play basketball, he was determined to excel at it. The priests had to put a light on the court because he began practicing day and night. His desire to win was so strong that on several occasions "El Loco, Fidel," as they called him, actually forgot who he was playing for, switching sides midway in the game and making a basket for the other team. The school coach admitted that Castro's passion to win at all costs almost drove him crazy, remembering that Castro was always asking him what he had to do to be a leader and to make himself better known. Given to rages and periods of brooding as a boy, he showed an implacable will and rebelliousness, even against his domineering father. At the age of thirteen he had the audacity to organize a strike of sugar workers on his father's plantation because, as he told an interviewer many years later, his father exploited the peasants, paid no taxes on his land or income, and played politics for money. In short, Fidel was an incipient leader desperately in search of a cause. With his passion for winning and defiance of authority, it was only a matter of time before he would be able to find an ideal outlet for his ambitions in his revolutionary activities and become an ultimate ruler himself.

The infamous five   Now let's shift the focus to a subgroup of twentieth-century rulers, whose utopian visions led to countless deaths and whose crimes to humanity are so great that they are almost beyond evil, to learn if they showed any distinctive characteristics as children. The critical question is whether this subgroup of rulers had the equivalent of cloven hooves, pointed ears, forked tongues, or hidden marks of Satan as youths. Did they torture animals or pull legs off of insects? Did they show signs of brutality toward their playmates? Even more important, was there anything in the child-rearing of these visionaries that possibly could account for their later insensitivity to human suffering? Let's examine their pasts.

First, let's review what we know about the infamous five rulers: Hitler, Mao, Mussolini, Stalin, and Pol Pot. Based on the biographical information available on them, it becomes possible to reach a number of important conclusions. Although all but one of these leaders had unremarkable relationships with their mothers during childhood, all five were alienated, estranged, or openly hostile toward their fathers. Joseph Stalin's father, who periodically beat him and his mother, was a violent alcoholic and was eventually killed in a brawl when Stalin was eleven years old. Pol Pot's parents sent him to live with an older brother and his wife, who adopted him when he was six, so his relationship with his parents was distant or resentful at best, despite his brother's claim about the lack of open conflicts with them. Adolph Hitler's father, who died when he was eight, drank heavily and was brutally violent toward his family. Mussolini's father drank too much, womanized, and was intermittently employed. Mao Zedong hated his father for beating him and his brothers and for shaming him in front of others, and constantly bucked his authority. In his autobiography, he said he learned to hate him.

The antagonism of this quintet toward parental authority seemed to spill over into other areas as well, especially toward their teachers. Mao bucked the authority of his teachers and was one of the first students to cut off his queue, or pigtail. He also was expelled from school for writing a declaration against the school authorities for raising fees. Adolph Hitler was a ringleader in elementary school. After he was asked to leave the Linz Realschule, his mother sent him to a boarding school, but he continued to be idle, willful, and disrespectful, reacting with hostility to any direction or advice. Benito Mussolini was always in trouble for fighting at school. He was expelled several times, once when he was ten for wounding a boy with a knife. At school, in his own words, he became "the desperation of my parents and a pest to the neighbors." Joseph Stalin was constantly defiant of authority. According to his school records, he was punished fifteen times for reading "prohibited" books and eventually was expelled before graduation. With Pol Pot there was no outright rebellion against the authorities at school. Rather, he simply neglected his studies and drifted along, losing his scholarship at the City University in France when he failed to take his exams.

As far as their schooling goes, none of the infamous five fully completed his education. They either dropped out of school at different points, failed to take final exams, or were expelled for poor grades, poor attendance, disrespect toward the teachers, or involvement in forbidden political demonstrations. Mao, for instance, completed normal school and took some college courses but did not pursue his university training, and Pol Pot failed to complete his advanced college degree in France although he went on to become a teacher in his homeland. Stalin did well enough in elementary school to win a scholarship to the Tiflis seminary but then, as he became more politicized, began to get poorer grades. Despite their quirky educational experiences, all were avid readers, fueling their ambitions for leadership by poring over biographies of great leaders like Julius Caesar, Alexander the Great, and Napoleon.

What do these disparities between their response to formal education and self-education suggest? All chafed under the constraints and regimentation of a formal educational system. It was not the process of learning that bothered them. Almost all of them were autodidacts, who read widely and learned what suited them. They just did not want anybody telling them what to read and learn and then passing judgment on how well they had performed.

While none of the infamous five showed any signs of precociousness or exceptional talent, all of them had some form of creative outlet.

As children, visionaries, more so than other rulers, are most likely to be precocious or gifted (25 percent). As already noted, Sukarno had a photographic memory and a remarkable facility for languages. Fidel Castro and Agostinho Neto had phenomenal memories. Vladimir Lenin was described as a "walking encyclopedia" by his classmates and teachers. By the time he was six, the Ayatollah Khomeini had learned the whole Koran by heart. As a child, Mikhail Gorbachev had memorized many of Pushkin's poems and could recite them by heart. Visionaries also are far more likely than other rulers to be avid readers (58 percent) and to engage in various creative activities (36 percent) such as playing the piano, painting, or writing poetry during their youths.

Stalin, Mussolini, Mao, and Hitler wrote poetry as youths, and Hitler played the piano and painted as well. Mussolini was drawn to writing as a teenager, and Mao was an excellent essayist. Little is known about Pol Pot as a teenager, but, judging by his early adult years, I assume he had begun writing anonymous political tracts by then.

Visionaries as a group are most likely among the different rulers to show the earliest signs of leadership (see figure 5.3 below). Among the infamous five rulers, three likewise showed early evidence of leadership. Pol Pot showed no signs of leadership or charisma as a child, and Stalin mostly engaged in his own personal rebellions without trying to get others to join him. But Adolph Hitler was a ringleader at elementary school, Mao was a respected student leader in high school, and Mussolini had a small following of thugs. What these general findings suggest, though, is that, compared to other rulers, visionaries are more likely to display leadership skills at an early age, perhaps because these skills are so essential to their success at a later age. Monarchs, authoritarians, and tyrants do not need to rely on these skills as much because they have nothing much to sell to their people, but visionaries need to get them to embrace their utopian or dystopian dreams as a way of wielding power over them.

What about the personalities of our infamous five as children? While all led relatively private, solitary lives with no real friends or confidantes, only Mussolini was an outright bully and thug who showed little promise of being domesticated. Stalin studied to become a priest and later sang in the choir. In an interview with journalists, his mother claimed, "Soso (Joseph) was always a good boy . . . I never had occasion to punish him. He studied hard, always reading or discussing, trying to understand

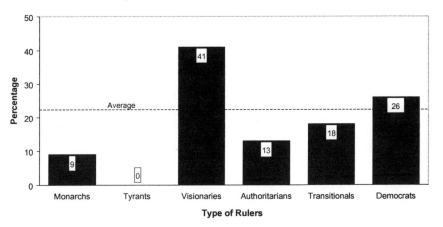

Fig 5.3: Exceptional Leadership Ability during Youth

Legend: The bars indicate the percentage of rulers who showed distinctive leadership traits as children.

everything.[20] Hitler was a choirboy in a Benedictine monastery and deeply loved his mother. In high school, Mao was voted "Student of the Year" by some four hundred students and won the highest rating for "moral and intellectual education." Pol Pot spent time in a Buddhist monastery as a child, where he learned obedience. In fact, if the words of his brother are to be believed, "the contemptible Pot was a lovely child," sweet-tempered, self-effacing, and unremarkable.[21]

What, then, distinguishes the childhoods of these infamous visionaries from those of their cohorts? Perhaps nothing. There was nothing distinctive about their backgrounds that convincingly hinted at the "villains" they would later become. Sure, as youths, most of these rulers were headstrong, defiant, unruly, stubborn, solitary, disrespectful toward authority, and determined to learn only what they wanted to learn at their own pace and in their own way, but these are the same qualities often found in creative geniuses as youths, not necessarily of monsters-in-the-making. While these rebellious qualities in children can make life hell for parents, teachers, and adults in general, they do not necessarily signify that these children are bad or evil. With only a couple of possible exceptions, these rulers showed few signs of deliberate cruelty, sadism, or a callous disregard for human life or suffering when they were youths. And by no stretch of the imagination could you have foretold their later notoriety and the fateful decisions they would make after they came to

As a group, the infamous five showed much of the same traits as other visionaries. Compared to other rulers, higher percentages of them became politicized before they were twenty-one. Kim Il Sung, for instance, began his political activities at the age of seven. By the age of fourteen, he had organized a union; by the age of fifteen, an anti-imperial youth league; and by the age of seventeen, a boycott against Japanese goods. And as a teenager, Chiang Kai-shek insisted on being the commander-in-chief while playing war games and was nearly expelled for leading a student protest. He also won the admiration of his fellow students by defiantly cutting off his queue, as did Mao, to show his revolutionary nature and disdain for imperial tradition. More so than other rulers, visionaries(50 percent) were hostile toward or alienated from their fathers, and about that same percentage were nonconforming and rebellious toward most forms of authority.

power by what you knew about them then. Though most were not obedient, conforming, and respectful as children, they likewise were not extraordinary or abnormal.

If Freud's maxim that the child is father to the man holds true, then crucial information must be missing about these leaders as children, or the explanation for their later behavior lies elsewhere. But if the reason for their behavior does not lie in the past, then where else can it be? In examining the early lives of these individuals, I have come to the conclusion that much of the answer paradoxically lies in their futures. What modern psychological theories fail to take into account is that certain extraordinary circumstances can transform the nature of people, perhaps not radically, but enough to make a difference. The very process of gaining absolute power seems to be such an extraordinary circumstance that it is capable of bringing out certain latent tendencies in rulers that might never have come into being under ordinary conditions. The child still gives rise to the man, but the wielding of ultimate power then may unleash the potential monster that later consumes the man. As I will show later, this notion helps to explain a lot of otherwise unexplainable actions of rulers.

Transitionals (Rulers of Emerging Democracies)

Presidents, prime ministers, and chancellors, including de Valera, Collins, Abdul Rahman, Figueres, Masaryk, and Ben Gurion:
During the twentieth century, many nations have gone on to copy the democratic system of government practiced by their foreign occupying powers

after having achieved independence. Other nations have instituted democracies after years of dictatorial or absolute monarchical rule. During this initial period of democracy, the rulers tend to be individuals who had been instrumental in helping to bring these transitions about, sometimes risking their lives or enduring privations to achieve these goals. Eamon de Valera, who took the Irish Free State out of the British Commonwealth in 1937 and made his country a "sovereign" state, renamed Ireland, and who served as prime minister (1932–48, 1951–54, 1957–59) and then president (1959–73), was one such leader.[22] A legend in his own country, he had a childhood befitting a legend, which certain of his biographers say he helped to create. His father, a Spanish immigrant who worked as a music teacher, abandoned his wife and son about one year before he died, when Eamon was only three. His mother, who was then living in America, sent Eamon away to live with his uncle in Ireland and had nothing more to do with his raising. With no father or mother about, his playmates teased and taunted him about being illegitimate. These usually were fighting words even for a half-blooded Irish youth, so he fought a lot, defending himself against accusations that probably were true. That led him to feel different from the other children, which was not an irrational response considering that he had a foreign surname and a lanky build and lived with relatives instead of his parents.

Educated by the Christian Brothers at Charlesville, Eamon was a good student who seriously considered entering the priesthood. From what I could gather, the only things that held him back were that he liked girls

A mixed parentage such as De Valera's was not unusual among leaders of emerging democracies. Sir William Alexander Bustamante, the first prime minister of Jamaica, from 1962–1967, used to boast, "I am one third Irish, one third Negro, one third Arawak, and one third white." When a journalist said that added up to 120 percent, he flashed a smile and replied, "That is why I am better than the other leaders,"[23] but did not comment on both his and the journalist's inability to add.

Be that as it may, de Valera's upbringing was not so different than that of many transitional democratic leaders. Seventeen percent came from broken marriages. Most (57 percent) were raised in small towns. They tended not to be firstborn children (68 percent). Compared to other rulers, their relationship with their parents was unremarkable, being neither especially close nor distant. Along with monarchs and visionaries, they (34 percent) were one of the most likely kinds of rulers to have lost one or the other parent before they were fourteen years old.

too much and he was not very religious. Later, at Blackrock College, he received honors in several subjects and a scholarship in mathematics and became Student of the Year despite almost being cashiered out of school for suspected cheating on a Latin exam. While at college, he ran and played soccer, but he was more an enthusiastic athlete than a gifted one. A healthy and energetic lad, he suffered from a peculiar handicap that was to plague him all his life: he constantly would have to fight to keep himself awake. This presented a problem at college until he hit on the idea of affixing himself in a tree while studying, knowing that if he did not keep himself alert he would go crashing to the ground. Once he entered politics, though, he apparently saw no need to take special precautions. In fact, his moments of somnolence were probably a great advantage, since he could catch up on his sleep during parliamentary debates and sometimes when he himself was holding meetings. He also noted that, because of his supposed handicap, he never lost a night's sleep no matter how much strain he had been under.

Except for leaders of established democracies, those of emerging ones spent the longest time in school, with many working toward advanced degrees, and they also got the best grades. Abdul Rahman, first prime minister of independent Malaya (1957–63) and then of Malaysia (1963–

Eamon was a bright but not especially precocious student, more diligent than brilliant, a student who already had surpassed his potential. Among the various ruler types, visionaries (25 percent), followed next by transitional rulers (13 percent) and democratic rulers (11 percent), were most likely to show special intellectual gifts as children. With transitional rulers, these gifts were mostly in the form of a prodigious memory or a facility for languages. David Ben Gurion, who was to become the Father of Israel, began learning Hebrew from his grandfather at the age of three and was able to read and write Hebrew and Yiddish when he entered school. Noted for his phenomenal memory, he was sent to school for the gifted. Tomas Masaryk, first president of Czechoslovakia (1918–35), acquired new languages easily and invented a new language with numbers as a child. Liaquat Ali Khan, the first prime minister of Pakistan, amazed adults with his excellent memory by quoting verses at length. Vaclav Havel, president of Czechoslovakia from December 1989 to July 1992 and president of the Czech Republic from January 1993, began reading and writing at a very early age. And reputedly an old scholar prophesied that Yasir Arafat was marked for greatness because of his photographic memory.

70), showed a persistence in his education that would make Sisyphus seem like a slouch.[24] But unlike many visionaries who simply flunked out or dropped out of school because of lack of interest or conflicts with school authorities, Abdul Rahman, much like other would-be transitionals, kept pursuing his education despite setbacks and failures until he achieved his goal, albeit in an unorthodox way. After flunking his final exams for a bachelor's degree, he tried again and got the lowest possible pass in history. He then spent about twelve years unsuccessfully studying for a law degree in England. Years later, after he was out of office, an academic failure in his own eyes but a political success by worldly standards, he finally realized his dream. He never did pass the bar exam, but he was ceremoniously admitted to the bar in his home country.

Other would-be transitional leaders likewise have doggedly pursued their studies despite academic difficulties or conflicts by taking unorthodox routes toward their goals. José Figueres, who as president of Costa Rica would be responsible for eliminating its military forces, found school unchallenging and constantly feuded with his teachers. So he took matters into his own hands and began teaching himself. With a strong interest in electrical engineering, he set up a lab in his bedroom and took international correspondence courses. At his father's insistence, Figueres attended the Colegio Seminario, taught by stern German priests. But this experience proved to be so traumatic that he ran away and unsuccessfully attempted suicide as a way of standing up to his father and never finished his final year of high school. Instead, he traveled alone to Boston and enrolled at MIT. But even there he had friction with the teachers, quitting after six months when told he had to take some courses that he felt duplicated ones he had already taken in Costa Rica. Instead, he put all of his fragmentary education to practical use by working for a while as an electrician while pursuing his own studies in the Boston Public Library.[25]

Tomas Masaryk eventually became a professor of philosophy only after a rocky educational experience. Intolerant of his teachers for their lack of erudition and unpopular with the other students, he mapped out his own course of study and pursued it single-mindedly. During his seventh form, he spent his time mostly in the library and got into trouble for truancy. He also was nearly expelled from school for his presumptuousness in telling the headmaster, "Whoever acts against his conscious is a scoundrel." But whatever his difficulties with the school authorities, he seemed to sense how far he could push the limits, always stopping short of getting kicked out of school.[26]

Only 18 percent of would-be transitional leaders showed signs of exceptional leadership abilities during their youths. Though this percentage was substantially less than for visionaries, the ways they displayed their leadership were similar.

Propelled by his sense of destiny—that he one day would be the leader of Israel—David Ben Gurion began his quest at an early age. At the age of ten, he founded a youngsters' Zionist Society but had to dissolve it because parents protested he was too young. At fourteen, he cofounded the Ezra Society, and at eighteen he founded the Herzl Society. He taught other kids Hebrew, gave Bible lessons, and read them Zionist poems to inspire them about his dream for a Jewish homeland. As his dream began becoming more of a reality, he was asked if he would like to be anointed King David. He graciously declined because then he would have to be King David II.

Yassir Arafat, with his opposing dream of a Palestinian homeland, was drilling other youths to become soldiers and Arab guerrilla fighters on the streets when he was ten. As he got older, he began to dominate almost all aspects of students' lives to the point that he often got on their nerves.

Leadership during childhood or adolescence was not necessarily a reflection of popularity. Many of these leaders simply took charge of other children or groups or, like Tomas Masaryk, simply started their own student organizations when such groups did not exist. Despite overthrowing the yoke of colonial powers or dictatorships before assuming office, transitionals as youths were surprisingly among the most conforming of the rulers, showing little evidence of the outright rebelliousness and confrontational behavior of visionaries. Compared to other rulers, they stayed in school, dutifully went to church, and, for the most part, respected their parents, elders, and superiors. When they were rebellious as children, they were more mischievous than revolutionary, qualifying their actions with a twinkle in their eyes, as did de Valera, or acting out in ways that did not antagonize too many people.

De Valera had a bit of Abdul Rahman's persistence, Figueres's obstinacy, and Masaryk's intolerance for imperfection. But he also had a bit of the fabled Irish charm, which let him buck authority, break rules, and exasperate his teachers without antagonizing them, while simultaneously winning the admiration of his fellow students for his audacity. This remarkable ability to tweak others without raising their hackles would stand him in good stead during his student years and later as a politician. It also would contribute to his assuming a leadership role in the many or-

Unlike the career path of authoritarians, visionaries, and tyrants, transitionals were not as likely to choose a military career as their route to power. Law (20 percent) headed the list, with teaching (17 percent) a second choice, followed next by the military (11 percent), journalism (9 percent), and farming (9 percent). What these varied professions suggest is that those individuals who would eventually lead their countries to independence and oversee its transition to democracy tended to be a heterogeneous lot, coming from a variety of occupational backgrounds. In the startup of a new government, there are few rules and precedents, little tradition to go by; and anyone who manages to come to the fore and win the backing of the people has a chance of becoming leader, regardless of his past profession. At the point that transitionals come to power, they usually do not have to contend with any military cliques or old-boy clubs of lawyers with an investment in perpetuating their kind. Those cliques and clubs will come later, after the fledgling democracy begins to come of age.

ganizations and clubs he joined, ranging from the College Literary and Debating Club to the Gaelic League, which was promoting Gaelic as the national language. Although Eamon was to gain a reputation for being hardheaded and opportunistic, indifferent to the feelings of other people, his critics did him an injustice, remaining ignorant of his occasional displays of sentimentality, seldom observed toward other people but once noted when he cried after the death of his family's canary.

Michael Collins, who would become president of the Provisional Irish Republic for ten days before being assassinated and was an enemy of Eamon de Valera after the nationally divisive treaty, paralleled de Valera's life in many ways.[27] Like Eamon, he too was a staunch Catholic, more ritual than spiritual. Although the youngest of eight children, he too was orphaned at a young age, losing his revered father when he was six and his mother when he was seventeen. Because his father had been seventy-five years old when he was born, Michael, like Eamon, probably was also the object of rumors about his legitimacy. Like Eamon, Michael was a leader as a child. From his earliest days, he always wanted to be in charge of everything; it made no difference what. His cousin noted that Michael always insisted on holding the pitchfork when they tried to spear fish. And his sheer size, good looks, and physical prowess added to his authority when he spoke. He too loved sports, but he was a more gifted athlete than Eamon. He too was an avid reader who would become head of his class in school, only to quit school at age fifteen after completing primary school. In disposition, though, Michael and Eamon were more complementary than alike. Michael was more outgoing and emotional, given to displays of great generosity and outbursts of temper. He laughed and wept easily. He also was more mischievous, wild, and cheeky. While Eamon was more calculating and rational, Michael was more daring and ruthless, making him the ideal person to head the elite hit unit, known as the "Squad," that built bombs, killed British detectives and G-men, arranged jail breakouts, and carried out kidnappings. Eamon seemed more interested in masterminding the strategy in their war for independence, while Michael seemed to thrive more on the thrill and excitement of participating in this deadly game.

Democrats (Rulers of Existing Democracies)

Presidents, prime ministers, and chancellors, including Nixon, de Gaulle, Churchill, and Theodore Roosevelt:

Compared to all other types of rulers, democratic rulers have more limits placed on their authority and power by all sorts of governmental regulations and rules. These constraints include having to be elected by popular vote, either directly or through elected representatives of the people; dealing with constitutional limits to their terms in office; and having to share power among the executive, legislative, and judicial branches of government. In a way, democracies invite rulers to lead the country with one hand tied behind their backs, sometimes two, and on rare occasions being hogtied, which can make it difficult for them to get things done or carry out their legislative agendas. They do not have the luxury of a dictator, like Nasser, who once proclaimed, "My parliament is the army," or of Oliver Cromwell long before him, who opined, "Nine out of ten citizens hate me? No matter, so long as the tenth one alone is armed." Because of these institutional constraints on their authority, you would suspect that the kinds of people drawn to becoming leaders in established democracies should be markedly different than those drawn to becoming dictators and, consequently, should have experienced different childhoods as well.

Obviously, no single ruler embodies most of the main attributes and early life experiences found in the broad array of democratic leaders. So to deal with this problem, I selected Richard Nixon, former president of the United States, as our modal democratic leader because he was forced to act at odds with his basic character, which should have made him one of the least-suited people to rise to political prominence in a democracy,

Although Nixon was handicapped by his personality and looks as a youth, both Churchill and Teddy Roosevelt had real physical disabilities to overcome, Churchill with his stammer and Roosevelt with his severe nearsightedness and asthma. Among the children who were to become leaders of established democracies, 8 percent had disabilities of some kind that put them at a disadvantage, the second-highest percentage among rulers. For example, Kato Takaaki had severe myopia. William Morris Hughes became increasingly deaf. Godfrey Huggins eventually lost hearing in his left ear after numerous surgeries for otitis media. Arthur Griffith was born with his two Achilles tendons contracted, which made him walk on the balls of his feet. Anthony Eden had poor eyesight. Jean Chrétien's deafness made it difficult for him to pronounce words and to learn at school. He also developed Bell's palsy at the age of twelve, which distorted his mouth. Boris Yeltsin had to have his left thumb and index finger amputated after a grenade exploded in his hand as a child. Woodrow Wilson, who was late in reading, did not know the letters until he was nine and had trouble with written words until he was about twelve, probably had undiagnosed dyslexia. Rene Waldeck-Rousseau had severely defective vision in his left eye. Harry S Truman was "blind as a mole" until he got glasses at age six. John F. Kennedy was born with an "unstable" back. And Mihály Károlyi apparently had a cleft palate, which was operated on at age fourteen.

to achieve his political goals.[28] The advantage in choosing Nixon is that the very ways he compensated for his lacks show almost in caricature what democratic leaders need to begin doing as youngsters to prepare them for gaining the highest office in the land. His youth should be an inspirational primer for how people can achieve prominence in politics when they seemingly are not suited for it by nature.

Richard Nixon was a man who became president despite an unprepossessing appearance (unattractive?), an absence of natural charm (little personal warmth? no sense of humor?), and a lack of social grace (awkward? nervous? fidgety?). Born the second of five children, all boys, he was raised in a relatively joyless lower-middle-class household located in the small town of Whittier, California. Frank Anthony Nixon, his father, was an argumentative, cantankerous, and opinionated man with a bad temper. A Methodist who did not smoke or drink, he converted to Quakerism after he married his wife, Hannah, a devout, tight-fisted Quaker who had spent two years at Whittier College. His conversion was not entirely because he suddenly saw the light but rather, I suspect, to assure his father-in-law that he was right-thinking so that he could get a loan from him to buy a small lemon ranch in Yorba Linda. After laboring unsuccessfully for several years, he quit the orchard, became a roustabout for an oil company, and eventually opened a relatively successful gasoline station and store.

Nixon was the last person you would imagine to be drawn to politics, where schmoozing and boozing were the norm. As a child, he seemed overly mature for his age, meaning he was shy, serious, stuffy, and deferential to adults. He also was persnickety, hating to ride the school bus because he did not like how the other children smelled. Even though his classmates in grade school grudgingly respected his knowledge and verbal skills, they ridiculed and teased him and mostly did not include him in their games. Rather than retreating into his shell, as most children might be inclined to do, Nixon was even more determined to win their respect and acceptance. Though awkward around people and petrified by girls, he hid his insecurities well enough to become a well-known student leader who excelled in debating and took part in many school activities. Despite his visibility in high school, he had no real friends or social life. A B+ and A student, he ran for student body president as a senior in high school but lost to a popular athlete. Then later, after he matriculated at Whittier College and failed to be accepted by the Franklins, he capitalized on his unpopularity by starting the Orthogonian Society for other unpopular students on campus and became its first president as a freshman. Determined to gain acceptance by his fellow students and teachers, he made the honor society for four years, won a number of prestigious speaking contests, and, despite his physical awkwardness, played on the football team but never won a letter. These achievements won him respect but not the popularity and acceptance he craved.

After winning a scholarship to Duke and graduating third in his class from Duke Law School, Nixon deliberately pushed aside his natural shyness and reclusiveness by joining every desirable organization he could get into and rapidly becoming its leader. When he began to practice law, it was impossible to have a meeting anywhere without him attending and assuming an important role. In his first three years as a lawyer, he served as president of four organizations and became the youngest member of the Whittier College board of trustees. He was president of the 20–30 Club for young businessmen and professionals, the Duke University Alumni of California, the Orange County Association of Cities, and the Whittier College Alumni Association. Amazingly, he later would become president without a natural inclination for the golfing, drinking,

What was most remarkable about Nixon was that, despite his basic shyness and reserve, he forced himself to be sociable, affiliating, and gregarious, belonging to many clubs and organizations at school and in the community and leading a busy social life, as did 39 percent of the other democratic rulers, the highest percentage among all ruler groups. He participated in competitive sports (18 percent) and was basically conforming and nonrebellious, as were 68 percent of the democratic leaders. Despite his relative unpopularity, he seemed to be an even-tempered youth with little tendency toward moodiness, as was the case for substantial proportions of children who likewise would later become leaders of established democracies (41 percent and 12 percent, respectively). Though not a precocious youth, he excelled in his studies; read widely; went on to get a graduate education, as did 41 percent of democratic rulers; and then chose to become a lawyer, the most common profession chosen by democrat rulers (33 percent) before they entered politics.

smoking, backslapping, cursing, and crude-joking world of businessmen; but, as the political stakes began getting higher, he even learned how to be as foul-mouthed, bigoted, hypocritical, and hard-drinking as the best of them. But even then, he rarely let down his reserve. While he was vice president, he confessed to Stewart Alsop, "In my job you can't enjoy the luxury of intimate personal friendships. You can't confide absolutely to anyone. You can't talk much about your personal plans, your personal feelings."[29] What he did not say was that he had been that way since childhood.

Despite his seeming social awkwardness, Nixon typifies the kind of childhood and youthful behaviors commonly found in leaders of established democracies. He had all the credentials and did everything he needed to do to prepare himself for a successful life in politics. Like Nixon, the greatest proportion of democratic rulers came from middle-class backgrounds with parents who had modest means or considerable wealth. Compared to children in most other ruler groups, their relationships with their mothers and their fathers were neither especially close nor especially distant. However, next to visionaries, they were the most likely among the different ruler types to come from intact families (89 percent) and, next to monarchs, to grow up in an urban area (44 percent).

Though possessing little personal magnetism or charisma, Nixon assumed a leadership role in the many organizations he joined because of deliberate decisions on his part. While children who later become visionaries are the most likely to show leadership skills, those who will become established democrats are the next most likely, suggesting the importance of these skills for their later political success. Within the sample of rulers, you can find many examples of impressive leadership during the youths of democratic leaders.

- Benazir Bhutto was elected president of the prestigious Oxford Union for a three-month term.
- At Yale University, George Bush was head of many committees, captain of the championship baseball team, and captain of the soccer team.
- William Clinton was elected president of his junior class. He also was president of the scholarly Beta Club, a member of the National Honor Society, a senator to Boy's Nation, and a Rhodes Scholar.
- As a child, Jean Chrétien was a leader in most activities because, for him, it was "the natural order of things." When he got to law school, he was elected president of his class for three consecutive years.
- By his senior year, Brian Mulroney had become a student leader and president of the student co-op, the biggest business on campus.
- As a teenager, Golda Meir organized a parade in downtown Milwaukee to protest the pogroms in Europe.
- In his senior year, Ronald Reagan was elected president of the student body. He became editor of the yearbook and head of the student council.
- Ian Smith became the head boy of the school and captain of the cricket, rugby, and tennis teams and, later, chairman of the students' representative council.

These examples go on and on.

The inclination of these children and youths to show leadership abilities even shows up in how they play games. To overcome her loneliness as a child, Indira Gandhi, for example, sometimes jumped on the dining room table and gave disjointed speeches to her parents' servants. As a teenager, she organized her own party, called the monkey brigade, and recruited many children to it. She drilled them, marched them, and issued orders to them about their duties. She divided her toys into freedom fighters and the British and began having Joan-of-Arc visions of martyrdom.

As a child, Charles de Gaulle was much the same. He often played tin soldiers with his brothers and other relatives. Xavier, his older brother, would be the king of England and command the British forces. Jean de Corbie would be emperor of Russia. Charles would assign Jacques to be king of the "Mysterious Island" and Pierre to be the pope, in charge of the Papal Guard. Another boy would be emperor of Germany. Charles always would be the king of France and commander of the French army. Whenever anyone else wanted to trade positions with him, Charles would indignantly protest, "Never! France is mine!"[30]

What becomes apparent from study of these democratic rulers as children is that their leadership abilities need not be natural or God-given. Future leaders can set out deliberately to transform their nature into one that is more suitable for rulers. This same dogged persistence that Nixon showed to overcome his reclusiveness, shyness, and social awkwardness shows itself in other ways than in the social arena. Winston Churchill, for instance, was determined to prove that biology was not destiny. Like Nixon, Churchill was not especially liked by his classmates, and a boy once even stabbed him in the chest during an argument while the other boys looked on. When he was seven, he deliberately decided to be different. Sickly, uncoordinated, and speaking with a lisp, he was teased and beaten by bullies, sometimes causing him to hide in the nearby woods to avoid them. Tired of being timid, fearful, and shy, he set out to become a great orator and a hero. By his teens, he already was imbued with an unbounded self-confidence. In a letter to his mother at that time, he wrote that he was prepared to risk his life in the army because "I am so conceited that I do not believe the gods would create so potent a being as myself for so prosaic an ending," since he was "intended to do something in the world."[31]

Theodore Roosevelt, like Winston Churchill, set out to change his nature.[32] At age three, he began suffering from severe bronchial asthma and had recurrent stomach ailments that continued well into his teens. Detesting his own body and weakness, he became preoccupied with exercising and workouts in the gym and deliberately tried to be more manly and heroic. He took up boxing and became quite adept at it. He also set out to be liked and respected. By his senior year in college, Theodore Roosevelt was president of ADQ, vice president of the Natural History Society, president of OK, secretary of the Pudding, editor of the Advocate, and librarian of Porcellian. Years later, as the commander of the Rough Riders and as a fearless hunter in Africa after having served his term as president, he embodied the image of robust health, masculinity, and courage, a far cry from the fearful, timid, and shy boy he once had been.

5.4: Winston Churchill's report card at age nine. He was last in class. His teacher wrote that he was "very feeble" in composition and "as bad as it well can be" in spelling. In his later life, he went on to win the Nobel Prize for Literature. Churchill Archives Centre, Churchill Papers, CHAR 28/44/4. Reproduced with the permission of the Sir Winston Churchill Archive Trust and St George's School, Ascot.

A Summing Up

The different characterizations of these six kinds of rulers as youths lead to an important but not astounding conclusion, which is that different kinds of children with different kinds of backgrounds ended up becoming different kinds of leaders. We also have noted that a large portion of these future rulers were relatively ordinary as youths, showing few early signs of exceptional ability that could serve to predict their later fame or infamy. This observation is consistent with legendary accounts of heroes. A common theme of these legends is that the true character of the hero becomes revealed only at the conclusion of the childhood cycle after a long period of obscurity. At that time, the hero begins to show powers he never displayed before, which he then employs to survive certain perils and eventually secure the throne.[33] To the extent that many aspiring rulers follow the script of heroes, we should expect that, in the process of their quest for ultimate power, they likewise should display previously unexpressed attributes that ensure their eventual success. What the legends do not say is whether the would-be ruler is now an entirely different person than he originally was or only an older version of his younger self. They also do not explain how these changes could have come about or what kind of personal attributes are best suited for each of the different kinds of leadership roles. Let's now see what light the results of my study shed on these matters.

Little Acorns into Mighty Oaks

> A male chimpanzee in his prime organizes his whole life around
> issues of rank. His attempts to achieve and then maintain alpha status
> are cunning, persistent, energetic, and time-consuming. They affect
> whom he travels with, whom he grooms, where he glances, how often
> he scratches, where he goes, and what time he gets up in the morning.
> And all these behaviors come not from a drive to be violent for its
> own sake, but from a set of emotions that, when people show them,
> are labeled "pride" or, more negatively, "arrogance."
> —R. Wrangham and D. Peterson, *Demonic Males: Apes and the
> Origins of Human Development*

Once many rulers assume power, they begin to suffer from what I call
the Louis XIV syndrome of *"L'etat, c'est moi."* As a feature of this syndrome, they seem to undergo a peculiar expansion in their personal identity and come to believe that they and their people are one. Like a spirit
guide that gives voice through a medium, they often act as if their people
give voice through them. Sukarno, for example, often claimed, "I am Indonesia, I am the Revolution." Charles de Gaulle, showing he had the
makings for a ruler, took it upon himself to speak for France long before
anyone actually asked him to do so. Jomo Kenyatta became the physical
incarnation of Kenya just as de Gaulle symbolized France, not only in
their fortuitous surnames but in how they actually saw themselves.
Nkrumah, who touted the view that he was "Messiah of Africa," named
his autobiography *Ghana*. As savior of the Spanish people, Franco re-
sented being thought of as an individual. Since he and Spain were one,
any criticism of him was an insult of all Spanish people. Sekoe Toure,
who headed the PDG one-party state of Guinea, referred to his writings
as *The Works of the PDG*. Hitler was the personification of the Third
Reich, just as Atatürk assumed the identity of Turkey. Kenneth Kaunda

believed himself to be the living incarnation of Zambia. And Bokassa began to see himself as the personification of the Central African Republic.

During my professional career, I have met many people who claimed to be God, but I have never met ones who claimed to be the living personification of their own country, perhaps because those claiming to be God usually get locked up on a mental ward, while those claiming to be one with their own country begin attracting a political following. What is so intriguing and so frustrating about these rulers who identify themselves with their nations is that, when interviewers ask them to tell them about themselves, they cannot get the rulers to reveal any intimate details. They prefer instead to interweave their prior lives with various political happenings within their country and interpret their pasts in that context rather than within a personal life story. However, on reflection upon this common practice among rulers, you cannot help but be struck by its basic absurdity. For instance, when Castro boasts to a lover, as he actually did, "I am Cuba," before bedding her,[1] is he implying that he will be having sex with this women on behalf of the roughly five million men and the five million women in Cuba as well? And if so, do you categorize this vicarious *ménage-à-millions* as heterosexual, homosexual, or bisexual? Or if he means that he is Cuba only in a political sense, should you then assume that his lover, like so many other people in the country, was truly getting #$%*&!d by her country?

Then let's take Bourguiba, who billed himself as the creator and incarnation of Tunisia. "The system? I am the system!" he proclaimed when asked to describe his government. With a peculiar kind of logic, he must have seen himself as greater than most men because he had only one testicle, else why did he proudly mention his undescended testicle in a public speech to the nation? From what I gather, he was saying that, since other men who had given birth to new nations needed both of their testicles to do so, he must be at least twice as great as they since he had been able to do so with only one testicle. He truly was numero uno in his country. But in fairness to him, his grandiosity seemed tempered by an iota of modesty. He did admit, "Bourguiba is mortal," but he qualified this by adding, "Bourguibism will live for ever."[2]

Then there is Francois Duvalier, who put a neon sign outside his palace that read, "I am the Haitian flag, One and Indivisible."[3] Was he saying it made no difference if the people pledged allegiance to the flag or to him because both were one and the same? Or was he simply trying to establish his uniqueness by saying he was one flag and not two or two halves of one? Unfortunately, I fear we shall never know the truth, since nobody, to my knowledge, ever questioned him about these crucial distinctions. Therefore, without evidence to the contrary, I assume that many of his countrymen would have preferred to give Duvalier the benefit of the doubt by accepting his literal contention that he really was the Haitian flag. That way, they would have had a better chance of hoisting him to the top of a flagpole.

Now having made a case for the bizarreness of this transformation in identity, I want to argue that what may strike rational humans as absurd may make a great deal of sense from an evolutionary perspective, representing a remarkable, socially adaptive response on the part of a ruler to being the head of his nation. Not only do rulers seem to physically grow in stature and exude more charisma by virtue of their office, often abetted by many artificial props and aids that heighten these impressions, but their sense of self slowly begins to expand like a molten lava flow to engulf all the people in the land and its terrain, too. And in a peculiar kind of way, which is consistent with Nature's intentions, this expanded sense of self represents a marvelous way for the ruler to fulfill his sociobiological role—as head of the body politic. Just as the male monkeys, chimps, or apes automatically begin to assume more responsibility for their particular community once they attain the dominant status of alpha male, human rulers begin to do so as well. This alteration in their sense of personal identity, sometimes expressed by the use the imperial "we" when they speak, is not simply an affectation or a matter of personal choice. According to my thesis, it represents a psychobiological response to their crucial social role. Just as many drugs, such as opium, alcohol, marijuana, and hallucinogens, can cause people to experience an expanded sense of self or a sense of cosmic consciousness, it is tempting to speculate that some natural internal neurochemical with similar identity-diffusing properties gets released within the brains of higher-order primates once they begin to wield absolute power, which then causes them to feel responsible for their people—or, at least, to rationalize away all their self-serving motives and actions with suitable socially sanctioned ones. It also may help to provide a kind of psychological cement that bonds them to their people and heightens their national sense of territoriality. This response is likely met by a complementary one on the part of the people, now functioning in the role of subordinates, who charge their ruler with speaking and acting on their behalf—at least until their social head gets lopped off and replaced by a new one.

Aside from the difficulty of penetrating beyond this peculiar identity shield of rulers, you are likely to encounter an even more formidable problem in getting meaningful personal information from them, especially dictators but often democratic leaders as well. They simply do not want to reveal anything meaningful or private about themselves; they only want to present a picture of themselves that is flattering and strengthens their grip on power. Sir Alan Bullock, the noted biographer of both Hitler and Stalin, for instance, informed me he had difficulty learning about Hitler's private self and became skeptical that he even had one.[4] Not only was Hitler enormously guarded about revealing anything personal, but he said more than once to people, "You will never know what I'm thinking." And the same went for Stalin. Bullock said Hitler and Stalin were two of the most secretive men in history. Hitler never would have let himself be interviewed, and, if he did, it would have been for his political purposes, and he would have dominated the interview and used it as a forum for his views. As for Stalin, who was suspicious of everything, he would not let you ask anything personal, not only because he would not trust you but because he felt it was none of your business. And if by accident he happened to reveal something personal or you learned it on your own, you probably never would live to report it.

The problem of getting to know rulers is not confined only to dictators. In my conversation with William Manchester, the noted biographer of Winston Churchill and John F. Kennedy and an interviewer of Harold Macmillan as well, he informed me of his difficulties in getting personal information from these leaders. Manchester said he found absolutely no distinction between Churchill's public image and his private life. He always was on stage. There was no difference in him whatsoever if he delivered a major political address or held a private conversation. During his many interviews with Churchill, Manchester said, "I didn't really converse with him. I was a one-man House of Commons listening to him. He had everything to say, and I had nothing to say." With Kennedy, it was different. Instead of Manchester getting a chance to ask his probing questions, Kennedy was interviewing him and trying to get at whatever information he had. Then, during a meeting with Macmillan at his country estate, Manchester found that, after he would ask a question, Macmillan would lapse into a long silence while he stared at the carpet and then finally nod and point his finger at the tape recorder, signaling Manchester to turn it on, and then "speak in sentences and paragraphs, which when I played them back were grammatically perfect and did look very well in print."[5]

What all this adds up to is that it is hard to get to know a ruler despite the efforts he may go through to seem personable and accommodating. The reason is that you not only have to get to know him as a person (= his fears, concerns, conflicts, aspirations), which is hard enough to do, but also the person playing the role of ruler (= acting decisively in crises, inspiring awe in subjects, showing a natural authority, being a forceful advocate for certain views), tainted by your personal perception of him (= caring, devious, moral, personable, intimidating, or manipulative). Whatever image you have of him will be complicated further by how forthright or deceptive he is. Then, even if he makes an effort to be frank, he may lack insight into his real motivations. As was so with many of the rulers in my study, he is more likely to be a man of action than of introspection, giving self-serving, selfless political reasons for his choices rather than more probable selfish, personal ones. All these factors leave you with three options in forming your impressions about the ruler: you can dismiss everything you learn about him as false; you can accept everything you learn about him as true; or, as I am inclined to do, you can take him at face value—what you see is what you get—social mask, private person, preposterous notions and all.[6]

In reality, except for those we know intimately, this also is how we tend to judge most people. When Dorothy and her whimsical cohorts pulled back the curtain to reveal the Wizard of Oz, they did not necessarily unmask the "true person." Though he actually turned out to be a frightened little man, the Wizard of Oz also happened to be a frightening tyrant who used all the means at his disposal to terrorize the inhabitants of the Emerald City. What all this means is that, if you hope to be able to characterize rulers, you are obliged to take the person with the public persona, along with your own attitudes toward people in authority. But despite any limitations with this approach, we now have one critical advantage over other people in getting to know rulers and even the biographers who study them for years: we have access to an extensive data base on 377 rulers that can transform any two-dimensional portraits of them into three-dimensional portrayals by placing our observations on any particular ruler within the context of many other rulers of his particular ilk.

ADDING DIMENSION TO THEIR CHARACTER

Monarchs

Kings, sheikhs, sultans, emperors, and other regal rulers, including Franz Joseph and Abdul Hamid:
Franz Joseph, emperor of Austria (1848–1916) and king of Hungary (1867–1916), is the gold-plated standard for monarchs not only because

of his amazingly long tenure in office but also because of his remarkable achievement of accomplishing so little of note over so long a period of time except perhaps to divert the murderous hatred his Austrian, German, Czech, Polish, Hungarian, and Italian subjects had toward each other, toward the Russians, Serbs, French, and English during the Crimean War, the war with Napoleon III, and World War I.[7] By temperament and training, he seemed well suited for ruling an unstable empire composed of different ethnic groups. Because of his phlegmatic nature, the emperor gave the impression of being more deliberate, thoughtful, and intelligent than he was. Earning the rank of regimental colonel at the precocious age of thirteen after only one year of military school, Franz Joseph later displayed a military genius as emperor that not only befuddled his enemies but confounded his own generals even more. What he did during war was to adopt a revolutionary strategy of first yielding territory to the enemy and then futilely defending it after it was gone because he believed it was dishonorable for the army to cede any territory without fighting for it. That way the enemy never could celebrate

after its seemingly easy victory because it was too busy fighting over what it previously had won, and his countrymen could preserve their honor by sacrificing more lives for a cause already lost.

During the past century, several monarchs came to power at a younger age than Franz Joseph, who became emperor of Austria at eighteen, but none reigned longer—sixty-eight years: over two-thirds of a century! almost three and one-half generations! and the average life span of people at that time! Reigning as long as he did, you would think he would have gotten bored and wanted to retire long since, or at a minimum experienced job "burnout." But that did not seem to be so, probably because there was nothing else he was suited for or apparently wanted to do. So without any alternative options for retirement, he simply pressed on in his

6.1: Emperor Franz Joseph, the longest reigning ruler in the study. © Corbis/Bettmann.

inimitable, unimaginative way, doing what he always did, over, over, and over, for God, for country, for duty, and forever. Unfortunately, although the problem of job burnout arouses little sympathy from the common people, that is a big problem with monarchs. Their parents train them almost from infancy to command but do not prepare them adequately for a life after ruling if they are lucky enough to escape with their lives after coups, forced abdications, and shifts to more democratic forms of government. Monarchs without countries to rule are like coaches without any teams or, even worse, authors without a publisher, so you can imagine how desperate their plight would be. All they know how to do is to rule, not necessarily wisely or well, but well enough to sit on the throne, issue orders, sign assorted documents their ministers tell them to sign, and stage royal ceremonies.

Though coming from an entirely different culture, Abdul Hamid II also likely never considered doing anything but rule.[8] Dedicated and hard-working, much like the emperor, he usually spent his days when he was not killing infidels attending to his royal duties, which mostly involved poring over the stacks of daily "journals" his palace guards, spies, and a special legion of black eunuchs prepared for him, containing accounts of suspected court intrigues, coups, and assorted treasons. In most instances, his underlings took the liberty to give free rein to their suspicions because they knew that if they did not concoct these potential conspiracies, their master, who was a lover of mystery novels, would begin to suspect them of hiding vital information and then begin to look upon them as intriguers. But Abdul Hamid knew that, if he wanted to keep mentally alert for these demanding tasks, he periodically needed to set aside some personal time for himself. His doctor insisted that he do so. So without any creative outlets for his paranoia, Abdul Hamid periodically forced himself to leave his heavily protected white villa on the hill to walk about in his heavily protected gardens and perhaps discharge some of his pent-up tensions by practicing pistol shooting in his heavily protected shooting range. Then, being a born collector at heart, he would go to his specially constructed, heavily protected zoo to inspect his cages of wild beasts he had gathered from all over the world, before wandering over to his heavily protected harem to inspect his assorted wives and concubines whom he had gathered from all over his kingdom. He probably could have continued this arduous routine on behalf of his empire until his eventual demise had he not been overthrown after thirty-three years by the Young Turks and then exiled to Salonica and placed under heavily protected house arrest.

Lacking any creative outlets like painting, composing, playing a musical instrument, or writing poetry, Franz Joseph and Abdul Hamid were more the rule than the exception among monarchs, although monarchs as a group indulged in artistic activities more than other ruler types. However, their preferred royal pastimes included hunting, flying, riding horses, driving fast sports cars, and collecting objects d'art and women—seldom anything to tax their brains or imaginations. There were exceptions. King Ferdinand of Bulgaria, for instance, was a skilled ornithologist and naturalist who built aviaries during his retirement and had a huge butterfly collection. King Albert I of Belgium collected art, flew airplanes, loved to watch movies, and had a passion for books, although he was not much of a reader. Rather than watch movies, King Sihanouk of Cambodia preferred to direct, produce, and star in his own films. He also edited a pornographic magazine, called *Different Things*, which he had printed at government expense.

Monarchs also showed little inclination to write their memoirs or publish "how-to" books about staying in power. Only 17 percent of them saw fit to document their achievements or excuse their lack of them in personal memoirs or to express their views in print about anything, either because of an admirable modesty on their parts, a lack of anything significant to say, or being too lazy to expend the mental effort to do so. In contrast, 46 percent of all the rulers in my sample wrote books about their reign or about related political matters or about how all their critics were cretins.

A staunch Catholic, Emperor Franz Joseph believed that all of his actions and pronouncements were divinely inspired, so he never had to endure the awful burden of having to doubt himself. Proclaiming himself an expert on military matters, he objected on religious grounds to any protests by his ministers as to his policies, because any criticisms of them were really attacks on God, who had chosen him to be His spokesman on foreign affairs, and he would not tolerate anyone being irreverent toward the Almighty. Committed to the perpetuation of the status quo and the eternal nature of the Hapsburg empire, the emperor tried to dispel the disquieting change going on around him by his refusal to entertain any new ideas. With his own brand of solipsism, he believed that, if his thoughts never varied, his empire would remain constant, too. Stability, constancy, and predictability were his trademarks.

Since he never wavered in his routine, his subjects could tell what he was doing at any moment in time. He was against all contemporary thought and modern contraptions like the telephone and the newfangled toilets. He hated intellectuals with a passion, especially liberals, because they questioned authority and tradition. His tastes were simple, if not banal. He never voiced any appreciation for music, art, or literature, because he seldom went to symphonies, visited art galleries, or read anything but official reports. He had little desire to learn anything new about science, philosophy, or any other topic if it did not have any military application. But whatever he lacked in imagination, curiosity, or intellect, he more than made up for in his diligence with paperwork. In fact he seemed to have impressed his ministers with his astuteness after poring over their reports and writing "explain!" or "clarify" or "why?" along the margins.

Of all the different kinds of rulers, monarchs were the most likely to make displays of being devoutly religious. None declared themselves to be agnostics or atheists, in contrast to the 60 percent of visionaries, 28 percent of authoritarians, 9 percent of tyrants, 23 percent of transitionals, and 23 percent of democrats who did. Ninety-four percent of monarchs also made a show of attending church or praying at a mosque or engaging in other expected religious rituals on a regular basis compared to 54 percent for all rulers combined. Monarchs (70 percent) also were the most outwardly conforming among all the rulers and committed to upholding established tradition, with visionaries (22 percent) being the least. None of these findings are surprising. Why should not monarchs be exemplars of religiosity when they are supposed to be guardians of their faith in Muslim countries or rely on the Church to support their authority to rule based on divine right? Also, just in case their powers of reasoning should cause them to question their beliefs, 23 percent of them conveniently also managed to have epiphany experiences during prayer or moments of doubt to strengthen their convictions in their own divine authority. Except for visionaries (56 percent), who probably needed the backing of some supernatural force more than other ruler types to implement their grandiose schemes, monarchs were the next most likely to have these revelatory experiences. As a matter of record, I have never come across an account of a monarch—or any other kind of ruler, for that matter—who ever had an epiphany experience in which he suddenly realized how ridiculous his inflated notions about himself were or where the experience revealed anything he did not want to hear. You can draw your own conclusions about what that means.

Among the different types of rulers, monarchs (14 percent) were much less likely than rulers as a group to be highly sociable or to form close long-term friendships (6 percent). These findings make sense. There was no reason for monarchs to schmooze with others to get ahead or seek their approval, since their status already was secure, and their singular, quasi-divine status separated them from all other humans. The burden of solitude that Emperor Franz Joseph complained about was shared by 22 percent of his fellow monarchs, a percentage similar to that for the rulers as a whole, suggesting that the burden had more to do with being a ruler than with being a monarch in particular.

Deeply committed to his own majesty, Franz Joseph played the role of monarch to the hilt. Although he always was courteous to his ministers and subjects, he retained his imperial prestige in his dealings with them through his air of reserve, aloofness, and imperturbability. This subjected him to the "ordeal of loneliness," as he liked to say, which he was all too willing to accept, probably because he lacked the capacity to be truly intimate with anyone anyway and would not have known how to relate to others as equals even if he had tried. Along with other monarchs, Franz Joseph probably did not welcome confidantes or close friends, because he did not want to let them discover his many human shortcomings, which rulers were not supposed to have. But the most likely reason he and other monarchs kept a royal distance from others was simply because he had a natural aversion to getting too close to nonregal beings. It was okay to act kindly and considerately toward them, just as he did toward his horses and hunting hounds, but being intimate with them was unthinkable!

Even if the emperor in a moment of weakness had decided to be more approachable, his regal bearing would have been too intimidating to others and would have protected him from himself. How much of his appearance was studied and how much was natural is hard to know, but whatever a "regal bearing" is, Franz Joseph had it. As I understand the notion of a regal bearing, it has to do with the combination of the monarch's posture (straight-backed, chest puffed out, shoulders back, head held high so that his eyes always seem to be looking down on others even if they are taller than he), gestures (graceful, deliberate, spare), speech (precise, proper, commanding), dress (royal robes, colorful uniform, medals, decorations), and courtly manner (courteous, assured, attentive without being solicitous), all of which give the impression of complete confidence, self-assurance, and superiority. Whenever you are in the presence of people with this bearing, you are apt to be naturally deferential toward them. Rulers who possess this air of authority do not need to rely on impassioned oratory or the attention-riveting charisma of a demagogue to command obedience. Simply speaking quietly and firmly and with authority stamps their remarks with the imprimatur of truth.

6.2: Male gorilla strutting to appear more impressive. Courtesy of George B. Schaller.

Capitalizing on their regal bearing and the splendor and pageantry of the monarchy, 42 percent of the monarchs in the sample usually inspired a sense of awe in their audiences. Even with all these impressive ceremonies and the trappings of their office, monarchs were not more inclined than rulers as a group to be seen as charismatic by their subjects. Visionaries (72 percent) and transitionals (51 percent) were far more likely to possess personal charisma. Also, since they had the power to persuade by a simple command, they had little need to be great orators. In fact, many monarchs seemed to feel it would be beneath them and the dignity of their office to appeal to the common people for support. It was no surprise to find, then, that only 20 percent of the monarchs were noted for their oratory; but, unlike democrats and visionaries, they probably were proud of their lack.

Although monarchs had no need to be outstanding at anything because their natural authority already made them superior to everyone else in their kingdoms, a substantial percentage of them (25 percent), including Franz Joseph, were noted for their excellent memories, although they did not necessarily use them for much worthwhile. King Boris of Bulgaria, for instance, could remember minute details of various events and could name the precise day they happened. He never forgot a name or face, no matter how many years earlier he had encountered it, and could remember much of what he read about botany, zoology, and engines. But despite his impressive mental faculties, he never managed to overcome his timidity and his sense of failure as a ruler. Blaming his father for molding his character "to be more like a lackey than like a master," he often would be out of town when he had to sign a decree he had doubts about or when he had to deal with unpleasant situations. According to his father, his son's problem as a ruler was that he thought too much about the consequences of his actions, and he tried to break him of that bad habit.[9] Any ordinary person could think before acting, his father seemed to be claiming, but only monarchs had the God-given gift to act without thinking first and, by virtue of their position, always be right, even when they were wrong.

Because monarchs can hide behind their cultivated, royal image, you often have trouble detecting any personal insecurities and intellectual deficiencies they possess. This not only was so for Franz Joseph. Tsar Nicholas of Russia, for instance, who was always polite and charming, avoided even the slightest attempts at intimacy for fear that others might discover how shallow he was.[10] Hampered by a mind that seldom entertained any thought deeper than whom he should invite to his next dinner party, he avoided using it as much as possible. Unlike Franz Joseph, who at least had a sense of "empire," Nicholas had no firm political ideology other than a vague royal authoritarianism, which dictated that he was ordained to be head of the state and that his subjects should obey him.

Despite the splendid isolation in which he lived, Franz Joseph seemed to have some capacity for affection, but it usually was muted and conditional. Being respectful of authority and tradition, he found it natural to remain close to his mother as an adult and to comply with her wishes, a filial devotion he shared with about one-fourth of all monarchs, the highest percentage among all the ruler groups. Unlike about two-thirds of his fellow monarchs who had antagonistic relationships with their fathers during their early adult years, Franz Joseph had a respectful but somewhat distant relationship with his father, Archduke Franz Karl, whose insipid personality and prosaic tastes he had inherited. The fact that his own father, born during Emperor Franz's second marriage, never was a contender for the throne probably helped to keep their relationship cordial, a situation that did not apply to the fathers of other monarchs.

Although he had many extramarital affairs, the emperor remained devoted to his wife, the duchess Elizabeth of Bavaria, throughout their long marriage. At least, that was the official word. His wife documented the closeness of their marriage in a note she wrote him, mainly because she seldom got to see him: "I know that you love me, even if you do not show it, and we are happy together because we do not interfere with each other's lives."[11] While I cannot agree with her assessment about the closeness of their relationship, perhaps this was as close as it could be, given her husband's personality and her own obtuseness. In any case, after she was stabbed to death by an assassin, she would have been pleased to learn that at her funeral her husband visibly grieved over her loss.

Tyrants

Oppressors, despots, and corrupt rulers, including Macias Nguema, Idi Amin, and the Shah of Iran:

The competition is tough for who among the twentieth-century despots qualifies as being the most despicable. You have your pick from among the cold-blooded murderers, the hot-blooded tyrants, and the ordinary bloodthirsty despots. Even with so many deserving of this signal honor, you cannot go wrong placing Macias Nguema, president of the Republic of Equatorial Guinea from 1968 to 1979, among the top ten finishers for fiendishness.[12] At least, you would be in good company. In Frederick Forsyth's novel, *The Dogs of War*, one of his characters describes the "fictional" representation of Macias, whose mouth twisted downward at each corner so that it always conveyed disapproval and whose eyes had the glazed fixity of a fanatic's, as "Mad as a hatter, and nasty as a rattlesnake. West Africa's own Papa Doc. Visionary, communicant with spirits, Liberator from the white man's yoke, redeemer of his people, swindler, robber, police chief and torturer of the suspicious, extractor of confessions, hearer of voices from the Almighty, seer of visions, Lord High Everything Else."[13] But this description is too flattering to him.

Macias was a persistent man. He would have to be after having failed the civil service examination three times before barely passing on the fourth try some years before he came to power. He also was a sensitive man. Touchy about his having had only an elementary school education and the failing grades he received, he developed an abiding hatred for anyone who was better educated. So instead of hiring tutors to help him learn and increase the breadth of his knowledge, he adopted an entirely different approach to remedying his deficiencies after he became ruler: adhering to the maxim, "In the Land of the Blind, the one-eyed man is King," he simply sought to eliminate anyone who had better vision than

---

Macias was not alone among tyrants in his hatred of intellectuals.[14] All of them did. Though most were lacking in academic smarts, tyrants took pride in their native shrewdness, craftiness, and practicality despite the many stupid decisions they made. As a group, only 9 percent of tyrants (the lowest percentage among all the rulers) showed any exceptional mental abilities, such as possessing a phenomenal memory. Aside from monarchs, they also were least likely to write memoirs about their rule or books about politics (18 percent), not only because many were semiliterate or got overthrown and killed before they could do so but because it took some mental effort and patience to compose their thoughts and lots of imagination to justify their reign.

Aside from their lack of intellectual pursuits, tyrants also were lacking in creative interests. Only 10 percent of them engaged in any form of creative activity as adults, such as music, art, or writing, a lower percentage than the 28 percent for all groups. Idi Amin, for example, who sometimes played the accordion, sang, and danced spontaneously, was one of the small minority of tyrants with any creative bent. But my criteria for creative expression may be too strict. I may be doing Macias an injustice by not counting his hobby of collecting human skulls as imaginative and expressive.

he. He harassed and persecuted the educated citizens in his country, forcing most of those with technical skills and know-how to leave the country; and, in one fell swoop, he removed any semblance of respect for scholastic accomplishments by banning the word "intellectual" from all conversations and writings. To make his point, he fired his minister of education for using the forbidden word. But that particular minister got off easy, because Macias ended up murdering his successor.

Macias was an ambitious man. After finally passing his civil service exam, he steadily worked his way up from being an orderly in the forestry service and then a clerk in the department of public works and then an assistant court reporter to being appointed by the Spanish government as mayor of a small town and then the head of Public Works in Consejo, and then, finally, getting himself placed on the ballot before independence and being elected president in a plebiscite. After that, Macias showed a side of his character that none of his superiors or colleagues had suspected. Shortly after he came to office, he banned all political parties, established one-party rule, repealed the constitution, and assumed absolute powers. But that was not enough. Reluctant to delegate authority, he appointed himself president for life; commander-in-chief of the army; and grand master of education, science, and culture, and assumed all executive, legislative, judicial, and military powers. With all these appointments, he was his own president and cabinet all combined in one. While this arrangement helped with efficiency, since he could assign himself tasks in his ministerial role without having to write himself memos and could keep after himself to get them done, it had serious administrative problems. Macias as president was reluctant to fire Macias as minister when he kept botching up his assigned jobs, and Macias as minister nursed a resentment toward Macias as president for making unreasonable demands on him.

Inspired by his past work in a civil-service job, Macias steadily lowered the bar for excellence within the government. When competent government workers and administrators kept exceeding that standard, he fired, tortured, jailed, or killed them. After all, it was not good for morale to have uppity and overly ambitious workers being superior to their coworkers. Then after he had filled all these now vacant positions with people he could trust, who were mostly relatives and thugs, he launched his ambitious economic plan for the country, which in record time brought economic chaos. Government workers were not paid, all public services were stopped, public transportation came to a halt, and all communications and utilities became inoperable. But Macias was not

Although Macias had no special political mentors to guide and facilitate his career, 55 percent of tyrants did, compared to an average of 36 percent for all rulers. Mostly, their commanding officers, senior politicians, or past presidents took an interest in them and put them in positions of authority that served as springboards for their gaining absolute power. What kind of loyalty and gratitude did these tyrants show toward their benefactors? All of them—100 percent!—turned against their sponsors, mentors, or influential supporters and were responsible for their political demise.

Tyrants may have been untrustworthy, disloyal protégés, but that did not mean they wavered in their personal convictions. Being hell-bent on gaining ultimate power, they were the mostly likely of all the groups of rulers (77 percent) to risk their lives in battle, wars, or coups and, as a result, often gained reputations as being heroes before coming to office. As people who pursued personal power so zealously and willingly risked their lives for it, they understandably showed no compunction in getting rid of anyone who stood in their way, former mentors and sponsors included.

deterred by the lack of money to pay workers. He simply decreed that all citizens over the age of fifteen had to work on government plantations and mines at their own expense, but, as I imagine it, in a goodwill gesture, he let them pay themselves anything they wished as long as they paid their income tax. Then rewarding himself for his entrepreneurial genius at finding ways to cut down production costs, he paid himself a handsome salary of five million dollars a year, naturally in U.S. currency.

Mostly tyrants were deeply religious people, or pretended to be so, and saw no contradictions between their avowed beliefs and their deeds, not the least of which was their failure to attend church. In Macias's case, he claimed to be a practicing Catholic, and even paraded a priest around with him to prove it, while still attacking the Church and being an atheist. Perhaps he felt free to attack the Church because he believed himself protected by a "juju" that was given to him by the spirits and made him invincible and immortal. Like Macias, other tyrants also believed that they possessed special powers. Samuel Doe, who was obsessed with witchcraft, proclaimed, "No bullet can touch me, no knife can scratch me." And it was rumored that, through voodoo magic, Francois Duvalier held conversations with the head of his former enemy, the former army captain Blucher Philogènes, which he had packed in ice, and it kept him informed about his enemies' plots.

It was not that Macias made decisions entirely on his own without benefit of any input by others. Deferential and insecure around Europeans and highly educated people, he was not somebody who thought he knew all the answers. So at times he freely consulted the voices in his head, which sometimes interrupted him in the middle of a speech to remind him of something he forgot or give him new insights. Then blessed with these penetrating perceptions, he would want to share them with his countrymen. In one of his disjointed, inspirational speeches, he proclaimed, while ranting and raving for effect, "I will tell you why Hitler liberated Africa in the following sense, even though his confusion which was human, for all men are human. . . . Knowledge is not important to me, what is important is man, and what my people wish is that man be given dignity."[15] Moved by the power of his own babbling, he would fail to detect the blank faces and puzzled looks of people in the audience.

Not being a devout, atheistic, non-churchgoing Catholic like Macias, Idi Amin felt free to mention God in his talks and gave the impression of being a prophet for the Ugandans. On one occasion he claimed he had a dream that told him how he should lead the army and the people. On another occasion, after he announced his expulsion of the Asians from the country in 1972, he said that God had told him in a dream to do so. At a news conference, a reporter asked him if he dreamt very often, and he answered without smiling, "Only when it is necessary."[16]

Idi Amin was not alone among tyrants in having revelatory experiences. Almost one-fifth of them likewise reported them. The former shah of Iran, for instance, conveniently had epiphanies at opportune times.[17] This divine sense of purpose made him question at times whether he had free will and a personality of his own. He shrewdly was able to resolve this philosophical issue by willingly putting himself in the hands of the CIA, which launched a coup that installed him in power, and then attributing the results to the will of Allah.

People who are level-headed and calm are not likely to become tyrants. Rulers like Hafiz al-Assad, known as "the sphinx of Damascus," who spoke with a quiet authority and seemed to have nerves of steel, were among the minority. Mostly, they were like Macias, who was known for his irascibility and irrational temper outbursts; or like Idi Amin, who often had violent, uncontrollable rages, sometimes contrived; or like Bokassa, who had wild mood swings and was impulsive and excessively emotional. But these rages and moods swings appeared to be an indulgence they allowed themselves mostly after gaining ultimate power. Beforehand, all of these rulers were deferential, obsequious, and compliant to their military or administrative superiors while they were advancing in their careers.

> About the same portion of tyrants (41 percent) as that of all ruler groups were effective orators, if you do not count ranting, raging, raving, and rambling as being elocutionary skills, and about the same percentage (45 percent) possessed charisma.
>
> Compared to other rulers, tyrants were most likely to shine in being moody (59 percent) and capricious (62 percent). The instability in their relationships with others seemed highlighted in their marriages. Fifty-six percent of them had serious conflicts with their first spouses that led to separations and divorces, compared to only 22 percent for all rulers.

Increased moodiness and capriciousness were not the only changes that tyrants showed once they gained ultimate power. The longer Macias remained in office, the more suspicious he became. In time, he suspected almost everybody of wanting to overthrow him, and he began isolating himself more and more within his own palace. There is no doubt he had justification for his growing distrustfulness, since he already had weathered at least two unsuccessful coup attempts, but he now was seeing potential enemies everywhere. Not one to take a passive approach to threats, he launched preemptive attacks on all his imagined and potential enemies and waged a reign of terror on the entire nation.

Visionaries

Social engineers and utopian socialists, including Mao, Atatürk, Hitler, Sukarno, and Mussolini:
If you buy into the ideology of visionaries, you can be consoled to know

> It is not surprising that tyrants are the most likely group of rulers to be suspicious of others (64 percent) and the least apt to have any close, enduring friendships (5 percent). That did not keep them, though, from being gregarious and charming at social gatherings or when dealing with leaders and representatives of other nations or during press conferences with reporters. Forty-one percent of them were highly sociable, compared to 29 percent for all rulers. Interestingly, only 14 percent of the tyrants were loners, compared to 21 percent for all the ruler groups combined. This combination of high sociability and a low tolerance for solitude suggests that tyrants had trouble being alone with themselves, showing that in at least some part of their minds they were capable of exerting good judgment.

that any suffering you and your loved ones endure because of them serves some higher purpose—History, Christianity, Freedom, the Masses, Society, Pan-Arabism, the Empire, The Father Land, Providence, you name it. With tyrants, you have no such consolation. Visionaries mean well; tyrants do not. Tyrants want your pocketbook and your submission. All visionaries want are your mind and soul. Tyrants tax your baser instincts for survival. Visionaries appeal to your lofty wish for immortality. Tyrants rob you of your dreams. Visionaries generously offer you their utopian vision. Tyrants command fear and hatred. Visionaries inspire awe and adulation. Because of their insincerity, tyrants are condemnable. Because of their sincerity, visionaries are commendable.

As a representative visionary, I have chosen Mao Zedong, who is still revered by many of his countrymen despite his ideological decisions as ruler of China that were directly or indirectly responsible for an estimated 40 million deaths due to war, famine, and starvation.[18] His Great Leap Forward, which was a crash program to industrialize China overnight by trying to raise steel production to levels comparable with Britain, turned out to be a disaster; and his later Cultural Revolution, which he launched to reestablish his control over the party by reasserting his revolutionary goals, set China back many years in its industrial development. Mao is an excellent example of a visionary not only because of the greatness of his accomplishments and the magnitude of his failures but also because of his quixotic and enigmatic nature.[19]

If there was one quintessential quality that characterizes Mao, it was his perverse capriciousness that managed to keep friends and foes alike off balance. It was as if he enjoyed befuddling those around him, who must have wondered at times if he was a genius or an idiot. He reveled in his unpredictability, even to the point of never taking the same path twice. Perhaps for shock value or to emphasize his peasant origins, he was known to pick lice off of his body deliberately while being interviewed by a woman reporter, who became increasingly incoherent and agitated as her eyes hypnotically followed his hands moving slowly within his baggy trousers and then suddenly pouncing like cats on the unseen vermin.

Mao also was someone who managed to raise crudity and vulgarity to an art form. He may not have been the only leader whose condition in his behind affected his mind, but he was one of the least abashed about it. Most of his aides knew that, when he had not moved his bowels for several days, he became increasingly grouchy and cantankerous and would be more likely to lash out at them or even foreign dignitaries. Mao's bodyguards were literally his body guards, trained not only to protect him against enemies but also to give him enemas if they failed in their attempts to relieve his constipation by putting their fingers up his anus to pry his impacted feces out. When he did not need assistance, Mao liked to go out to the fields alone to defecate because he felt toilets were too stinky. When he went out into the fields, he often picked up a piece of human turd that was being used as fertilizer and smelled it before squatting down. Once, when a guard had the audacity to ask why he did that, Mao patiently replied, "I like to sit and think while I'm relieving myself. If it smells too bad I can't think."[20] Mao waged heroic struggles daily to loosen his bowels, with the main topic among his concerned intimates being whether he had the male equivalent of a false labor or not. Once after he had been severely constipated for about nine days in Yanan and finally got unplugged, the word spread rapidly among his staff, who joyfully shouted: "The chairman's bowels have moved! He has had a good shit!" In time, though, much to the relief of his staff, Mao's constipation did improve somewhat after he began using a specially designed upholstered chair with a toilet bowl in it.[21]

These earthy behaviors are from the same man who incongruously was a compulsive reader of Chinese literature and history, who published classical poetry, and who wrote articles and served as editor for several political journals. As noted in his youth when he rebelliously cut off his pigtail and had confrontations with teachers, Mao had an antipathy toward all forms of outside authority, the most notable one being his father. This attitude seemed to shape his personality and dominate his interactions with others. It was not that he openly confronted people who presented themselves as equals or superiors to him. He just kept them completely off balance with his unpredictable and contradictory remarks. During serious conversations, for instance, he would make a tactless joke or say something absurd or speak in riddles. He could be grim when a visitor made an attempt at humor and be maddeningly silent and enigmatic when others expected him to speak. He acted on whim at times when serious deliberation was called for and indefinitely put off decisions of little consequence. At times he could become combative and pugnacious with little provocation, and at other times he could remain calm and serene when he had cause to be upset. He even befuddled foreign diplomats who had been briefed about his being unpredictable, capricious, and enigmatic but who then found him to be rational, analytical, and pragmatic.

Two anecdotes relating to his interactions with Khrushchev highlight Mao's characteristic orneriness. Once he and Deng Xiaoping, who

Mao's strong antagonism toward all authority figures was not unusual for visionaries (60 percent), who, along with tyrants (59 percent), were the most likely rulers to exhibit this trait. This antagonism toward authority showed itself in other ways as well. Along with tyrants (60 percent) and monarchs (64 percent), most visionaries (53 percent) were hostile toward and alienated from their fathers during their adult years. They also had trouble dealing with father figures in their political life. Although 44 percent of them had political mentors who had helped them advance their careers, they resisted being beholden to them. And because of their cocksureness and lack of proper deference, many potential benefactors were put off by them. Responding to authority figures in this fashion, visionaries naturally turned out to be the most rebellious and the least socially conforming (48 percent) of all the ruler groups. Perhaps their ultimate rejection of authority involved their attitudes toward the church and their beliefs in God. Visionaries were by far the most likely of the rulers to be agnostics or atheists (60 percent) and, consequently, the least likely to go to church or partake in prescribed religious practices. With attitudes such as these, visionaries, predictably, tended to be loners, have few if any close friends, and be highly suspicious of others.

was one of his top foreign policy advisors at the time, were meeting with Khrushchev, who not only wanted to set up wireless stations in China that would let the Russians communicate with their fleet in the Pacific but to build and operate these stations themselves.[23] Deng voiced no objection to the idea of these stations in China, but he insisted that they would have to be built, operated, and controlled by the Chinese; otherwise the Russians would be installing military bases on Chinese soil. Khrushchev kept insisting on the right to do this, while Deng argued that this would be violating China's sovereignty. When it was finally time to break, Mao, who silently had been taking all this in, bid Khrushchev good evening and directed an aide to take the Russian party to a hotel and restaurant at Jade Mountain in the Fragrant Hills, where there was no air-conditioning. Because it was so hot that night, Khrushchev had to sleep out on the terrace, where the mosquitoes feasted on him. The next morning, after a poor night's sleep and being mildly anemic from blood loss, Khrushchev now was a lot more reasonable and accommodating when he met with Mao again, probably because he feared having to sleep at the same hotel again that night.

Mao's composing of poetry was not unusual for a visionary. Thirty-three percent of them engaged in some form of creative activity, somewhat above the average for all rulers. Sixty percent of visionaries (by far, the highest percentage among the ruler types), including Mao, compared to an average of 46 percent for all rulers, likewise published their memoirs or political views or homilies as ideological guides for their subjects or as historical testaments to their genius and accomplishments in case nobody else was going to do it for them.

As a cold and calculating materialist, Mao never claimed to have had any revelatory experiences that helped him crystallize his resolve. In this respect, he was different from the 56 percent of visionaries who claimed to have had such epiphanies, more than three times the percentage for all rulers (17 percent). Hitler, for example, while he was lying in a hospital bed after having been gassed in the war, committed himself to restoring Germany's honor when he learned about her defeat. Then later, after he survived a second assassination attempt, he became convinced that he was invincible and saved by Providence. Atatürk also became convinced of his own invincibility after an incident at Gallipoli when a piece of shrapnel struck his watch.

Then there were pragmatists like Bourguiba, who never had a revelatory experience but had to manufacture a rationale to account for his own specialness. When asked if he believed in God, he answered, "I have decided to deal with this question thus: If God exists, He must be pleased with me. If He does not exist, then I am quite pleased with myself."[22]

At another high-level meeting in China, Mao declared that he and Khrushchev should hold their conference in his swimming pool.[24] Refusing to yield to Khrushchev's protests about his not knowing how to swim, Mao outfitted him with a pair of baggy green trunks and a life preserver and then leaped in the water, urging Khrushchev to follow. Since he hoped to wrest some important concessions from Mao, Khrushchev did not want to offend his host, so he did as he was told. With his boxer swimming trunks strung tightly above the equator of his globular belly to keep them from falling off, Mao maneuvered around with a powerful sidestroke, jabbering away, while his guest floundered after him, coughing up water, sputtering, and giving short answers between gulps when he tried to respond. The frantic translators, who were too busy scurrying around the slippery edge of the pool and trying not to fall in as they struggled to catch what was being said, gave imaginative translations that may or may not have had any relationship to the spoken words. But that did not matter, because even if the communications between these two leaders had been translated with utter fidelity, Khrushchev still would have had trouble deciphering Mao's enigmatic responses.

Listen to Khrushchev's own account of one of these swimfests, or pool-side meetings. "After I had arrived, Mao and I embraced each other warmly and kissed each other on both cheeks. We used to lie around a swimming pool in Peking, chatting like the best of friends about all kinds of things. But it was all too sickeningly sweet. The atmosphere was nauseating. In addition, some of the things Mao said put me on my guard. I was never exactly sure that I understood what he meant. I thought at the time that it must have been because of some special traits in the Chinese character and the Chinese way of thinking. Some of Mao's pronouncements struck me as being much too simplistic, and others as being much too complex."[25]

Poor, well-meaning Khrushchev, he did not have a clue about what was going on, since he was simply out of his league when it came to teasing, tweaking, and keeping someone else intellectually off balance who thought he had the upper hand.

If you still have any doubts about Mao's squirrelly taunting of his dogged colleagues, then read this exchange between these leaders of two of the most populous and powerful countries in the world, taken again from Khrushchev's diary, which documented another conversation they had while both were lying next to the swimming pool in their bathing trunks, like two beached whales.

While discussing the problems of war and peace, Mao said, "Comrade Khrushchev, what do you think? If we compare the military might of the capitalist world with that of the socialist world, you'll see that we obviously have the advantage over our enemies. Think of how many divisions China, the U.S.S.R., and the other socialist countries could raise."

"Comrade Mao Zedung," Khrushchev replied, "nowadays that sort of thinking is out of date. You can no longer calculate the alignment of forces on the basis of who has the most men. Back in the days when a dispute was settled with fists or bayonets, it made a difference who had the most men and the most bayonets on each side. Then when the machine gun appeared, the side with more troops no longer necessarily had the advantage. And now with the atomic bomb, the number of troops on each side makes practically no difference to the alignment of real power."[26]

It is hard to believe this hilarious and preposterous conversation actually happened. Mao had to be teasing Khrushchev when he suggested that because of the sheer size of their numbers, a coalition of socialist nations would give them a strategic advantage over their capitalist enemies, although their weapons were not as advanced. Then Khrushchev, playing the unwitting straight man to perfection, presumptuously begins to lecture Mao, an expert on tactical warfare and the leader of hundreds of millions of people, about how, when the machine gun appeared, it more than made up for any deficiencies in manpower, and then with the addition of the atom bomb, troop size no longer made much difference. That was bad enough. Then when Mao treats this information as a revelation, as though he never considered the devastating effects of the atom bomb before, it is hard to believe that Khrushchev had no notion that he was being led on. What is even more remarkable is that he even went to the trouble of documenting his comments in his diary so that posterity might appreciate how he educated Mao about certain realities in the world.

Other seeming contradictions show up in Mao's character. As he grew older, his colleagues found it impossible to tell him anything he did not want to hear. He would not let any of his party colleagues criticize his decisions, but he sometimes let his personal servants and bodyguards do so after asking their opinions. Those who had dealings with him also needed to remember that the benign, monkish figure with his unwashed look and "natural" smell was an extreme ideologue who was vindictive toward those he saw as his enemies and his critics. If Mao could go days without a bowel movement, he was a tireless and indefatigable worker who also could go days without sleep in a crisis. Along with his intransigence, his personal arrogance and self-confidence gave him no compunctions about making decisions that could cause the suffering and deaths of others or about risking his own life for his beliefs, as he did during the legendary Long March, or during a bombing raid when he refused to take shelter until he finished smoking his cigarette, proclaiming, "If a bomb falls on my head, it won't dare to explode."[27]

Sometimes a personal sense of specialness, a common feature of epiphany experiences, is hard to distinguish from an overweening self-confidence and sense of mission, which often leads would-be rulers to experience a sense of immortality and take inordinate risks. This transcendent sense of certainty often gives others the impression that they hold a special lien on truth. "A man like me comes along once every five hundred years," Ceaucescu proclaimed. And "Thank God," his Roumanian countrymen must have sighed in relief. Benito Mussolini seemed to create his own artificial epiphany when he began believing his own press clippings that he was a divine Caesar, even greater than Napoleon, and miraculously had halted the lava on Mount Etna before it destroyed a village. Hitler, who saw himself as an infallible military genius, felt that Providence had chosen him to fulfill his mission. Josip Broz Tito would inspire himself periodically by watching the film he had made, *The Battle of Sutjeska,* starring Richard Burton in the role of Tito, which documented his legendary military exploits.

Closely allied to this quality of self-possession and supreme confidence is the display of personal charisma, which sometimes is so powerful that it becomes almost palpable. I am not referring to the kind of awe and respect you confer upon rulers by virtue of their being in high office but to a kind of energy and aura that emanates from certain of them. Mao, Stalin, Ceaucescu, or Tito did not possess this kind of charisma, but visionaries like Hitler, Mussolini, Bourguiba, Sukarno, Castro, and Atatürk did. Atatürk, for example, had almost a physical magnetism that drew people to him. One of his admirers claimed she could sense his presence even in an adjoining room, and, when he entered a room, he was too awesome to look at. If he shook hands with a child, the child would not wash his hand for weeks, fearful that the virtue would depart it. An old peasant woman claimed to be seventeen, dating her age from the time she first saw him.

Although perhaps not showing any natural charisma in their manner or bearing, a substantial percentage of visionaries were compelling speakers who had the ability to rouse the passions of their people and get them to suspend their critical judgment regardless of what they actually had to say. Mao did not have this oratorical ability. Instead, he had to rely on his personality cult to imbue his writings and sayings with special meaning. Sukarno, known as the "Lion of the Podium," did have this ability. An intoxicating, spell-binding orator, he could mobilize the masses into action and often get the different ethnic groups to put aside their murderous hatred toward each other for variable periods of time with such meaningless claptrap as "Revolution is a dynamically dialectical process or a dialectically dynamic process."[28] Mussolini caught the imagination of the crowd with his theatrical, staccato style of oratory, with his dramatic, repetitive arm movements serving as distractions for his many contradictions, outright lies, and misleading metaphors. Among all the visionaries, Hitler perhaps was the most extraordinary in his ability to sway almost an entire nation with his oratory. Possessing an uncanny

Almost all visionary leaders (92 percent) showed an unshakable conviction in their opinions, which undoubtedly let them sway others to their cause. This great self-confidence, naturally, contributed to their personal magnetism. Among all the rulers, visionaries (72 percent) were the most likely to be charismatic. Fifty-two percent of them also were good speakers. However, if you include only exceptional orators—those who had the ability to captivate their audiences—then only 28 percent fit that criterion, but that was more than twice the percentage for any other kind of ruler. See figure 6.1 below.

ability to sense the secret sentiments of the German people, he played on their emotions like a virtuoso and orchestrated their response.

Writing years before Hitler came to power, Nietzsche claimed that every great demagogue has the capacity to become overcome by his belief in himself and that it was this very belief that spoke so persuasively to his audience. All great orators manage to establish a special personal bond with their audiences by putting into words what their audiences want to hear and then by becoming invigorated by the adulation they evoke, which lets them continue to believe that they are really as great as they imagine themselves to be.

Fig 6.1: Cultivated or Natural Charisma of Rulers

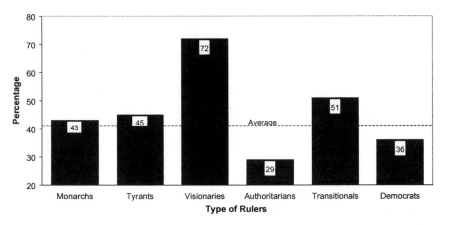

Legend: The bars represent the percentages for the different kinds of rulers who display personal charisma.

Although Mao usually was a remote, insensitive, and cold figure who showed little compassion toward others, even members of his own family, he could be very emotional and caring, but usually under special circumstances, as when his comrades had died in battle or when he was absorbed in an opera. One of his bodyguards once witnessed Mao break into tears and start bawling during a performance of *The White Snake Fairy Tale* at the Beijing Opera. Mao became so upset while watching the opera, he forgot he was holding a cigarette and burned his fingers. He began yelling several times, "We've got to have the Revolution!" His guards whispered, "Remember the audience," and tried to calm him, but he ignored them and got more agitated. Finally, he struggled to his feet and shouted for someone to rescue the heroine. As had become the custom, the guards had unbuckled his belt so that the chairman, with his huge belly, could be more comfortable sitting through the performance. When the tearful Mao stood up, his pants dropped before his guards could form a human screen around him and refasten his belt. Hardly conscious of his surroundings, he pushed the helpful hands aside and rushed toward the stage to congratulate the performers, clutching his pants with one hand.[29]

Authoritarians

Military rulers, caudillos, apparatchiks, and appointed leaders, including Admiral Horthy, Ubico, Ulbricht, and Peron:
The role of the authoritarian ruler is to preserve the institution of society, sometimes relying on harsh measures to do so. Unlike the visionary, he is not interested in making wholesale changes in society, and, unlike the tyrant, he is not interested in exploiting or plundering it. Mostly, he is dedicated to keeping it like it is except for times of civil war or social unrest, when, as a military commander, he acts to overthrow an elected leader and then takes drastic measures to stabilize the government until conditions are right to hold democratic elections again.

There are different kinds of authoritarian leaders, some of a military and others of a civilian stripe. Adm. Miklos Horthy, regent of Hungary from 1920 to 1944, will serve as a prototype for an authoritarian ruler who, as head of state, remained committed to the goals of tradition, discipline, and honor.[30] Exuding a patriarchal manner, he could expound at length on subjects he knew nothing about or, even worse, was grossly misinformed on. He compounded the absurdity of his views by blurting them out almost before they entered his head. Unlike many authoritarian rulers whose minds accepted no ideas but their own and whose own ideas were a potpourri of popular prejudices and preconceptions, Horthy did have the capacity to absorb new information after listening to others if it was consistent with his narrow-minded, ultraconservative, right-wing, orthodox-but-highly-idiosyncratic views. Incapable of honest introspection or critical self-analysis, he saw no contradictions or inconsistences in anything he said.

There was one area in which Horthy was an acknowledged expert: in matters of bigotry, his countrymen looked upon him as a sage, since he articulated prejudices that mirrored their own and did so with the full weight of his authority. Consistent with the military mind, he interpreted history as a series of conspiracies and conflicts between good and evil, with the Magyar people always on the side of virtue. He held that all the bordering countries were ethnically inferior. An aristocrat at heart, he derided democracy and socialism as unworkable systems. He claimed that Bolshevism was a Jewish conspiracy. He preached about the importance of eugenics, the evils of Zionism, the cowardliness of all Czechs, and the dangers of racial contamination. Horthy had the kind of conceit that made him proud of his ignorance, and, when challenged for facts or proof, he simply reaffirmed his position more adamantly. For a man who hardly ever read a book, paid no attention to the cultural trends of his day, knew little about the world, and had no intellectual curiosity, he held firm convictions about everything, even topics and issues he had never thought about before.

As his country's leader, he devoted much of his time to ceremonies that would help to restore the people's faith in their government and promote the ideals of Christian nationalism. On his white steed, he symbolically carried out the "liberation" of towns and cities that recently had been evacuated by Romanians, Slavs, and French; presided over military parades; and made ceremonial visits to hospitals. Wherever he went, he preached the virtues of hard work and discipline as a prerequisite for Hungary's regaining its old grandeur. If the villagers, who were rounded up for his visits, did not show the proper respect and adulation when he passed, they were summarily fined or imprisoned.

Perhaps the crowning achievement during his twenty-four-year rule, which roused his countrymen to look upon him as their benefactor, was his creation of the Order of Heroes to reward those Hungarians who had shown bravery during World War I or resisted the Bolshevik campaigns. Only Christian men with Magyar names and an unblemished record of patriotism were eligible for the title of "hero" and the reward of a hero's estate, which included a house, a stable, two horses, and a cow.

The regent then would induct the hero into the order during a solemn ceremony by touching his shoulder with a sword, like the dubbing of a knight during the Middle Ages, and the newly anointed hero would swear an oath of allegiance to him. During his reign, he swore in more than twenty-one thousand men as "heroes," whose supposed cumulative bravery could have conquered the world three times over. It made no difference that the closest many of them had ever come to facing danger was when he touched them with a sword. But by this relatively inexpensive means, Horthy was able to create a legion of vassals who were now sworn to obey him.

Horthy was so caught up with the old-world values of chivalry and gentlemanly conduct that he made dueling legal again in Hungary. In fact, in 1935, he set an example for his countrymen on how true gentlemen should defend their honor. Upset by the insulting articles in the Prague press that referred to him as a bloodthirsty admiral, he drafted a letter to Tomas Masaryk, the president of Czechoslovakia, demanding a formal apology. If no formal apology was given, he told Masaryk, he then demanded satisfaction through a duel. His courage was inspiring to his countrymen despite the fact that Masaryk was eighty-seven at the time and known to be infirm, and Horthy was a healthy sixty-seven. Then, thinking that his bold intentions might be misconstrued, he expressed his willingness to duel Eduard Benes instead. Benes, Masaryk's vice president, was fifty-one at the time and probably had not bargained for being a surrogate duelist for the president when he had been sworn into office. Still, this whole episode must have made the Hungarian people proud to know that they had a leader who was willing to risk his own life defending his good name and, by extension, the reputations of all his countrymen.

Authoritarian rulers, not surprisingly, have what is known as an "authoritarian personality," which tends to be characterized by a reverence for tradition and convention, a dislike for introspection, a distrust of others, and a hierarchical view of relationships in which they are obedient to those above them and demand absolute obedience from those below.[31] Unlike most tyrants and visionaries, who acknowledge no other authority but themselves, authoritarians prefer to rule their countries under the symbolic aegis of some higher authority or agency such as a military junta, a political party, the Church, or a revolutionary organization that legitimizes their autocratic actions. In Horthy's case, he justified all his decisions on the basis of God and country. Claiming to be devoutly religious, he set an example for his countrymen by not only

Authoritarians, by definition, had a healthy respect for all forms of authority and tradition, with 74 percent showing loyalty to those above them. A substantial portion of authoritarians (39 percent) also were most likely among all rulers to depend on mentors to help them advance in their political careers. In attending church services regularly, Horthy was among the large percentage of authoritarians (50 percent) who likewise did so, a lower percentage than for monarchs (94 percent) but a much higher percentage than for tyrants (27 percent) or visionaries (24 percent).

Naturally, you would expect that a leader's attitudes as a adult toward authority figures should mirror his attitudes toward his parents, who represented the original authority figures in his life. This expectation held true, dramatically so for authoritarians. Although the vast majority of them continued to have unremarkable relationships with their mothers, a category I used to cover a broad range of normal interactions, 18 percent of them remained exceptionally close with their mothers as adults, with only 9 percent becoming alienated from them, one of the lowest percentages among all rulers. The situation was much the same with their fathers. Although none seemed to be especially close to their fathers, as also was so for rulers in general, only 11 percent of them were openly antagonistic toward them, by far the lowest percentage among all rulers. Nonrebellious toward parents and teachers while growing up and toward superiors while adults, authoritarians expected others to behave likewise toward them once they became rulers.

attending Protestant services but going regularly to the Roman Catholic church as well. It was not what church you belonged to that mattered, he held, but whether you believed in God (and also, I should add, whether you wanted to gain the broad backing of your subjects).

While Admiral Horthy remained a respected figure in his country, he had less than a glowing reputation abroad. The prevailing attitude of other world leaders toward him was exemplified by the imagined exchange between President Franklin D. Roosevelt and his secretary of state, Cordell Hull, at the beginning of World War II.

> Hull: "I am sorry to announce, Mr. President, that Hungary has declared war on us."
> Roosevelt: "Hungary? What kind of country is it?"
> Hull: "It is a kingdom."
> Roosevelt: "Who is the king?"

Hull: "They have no king."

Roosevelt: "A kingdom without a king! Who is the head of state?"

Hull: "Admiral Horthy."

Roosevelt: "Admiral? Now, after Pearl Harbor, we have another navy on our neck!"

Hull: "No, Mr. President. Hungary has no navy, not even a seacoast."

Roosevelt: "Strange. What do they want from us? Territorial claims, perhaps?"

Hull: "No, sir. They want territory from Romania."

Roosevelt: "Did they declare war also on Romania?"

Hull: "No, Mr. President. Romania is their ally."[32]

Now the question remains how such a dunce could have remained head of a civilized nation of reasonably educated people for as long as he did and be so beloved by his countrymen. The answer, it seems, is that his long tenure in office had nothing to do with his intellect or competence, which, as we already have seen, often has no bearing on being a ruler. The reason was based entirely on his personality. Horthy had an old-world charm and congeniality that captivated his countrymen. Though lacking in diplomatic skills, economic knowledge, intellectual breadth, and vision, he oozed with sincerity and had a remarkable ability to make everyone feel comfortable, even those who found his prejudices offensive. With his impressive appearance, informal manner, and anecdotal style, he charmed his audiences late into the night at social gatherings or dinner parties, playing the piano and regaling them with endless accounts of heroism from the war, demeaning ethnic jokes, and amusing uninformed expostulations about everything and anything. Tipsy with brandy or cognac, his audiences found him to be a spellbinding raconteur who could make them cry or laugh at will. Some might not approve of his policies, bigotry, or closed-mindedness, but they had to concede he was honest and well-meaning and had a knack for telling a good story. What more could you ask of a leader?

In Latin-America, Africa, and certain other regions, leaders often are autocrats who operate outside the bounds of democratic constitutional law. Typically, these strongmen, who often come from military backgrounds, play up the virtues of courage and gentlemanly courtesy and are men of action more than of thought. When a strongman begins to use his power for his own personal gain or for the benefit of his supporters, much like Cipriano Castro of Venezuela did, he becomes a tyrant. When he exploits his power to promote his ideology, much like Fidel

Admiral Horthy was a relative anomaly among authoritarians in his sociability, openness, and gregariousness. Only 16 percent of authoritarians appeared to enjoy partying or informal social interactions with others, about half the percentage for all the ruler groups. Though authoritarians tended to be lacking in social skills, they more than made up for that in their reliability and steadfastness, reflected in their low rates of moodiness (16 percent) and impulsiveness (6 percent), which made them especially suited for their roles. Along with the other dictators, only a small percentage of them were trusting of others (17 percent) or formed close friendships (12 percent).

Entertaining companions with witty accounts of bloody battles and playing the piano at banquets were unusual activities for these serious-minded rulers. Like Horthy, Augusto Pinochet, a typical authoritarian, also could be charming at dinner gatherings, but he mostly was ill at ease and had trouble with small talk. The only topics he freely could talk about were the military, the weather, his political accomplishments, and his family. When the conversation turned to cultural events, philosophy, literature, or academic topics, he seemed to become discombobulated. He then would try to compensate for his social ineptness by turning on his charm and becoming more solicitous toward his companions, who then would become discombobulated and forget what they had been talking about. Perhaps he would have felt more at home at social gatherings if he had been able to entertain his guests at the piano, as did Horthy, one of the 21 percent of authoritarians who played a musical instrument, painted, or wrote creatively as a hobby. Unfortunately, Pinochet had no special artistic interests, although he did manage to publish four unoriginal books on military topics, which helped him advance in his career. As a group, authoritarians (41 percent) were somewhat less inclined than rulers as a whole (46 percent) to publish their memoirs or political books. When they did, the dryness of their accounts often matched their personalities and seldom had the impact on their countrymen that the writings of visionaries did.

Castro did, he becomes a visionary. When he uses his power to promote social stability and maintain law and order during his rule, much like Alfredo Stroessner of Paraguay did, without showing evidence of gross corruption in office, he qualifies as an authoritarian. Unlike rulers who gain their authority through popularity or seeming sociability, authoritarians often gain and retain power through being cold, efficient, methodical, dedicated, and ruthless; and they have little outside pressure to portray themselves otherwise. Being impersonal suits their purposes well. Jorge Ubico, dictator of Guatemala, a strongman of the caudillo mold, claimed, "I have no friends, but only domesticated enemies.... Be careful! I am a tiger, you are monkeys."[33]

Actually, Ubico may have been underestimating his fierceness by comparing himself to a tiger. According to one characterization of him, he was far more ferocious and intimidating. As the story goes, Ubico lamented one day to his minister of war that there no longer were any brave men in Guatemala. The minister relayed the president's concern to the director of the military academy, who then recruited ten cadets to uphold the honor of the army. When the news was communicated to Ubico, he ordered the ten men to come to his office the next day. After they appeared, without saying a word, he personally drove them to the national zoo and ordered them to show their bravery by entering the lions' cage. The cadets dutifully obeyed and stood shakily at attention for several minutes as the lions snarled and growled at them. When they left the cage, the hair of all ten men had turned gray from their ordeal. Un-impressed by what he had witnessed, Ubico declared he'd show them how a truly brave man conducted himself. He then stepped in the cage, closed the door behind him, and began screaming at the lions and kicking them. The lions retreated in terror from this horrific apparition, cowering in the far corner of the cage until this wild creature left. When he finally did leave—and supposedly there were eyewitnesses to confirm this—the fur and mane of the lions had turned completely gray.[34]

Though uniformly authoritarian in their governing style, apparatchiks stake their claim for power more on their mastery of the bureaucracy than on their personal charm, heroic deeds, or rhetorical abilities. They may be deficient in their imaginations, but they have a remarkable "social maze brightness," a term I use to refer to their ability to get things done in organizations with all kinds of confusing rules and regulations that seem designed to preserve the status quo and hamper individual initiative. One of the ways that psychologists test the intelligence of rats is to put them in a maze and time how long it takes them to get to the food at the end. Those who take the shortest time are considered to have the greatest maze brightness. In a complex bureaucracy, not many people are clever enough to maneuver their way to the top and, once there, know how to manipulate the bureaucracy for their purpose. Among the authoritarians, particularly the apparatchiks, there were a number of rulers who showed a kind of maze brightness that would be the envy of any rat. By being able to wend their way quickly through the labyrinthine pathways of the system, they learned how to manipulate the system to their advantage and use it to befuddle their competitors.

Walter Ulbricht was one such person.[35] Though lacking in social grace, originality, education, brilliance, charisma, persuasiveness, style, popularity, wittiness, or any of the other attributes that go with having a winning "personality," he more than made up for these deficiencies by his amazing capacity for work, his being better informed than others, his command of bureaucratic details, his organizational talent, and his steadfast adherence to the party line, whatever it happened to be at the time, without seeming to be cynical or opportunistic. As an apparatchik par excellence, he also carried out orders efficiently and without any qualms of conscience before he came to power, and issued orders efficiently and without any qualms of conscience afterward. Abhorring factional struggles and "ideological chatter," he managed to show a loyalty to whoever was in power at the time and cleverly avoided the charge of deviationism that proved to be the ruination of so many of his colleagues. The way he did this was to steer clear of the rampant factionalism in the party while at the same time seeming to take positions on the issues by qualifying everything he said that could in any way be construed as being favorable to one side or the other. Once he was in power, he demanded complete loyalty from all his subordinates and ruthlessly got rid of them if they showed the slightest signs of deviationism.

Todor Zhivkov of Bulgaria (1971–89), Yuri Andropov of the Soviet Union (1983–84), Georgy Malenkov of the Soviet Union (1953–55), and Erich Honecker of East Germany (1971–89) also were of this ilk. They all were excellent bureaucrats who worked their way to the top by not giving others the impression that they were scheming or hatching plots. They all held a dislike for freethinkers and intellectuals, whom they saw as dangerous and naive. They all had a knack for simplifying confusing notions and for organizing facts and information in ways that could be palatably believed even if they did not make sense. They all showed an unquestioned loyalty to the party and whatever dogma was regnant at the time. And they all cultivated convenient scapegoats to blame if anything went wrong.

Bureaucratic competence is not always necessary for becoming a successful authoritarian. Sometimes authoritarians come to power because outside nations put them there to do their bidding. The Soviet Union did that with Janos Kadar after the Hungarian Revolution. The United States, likewise, was not immune to this practice. For instance, the Central Intelligence Agency backed Carlos Castillo Armas in a coup to become president of Guatemala in an effort to preserve the business interests of the United Fruit Company and other U.S.-owned companies. In many ways, he was an ideal choice for the Americans. He had a vague reputation as a hero among the exiles and presumably was someone who would listen to reason, which meant he was malleable and bribable. He had no strong political ideology except for a vague commitment to nationalism and anti-Communism, without exactly knowing what each of these isms meant, and so supported American foreign policy. He had a "good Indian look," which would appeal to the people. Most important, as a former Time Magazine correspondent remarked, the Americans picked him "because he was a stupid man" who would be way over his head and would have to turn to them for direction.[36]

Authoritarians, and especially apparatchiks, tend to be dull, dull, dull, reminding me of Winston Churchill's characterization of John Foster Dulles, secretary of state under President Dwight D. Eisenhower, as "Dull, Duller, Dulles." Showing any joie de vivre, exuberance, or sense of humor apparently smacked too much of bourgeois frivolousness for someone working within a bureaucratic structure, devoted to the sober task of preserving the status quo. Oliver North's depiction of Manuel Ortega, onetime dictator and president of Nicaragua, as exuding "negative charisma," captures the typical authoritarian best. "When this guy enters the room," North wrote of Ortega, "it feels like three people left."[37]

Though blessed with modest oratorical gifts, Juan Peron was not much more dynamic than Ortega. But he had one important asset that Ortega did not, which improved his oratory immensely: he had his wife. Standing on his balcony with Evita by his side, he would proclaim Truth Number One to the crowd in the courtyard below from his Twenty Truths of justicialismo,[38] which was his new, revolutionary approach to government—"True democracy is the system where the government carries out

Only 29 percent of all authoritarians showed any signs of charisma or even a personal spark, the lowest percentage for any ruler type. Though a smattering of authoritarians had epiphanies (15 percent), mostly dealing with a sense of destiny or mission, they did not necessarily capitalize on their rejuvenated convictions to fire up their subjects. Their lack of personal dynamism usually matched their lack of oratorical skills, with only 26 percent showing the ability to arouse audiences during their speeches without having to call out "Fire!" or "The drinks are on me."

the will of the people defending a single objective: the interests of the people." As I imagine it, he then would pause while the crowd roared its approval at this profound revelation. By the time he got to Truth Number Four—"There is only one class of men for the Peronist cause: the workers"—the crowd likely would be worked up to a feverish pitch. No one before, in the history of the country, had enunciated such pithy insights so well! After an hour or more, he would shout out Truth Number Eleven—"Peronism desires the establishment of national unity"—and by now the crowd would be ready to go wild. Basking in the genius of his truly heady ideas, which his speechwriter had concocted for him, Peron likely stopped momentarily to beam at his wife before pressing on. When he finally declared his last Truth—"The best of this land is its people"— the crowd would be unable to contain its enthusiasm any longer. Stomping its collective feet and waving its collective fists, it would shout in its collective voice, "Peron! Peron! Peron!"—once for the Father, once for the Son, and once for the Holy Ghost—in response to his modern-day Sermon on the Mount. But if you were to circulate among the people in the crowd below and ask them what they found so enthralling about his speech, you would probably elicit blank stares and incoherent replies from them, largely because all the twenty-one Truths would have become so jumbled in their minds, and, besides, they really were not listening to the speech anyway. The reason they were there was to watch their beloved Evita, who likewise had no idea what her husband's speech was all about, since she was too busy blowing kisses to them and seemingly waving personally to each and every one of them.

Transitionals (Rulers of Emerging Democracies)

Presidents, prime ministers, and chancellors, including Kenyatta, Aguinaldo, and Adenauer:

Transitionals, otherwise known as leaders of emerging democracies, appear to have some of the characteristics of visionaries and established democrats. They resemble visionaries in their desire to bring into being a new form of government that conforms to their ideals, but, unlike visionaries, their ideals include greater freedoms for their people rather than compliance with a particular ideology. They resemble established democrats in their commitment to freedom and democracy, but, unlike established democrats, they tend to be more paternalistic, perhaps because in many instances they really are the fathers of their country or have stewarded it from a more oppressive government to a more liberal one.

As one example of a transitional, I have chosen Jomo Kenyatta, the acknowledged father and first president of Kenya, who managed to combine the opposing characteristics of a revolutionary and a traditional leader.[39] Kenyatta was as complex and controversial in his private life as he was in his public life. Having studied anthropology at London University, where he wrote *Facing Mount Kenya,* an analysis of the colonial impact on Kikuyu life, he straddled both the European colonial and African tribal cultures, incorporating both in his lifestyle and values. While he supported the Kikuyu custom of female circumcision, a ritual Europeans typically saw as barbaric, Kenyatta identified himself as a Christian without a denomination and even claimed to have had a "profound religious experience" while in prison that transformed his life.

Vacillating between his African roots and his British tastes, Kenyatta shifted at times between wearing traditional tribal clothes and European-style suits. Once he became president, he was freer to be a nonconformist and cultivate his own idiosyncrasies, like writing with green ink and adorning himself in lion skins, especially in the presence of Europeans. As a showman and extrovert, he enjoyed being the object of people's attention and curiosity, sometimes provocatively so. But despite his seeming gregariousness, he basically remained a loner who trusted few people and kept his own counsel.

Not all transitionals have Kenyatta's dash and panache. Some of them are more sober-minded and solemn and have little of the visionary zeal about them. Konrad Adenauer, who was to become the first chancellor of the Federal Republic of Germany (1949–63) after being confirmed by

---

Fifty-one percent of transitionals were described as being charismatic leaders, almost the same percentage as for visionaries and a higher percentage than for other rulers. Along with visionaries (52 percent) and democrats (52 percent), transitionals (53 percent) also were excellent speakers, superb debaters, or spellbinding orators, blessed with the capacity to inspire legislators or the public at large. What also helped many of these leaders to inspire others was their inner confidence (77 percent), which sometimes came from a religious experience or epiphany (17 percent), as happened with Kenyatta. But epiphanies were not always essential for giving leaders a strong sense of mission. Nelson Mandela, for example, who gave the impression of possessing an inner calm, had no definable crystallizing experience. Instead, he developed his intense resolve to fight apartheid and rebel against white rule only after an accumulation of many degrading and belittling incidents.

the Bundestag by a one-vote margin, is a good example of this subgroup.[40] Though he was not a founder or liberator of a new country, as were many transitionals, he played a crucial role in overseeing the transition from a past dictatorship and the Allied occupation of his country to an independent new Germany and the shaping of a political entity that had not existed before. Under his stewardship, West Germany also managed to achieve a complete economic recovery and reestablish ties throughout the Western world.

When he was about forty-one years old, Adenauer broke his nose, cheekbones, and jaw in a serious car wreck. This turned out to be a blessing in disguise. Because of surgery, his facial features froze into an enigmatic mask, which gave him certain advantages as a diplomat and politician. Without an expressive face, he did not have to worry about betraying his emotions or always having to smile, as so many politicians did, or manipulating his features to show emotions he did not feel. People would have to judge him by his words and not his looks. But his words were not much to go on either. An opposition leader once said, "Goethe had a vocabulary of 29,000 words; Herr Adenauer only has 200 words at his disposal." "And even if he had another 200 words," a colleague responded, "he wouldn't use them. That's precisely his strong point."[41]

It probably was a good thing. "Der Alte," as he was known, did not use a broader vocabulary, since he might have made even more enemies than he already had with his biting, critical remarks. His real claim to leadership was not based on any personal magnetism (he lacked warmth and ebullience) or oratory (his speech was slow, heavily accented, wooden, and matter-of-fact) or inspired writing (his memoirs were dry and boring), but on his ability to get people to do what he wanted. He was intolerant of incompetence and stupidity, and he usually let those involved know it. However, when backed into a corner, he recognized the value to rulers of ignorant people. One of his favorite sayings was, "If God had made men cleverer, they could have ruled themselves better. If he had made them stupider, I could rule them more easily." When asked his preference, he said, "Stupider, of course."[42]

Adenauer's interest in other people had nothing to do with any genuine curiosity about their lives or their families or their opinions but only with getting them to do what he wanted. With his general contempt for humanity (which he had good reason to despise after all he had witnessed in Germany during the war), he did not feel others had much to teach him, so he seldom consulted them. Confident in his own judgment, he became irritated whenever anyone else was presumptuous enough to offer him unsolicited advice. But his general mistrustfulness of others did not mean he was completely insensitive to their needs for approval and appreciation. He was quite capable of being charming and friendly and courteous toward fellow politicians if he felt they could be useful to him. However, the longer he was in power, the less need he had to engage in this hypocrisy.

All that mattered for Adenauer was his work. He rose early, drank in moderation, and seldom took vacations. He had an aversion to idleness, and he imparted this attitude to his staff. With little artistic inclinations or intellectual accomplishments (he wrote three volumes of memoirs but did not finish them), he funneled all his energies into his job and expected everyone else to do so, too. An unapproachable, scrupulous man with no close friends, he dealt with most people mainly by keeping a comfortable distance from them. Though many thought he had a thick skin because he rarely lost his temper under provocation and could hide his feelings behind his frozen face, he actually was very sensitive to criticism. Anyone even mildly criticizing him or his decisions could expect to become his enemy.

Der Alte was a master of manipulation and managed to get his way at almost every meeting. His tactics were straightforward and simple, but few of his colleagues ever deciphered them. His first tactic was to prepare thoroughly for every meeting about the topic under discussion.

A practicing Catholic, Konrad Adenauer relied more on faith and prayer than on any human agency to sustain him. As with 60 percent of transitionals, he attended church services regularly, but he had no need to proselytize about religion. Unlike the 35 percent of his fellow transitionals who had some form of creative outlet, Adenauer channeled all of his energies into his political work. Perhaps because he was such a private person, he had difficulty completing his memoirs or writing any books, although 49 percent of his fellow transitionals had been able to do so.

Compared to other rulers, transitionals were about as likely to be loners (17 percent). However, they had a greater tendency to be level-headed and even-tempered (45 percent). Along with democrats (47 percent), they were more apt to be trusting of colleagues (38 percent) and capable of forming close friendships (38 percent). Perhaps that was because, as rulers of democratic countries, they did not need to worry constantly about being forcibly overthrown, so they did not need to relate to everybody as potential enemies.

He would appear at the meeting with a bevy of experts and a briefcase stuffed with facts and figures. That let him immediately counter any objections brought up by the opposition. When that first tactic did not seem applicable, he resorted to his second, which was never to interrupt his opponent while he was speaking. The opponent should have every opportunity to exhaust his views so that he had no arguments left to offer. Adopting that approach, he deliberately arranged to have council and committee meetings dealing with topics dear to his heart drag on well into the night. All during this time Adenauer simply sat, listened, and raised questions. Then when the yawns started and people began shifting restlessly about in their chairs and glancing at their watches and seemed irritated and exhausted from the endless pros and cons of the debate, he finally would voice his own proposal or motion, which to the benumbed and tired minds of the participants would seem like a brilliant recapitulation of their own views, and they would immediately adopt it without objection. Time and time again he was proven right in his dictum that "the most successful man in politics is he who can out-sit the rest."[43]

Democrats (Rulers of Established Democracies)

Presidents, prime ministers, and chancellors, including Diefenbaker, Churchill, de Gaulle, JFK, and LBJ:
Leaders of established democracies are capable of wielding great power, but they need to do so within a governmental system that imposes many constraints on them. Since they usually are dependent on a legislative body to enact laws and approve key appointments and have many constitutional curbs on their power, they often find themselves, like Gulliver, immobilized by countless Lilliputian ropes that represent the different constituencies they must please. The willingness to negotiate, strike compromises, manipulate others, and exploit the prerogatives of their office to achieve their political ends requires different kinds of leaders than those who primarily rely on force.

Although he is a hard person to characterize, John G. Diefenbaker, prime minister of Canada from 1957 to 1963, seems well suited to serve as a prototypical leader of an established democracy.[44] Like so many populist leaders, he tried to be all things to all people and ended up satisfying few. He also embodied the democratic dream, achieving ultimate power almost entirely on the basis of his own initiative and personality. Remarkably, he became head of his party and later prime minister without ever having worked for anyone but himself, without ever having hired or fired anyone, and without ever having administered anything more complicated than a small law office. Whether his lack of administrative experience had any real bearing on his accomplishments and failures while in power is debatable, since it is not clear that those with far more experience have done as good a job.

From his early beginnings, Diefenbaker seemed destined for success. At the age of eight, he declared he was going to be prime minister, and he single-mindedly set out to become one. At the university, he was a campus power—a member of the student council, an excellent debater, an editor of the student paper—and was enrolled in the Officers' Training Corps. Then he spent two years as a second lieutenant and won service ribbons in World War I before being invalided home, supposedly after an accident, although evidence suggests he may have been suffering from panic attacks. In any event, he arrived home a patriot but not a hero.

Interestingly, while being a war hero has great public appeal, not being one is not necessarily detrimental for democratic leaders. Democratic leaders simply do not have as many chances prior to election to show their manliness as do other kinds of rulers, who often rise to power after insurrections, wars of liberation, and military coups. Despite more limited chances to be heroes, there is little question that democratic leaders can be as courageous as other kinds of rulers when the occasion arises. For example, after being wounded three times and eventually captured by the Germans at Verdun in World War I, Charles de Gaulle unsuccessfully tried to escape five times and spent about four months in solitary confinement. Prime Minister Ehud Barak of Israel masterminded the successful raid on the hijacked plane at Entebbe, tracked down and killed the three Palestinian terrorists blamed for the murder of the Israeli Olympic athletes, and supervised the assassination of Abu Jihad, a top aide of Yasser Arafat. The biographies of democratic rulers are filled with other remarkable exploits.

Knowing that the public tends to equate heroic deeds with political wisdom, aspirants for high office naturally want to capitalize on this when they can. So it is not surprising to find that a democratic leader such as John F. Kennedy should make the most out of the Japanese's sinking the PT 109 boat he commanded while in the Pacific in 1943. In masterminding his son's political career, Joseph Kennedy deliberately sought to immortalize this incident by lobbying to get his son a medal and then, after publication of the account in the *New Yorker*, being instrumental in getting it reprinted in the *Reader's Digest* and later made into a movie.[45]

For complex reasons, the public often looks upon war heroes, especially those in responsible military positions, as automatically being qualified to run a country. In Diefenbaker's case, his backers did not want to play up his service experience for fear of what the press might learn about the reasons he was invalided home. As a democrat, Diefenbaker's failure to make political capital out of his war record was not unusual for democratic leaders. Only 23 percent of them, by far the lowest percentage among all the ruler types, had been in battle before gaining office, with 20 percent winning medals for bravery or gaining a reputation as heroes (see figure 6.2 below).

Lyndon Johnson, Kennedy's successor, had no such ambitious father to craft his image, so he had to do it himself. Serving only a brief tour on active duty with the U.S. Navy in the Pacific during World War II, Johnson returned to Washington when Roosevelt recalled members of Congress from active duty. Commissioned as a lieutenant commander, he worked mainly on production and manpower problems. On one of his official trips, he wrangled an opportunity to go out on a bombing mission as an observer. To add to Johnson's excitement, his plane was shot at by Japanese Zeros. To his credit, he remained calm in the face of danger, but he likewise played no active role in the action. Nevertheless,

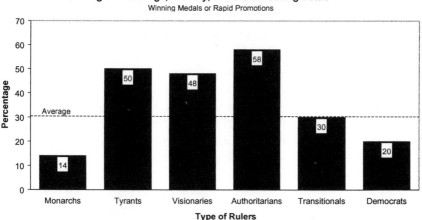

Fig 6.2: Courage, Bravery, or Heroism during Battle
Winning Medals or Rapid Promotions

Legend: The bars represent the percentage of rulers who were courageous, brave, or heroic during battle.

Gen. Douglas MacArthur, perhaps hoping to recruit a political ally, awarded him a Silver Medal. At first, Johnson felt that the medal was undeserved and debated returning it; but, as time went on, he began embellishing his role to listeners and soon transformed himself into a genuine grade-A war hero who proudly wore the symbol of the Silver Medal on his lapel.[46]

Once he got settled, Diefenbaker returned to college to complete his studies for a law degree. He then went on to establish a highly successful practice, aided in part by all the connections he made as a thirty-third-degree Mason and as a member of assorted social, religious, and political organizations. Becoming involved with the Conservative Party, he rose rapidly to become its leader. In a short while, he made his bid for ultimate power. Undaunted by being defeated five times for prime minister, he finally won, as he was confident he eventually would, and made his childhood dream a reality.

As prime minister, John Diefenbaker roused extreme reactions toward himself, both good and bad. Much like Teddy Roosevelt, who, according to his son, had to be the bride at every wedding and the corpse at every funeral, Diefenbaker also had to be on center stage even when he was out of the political limelight. Some saw him as the Savior of Canada, others as a Great Plague. But he saw himself as a folk hero who believed his authority came from a special mystical contact he had with the people. Much of the power of his appeal for people was his ability to fire them up with a similar sense of purpose and make them feel they were part of some grander scheme. When he traveled about the country, his audiences came away as fervent converts to a cause they could not fully understand. Women swooned and men shouted and clapped loudly during his public speeches or television addresses as he proclaimed, "I'm asking you to catch a Vision of the greatness and potential of this nation." "Join with me," he pleaded, with his eyes ablaze, "to catch the Vision of men and women who rise above these things that ordinarily hold you to the soil. Join with me to bring about the achievement that is Canada, one Canada, the achievement of Canada's destiny!"[47]

In response to these inspirational speeches, Diefenbaker clubs began sprouting up around the nation, poised for action but not sure what they were supposed to do. With his adherents clamoring for direction, he continued to light their emotional wicks with impassioned speeches that were replete with inconsistences, contradictions, and non sequiturs, along with some old-fashioned malarkey and a liberal sprinkling of cliches, which he admitted he liked to use, because then "they can't catch me out." The more the people got caught up in his Vision, the more sure he became of his own greatness, which I suppose he had every right to feel, since it is probably more difficult to fire people up when you do not have anything substantial to say than if you do. But when you think about it, maybe it is the other way around.

A practicing Baptist who attended church regularly, Diefenbaker believed he had a divine mission and was destined to lead the country. Other democratic leaders likewise credited their religious beliefs either for their motivation to rule or for the courses of action they took. But belief in the Bible, Koran, Talmud, or Upanishads never stopped them from interpreting these holy scriptures as they saw fit. Daniel Malan, for instance, was a very religious man with an iron will who believed he was chosen by God to act in the best interests of his people, which was to establish a segregated society in South Africa based entirely on race. Later, Hendrik Frensch Verwoerd, who served as prime minister of South Africa from 1958 to 1966, extended his predecessor's notions of racial segregation and transformed them into an elaborate system known as apartheid. Likewise claiming to be inspired by God, he credited Him as being the true architect for his "pigmentocracy" and could cite passages from the Bible as proof. From the visions offered by these various white South African leaders, the message was unmistakable that God was the source of all racism.

Although charisma may help in the delivery of a speech, oratorical ability does not depend on charisma. A leader can possess natural charisma without opening his mouth, and he can potentially lose it if he is a poor speaker. An otherwise colorless leader can become transformed into a spellbinding orator once he rises to the podium. Being a gifted speaker often has less to do with what someone says than with how he says it. Arturo Alessandri Palma, Chilean president (1920–25, 1932–38), for instance, was such a phrase-monger that some of his enemies refused to talk with him for fear they would be converted to his point of view, or at least begin to have doubts about their own. Georges Clemenceau, premier of France (October 25, 1906–July 20, 1909; November 1917–January 28, 1920), was a powerful speaker whose effectiveness came from the force of his personality and his quaint habit of challenging his colleagues to deadly duels with swords or pistols if they offended him.

An adept debater who scores points with bon mots and clever attacks on the arguments of his opponent is not necessarily silver-tongued. Of course, any judgments you make about a leader's eloquence have to be tainted by your personal biases. Teddy Roosevelt put this well when he claimed, "The most successful politician is he who says what everybody is thinking most often and in the loudest possible voice."[51] But regardless of whether the oratory of leaders is mostly substance or fluff, the relatively high rates of gifted orators among democratic leaders should not be too surprising when you consider the relatively high percentages of lawyers among them and the high premium placed on words in democracies. In awe over Churchill's verbal facility, President John F. Kennedy said, "He mobilized the English language and sent it into battle."[48] Eleutherios Venizelos, prime minister of Greece (1910–15, 1917, 1924, 1928–30) was such a dynamic speaker that King Constantine admitted that Venizelos could convince him about anything. Many of his political opponents refused to meet with him because they were afraid he would

> In established democracies, a leader gains and retains power by his ability to draw people to him and command their support. Not having access to the military or a totalitarian government to force the people to do his bidding, the democratic leader relies heavily on the impression he makes on others as a means of exerting influence over them. Although 48 percent of democrats gave the appearance of being highly self-confident, this did not always translate into personal charisma. Leaders of established democracies (37 percent), along with authoritarians (29 percent), were the least likely of all the rulers to be charismatic. But whatever these democratic leaders lacked in personal charisma, they more than made up for in the oratory. Democrats (52 percent), along with visionaries (52 percent) and transitionals (53 percent), were much more likely to be gifted speakers than tyrants (41 percent), authoritarians (26 percent), and monarchs (20 percent).
>
> As already noted, a number of democratic leaders cited their religious convictions either as a basis for their seeking high office or as influencing their political views. Whether these claims were simply for public consumption or true is hard to know, but it is a fact that a majority of democrats (53 percent) attended church regularly and less than one-fourth were agnostics or atheists (23 percent). Surprisingly, for leaders who mostly professed to be religious (or at least made a show of being so), democrats were the least likely (11 percent) of all the ruler groups to credit religious revelations or epiphanies as contributing to their political careers, perhaps because they had no need for them or, if more actually had them, believed that revealing them might turn many voters off.

convert them to his views. His powers of reasoning were so great that angry crowds that had been ready to deride him left muttering words of praise. It also was not uncommon for the opposition members in Parliament to erupt into cheers when he finished his speeches and then later, when they came back to their biased senses, begin attacking him again.

Despite the power of words, democratic rulers often have access to a number of other personal influencing techniques to get others to do their bidding. Lloyd George, who was credited in Britain as the prime minister who won World War I, essentially did whatever it took to get his way. He could be conciliatory, generous, seductive, and reasonable with colleagues; but, if that did not work, he could become furious, threatening, and vengeful. And when being frank and open did not bring about the desired results, he could be deceptive and manipulating.[49]

President Lyndon Johnson had much the same kind of bullying personality as Lloyd George. Though not a great orator, he could dominate others by the sheer force of his personality. Johnson used what the journalists Evans and Novak called "the treatment" to stun and browbeat individual senators and small caucuses, an overpowering combination of pleading, accusing, trickery, complaining, enthusiasm, and the hint of threat, along with clippings, memos, and statistics to support his requests. Benjamin Bradlee of the *Washington Post* gave a vivid description of Johnson in action: "You really felt as if a St. Bernard had licked your face for an hour, had pawed you all over. He never just shook hands with you. One hand was shaking your hand; the other hand was always someplace else, exploring you, examining you. . . . And at the same time he'd be trying to persuade you of something, sometimes something that he knew and I knew was not so, and there was just the trace of a little smile on his face. It was just a miraculous performance."[50]

Although Johnson himself discounted descriptions of his "treatment" as ridiculous, he did admit to a strategy underlying his approach. "There is but one way for a President to deal with the Congress," Johnson explained, "and that is continuously, incessantly, and without interruption. If it's really going to work, the relationship between the President and the Congress has got to be almost incestuous. He's got to know them even better than they know themselves. And then, on the basis of this knowledge, he's got to build a system that stretches from the cradle to the grave, from the moment a bill is introduced to the moment it is officially enrolled as the law of the land."[51] As a master of this approach, he then singlehandedly pushed through the legislation that defined The Great Society.

Brashness, arm-twisting, and the "treatment" are not always the most suitable tactics for swaying legislators. Sometimes, in certain parliamentary systems, humility can be a highly effective tactic. Clement Atlee, the prototypical respectable British prime minister, was so lacking in charisma and so ordinary, modest, and humble a person that his colleagues often did what he wanted because they did not want to offend so nice a chap. Stanley Baldwin, three times prime minister of Britain between 1923 and 1937, like Atlee, also was diffident to a fault. He seemed so indecisive at times that his colleagues compensated by wanting to act rapidly on measures that they ordinarily would have debated about endlessly. When he took so much time naming his minister of defense, Churchill, who was not taken by his manner, claimed, "Baldwin has to find a man of inferior ability to himself, and this Herculean task requires time for its accomplishment."[52]

Diffidence was not one of Diefenbaker's characteristics, but indecision was. The seeming confidence and conviction he exuded on the podium and on stage were not obvious in his administrative style. During cabinet meetings, he could be maddeningly indecisive about making tough decisions. He seldom approved any course of action until he could get the full support of all his ministers—and, on some issues, not just their support but their enthusiastic endorsement. He dominated cabinet meetings not by keeping his ministers from expressing their opinions, which mostly involved complaints about his lack of action, but by scheduling endless meetings and encouraging endless debates and forcing them to go beyond consensus to a unanimity of opinion. But he was not as unfeeling a taskmaster as this might seem. If the ministers began complaining of exhaustion, he willingly called an end to these meetings and then rescheduled them for the next day. It was better to postpone a decision than to be blamed for making a wrong one. And by forcing unanimity among his ministers, he could spread the blame if the decision turned out wrong, and take credit if it worked out.

On more informal occasions, Diefenbaker was a charmer. With his phenomenal memory for names and his clever impersonations of past prime ministers and his delightful anecdotes about them, he was able to dominate conversations at social gatherings. To most people who did not know him well, he gave the impression of being open, jovial, and uncomplicated. But despite his seeming friendliness, Diefenbaker actually remained suspicious of others' intentions and had few if any really close friends. The reason was partly because he was overly sensitive to any kind of criticism, nursed grudges whenever he felt wronged, and

> Being sociable, gregarious, or affiliating—or the appearance of it—seems to be a far more common in democratic leaders (35 percent) than in other kinds of rulers, perhaps because the more consensual nature of democracies favors leaders who show these qualities. As a corollary, it follows that leaders of established democracies (18 percent), along with those of emerging ones (17 percent), should be the least likely among all the rulers to prefer solitude, which, with the exception of tyrants (14 percent), happens to be the case. Thriving on social interaction, they seemed to be either working the crowd for votes or simply seeking constant approval. Being more even-tempered (40 percent) and less emotionally volatile (17 percent) than most of the other ruler types, they also were more likely to have close friends (41 percent) and form trusting relationships with colleagues (47 percent).

brooded over any perceived slights. In parliamentary forms of government and probably in life in general, responding in this way not only makes it hard to trust others but also to have any personal peace of mind.

Aside from possessing a prepossessing personality and a gift for oratory, as Diefenbaker did, would-be democratic leaders are likely to find it politically advantageous to have excellent memories. Nothing increases their popularity more than the personal touch of being able to remember the names, faces, and certain personal tidbits about the members of their constituency or the people they have to deal with. Absolute dictators do not have to rely on memory as much. If they want somebody to do things, they simply say, "Hey, you, do that!" and if he says "No" or hesitates, they have him hauled off to prison even if they do not know his name. The statistical results partly support the expectation that democratic rulers should have exceptional memories. About one-fourth of them did, roughly the same percentage as found in monarchs and visionaries, but a higher percentage than in other ruler groups. For instance, Sir Francis Bell, whose main form of communication consisted of a variety of growls that signified agreement, dissent, noncommitment, or puzzlement, could quote from memory nearly all the Bible and large portions of many classics. Indira Gandhi had a fantastic memory for names and faces. Ben Gurion had almost a photographic memory. Winston Churchill had a photographic memory, which he put to good use in memorizing large sections of *Bartlett's Familiar Quotations* and developing a tremendous facility with words. Charles de Gaulle likewise had a prodigious memory,

Perhaps because they rely on popular support to gain high office and retain power, leaders of established democracies (along with monarchs) also were the most outwardly conforming among all the rulers and the most sensitive to public appearance and decorum. The shock displayed by political colleagues toward Joseph Caillaux, who served briefly as prime minister of France in 1911, for his minor nonconformities, shows the kinds of social pressures exerted on these leaders. As a young cabinet member, Caillaux created a scandal in the senate one hot July day by appearing in fashionable summer clothes. Worse yet, when he decided to announce his resignation as prime minister, he went straight from a hunting expedition to see the president of France without bothering to change his English outfit. And then, on another occasion, "His Puffed Up Majesty" or "His Boastfulness," as the press sometimes referred to him, had the audacity during an investigation into his misconduct to lean back and light up a cigarette in a room with a "Smoking Prohibited" sign. "What a man!" exclaimed one of the reporters covering the trial.[53]

which he deliberately trained by memorizing French words and sentences spelled backward and by learning how to repeat whole sentences backward in Latin. He also memorized hundreds of lines of French poetry, all of Cyrano de Bergerac, and even parts of Antigone in classical Greek.

As they say, all work and no play makes Jack a dull boy. Although the ranks of democratic leaders are filled with dull boys, with Diefenbaker among them, almost one-third had some sort of creative outlet to defuse their tensions and restore their energies. Some of them produced works of professional or fine amateur quality and others produced works that were pretty bad. But the quality of their work made little difference. What mattered was that they could turn to these activities for relaxation and as ways to cope with stress. Bill Clinton is a fine saxophone player. Tony Blair, his colleague in Britain, is a rock guitarist and singer. Though Leon Blum was able to publish some of his poetry and sonnets, Andre Gide remarked that he had "the most anti-poetic mind in the world." Stanley Baldwin played the Pianola and sang in a choir. Clement Atlee wrote poetry and limericks. Dwight D. Eisenhower was an oil painter. Richard Nixon played the piano. André Tardieu composed satirical ditties and was a great caricaturist. Alec Douglas-Home painted wildlife. Woodrow Wilson wrote poetry. Ronald Reagan drew caricatures. Shimon Peres played the guitar and wrote stories, articles, and poems.

Leaders of established democracies (28 percent) were somewhat less inclined than monarchs (38 percent), transitionals (35 percent), and visionaries (33 percent) and more inclined than authoritarians (21 percent) and tyrants (10 percent) to have creative outlets or hobbies. Where democrats led all other rulers was in their continued participation in sports like tennis, cricket, tag football, softball, horseback riding, or golf during their leisure time. A greater portion of democratic leaders (28 percent) actively engaged in sports during their adult years than all other ruler groups. The reasons this relatively high percentage of democratic leaders should have been more involved in sports are speculative. Being more sociable than other rulers, perhaps they were more inclined to participate in team sports or express their competitiveness in athletics. Involvement in athletics also may have been their route to popularity. In contrast, the various kinds of dictators may not have found sports necessary as outlets for their pent-up aggressions or competitiveness when they had opportunities to engage in the real thing—coups, wars, riots, foiling plots, and rebellions. As a result, they may have looked upon athletic activities as frivolous. Then again, they may not have wanted to engage in competitive sports because of the possibility of losing or being forced to acknowledge that others showed greater athletic prowess than they.

A Summing Up

What these brief sketches of the different ruler types suggest is that, despite all the seemingly chaotic and random political activities occurring throughout the world, a certain natural order may govern the actual rise to power of rulers. Just as the process of natural selection seems to favor the survival of organisms with traits that let them cope optimally with their environments, some unknown sociobiological process also seems to have been at work to select individuals with certain distinctive traits that seem well-suited for their role as rulers within different societies with particular kinds of governments, histories, and expectations. If these individuals do not happen to show these essential traits before becoming a ruler, then the particular leadership role itself and the political demands at the time often have the power to draw them forth. That likely is why each of these six different types of rulers seems to fit a certain general mold, each with a different set of characteristics. Although aspiring rulers tend to display a certain plasticity in responding to these social and political demands, some simply will constitutionally lack the capacity to adapt. When that happens, the misfits are apt to try changing the political system to suit their personal needs or to rely on others to compensate for their lacks or simply to founder in their ill-suited roles.

OF SOUND MIND??

I have seen long-tailed macaques run to their swimming pool to threaten their own images in the water; a dozen tense monkeys unified against the "other" group in the pool. The need for a common enemy can be so great that a substitute is fabricated. If such invention is not necessary because of the presence of a suitable target, internal tensions may stir up external relationships. Battles between different bands of wild hamadryas baboons often start when members of one band "solve" a dispute among themselves by jointly threatening the members of another band.

—Frans de Waal, *Peacemaking among Primates*

The fact that many artists, poets, writers, actors, and entertainers drink heavily, use drugs, or suffer from depression or mania is not surprising. What more can you expect from people who live on the social fringe, cultivate their eccentricities, take pride in their nonconformity, and deliberately exploit their emotional difficulties for the purpose of their art? But the expectation for political rulers is different. As symbols of their countries and as spokesmen for their people, they are supposed to be conforming, traditional, and emotionally stable. They are not supposed to hold daily conversations with the voices in their head (as did Macias Nguema), wrestle for months with the urge to commit suicide (as did Salvadore Allende), drink more whiskey in one day than many people do in a year (as did Yahya Khan), have grandiose delusions that they are God (as did Bokassa), make high-level decisions after snorting cocaine (as did Manuel Noriega), show signs of being demented (as did Habib Bourguiba), or see enemies and conspirators everywhere (as did King Zogu), sometimes even in their own mirror. The only way you would be able to accept these behaviors in your ruler is if you were forced to, if you interpreted his madness as genius, or if all of his irrationalities reflected your own.

While my past studies showed that the lifetime rates of mental illness among well-known creative artists as a group were over twice as high as those for the population at large—74 percent compared to 36 percent—nothing is known about these actual rates for rulers around the globe.[1] Most impressions about mental illness in rulers come mainly from overworked anecdotal accounts about Hitler, Stalin, Mussolini, Saddam Hussein, or Idi Amin, which suggest that dictators tend to be vindictive, power-crazed paranoiacs and that democratic leaders are models of sanity in comparison. There is good reason that so little is known about the actual rates of mental illness in rulers: rulers go to great lengths to conceal this kind of information. They realize that, once the public begins doubting their sanity, their hold on power becomes threatened.

GETTING RELIABLE INFORMATION

How then do you go about collecting information about the mental aberrations in rulers? The usual way of gathering highly personal information about people by asking them pointed questions about themselves won't work. Most of the rulers in my study have long since died, and, if you tried to interview many of those still alive about their mental aberrations, they would have you tossed out of their office or hauled off to a mental ward or they would simply shoot you on the spot. Even if you somehow could establish contact with dead leaders during seances, they likely still would not reveal any sensitive information about themselves that might stain their carefully crafted, sanitized personal legacy.

So if you cannot get this material directly from rulers, you are obliged to switch to the next best option, which is to get it from others. The best way to do that is to rely on scholarly biographical accounts of rulers that include multiple sources of information. That is easier said than done. The problem is that, in the political arena, leaders have an important stake in hiding their emotional difficulties from others, even their official biographers, and their followers and opponents interpret their actions differently. Some biographers may portray a leader's actions as inspired, others may portray them as insane, and yet others as both. But despite the difficulty of getting accurate information about the mental stability of leaders, it is not an impossible task. In many instances, the observations of those who knew them intimately or through personal encounters, as noted in the various biographical sources, offer the best basis for judging the mental stability of the rulers in much the same way that the observations by parents, teachers, and pediatricians of children are invaluable aids for the child psychologist in formulating opinions about the child's emotional difficulties. However, if you do turn to biographical sources to form judgments about the mental stability of rulers, you then are obliged to make sure the information is reliable. The best way to judge this is on the basis of its consistency, plausibility, and correspondence with other available material.[2] As in my past studies on the relationship between "madness" and creative achievement, I have tried to rely only on reasonably reliable sources of information about the rulers in my sample to tell if they suffered from mental illness.[3]

Syndromes Rather Than Diagnoses

At this point I need to explain how judgments about these mental disturbances were made. My aim was to establish whether certain clusters of psychiatric symptoms and signs, known as "syndromes," occurred at any time in the lives of these political rulers. The criteria I used for these different syndromes were those listed in the glossary descriptions in the *Ninth Revision of the International Classification of Disease.*[4] Given the changing nature of psychiatric diagnoses, I felt that the identification of different psychiatric syndromes would give a better picture of the emotional disturbances experienced by rulers during the course of their lives than would any specific clinical diagnoses. This descriptive approach was consistent with the growing recognition that multiple psychiatric disorders (known as "comorbidity") may exist simultaneously or over time within many individuals. With this approach, I could record if rulers suffered from two or three separate psychiatric syndromes simultaneously, such as depression, alcoholism, and drug abuse, or suffered from them at different times in their lives, without assuming that these syndromes shared a common cause or qualified as "official" diagnoses.

Because this syndromatic rather than diagnostic approach was central to the classification of these mental disturbances, I have selected a couple of rulers as examples to show how it was applied.

Drugs, insomnia, and Mao Zedong:

According to his personal physician, Dr. Li Zhisui,[5] Mao Zedong had been taking Veronal, a barbiturate, in the 1930s and then later up to four or more 0.1 gram gelatin capsules of sodium amytal every night for chronic insomnia without much success. Hoping to break him of this habit, his physician tried to reduce the dosage of amytal without his patient's awareness by cutting the strength of the capsules, but Mao countered this by taking more capsules. His physician then switched to chloral hydrate, another sedative-hypnotic drug, which worked dramatically at first, but soon Mao began taking it with his evening barbiturate and regularly during social occasions to induce euphoria. *(This cluster of behaviors was coded as a "dependence on sedative-hypnotic drugs.")* His physician also treated him with ginseng and various drugs for "neurasthenia." By neurasthenia, his physician meant anxiety attacks, along with dizziness and depression. These attacks were brought on by worries about ranking leaders not being loyal to him and were relieved by relaxation. *(This cluster of behaviors was coded as "anxiety.")* Mao also spent days disengaged from government, lying around his bedroom, withdrawing from most social encounters, and responding to questions about the business of the day with enigmatic statements, if he responded at all. *(This cluster of behaviors, along with other observations about his tendencies for depression, was coded as "probable depression.")* In sum, then, this information revealed that Mao suffered from anxiety, depression, and drug dependence over the course of his life.

The "black dog" and Winston Churchill:

Winston Churchill was plagued for much of his life with spells of prolonged depression, which he referred to as the "black dog." During these times, he had trouble reading and writing and tended to be more socially

7.1: Winston Churchill often turned to painting as a way to cope with "the black dog" of depression. © Corbis/Hulton-Deutsch Collection.

withdrawn. He became very depressed in 1915 after his problems at the admiralty. At that time, the "muse of painting" rescued him from depression. After that, painting became a kind of opiate for him, which helped him to cope with his many episodes of depression. (*This cluster of behaviors was coded as "depression."*) He began drinking heavily in 1921 and continued doing so throughout his life.[6] Typically, he started the day drinking with a whiskey and soda before lunch; had champagne at lunch, followed by port, brandy, and a cigar; and then had another whiskey and soda about 5:00 P.M., along with the fifteen cigars he smoked a day. (*This cluster of behaviors was coded as "alcoholism."* Had I been recording nicotine dependence, he certainly would have qualified for that.) Oftentimes he would consume more alcohol, and sometimes less, especially in his later years. For instance, in a meeting with Tito, after Churchill had left office, he accepted a small whiskey, while Tito had his usual large one. "Why so little whiskey?" asked Tito. "You taught me to drink big ones." "That was when we both had power," Churchill answered. "Now I have none, and you still have yours." But alcohol and tobacco were not the only substances he was dependent on. During his last years, he became dependent on the drugs prescribed by doctors: barbiturates to sleep and stimulants to get through the day.[7] (*This cluster of behaviors was coded as "dependence on sedative-hypnotic drugs."*) In Churchill's case, the assorted information revealed that he suffered from depression, alcoholism, and drug dependence at various times in his life.

Base Rates and Sampling Methods

These abbreviated accounts show the usefulness of a syndromatic approach to the classification of psychiatric difficulties. Aside from identifying these different mental syndromes, we also need to know if their rates are more or less than those found within the general population. Fortunately, this information is available through the results of the Epidemiological Catchment Area (ECA) survey, a monumental study involving interviews at five different sites with about twenty thousand individuals who typified the entire United States population.[8] Although these results do not take into account cultural differences among the many nations, they are the best population statistics available and offer a yardstick for gauging the relative extent of mental disturbances among these rulers.

What also needs to be recognized is that differences in sampling methods, diagnostic criteria, and population groups can lead to wide disparities in the lifetime rates of mental disorders. The results of past epidemiological surveys clearly show this. In the Stirling County study, the lifetime prevalence for *any* psychiatric disorder defined in the first edition of the *Diagnostic and Statistical Manual of the American Psychiatric Association* (1952) was 57 percent.[9] Although the Midtown Manhattan study did not try to establish base rates for specific mental disorders, it did report that 23 percent of the sample population had significant psychiatric impairment, and over 80 percent had at least some mild impairment.[10] If you define the normality of certain behaviors on the basis of what most people do, then these results dramatically show that it is "normal" to have a mild mental impairment and "abnormal" not to. Although some argue that the 80 percent estimate is still too low, considering the craziness of people living in large metropolitan areas or the kinds of leaders people tolerate, we really need to question the criteria these researchers used and their use of the pejorative term "impairment." Fortunately, the results of the ECA study revealed a more respectable lifetime prevalence of 32 percent for *any* psychiatric disorder within the general population, so that saves us from having to deal with the disturbing implications of the Midtown Manhattan study.

With the present study, I made allowance for a certain degree of uncertainty in classifying syndromes as "definite" or "probable," depending on the supporting evidence. For the purposes of my analyses, I have decided to adopt the more liberal criteria for identifying the existence of an emotional disorder (by combining the "definite" and "probable" categories), mainly to compensate for the concerted effort by most politicians to disguise all signs of mental illness. The lifetime rates of mental illness I will be reporting in rulers are still likely to be on the low side because of the difficulty in gaining adequate information in this area, but they are the best approximations available. More to the point, *they are the only ones available on the largest collection of rulers ever studied.* As it turns out, they not only clarify the susceptibility of the different kinds of rulers to the different kinds of mental disorders but, even more telling, suggest that certain kinds of "mental disorders," under certain circumstances, actually may be relatively adaptive for them. With this the case, the results also challenge certain basic notions about the nature of mental illness.

A POTPOURRI OF MENTAL ABERRATIONS

Although the current official classification of mental disorders lists over a hundred disorders, I have simplified matters by limiting them to six general categories—alcoholism, drug abuse, depression, mania, anxiety, and paranoia—and an unclassified category for the remainder (e.g., "nervous breakdown," "shell shock," and other ill-defined conditions). This simplified classification should suit our purposes.

Alcoholism

Alcoholism refers to some combination of the following criteria: in its most severe forms, individuals show a physical addiction to alcohol that involves an intense craving for alcohol, uncontrolled drinking ("loss of control"), the consumption of increasing amounts of alcohol over time to get the same psychological effects ("tolerance"), and physical signs of alcohol withdrawal (such as getting the "shakes" or becoming confused or developing delirium tremens after stopping alcohol). Dependence on alcohol can affect almost every aspect of a person's life. Compulsive, excessive, or continuous drinking can cause physical problems (e.g., liver damage, delirium tremens, gastric ulcer), vocational problems (absenteeism, impaired job performance, decreased productivity), personal problems (divorce, alienation of children), social problems (increased friction with friends, colleagues, employees), or legal problems (e.g., arrests for assaults, driving under the influence of alcohol, or public intoxication). Usually, alcoholism is a chronic, relapsing condition, associated with periods of continuous or binge drinking intermixed with variable periods of sobriety.

Despite these clear-cut criteria, it is still sometimes hard to judge if certain rulers meet them. Take Slobodan Milosevec, for example. According to his biographer, Milosevec supposedly only gulped alcohol "under stress."[11] But since he has been under stress a lot, it is likely that he must gulp a lot of alcohol. Fortunately, information from other competent observers helps to clarify the situation. For instance, Peter Galbraith, formerly the U.S. ambassador to Croatia, remembered when Milosevic arrived late for an important meeting slightly disheveled, tie askew, fresh from a meeting at the officers' club. "He'd obviously had a liquid lunch," Galbraith recalled.[12] Additional observations by others about Milosevic's fondness for alcohol made me lean toward a judgment of "probable" alcohol dependence.

As you learn about the drinking practices of many rulers, you cannot help being struck by how much alcohol figured in their daily duties and functions and the many ways they used it. Wine and whiskey flow freely at their diplomatic meetings, social gatherings, and state dinners. In man-to-man negotiations between rulers, leaders often consume stiff drinks of the finest bourbon or scotch as "ice-breakers" or for male bonding or to enhance their own macho image. Many rulers use alcohol as a way to wind down or to relieve tension or to help them sleep. Others use it for pleasure or, as William James might say, to make their thoughts and perceptions seem "more utterly utter." Some use alcohol for pleasing or appeasing other rulers during state visits or other encounters and sometimes even for teasing their guests, just as Tito enjoyed doing with royalty. On one occasion, for instance, when Sir Fitzroy Maclean joined Prince Charles on his official visit to Yugoslavia, he gave Tito some of his celebrated MacPhunn malt whisky as a gift. Later that evening, at the official reception, Tito served Chivas Regal to the prince. Disappointed, the prince asked, "Can't we broach some of Fitzroy's malt!" "Oh no," replied Tito, "we keep that for special occasions."[13]

Perhaps the way rulers use alcohol is no different than how many people use it in society. In some fashion or other, alcohol seems to have insinuated itself into all aspects of social life. Used in moderation and with discretion, it creates no problems for individuals. The difficulty is that many people cannot keep their drinking within bounds. Because too much alcohol can impair concentration and judgment, rulers who have trouble controlling their drinking usually cannot effectively discharge their duties. For instance, by 1955 King Saud of Saudi Arabia had become so addicted to alcohol, especially Cointreau, that he repeatedly had to be flown out of the country to dry out. Yahya Khan, who was president of Pakistan from 1969 to 1971, drank over two bottles of whiskey a day during the war with India and supplemented that with vodka, disguised as water, when he had to deal with the public during meetings or television speeches. It seems reasonable to assume that his consumption of this enormous amount of alcohol impaired his judgment, contributing to the loss of East Pakistan, and eventually led to his "nervous breakdown."

Protective cover-ups:

Unfortunately, because of the widespread use of alcohol and a certain toleration of excessive drinking in society, it is common for the colleagues, staff, and friends of alcoholic rulers to cover up for them, even in democratic societies. Here are several examples.

- Harold Wilson, prime minister of the United Kingdom from 1964 to 1970 and from 1974 to 1976, developed a strong reliance on brandy and would sip on it alone during ministerial meetings. By the age of sixty he had lost the capacity for original thought, had trouble with his short-term memory, and was covering up for his memory defects with false recollections and lies, all typical signs of an alcoholic dementia.[14]

• John Curtin, prime minister of Australia during most of World War II, became more and more unreliable as his drinking increased. His judgment became so poor that sometimes he wandered into choir practice drunk, sat down, and immediately fell asleep. Concerned for his future, his friends tried to save him from complete collapse and ruin and finally got him to promise to stay sober.

• Robert Hawke, prime minister of Australia from 1983 to 1991, continued his winning ways from being a champion at drinking fellow students "under the table" at Oxford to outdrinking his political colleagues on frequent social occasions.

• Ito Hirobumi, Japanese elder statesman (*genro*) and premier (1885–88, 1892–96, 1898, 1900–01) who played a crucial role in the building of modern Japan, often drank sake late into the night until he passed out.

• Brian Mulroney was a certified drunkard throughout much of his political career. Faced with the collapse of his marriage and the ruination of his reputation, he finally quit drinking and joined Alcoholics Anonymous several years before becoming prime minister of Canada.

Lifetime Rates of Alcoholism: In the ECA survey, the total lifetime prevalence for both alcohol abuse and dependence was 14 percent for the general population. Among our rulers, the lifetime rate of alcohol-related problems was 15 percent, almost the identical percentage as in ECA survey. While it is reassuring to find that the percentage of alcoholism among rulers is not substantially higher than for the population at large, this is still a high figure for people entrusted with such enormous responsibilities. Although all types of rulers were susceptible to this disorder, one type towered over all others: over 40 percent of all tyrants were alcoholics, two to three times the percentages found in the other ruler groups. Typical of these tyrants were Omar Torrijos, dictator of Panama, who stayed drunk all day; and Bokassa, self-appointed emperor of his Central African Empire, who drank about a fifth of Chevas Regal a day and had someone always nearby waiting to refill his glass.[15]

Fig. 7.1: Lifetime Rates of Alcoholism in Rulers

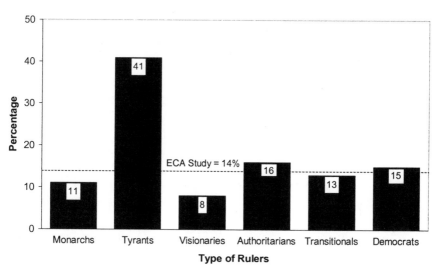

Legend: All ruler groups except for the tyrants display roughly the same percentage of alcoholism as noted in the ECA study.

As figure 7.1 above shows, the lifetime rate for alcoholism is highest by far for tyrants. Why should this be so? I will return to this question later after we examine the lifetime rates for the other psychiatric syndromes, which show that tyrants have other emotional problems as well. For now, it is sufficient to say that, among the six different kinds of rulers, tyrants are the only ones without either a legal, traditional, or hereditary basis for their authority and without any vision or ideology to guide them. They also are not likely to have any trusted friends, colleagues, or advisors to whom they can turn for support and understanding in times of stress. Because of the tension generated by the tenuousness, insecurity, and isolation of their position, many seem to rely on alcohol as a way to buoy up their flagging spirits and for its relaxant effects.

One last word about alcoholism in rulers. Despite the erratic behavior of rulers who drink too much, it is wrong to assume that their excessive drinking inevitably led to disastrous consequences. At times I have been astounded by how well certain rulers were able to run their countries and accomplish impressive deeds despite their periodic drunkenness and lapses of judgment. For instance, Kemal Atatürk still managed to transform Turkey and be revered by his countrymen despite being grossly intoxicated much of the time and eventually dying of cirrhosis of the liver at the relatively young age of fifty-seven. When drunk, he might order a minaret destroyed because of the annoying music coming out of a mosque. The next morning, after he sobered up, he would rescind the order if it had not yet been implemented. But sometimes he was not in a position to undo his orders, as when he told a singer to put a glass on top of his head and then shot at it with his pistol à la William Tell. In time, though, his liver began to fail, his memory got worse, his behavior became more erratic, his temper worsened, and depression set in, but, amazingly, as debilitated as he was, Atatürk never lost his sense of humor. A French journalist wrote that Turkey was governed by one drunkard, one deaf man (referring to Ismet, the vice president), and three hundred deaf mutes (the deputies). Kemal responded, "This man is mistaken. Turkey is governed by one drunkard."[16]

Drug-Related Problems

Although drug dependence usually refers to a powerful craving for a drug, it is often marked by the need for more and more of the drug over time to produce the same psychological effects and by the presence of physical withdrawal symptoms once the drug is no longer available. Previously, a combination of these criteria were used to define "drug addiction." Substance abuse refers to physical, vocational, interpersonal, or legal problems due to compulsive, excessive, and sustained legal or illegal drug use. Often, drug dependence and abuse are part of the same syndrome, but sometimes they are not, as when a person becomes addicted to a drug prescribed by a physician and tries to deal with the problem by legal and medical means. The criteria for drug dependence or abuse do not cover the experimentation with certain psychoactive drugs such as marijuana. For example, in the absence of contradictory information, President William Clinton, who admitted to smoking but "not inhaling" marijuana as a student, was not counted as a drug user.

A cornucopia of drugs:

Unlike the use of alcohol, drug use or abuse covers many different drugs, which have many different effects and many patterns of use. As it happens, the rulers in my study used almost every available kind of drug that could affect their moods and minds and produce physical or psychological dependence. These drugs included barbiturates, narcotics, marijuana, hallucinogens, amphetamines, cocaine, and assorted aphrodisiacs.

• Patrice Lumumba, prime minister of the Republic of Zaire, smoked hemp regularly.

- Nicholas II, the last Russian emperor (1895–1917), took cocaine for fatigue for months during his last year in power.
- Jean-Claude Duvalier, also known as "Baby Doc," likely smoked cocaine, since he attended many parties with his wife, who allegedly supplemented her government salary of a million dollars a month by trafficking in cocaine and assorted other drugs.
- According to a CIA report, Muammar Qaddafi regularly took enormous doses of sleeping pills to help him sleep, followed by other pills to wake him up in the morning.[17]
- John Fitzgerald Kennedy, thirty-fifth president of the United States, received injections of steroids and amphetamines from a Dr. Max Jacobson, known among many celebrities as "Dr. Feelgood" for his willingness to inject stimulants. By the summer of 1961, he reportedly had developed a strong dependence on amphetamines.[18]
- Macias Nguema consumed marijuana regularly and drank a hallucinogen, *iboga*, which was a local drug used in traditional ceremonies.
- Anthony Eden, prime minister of Great Britain, likewise became dependent on stimulants to counter depression and to help him function.
- Leonid Brezhnev, according to Mikhail Gorbachev, stayed "whacked out" on tranquilizers and often seemed more dead than alive.
- Some question exists about whether the stimulants Hitler's doctors regularly prescribed for him and the cocaine solution he took for his sinus pain increased his paranoia.[19]
- Manuel Noriega, commander of the Panamanian Defense Forces

Lifetime Rates of Drug Abuse/Dependence: With the ECA findings, the lifetime prevalence of drug dependence or substance abuse was about 6 percent. Among our rulers, 5 percent experienced drug-related problems or used psychoactive drugs regularly at some time in their lives, almost the same rate as in the ECA study. As with alcohol-related problems, tyrants had the highest lifetime rate of drug use (23 percent). Except for the elevated rate in visionaries (16 percent), the rates of drug use among the monarchs (6 percent), authoritarians (3 percent), traditionals (4 percent), and established democratic rulers (2 percent) were relatively similar. See figure 7.2.

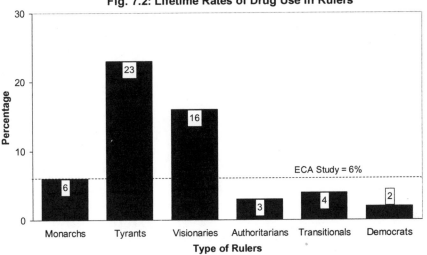

Fig. 7.2: Lifetime Rates of Drug Use in Rulers

Legend: Note that all groups of rulers except for tyrants and visionaries have a somewhat lower rate of drug use than that noted in the ECA study for the U.S. population at large.

(1983–89), who was the actual power behind the civilian president during the years of his command, snorted cocaine while he held power.[20]

Of course, the matter of drug use by dictators takes on a different meaning when they have the prerogative to define what is and what is not legal. If the worse thing about taking psychoactive drugs is breaking the law, then casual experimentation with them would not be too awful if there were no laws against doing so or the ruler made an exception in his own case. In the absence of physical dependence or constant intoxication, we now face the intriguing question of whether we should consider the use of cocaine, marijuana, stimulants, or narcotics by tyrants as *drug abuse* if they are the ones who define what is or is not "abuse."

Depression or Melancholia

Depression refers to at least one several-week episode of some combination of the following symptoms: a melancholy mood, a sleep disturbance, increased or decreased appetite, lack of energy, excessive tearfulness, a sense of dread or futility, social withdrawal, morbid thoughts, or suicidal preoccupation. Unless evidence to the contrary existed, I interpreted ac-

Lifetime Rates of Depression: The results of the ECA study revealed a combined lifetime rate of about 6 percent for major depression or dysthymic disorder for the population at large. The lifetime rate for severe depression was 14 percent for all the rulers in the sample, over twice the percentage found in the ECA findings. Because the ECA study did not interpret dysphoria, frequent thoughts of death, and appetite changes lasting longer than two weeks as indicative of depression (symptoms I would have regarded as probable signs of depression), I decided to use only those rulers with definite signs of depression as a more appropriate basis of comparison to the ECA sample. Had I included those rulers with "probable" depression, the overall rate would have been 31 percent, about the same rate the ECA study reported for dysphoria but substantially above the rate it reported for depression. However, about 12 percent of the rulers who had definite or probable depression by my criteria also suffered from mania or had periods of sustained emotional "highs." As figure 7.3 below shows, visionaries (24 percent) were the most likely to become depressed, and tyrants (0 percent) were the least likely.

tual suicide attempts as signs of depression, although in certain instances they happened in a political context. The "probable" signs of depression included moodiness, unhappiness, pessimism, gloominess, and general dysphoria. For my study, I reserved the term of depression or melancholy only for those instances in which obvious personal crises, such as bereavement, imprisonment, ill health, or the loss of a job, did not seem to be responsible or when the emotional response to these crises was out of proportion to their significance and lasted longer than normally expected. Common psychiatric conditions that qualified as depression included major depressive disorders, dysthymia or "neurotic" depressions, depressive episodes associated with bipolar disorders, and adjustment disorders with depression that lasted more than six months or resulted in severe consequences such as suicide attempts.

The many faces of depression:

Depression occurs in many varieties and forms. As with other mental disturbances, depression, depending on its kind and severity, can affect the lives and works of people in different ways. Those who suffer from chronic low-grade forms of depression may be affected differently than those who have only one or two incapacitating episodes or those who experience depressions as preludes to manic highs or those who stay seriously depressed for many years.

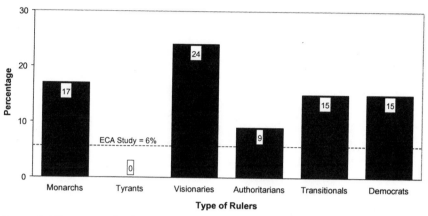

Fig. 7.3: Lifetime Rates of Depression in Rulers

Legend: All groups of rulers except tyrants have higher rates of depression than that reported in the ECA study for the U.S. population at large.

Let's first note some instances of depression in the most vulnerable groups of rulers. Among the monarchs, Alfonso XIII, king of Spain (1886–1931), periodically suffered from "fits of the deepest depression." King Ferdinand of Bulgaria became a "morbid recluse" in 1915. His son, Boris III, king of Bulgaria from 1918 to 1943, often spoke during his dark moments about abdicating or shooting himself. During Carol II's last two years in office before fleeing his country, he was in a state of severe depression, which he described as "two years of agony."

Among the visionaries, Atatürk drank heavily to quell his frequent depressions, but the drinking often only served to make his depressions worse. Leopold Sedar Senghor, president of Senegal from 1960 to 1980, suffered from bleak periods of depression throughout his life. At those times, he had great difficulty concentrating, so he had to slow down and do more methodical work.[21] Fidel Castro's severe depression and reclusiveness after the death of Celia Sanchez, his lover, led to a slow-down in many governmental activities for several months.[22] Adolph Hitler had at least three episodes of deep depression, the worst one being after his niece, Geli Raubel, committed suicide.[23] After the Six-Day War disaster with Israel, Gamal Nasser, president of Egypt, went into a long funk. He began taking sleeping pills for insomnia, lost more than thirty pounds in weight, and suffered a great loss of self-confidence. He went on the air and, with a choked voice, resigned his position, but the people refused to accept his resignation. For the first few weeks after the defeat, he was in a state of shock, with his depression lingering on for almost a year. During that time, Nasser described himself as "a man walking in a desert surrounded by moving sands."[24] Though he supposedly eventually recovered, the defeat had taken its toll, and he never was the same afterwards.

Among the democratic rulers, Menachem Begin suffered from recurrent melancholy and went into a severe depression after the Lebanon massacres and again after his resignation from office. Louis Botha suffered from a prolonged bout of "black depression" during which he became obsessed with dying, felt disillusioned and exhausted, and had trouble sleeping. Willy Brandt suffered from periods of deep depression and brooding. Arthur Griffith had to be hospitalized once for a bout of severe depression. Poincaré experienced long periods of melancholy when he felt that everything was futile and bleak. While in prison, Alcide De Gasperi, who later became the prime minister of Italy (1945–53), had a several-month period of torpor and numbness when he could not pray or study and was incapable of experiencing enjoyment. Though this was his first episode of depression, it reappeared years after he was released. Indira Gandhi went into a deep funk that lasted for years after her estranged husband died of a second heart attack.[25]

The special case of the British prime ministers:
Although roughly one-third of all rulers suffered from depression at some point in their lives, I found some intriguing "coincidences" when I analyzed the data more closely. For instance, at least 60 percent of British prime ministers suffered from this malady. Of the twenty individuals who served as prime minister during the twentieth century, Herbert Asquith, Stanley Baldwin, Arthur James Balfour, James Callaghan, Neville Chamberlain, Winston Churchill, Edward Heath, Andrew Bonar Law, David Lloyd George, Ramsay Macdonald, Harold Macmillan, and Robert Arthur Salisbury all suffered from depression, and it is likely that Anthony Eden did as well. This astounding percentage of afflicted persons raises the question of whether this was just coincidence, whether the political system tended to favor those with a depressive bent for prime minister of Britain, or whether working in that particular political system made people get that way.

Let's take a closer look at how depression affected some of those afflicted.

• As was the case with Winston Churchill, Harold Macmillan, British prime minister from January 1957 to October 1963, was plagued by the "black dog" throughout his life. Ever since childhood, he was oppressed by some kind of mysterious power that he believed would get him in the end.[26] In 1931 he actually suffered from a "nervous breakdown" and apparently attempted suicide when he could not go on.

• Henry Asquith, Liberal prime minister of Britain from 1908 to 1916, had occasional bouts of melancholy, aggravated in the years before his becoming leader of the nation by his frustrated ambitions. In a letter, he wrote, "Of all human troubles the most hateful is to feel you have the capacity of power and yet you have no field to exercise it. That was for years my case and no one who has not been through it can know the chilly, paralyzing, deadening depression of hope deferred and energy wasted and vitality run to seed."[27] In a sense, he eloquently voiced the anguish of all driven people who yearn for power yet find themselves thwarted by their own lacks or by external factors beyond their control.

• Ramsay MacDonald periodically grieved for his wife for about twenty-five years after her death and never remarried. He said some part of him died with her and "my heart is in the grave." In his diary, he recorded his many black moods, and, in his later years, he displayed a brooding melancholy that made him unapproachable to all but a few close friends.[28]

• Already prone to despondency, Bonar Law, prime minister of Great Britain from October 23, 1922, to May 20, 1923, never fully overcame the deaths of his two oldest sons during World War I. The only way he was able to deal with his melancholy was to keep busy every waking hour of the day.

• Robert Arthur Talbot Gascoyne-Cecil Salisbury, three-time prime minister of Britain (1885–86, 1886–92, 1895–1902), whose tenure in office just made it into this past century, had his first bout of melancholy at Eton and, though he was relatively free of depressions during his late twenties, continued to suffer from "black glooms" and "nervous attacks" throughout the remainder of his life.

The emotional toll of eroding power:
In reviewing these data on depression, I was struck by how many of these democratic rulers went into a deep funk once they began to experience their power slipping away and especially after they lost it. They tended to react to these events as though their entire universe had collapsed or, at least, as if they had irretrievably lost something very dear to them.

- Winston Spencer Churchill, for example, became very depressed and had trouble reading and writing in 1915 along with experiencing morbid worries about his political career after he was criticized for his performance at the admiralty. He also became severely depressed after he left office in the 1930s, again after his election defeat in 1945, and again after his final resignation.
- Charles de Gaulle became very upset about the student-worker protests near the end of his presidency. After a poor showing in a public referendum, he became depressed over what he perceived to be a personal rejection by the populace and decided to resign the presidency. Once he left office, he went to Baden for a "rest," which I interpreted to mean that he went there to be cured of his mental funk.
- Indira Gandhi remained depressed for months after losing the election in 1977, even crying in public.
- Mohammad Ayub Khan became increasingly demoralized in response to his deteriorating political situation, during which his family was being attacked for corruption. By 1969 he was feeling isolated and helpless, and many of his associates felt he had lost the will to govern. Some of his ministers kept futilely trying to get him to act decisively. A gloom settled over the president's house, and everything came to a standstill. The pretense of official routine still went on, though nobody was doing anything. For a long while before his final abdication speech, Ayub would go to sleep at night and wake up with the question that probably haunted most rulers who lost power: "How did it all go wrong?"[29]

One of the main reasons the erosion of power and its eventual loss hits so many rulers with a susceptibility to depression so hard is that the very exercise of power often serves as a powerful prophylaxis and antidote for depression. Teddy Roosevelt, whose mercurial temperament fluctuated between elation and depression, described this situation well: "Black care rarely sits behind a rider whose pace is fast enough."[30] He was saying that if he kept busy enough, driven enough, and focused enough on his ultimate goal, then he could avoid being sucked into the black hole of his own morbid thoughts. But once his work, drive, and ambition were gone, he would have no defense against the looming gloom.

Suicide attempts:
Suicide attempts are common signs of depression but not always so. For the purpose of these analyses, I judged any successful or unsuccessful

effort on the part of a ruler to end his life as a suicide attempt, whether he did so seriously or for attention-gaining, manipulation, or other obscure reasons. In many instances, the reasons rulers tried to commit suicide seemed to be entangled with their political lives. Several rulers, for example, unsuccessfully attempted suicide to avoid prison or escape execution for their political deeds. Tojo Hideki, prime minister of Japan during World War II, asked a doctor to draw a spot on his chest with ink marking where his heart was located and then shot himself there. But his aim must have been poor or his doctor did not know his anatomy, since Tojo survived his wound. After being doctored back to health, he was tried, found guilty of being a war criminal, and then hanged. Pierre Laval, French politician who led the Vichy government in France during World War II, tried to poison himself before he was tried and then was ultimately executed as a traitor to France. Mohammad Mossadegh twice attempted suicide in prison. He was regarded as such a risk that the prison guards had to watch him in the morning when he was shaving to make sure he did not hurt himself. When briefly imprisoned toward the end of the war, Benito Mussolini cut his wrists in an apparent suicide attempt.

In other instances, the rulers attempted suicide for more personal reasons. Reputedly, Boris Yeltsin once attempted suicide, probably while in one of his depressed moods and under the influence of alcohol, according to his chauffeur. Harold Macmillan, who suffered from severe recurrent depressions during his lifetime, also made an unsuccessful suicide attempt, as reported by an old family nanny.

Initially, I was surprised the actual suicide rate for rulers was no higher than that for the general population at large because I assumed that the

---

Lifetime Rates of Suicide Attempts: Within the sample of rulers, the lifetime prevalence for both unsuccessful and successful suicide attempts was about 3 percent. Visionaries (12 percent) had the highest rate of suicide attempts, and monarchs (0 percent) and tyrants (0 percent) the least.

Among all the leaders in the world during the past century, the *actual suicide rate* among the various causes of death was 0.9 percent. Only 4 rulers out of the 377 in the sample actually managed to commit suicide, a rate of about 1 percent, which not only mirrored the rate for the total sample but corresponded exactly to the mortality statistics by suicide in the United States over seven separate sampling periods during the twentieth century.

stress of the job would bring more of these people to the breaking point. Then I realized my assumption did not take into account the kind of people rulers are. These were basically men of action, not prone to morbid ruminations or self-destructive thoughts. As such, they were more adept when distressed at increasing the death rates of others than at turning their aggression and frustrations against themselves.

Even those four rulers in the sample who killed themselves did so under special circumstances. Getulio Vargas committed suicide with a shotgun at the age of seventy-one rather than accept forced retirement in response to widespread criticisms of his government from both the public and the military. As sometimes happens with dramatic deaths, his suicide note, in the form of a farewell message to the Brazilian people, helped to transform him from a despised politician into a patriotic martyr. The situation was much the same with Salvadore Allende, the Marxist president of Chile, who became a political martyr and hero of the Left when he shot himself rather than be captured during the coup by General Pinochet. What his many posthumous admirers do not realize is that, at the time he committed suicide, he was frustrated with the growing national discontent over his economic and social policies; was recuperating from a heart attack; had suffered two strokes, one leaving the right side of his face partly paralyzed; was deeply depressed; and probably used the occasion as an excuse to follow through on threats of killing himself that he had made numerous times before. Konoe Fumimaro, prime minister of Japan (1937–39, 1940–41), committed suicide in late 1945 by drinking poison after he was served with an arrest warrant by the occupation army on suspicion of being a war criminal. And lastly, Adolph Hitler and his new bride, Eva Braun, took their lives in his bunker when he finally realized all was lost and that suicide was the only way to avoid capture by Allied forces.

Mania, or "Highs"

Mania refers to at least one sustained episode of elation, grandiosity, excessive energy, unusually poor judgment, racing thoughts, social intrusiveness, insomnia, excessive buying, or juggling too many activities in comparison to the person's ordinary behavior. "Probable" indications of mania involve major mood swings with periods of heightened well-being, marked irritability, poor sleep, lapses in judgment, and increased physical activity. Mania should not be attributed to people if they simply feel "good" after a long period of depression, experience a "flow state" or "creative high" while engaged in their work, or become "hyper" or energized while immersed in a major project. In other words, mania or hypomania represents an "abnormal" state of sustained arousal.

Mania usually has a chronic, relapsing course. Although a small minority of people with depression also have mania, a large majority of those with mania also have depression. Many people with mania manage to endure their emotional peaks and valleys without irreversible damage to their personal relationships and continue to be creative and productive, but others, especially those with severe episodes or "rapid-cyclers," do not.

An emotional roller coaster:
When a ruler lives his life on an emotional roller coaster, he is apt to be erratic and unpredictable. Here are some examples.

- William II, German emperor (kaiser) and king of Prussia from 1888 to the end of World War I in 1918, had long periods of euphoria following bouts of the blackest depression.
- Habib Bourguiba, first president of Tunisia (1957–87), alternated between bouts of mania and depression that were so incapacitating at times that he had to leave the country for psychiatric treatment.
- Joseph Caillaux, a former French prime minister whose opposition to World War I led to his imprisonment for treason in 1920, vacillated between highs of self-exaltation and lows of nervousness, self-doubt, and depression. During highs, he commanded the attention of crowds. But when his moods were dark, he withdrew from social contact.[31]
- After coming out of one of his frequent depressions, Menachem Begin, prime minister of Israel from 1977 to 1983, had periods of ecstasy during which he became boastful, showed poor judgment, and was extremely talkative.
- On occasion, Alexandre Fyodorovich Kerensky, who served as head of the Russian provisional government from July to October 1917, became excessively talkative, humorous, dramatic, and energetic and could go for long stretches of time without sleep. As revolution began sweeping his country, he feverishly rushed about the countryside and gave impassioned speeches to his troops, inspiring no one but himself, mainly because he was the only one who seemed to make any sense out of his semi-delirious rantings.

What these results show is that those leaders who relied mostly on their personal charisma, ideology, or personalities for their authority to

Lifetime Rates of Mania: In the ECA study, the lifetime rate of mania was 0.8 percent for the population at large, with the range varying from 0.4 to 1.2 percent among the five research sites. As noted in the figure below, 7 percent of rulers in my sample had at least one episode of mania during their lives—remarkably, the same percentage I found for over a thousand eminent individuals within a wide variety of professions in my prior study of creative achievement. Among these rulers, tyrants had over three times the average percentage of mania (23 percent), followed next by visionaries, who had over twice the percentage (20 percent). Among the remaining rulers, authoritarians (4 percent) and rulers of established democracies (3 percent) were the least likely to become manic during their lifetimes. See figure 7.4.

rule—namely, visionaries and tyrants—were much more likely to become manic than those who justified their authority to rule on legal or institutional grounds. Rulers with manic tendencies are more likely to be confident, passionate, grandiose, charismatic, and verbally facile, all of which tend to attract followers to them. Whether political aspirants with mania tend to be drawn to more totalitarian forms of rule or whether these forms of rule draw out manic tendencies latent in these rulers is often hard to

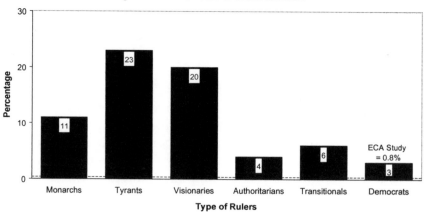

Fig. 7.4: Lifetime Rates of Mania in Rulers

Legend: Note that except for authoritarians and democrats, all other groups of rulers have a substantially higher percentage of persons with mania than that noted in the ECA study. The percentages in tyrants and visionaries are especially high.

sort out. In the case of visionaries, whose persuasiveness, forcefulness, and grand designs vault them into positions of prominence, these tendencies seem more apparent before they reach ultimate power. In the case of tyrants, many of whom were relatively colorless persons lacking in charisma and oratorical skills before rising to prominence, these tendencies became more apparent after they began exercising ultimate power.

In contrast, the relatively low rate of mania in authoritarians and established democrats makes sense. Since governmental bureaucracies, traditional political parties, and military organizations depend on predictability, procedure, and protocol, authoritarians and leaders of established democracies would likely have trouble gaining broad-based political support if they were as erratic, impulsive, and grandiose as persons with mania.

What this suggests is that the emotional tendencies of rulers need to be examined within the context of their particular forms of government to determine if they prove to be politically advantageous or disadvantageous for them. So far the findings show that certain kinds of government tend to attract leaders with certain kinds of emotional tendencies, perhaps even fostering their expression, while other kinds of rule select for leaders with other kinds of tendencies. Therefore, the kinds of emotional expressions and behaviors that may be "normal" in one political context may be "abnormal" in another.

Anxiety-Related Disorders

Pathological anxiety can be defined as an extended period of fearfulness, apprehension, dread, agitation, restlessness, tension, and shakiness—all without any adequate physical or psychological basis. Besides being a distinct syndrome in its own right, this symptom complex also includes obsessive-compulsive disorders, major phobias, post-traumatic stress responses, panic disorders, and cases of severe "nerves." Naturally, the designation of anxiety does not apply to all those instances when rulers are under a lot of natural stress because of civil wars or riots or other problems that directly threaten their tenure in office or even their lives. In these instances, a certain measure of anxiety is appropriate and normal.

Some instances of pathological anxiety:
Many rulers in the study were plagued by severe and at times incapacitating anxiety.

- Lester Bowles Pearson, prime minister of Canada from 1963 to 1968, had a long history of severe anxiety extending back to age twenty while he was in the military service when he was hit by a bus, after which he developed "neurasthenia." Even after discharge, he remained emotionally unstable, suffering from daily headaches, startle responses to noise, insomnia, drowsiness, edginess, stuttering, and nightmares about flying.

• Kurt von Schuschnigg, chancellor of Austria from 1934 to 1938, remained in a state of shock and agitation for a long while after being humiliated by Hitler in 1938.[32] During his last days in office, he was having a "crisis of nerves": smoking more than three packs of cigarettes per day, being unable to sleep, experiencing a loss of confidence, and being erratic and irritable. His anxiety got worse after he was arrested and taken off to prison and became almost incapacitating when he learned that his father had died under mysterious circumstances.

• Talbot Gascoyne-Cecil Salisbury, prime minister of England, had "nervous attacks" that would lay him up for days.

• Stanley Baldwin, another English prime minister, was a "bundle of nerves," constantly sniffing at blotting paper or books, snapping his fingers, or showing his tension in other ways. He worried constantly, had trouble making decisions, and could not sleep. By 1936 he was under such great pressure that he "nearly broke down." To prevent his having a complete "nervous breakdown," his physician ordered him to take three months off from work for total and complete rest[33]—which itself could be anxiety provoking for someone used to keeping busy.

Although the lifetime rates of anxiety in rulers are considerably less than for depression, both syndromes share similar patterns. Monarchs and visionaries were most prone to anxiety, and authoritarians were the

---

Lifetime Rates of Anxiety: The results of the ECA study revealed that about 9 percent of the general population experienced some sort of generalized anxiety disorder. In the sample of rulers, the lifetime rate of generalized anxiety was 8 percent, essentially the same percentage as for ordinary people at large. Among the rulers, monarchs (19 percent) and visionaries (20 percent) were most likely to experience some form of morbid anxiety, followed next by transitionals (6 percent) and democrats (7 percent). Tyrants (4 percent) and authoritarians (3 percent) were least likely to suffer from crippling bouts of anxiety. See figure 7.5.

Fig. 7.5: Lifetime Rates of Anxiety in Rulers

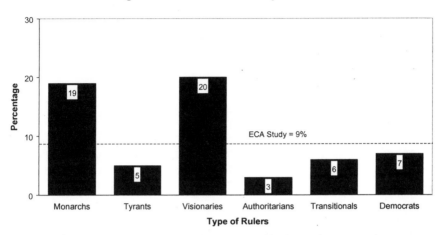

Legend: Except for monarchs and visionaries, all other ruler groups have comparable or lower rates of anxiety as noted in the ECA study for the U.S. population at large.

least. Why this pattern of differences among the different kinds of rulers? It is hard to be sure. We do know that a substantial overlap exists clinically between anxiety and depression and that people who suffer from one of these primary syndromes usually have secondary symptoms of the other. So at least these findings are consistent. Why, then, should visionaries and monarchs be more susceptible to depression and anxiety than other rulers? Accounting for the situation with visionaries does not offer as much of a problem as for monarchs. With their greater tendency for mania, visionaries should be more vulnerable to depression when the mood pendulum swings the other way. Then, with their increased susceptibility to depression, they likewise should experience more severe anxiety on occasion, too, because of the close association of these syndromes.

The real puzzle has to do with the monarchs, who have the highest rates of depression and anxiety among all rulers. Although I cannot be sure why, I wonder if it somehow has to do with the rapid disappearance of absolute monarchies over this past century, with the shift toward more constitutional monarchies or even the elimination of royalty entirely, as happened in Russia, Egypt, and elsewhere. More than any other group of rulers, monarchs get their authority to rule on the basis of their lineage and tradition. With the changing social and political climate, monarchs not only have had to face the steady erosion of their powers over time but the eradication of everything they stood for as well—their quasi-divinity, their genealogical rootedness, and their special status. The realization of their eventual extinction certainly is not designed to raise their spirits. But all this is surmise.

Paranoia

Unfounded beliefs in conspiracies by certain ethnic, religious, or racial groups, and extreme prejudices toward them, unfortunately, are commonplace in the general population. Where this hate-mongering, narrow-mindedness, extreme suspiciousness, and bigotry end and paranoia begins sometimes may be hard to figure out, especially when others share similar beliefs. Nevertheless, a line (albeit blurred) does seem to exist beyond which the suspiciousness of people assumes almost delusional proportions although it may not be severe enough to incapacitate them completely. When people pass over this line, they become more obsessed with conspiracies against them or their families or their countries than any objective evidence warrants and begin entertaining bizarre and sometimes incoherent beliefs. Grandiosity and religious ideation, often tinged with a vindictive, self-righteous, or persecutory tone, tend to color these beliefs. Because paranoid leaders may be so forceful in their convictions, credulous listeners may embrace them wholeheartedly even when they make little sense.

In a clinical context,

7.2: Humans are not the only primates to imagine enemies. Note the bristled hair as the chimp threatens its own image in the mirror with a stick. Photograph by Hugo van Lawick, courtesy of the Jane Goodall Institute.

paranoid states of this sort usually evolve gradually over time, becoming more apparent between the ages of forty through sixty. They have a relatively stable course over time and tend to be well integrated into the lifestyle of the person. The person's intellectual functioning and occupational skills may remain intact, but, as expected, his social and personal relationships with others usually suffer.

Paranoid states are distinguishable from acute paranoid reactions in which the delusions are less systematized and coherent. These acute reactions tend to be more time-limited and related to sudden situational stresses such as after emigrating from one country to another, exposure to bloody battlefront conditions, or assassination attempts. These states are also distinguishable from full-blown paranoid schizophrenia, a condition that leads to severe social deterioration. Technically, paranoid states qualify as being "psychotic" because the person's beliefs have no grounding in reality and, because they usually are not shared by others, keep the person from functioning optimally in society.

Although paranoid conditions take different forms, they all tend to share certain features.[34] The person has an extreme suspiciousness about the intentions of others. He suspects that these other people mean him harm. He attributes malevolent powers to these people. He believes that these people are in league with other conspirators to harass him. He is a collector of injustices and constantly keeps looking for evidence to support his suspicions. He believes that most of his problems are due to the machinations of these people and that, if he can thwart their intentions, his difficulties will be solved. Therefore, the best defense is a preemptive offense. And although his overall beliefs are false, they often contain a kernel of truth, which the person clings to as justification for his convictions.

As I surveyed the presence of frank paranoia within my sample of rulers, I found the percentages displaying the features of this syndrome at some point in their reign to be substantially higher than any estimates of lifetime rates in the general population at large (see the figure below). With percentages this high, some critics may regard my criteria for paranoia as being too liberal, wondering if I simply interpreted many instances of extreme suspiciousness or realistic worries about treachery as "psychotic" or "delusional." Since I included the "probable" cases of paranoia along with the "definite" ones in my calculations, there may be some validity to this concern. However, when you examine each of these particular rulers on a case-by-case basis, it is hard not to conclude that for at least some extended period of time they were out of touch with reality

Lifetime Rates of Paranoia: Unfortunately, information about the prevalence of these states within the general population is sparse, mainly because these persons resist mental health care and tend to be uncooperative in epidemiological surveys. Although the method is imperfect, a rough notion of the lifetime prevalence of paranoia within the general population can be determined by noting the prevalence for the psychoses in general, including all forms of schizophrenia. In a 1994 United States mental health survey of over eight thousand persons, 0.7 percent were found to have a psychosis.[35] In the ECA study, the lifetime prevalence for schizophrenia and schizophreniform disorders (which likely included paranoid disorders) for the population at large at was about 1.5 percent. On the basis of these figures, the lifetime rate for paranoia within the general population should fall somewhere between 0.7 percent and 1.5 percent, or even double or triple that percentage, say, 3 percent to 5 percent, if you assume that many of these states never get detected. Since no past surveys ever studied the rulers of nations to discover what percentage of them went beyond the normal bounds of suspiciousness in their dealings with others, no conclusive information yet exists about what percentage of them have been psychotic, paranoid, or delusional at some point in their lives. Fortunately, we are now in a position to partly remedy this lack.

According to the criteria used in my study, 4 percent of the sample of rulers were definitely paranoid, and an additional 9 percent were probably so, for a combined 13 percent, which is substantially above any estimates for the general population at large. Among the different categories of rulers, visionaries (68 percent) and tyrants (55 percent) were most likely to be paranoid, and rulers of established democracies (3 percent) were the least likely. See figure 7.6.

and that their suspiciousness exceeded normal bounds. Judge for yourself from the following sampling of rulers.

Examples of "paranoia":

- Nicholae Ceausescu lost all sense of proportion after a key man in Romania's espionage system defected to the United States. In the witch-hunt that followed the defection, he got rid of whatever talent was left in his inner circle, forcing his wife, Elena, to take over more responsibilities. Growing even more suspicious of everybody, he insisted that his food be first inspected by a hospital laboratory, certifying that it had no contaminants, and then be tried out on an official taster. When he traveled abroad, he took along his own dietitian,

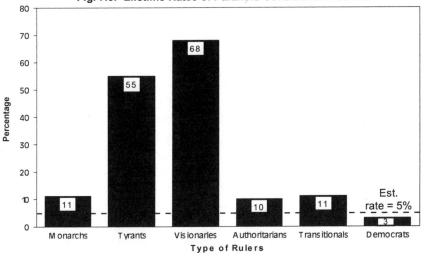

Fig. 7.6: Lifetime Rates of Paranoid Conditions in Rulers

Legend: Except for democrats, all other ruler groups show higher rates of paranoia than reported in the ECA study for the U.S. population at large. Exceptionally high rates of paranoia are found in tyrants and visionaries.

taster, and approved food supplies. Constantly preoccupied with coups, he constructed an elaborate maze of underground tunnels as a potential escape route, which were connected to his residence and government buildings.[36]

• Habib Bourguiba, ruler of Tunisia, became so paranoid in his last years that he dismissed his loyal friend as prime minister, divorced his devoted wife of many years for intriguing, and fired and banished his son, who was to be his successor.

• Because of Saddam Hussein's grandiosity, cruelty, extreme suspiciousness, constant preoccupation with plots and conspiracies, and the extreme precautions he took against being assassinated, a surgeon who treated him diagnosed him as having a clear case of "paranoia."[37] Saddam was so fearful about been overthrown that he slept in a different house every night, had an official taster, and hired at least one full-time double who would take off in a different direction whenever Hussein traveled and maybe even conducted certain official functions, like dedicating monuments to himself.

• Pol Pot was so paranoid that he made few public appearances even when in power, concealed his identity, changed residences frequently, and warned of treachery from every quarter. Whenever he had a stomach ailment, he believed his cooks were trying to poison him.

When the power at his residence failed, he had the maintenance workers killed. This fear of treachery—by foreign nations or by poisonous "microbes" within his own organization—dominated his behavior, from his personal secretiveness to the bloody purges he launched during his revolution beginning in 1977. Speaking before his followers in 1976, he warned, "We search for the microbes within the party without success; they are buried. As our socialist revolution advances, however, seeping into every corner of the party, the army and among the people, we can locate the ugly microbes."[38]

• Sekou Toure, president of Guinea, instituted the largest purge in modern West African history against imagined enemies who supposedly were engaged in conspiracies or were hatching bizarre plots to overthrow him. No group or profession was immune to his suspicions, including the military and doctors. Toure believed that a medicine shortage in 1972 was a physicians' plot. He even saw Guinea's defeat in the 1976 African Soccer Championship finals as a plot, and launched purges and arrests. His speeches became increasingly inarticulate as he offered irrational justifications for his actions against these satanic counterrevolutionary forces.[39]

• Idi Amin's predecessor and later successor, Milton Obote, likewise became increasingly suspicious and removed from reality, almost to the point of incapacitation, after two failed assassination attempts against him. He hardly went out in public and spent more and more time reviewing reports of thwarted assassination plots that his special police manufactured because they knew that was what he wanted to hear. At times, this taxed their imaginations, but they realized that, if they did not comply, he would accuse them of being in league with the conspirators.

• Eric Williams, longtime prime minister of independent Trinidad and Tobago (1962–81), became increasingly suspicious over the years and began leveling fantastic charges about an absurd Chinese coalition conspiring against him.[40]

• Muammar Qaddafi reportedly takes extraordinary precautions against being attacked. When he leaves his barracks, two convoys of armored cars take off in opposite directions, one as a decoy and the other with him. When he flies, two planes take off. The jet he plans to use flies for up to two hours before he boards in case a bomb, triggered by altitude, has been hidden onboard. He often won't announce his arrival in other countries until the plane is in their air space. And he considers all Western ambassadors and diplomats as spies and won't deal with them, a belief that may not be without foundation.

• Macias Nguema, president of Equatorial Guinea, became increasingly paranoid and mistrustful and began surrounding himself only with clan members and family. He only would eat food that was prepared by relatives and had been imported from Spain. He once ordered the table laid for eight people, then sat down alone and kept up a conversation with the dead people for whom the table had been set. He constantly heard voices, which sometimes interrupted him during a speech. As signs of his growing grandiosity and irrationality, he ordered the electricity generating plant to stop using lubricating oil because he claimed only his magical powers were necessary. He still clung to his claim even after the plant blew up.[41]

• When under stress, Abdul Hamid's morbid strain of suspiciousness turned into frank paranoia. As he got older, he became increasingly preoccupied with his personal safety, mistrusted everybody, lived in constant fear of assassination, surrounded himself with informers, and blamed all domestic and international crises on some conspiracy or another. In addition, he refused to submit to surgical operations, carried a revolver at all times, and was overly fearful about being poisoned. Sometimes his paranoia made him so agitated that he could not function for days.

The paranoid lifestyle:

The situation with President (and self-proclaimed king) Zogu of Albania offers a representative portrait of a paranoid ruler who can become almost incapacitated by his security arrangements.[42] Zogu spent most of his time shut away in his palace, working in his overheated office and chain-smoking cigarettes while poring over reports of his informants. His mother, who lived in a villa near the palace, prepared his meals and had an armed guard deliver them to Zogu's office in a locked container. When receiving visitors, Zogu sat warily behind his desk, ready to grab the revolver that was covered by a handkerchief on his desk if he noticed any unexpected movement. Heaven help a visitor if he should suddenly have to sneeze and reflexively reach for a hanky. Zogu also carried his gun with him as he wandered about the palace and often drew it on the slightest provocation. The information is not available on how many ministers and aides he accidentally managed to kill because they happened to scratch themselves inadvertently at a time when he happened to walk by, but I suspect the number is substantial.

On those rare occasions when Zogu did leave his house, he usually followed a prescribed routine. He felt relatively safe from attack when he left the palace in the company of his mother because it was contrary to Albanian custom to risk the safety of women in blood feuds. When Zogu did appear in public unattended, as when he took a short horseback ride for relaxation, he never announced these outings. Once he mounted the horse, he immediately took off at a fast gallop while a detachment of his cavalry followed, frantically trying to keep up. When on his way to an official function, Zogu never traveled without a large contingent of troops of his own loyal Mati tribesmen. He kept his travel plans secret until the last moment and then changed them abruptly again once he was under-way. On his way to parliament, his security troops cleared the roads of people; closed up any doors or windows behind which a potential assassin might lurk; lined the streets with troops, police, and secret agents; and clipped the branches off trees and cut back any bushes large enough for potential assailants to hide behind. He often rode down streets quickly in an armored car, built to protect him against bullets and bombs, and arrived at his destination much earlier than scheduled, then fumed over why those he visited kept him waiting. As a brilliant solution to keep from ever being attacked during his travels and as a way to save money on security precautions, he eventually got to the point that he hardly ever left his palace, except for in summer when the heat of the city be-came unbearable.

Perhaps the ruler who elevated paranoia to an art form was Joseph Stalin, who would react to any criticism of his policies or any bad news or any hesitancy on the part of his staff as if it was a personal attack on him. Aside from the customary practice by paranoid rulers of sleeping in different bedrooms at random or taking precautions about being poi-soned, Stalin saw potential conspiracies everywhere, even refusing to be treated by a dentist or having a doctor examine him when he became sick, especially at the time he launched his infamous "doctor's plot." Stalin apparently saw himself as a great man facing a hostile world peopled with jealous and treacherous enemies who were conspiring to pull him down if he did not destroy them first. Since he regarded his judgment as infallible, he was always on the lookout for evidence of these supposed conspiracies, even when it came from the forced confessions of the imag-ined perpetrators. In this atmosphere of fear and distrust, he was sure to find members of his entourage whose loyalty was less than total, con-firming what he knew all along. During the period of forced collectiviza-tion, his paranoia ran rampant. He blamed his victims for everything that went wrong. He trusted no one but himself. Enemies lurked everywhere, even among his closest collaborators. He believed that even his own wife had betrayed him by committing suicide.[43] Stalin's daughter, Svetlana, wrote: "When the 'facts' convinced my father that someone he knew well had turned out 'badly' after all, a psychological metamorphosis came over him. . . . At this point, and this was where his cruel, implacable nature showed itself, the past ceased to exist for him. Years of friendship and fighting side by side in a common cause might as well never have been. He could wipe it all out at a stroke—and X would be doomed. 'So, you've betrayed me,' some inner demon would whisper. 'I don't even know you any more.'"[44] And so, once he began entertaining even his slightest suspicion about someone's loyalty—and his pervasive paranoia predisposed him to do this continually—there was no turning back. His mind immediately marshaled forth the necessary evidence to buttress his conviction that he cleverly had uncovered yet another person who was planning to betray him.

Although a paranoid orientation toward ruling seems more suited for dictatorial rule, it is not uncommon to find instances of it among the democratic leaders who feel under siege by their political opponents, the popular press, or public protests against their policies. While these situational instances of extreme suspiciousness do not qualify as paranoid states, they do bear a certain resemblance. When under attack, these rulers tend to overreact, see potential enemies lurking everywhere, and become highly defensive. Toward the end of World War II, for instance, Charles de Gaulle's judgments and convictions at times bordered on paranoia after his various dealings with the British and Americans. According to one of his biographers, he twisted and interpreted even minor or innocuous happenings as signs of Anglo-Saxon plotting against him.[45] Toward the end of his term in office, Lyndon B. Johnson became increasingly suspicious and vindictive toward the press and certain "intellectuals" who, he believed, were unjustly blaming him for Vietnam.[46] President Nixon ruled with a siege mentality after the revelations of Watergate and began to view all "liberals" and Eastern "intellectuals" as his enemies. The major difference, of course, between democrats who get highly suspicious under stressful circumstances and dictators is that the democrats have more limited options in responding to these perceived threats. However, if they had held absolute power, their vindictiveness might have taken other forms.

The advantages of being paranoid:

There is still another way to look at this situation. Although paranoia is an abnormal condition, it is not always a political liability. Many leaders are able to exploit their beliefs in conspiracies and misinformation about the intentions of various ethnic, religious, or racial groups for their political advantage. Hitler, of course, proclaimed that the Jews had stabbed Germany in the back after World War I with the Versailles Treaty and were a threat to the entire Aryan race. Stalin saw the kulaks as betraying the revolution, and his definition of a kulak progressively expanded to include almost anyone with financial initiative, a notion that was not unacceptable for many peasants. Ruhollah Khomeini promoted the notion of a satanic conspiracy by Jews and the United States as a way of capitalizing on the xenophobia of the Iranian people. Mao Zedong launched the Cultural Revolution as a way of countering the perceived threat of the intellectuals and liberals against his power.

One of the problems in judging how pathological it is for leaders to be preoccupied with conspiracies, plots, and coups, no matter how preposterous their reasoning or how flimsy their evidence, is the reality that they do have enemies among their own people who would like to kill them and others who want to overthrow them. Just how much suspiciousness is realistic and adaptive and how much is psychotic and maladaptive is sometimes hard to say. It depends on your criteria. In the field of politics, if your criteria for adaptive behavior is doing what keeps you alive, then the proof is in the pudding. The most opportunistic rulers are those who get rid of all opposition before the opposition gets rid of them, even if many of the opposition are figments of their imaginations. Stalin, Pol Pot, Mao, Saddam Hussein, Muammar Qadaffi, and Tito, for example, who wielded tremendous power over a long span of time, were ruthless in their elimination of political opponents and potential enemies. In contrast, you could say that Indira Gandhi, Zulfikar Bhutto, Rajiv Gandhi, and John F. Kennedy, who were assassinated or executed, were not "paranoid" enough. Which of these groups is the sanest and most rational—the one that managed to avoid being killed in office or the one that did not?

It may not be much of a life for a ruler to have to be constantly on guard, have food-tasters, sleep in different rooms or homes every night, or hire imposters to act like him, but at least he stays alive and rules a while longer than those who supposedly are more mentally stable than he. By ruthlessly taking steps to destroy all his real and imagined enemies, he may be delusional, paranoid, and maladjusted by the usual mental health standards, but by the rules of the political jungle, which reward survival more than mental stability, he paradoxically may be more socially adaptive than if he was completely rational and sane.

THE SPECIAL PROBLEM OF PERSONALITY DISTURBANCES

In the field of clinical psychiatry, there are two categories of diagnoses: symptomatic disorders such as depression, anxiety, mania, or schizophrenia, which are mostly associated with disturbances in mood, thought, and behavior in afflicted individuals, and personality disorders, which mainly are associated with disturbances in relationships with other people. Because so much of political behavior involves dealing with other people and, in particular, manipulating them to achieve certain desired ends, I originally set out to document the existence of personality disorders within rulers, expecting the rate to be fairly high. But no sooner did I start to do so than I hit a conceptual brick wall. The problem had to do with the nature of personality disorders, especially as applied to rulers. Here are some of the issues.

Let's start with the definition of personality disorders. According to the tenth revision of the *International Classification of Diseases* (ICD-10), which essentially mirrors the position adopted in the *Diagnostic and Statistical Manual (IV-Revised)* of the American Psychiatric Association, personality disorders should meet the following criteria (each of which, in my opinion, is either imprecise or unclear):

- They are deeply ingrained and enduring behavior patterns, manifesting themselves as inflexible responses to a broad range of personal and social situations. *(But so, too, are most human traits, fixed attitudes, and firm beliefs.)*
- They represent either extreme or significant deviations from the way the average individual in a given culture perceives, thinks, feels, and, particularly, relates to others. *(To my knowledge, no scientific studies to date have documented the way an average individual in a given culture perceives, thinks, feels, and, particularly, relates to others. Besides, who is this "average individual" that this criterion refers to?)*
- These behavior patterns tend to be stable and to encompass multiple domains of behavior and psychological functioning. *(Yes, but so, too, by definition, does any behavior pattern.)*
- They are frequently associated with various degrees of subjective distress and impaired social functioning, and, according to the DSM-IV-R, occupational functioning as well. *(But with rulers, their behavior patterns enable them to become highly successful in their social and occupational functioning. More on this matter below.)*

These ambiguous criteria for personality disorders are problematic enough, but there are other difficulties as well. One of the reasons I have become opposed to the use of personality disorder diagnoses has to do with their negative connotations. As it happens, virtually all of the diagnostic features for any personality disorder involve unsavory character traits such as self-centeredness, narcissism, schizoid withdrawal, impulsiveness, attention-seeking, manipulativeness, uncontrolled anger, or inflexibility. So whether clinicians realize it or not, whenever they diagnose personality disorders, they are making pejorative judgments about people, indicating that they not only are unlikable and unpleasant but are difficult, ungrateful, and untreatable as well. Judgments of this kind are apt to be especially biased and unreliable with political figures. Since politicians commonly have a polarizing effect on the populace, opinions about their character traits are likely to vary greatly depending upon whether they happen to be expressed by their admirers or their detractors, as well as at what point in their reign they are given.

These are formidable problems, but perhaps the biggest conceptual problem has to do with the most important feature of personality disturbances—namely, *the trouble these persons have functioning in society and succeeding in their jobs.* This feature presents special difficulties in the case of rulers. Within my sample of rulers, there certainly are many who have shown character traits commonly found in persons with personality disorders—emotional instability, vanity, lying, exploitation, impulsiveness, inappropriate anger, or mistrustfulness— that are bound to contribute to rocky relationships with their spouses, children, colleagues, and superiors. But despite these character traits, these particular rulers, by definition, cannot qualify as having a personality disorder, since their attitudes and behaviors are not socially or vocationally maladaptive. In fact, the paradox is that perhaps because of these very traits, which are not considered to be normal for ordinary people, *those would-be rulers actually manage to achieve the greatest social and occupational success possible for any humans*—becoming the heads of their nations and being looked up to by a large segment of the populace. Some of them even achieve a quasi-divine status. With this the case, I did not see how I legitimately could diagnose the existence of personality disorders in individuals who capitalized on their supposedly undesirable character traits to gain the highest position in the land.

THE SEARCH FOR PATTERNS

Now that we have examined the lifetime rates for each of these different psychiatric syndromes in rulers, we are in a position to identify patterns of syndromes within each of the different types of rulers. Table 7.1 below summarizes the various findings.

Impressionistically, what these findings show is that each of the different kinds of rulers seems to have a distinct pattern of "psychopathology." Monarchs are most prone to anxiety. Tyrants are the most likely to be emotionally disturbed, showing the highest rates of alcoholism, drug use, mania, paranoia, and an assortment of other unspecified conditions. In contrast, they are the least likely to suffer from serious depression. Visionaries are prone to depression, mania, and paranoia, along with some miscellaneous related syndromes. While the leaders of emerging and established democracies have a heightened tendency for depression, they, along with authoritarians, are the least likely to have any form of mental disturbance.

Table 7.1: Different Psychiatric Syndromes in Rulers
Lifetime Rates (%)

	Monarchs	Tyrants	Visionaries	Authoritarians	Transitionals	Democrats
Alcoholism	_11_	**41**	_8_	16	13	15
Drug Use	6	23	16	_3_	_4_	_2_
Depression	17	_0_	**24**	9	15	15
Mania	11	**23**	20	_4_	6	_3_
Anxiety	**19**	5	20	_3_	6	7
Paranoia	11	55	**68**	10	11	_3_
Unclassified	8	14	**20**	_7_	_6_	12
Any Syndrome	64	**91**	76	_48_	_51_	_49_

Legend: The numbers in bold type indicate the rulers with the highest percentage of individuals with that particular disorder. The numbers italicized and underlined indicate the rulers with the lowest percentage of individuals with that particular disorder. The "Unclassified" category refers to vague, nonspecific conditions such as "nervous breakdowns," "nervous exhaustion," or a prolonged state of "emotional numbness."

Psychiatric Comorbidity

With the establishment of the lifetime rates for these different psychiatric syndromes or for the presence of any psychiatric syndrome, we now need to answer the question of whether rulers who have one kind of mental disturbance are likely to have another. A different perspective of mental illness arises if the same people have the bulk of all the emotional disorders than if the different disorders are distributed uniformly over all members of the group.

Another way of representing the above results is simply to calculate the average number of distinct psychiatric syndromes for rulers within each group occurring during their lifetimes. The bar graph below shows these statistically significant differences among the different groups. As with the comorbidity results, visionaries (2.1) and tyrants (1.7) average almost two psychiatric syndromes each as a group; monarchs (1.1), transitionals (0.8), and established democrats (0.8) average about one; and, as expected from all the above results, authoritarians (0.7) average the least (see figure 7.7). Later in the chapter, I will try to account for these differences.

Lifetime Comorbidity Results: According to the results of the National Comorbidity Survey, 52 percent of a national sample had no psychiatric disorders, 21 percent had one, 13 percent had two, and 14 percent had three or more.[47] The finding that more than 50 percent of those with at least one lifetime disorder had two or more disorders suggested that most psychiatric disorders tended to be concentrated in a group of highly comorbid persons. The results with my sample of rulers are similar. Forty percent had no psychiatric disorders, 28 percent had one, 17 percent had two, and 15 percent had three or more. This meant that over 50 percent of rulers with at least one emotional disorder had two or more psychiatric syndromes during their lifetimes.

Among the different categories of rulers, tyrants (55 percent) had the highest rate of comorbidity, defined as having two or more psychiatric syndromes, with visionaries (53 percent) a close second. On the second tier were monarchs (31 percent), transitionals (22 percent), and democrats (22 percent). The rulers least likely to suffer from two or more psychiatric disturbances were authoritarians (14 percent). They are the emotional equivalent of the Rock of Gibraltar.

Fig. 7.7: Total Number of Psychiatric Syndromes in Rulers

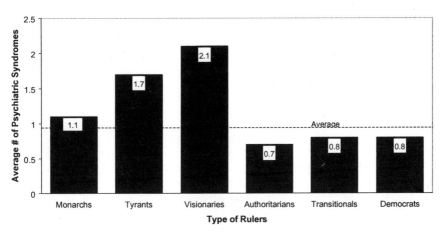

Legend: The figures in each bar indicate the average number of distinct psychiatric syndromes for each group of rulers occurring during their lifetimes.

NEUROFIBRILLARY TANGLES AND DEMENTIA

With responsibility for making decisions that can affect the lives and welfare of their people, rulers are expected to be of sound mind, which means not only being emotionally stable but also having all of their mental faculties intact. In fact, in most democratic nations, there are constitutional provisions for removing a leader from office if he is deemed to be cognitively impaired. By cognitively impaired, I mean the relative inability of a leader to comprehend verbal or written communications, to make his intentions known, to remember critical information, to pay attention to important matters, to be able to solve problems, or to extrapolate from one set of circumstances to another. Gradual deficiencies in memory and mental agility may be part of the normal aging process, but when they are more than what might be expected, they represent a form of dementia.

Dementia can be caused by many factors, ranging from Alzheimer's disease to head injuries, strokes, and vitamin deficiencies. Regardless of the cause, all forms are associated with brain damage, neuronal loss, or destruction of cortical tissue and, in contrast to delirium, which is reversible, tend to be persistent, irreversible, and sometimes progressive. Because dementia can profoundly affect judgment, you might think that its presence should automatically disqualify rulers from holding office. Yet it is the nature of politics that rulers can be not only illiterate, ignorant, or mentally disturbed but, as it happens, seriously demented as well, even in supposedly advanced countries.

The detection of dementia:

In documenting whether rulers suffered from dementia, I decided to use a lower threshold for identifying it, mainly to compensate for the practice of governments to hide that information from the public. In the absence of medical documentation, I sometimes accepted statements by reliable observers about a ruler's impaired state of mind as presumptive evidence of dementia (or at least impaired brain functioning), especially when there was a medical reason to do so. For example, if a ruler suffered from several strokes, advanced kidney failure, tertiary syphilis, or severe alcoholism, and informants commented on his failing mental faculties, I relied on my clinical experience to judge whether some degree of dementia existed (perhaps also complicated by delirium).

The results revealed that about one in every twenty rulers showed signs of being demented at some point during his reign. By far, visionaries showed the highest percentage of those affected, about one in five. Figure 7.8 below shows these differences.

There is no way to be sure about the reason for these differences. My guess is that if tyrants showed significant signs of impaired memory, comprehension, problem-solving, or abstraction, they would not last long in power. They are not necessarily the smartest or most charming rulers, nor do they inspire great loyalty among their backers, so they need all of their wits about them simply to survive in office, and, even so, they do not do too good a job at that. The likely reason for the absence of dementia in transitional leaders is that they need to stay mentally sharp to handle all the complexities of running a newly independent democratic nation and cannot use force to stifle criticism from opponents who might pounce on any of their mental deficiencies. In contrast, the likely reason

> *Lifetime Rates of Dementia:* Within the sample of rulers, 5 percent appeared to be cognitively impaired while in office. Among the different groups of rulers, visionaries (20 percent) were most likely to suffer from dementia, especially toward the latter part of their terms, while tyrants (0 percent) and transitionals (0 percent) were the least likely.

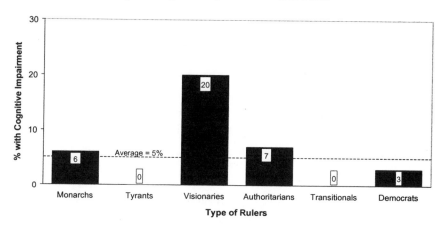

Fig. 7.8: Cognitive Impairment While in Office

Legend: Visionaries show the highest percentages of individuals with dementia or cognitive impairment of all groups of rulers.

for the relatively high percentage of dementia in visionaries, who are expected to be dreamers anyway, is because many of them remain in power even in their waning years, and their listeners may not be able to differentiate what they say in a nondemented state from what they say with increasing dementia. As long as they keep their zeal, passion, and ruthlessness and espouse a confusing ideology and as long as their subjects revere them, being demented need not keep them from ruling, especially when their existing personality cult continues to transform their deficiencies into virtues.

Examples of impaired cognitive functioning:

There are many kinds of dementia. The brief examples that follow show some of the ways it appeared in rulers. The examples also show some of the problems in getting detailed and accurate information about the actual brain pathology to make a definitive diagnosis, mainly because the rulers and their governments and their families do not want this information known.

• Alfred Deakin, prime minister of Australia (1903–4, 1905–8, 1909–10), disqualified himself from office because of his rapidly failing memory. By 1913 he began showing clear signs of Alzheimer's disease. In his diary, he wrote, rather pathetically, "Life has ended—in truth in fact & in judgment—None can know, not even my self,—what once I was capable of doing or did. The bell has struck its last final warning. My memory is but a little fiction, a chance return of the pitiful & a withering memorial of AD." (NB: AD=Alfred Deakin, although the same abbreviation often is used for Alzheimer's disease.)[48]

• During the last years of his reign, Habib Bourguiba had probably become senile. Based on the information available to them, a team of psychiatrists signed a document to that effect although they had not examined him in person.

• In 1949, Winston Churchill had a light stroke. After another stroke in 1951, he went downhill medically and emotionally. By 1954, colleagues noted his failing mental faculties, his increasing difficulty with speeches, and his trouble carrying out his duties as prime minister. Still, Churchill had so much reserve brain power that, even with the damage cause by his strokes (and perhaps his many years of heavy drinking), he continued to surprise people with his occasional witticisms and perceptive comments.

• Woodrow Wilson had the first of a series of strokes at the age of thirty-nine. In 1919 he had a massive stroke, followed by a paralysis of the left side of his body and marked mental changes. Within the White House, his wife and members of his staff tried to cover up his failing cognitive abilities and made major presidential decisions in his stead.

• Antonio de Oliveira Salazar suffered a severe stroke in 1968. Despite his mental debilitation, he remained officially in charge of the country for about three weeks. At that time, when it became obvious that he would not recover his mental faculties, the president of Portugal and some of Salazar's ministers and close political collaborators perpetrated a pious conspiracy to protect him from the knowledge that he had been replaced by Marcello Caetano, who was appointed acting prime minister, while Salazar was allowed to keep his now titular position for life. Until his death in 1970, Salazar remained oblivious to this bizarre ruse and continued to issue orders as dictator, while those closest to him went through the motions of complying. Salazar was so unaware of what was going on that, during an interview with a French journalist, he mentioned that Caetano, who now was effectively ruling the country, was out of politics. And when Dona Maria de Jesus, his lifelong housekeeper, kept trying to persuade him to retire because of his age and poor health, Salazar repeatedly answered that he could not because there was no one else.[49]

• Toward the end of his rule, Mao Zedong's health continued to deteriorate until he eventually was unable to speak coherently. Most accounts claim that he suffered from advanced Parkinsonism, although his personal physician said he had amyotrophic lateral sclerosis. Other accounts made mention of a stroke as well as heart and kidney failure. Authoritative rumors also surfaced that Mao had become "senile."[50]

• Harold Wilson, prime minister of the United Kingdom from 1964 to 1970 and from 1974 to 1976, began showing signs of mental deterioration at the age of sixty, either as a result of alcoholic dementia or early Alzheimer's disease. He had lost the capacity for original thought and had begun confabulating to cover up his increasing difficulties with short-term memory.[51]

• Sukarno, Indonesia's first president, began showing signs of mental impairment during his last years in power, which may have been due to his advanced kidney disease.

• Menelik II, king of Shewa (or Shoa, 1865–89) and emperor of Ethiopia (1889–1913), had been infected with syphilis as a youth. Despite showing neurological evidence of advanced syphilis, including seizures; decreased tendon reflexes; several strokes, followed by general paralysis after a major one; and signs of "senility," he continued to rule his kingdom until his death.

• Since November 1995, King Fahd of Saudi Arabia had survived several strokes and major surgery and was confined to a wheelchair. Although he responded politely to conversations, recent visitors came away with the impression that "he is not fully engaged."[52]

• Although not holding an official title, Jozef Pilsudski remained the most powerful person in Poland until his death in 1935 at the age of sixty-seven. At least one year before his death, certain observers noted that his mind had failed and that he showed signs of senility.

Doonesbury and Ronald Reagan:

Perhaps the most intriguing case of dementia involves Ronald Reagan, president of the United States from 1980 to 1988. It is hard to pin down exactly when Reagan's Alzheimer's disease began, because he showed certain cognitive features of a mild dementia long before it was officially diagnosed in 1994—a difficulty forming close meaningful relationships; significant memory gaps, especially recent memory; problems with sustaining attention; and a remote, disengaged quality. After his Alzheimer's disease was no longer a secret, his son, Ronald Prescott Reagan, reputedly said in a documentary that, while Alzheimer's was a terrible thing, some of the pain may be lessened by the fact that things have not changed that much because he was not missing something that he had before. One of his biographers, in an interview, claimed that Reagan first showed signs of dementia after he was shot in 1981, seven years before he left office.[53] Over that period, there were a number of telling observations, no single one of special diagnostic significance but, together, a strong indication that something was mentally amiss.[54,55] During his second term, he allegedly seemed unaware at first of the switch between his chief of staff, James Baker, and his secretary of the treasury, Donald Regan. At the 1987 Iran-Contra Senate hearings, his memory gaps were so bad that many assumed he was being deliberately evasive, although he may not have been.

With remarkable prescience, Garry Trudeau first launched a series of *Doonesbury* cartoons in 1980 having to do with Roland Hedley's search of Reagan's brain.[56] In his visit to the left hemisphere of Reagan's cerebrum; the home of logic, analysis, and critical thinking; Hedley, bedecked for his expedition in a Sherlock-Holmes hat and parka, noted that many of the nerves in that part of the brain were frayed. Seven years later, Trudeau had Hedley return to Reagan's brain to try to jar loose Iranscam memories. Traveling with a sherpa, Hedley comments, "What a bleak, ravaged landscape greets us. Cranial coils lay heaped in lifeless disarray. Neurons are stretched and frayed, their dendritic spines worn away. In short, nothing has changed."

All told, what Trudeau did, whether intentionally or not, was to give a reasonably good neuroanatomical description of the neurofibrillary tangles and senile plaques within the brain tissue that tend to be diagnostic of Alzheimer's disease. Although observations of this sort about the soundness of the president's mind should be vital to the security and welfare of the country, many publishers refused to print this series of cartoons, and, for all intents and purposes, no one officially raised the issue of Reagan's competence or mental fitness to rule the nation during his entire term in office. To Reagan's credit, his sense of humor never failed him even as he was fading out mentally. When shown the wickedly vicious *Doonesbury* cartoons, he graciously commented, "Cartoonists occupy a special place in my heart. I hope that Garry Trudeau will remember that. It's heart. Not brain, heart."

Now that we have established the presence of dementia in rulers, we need to address a question nobody has bothered to ask before: Does it make any substantial difference to the fate of a nation if its ruler is demented? As it happens, I could find no instances among all the rulers of the twentieth century in which their becoming demented led to any worse consequences for the nation as a whole or any more suffering, casualties, or deaths for their subjects than when their brain functioning was intact. It is not the dementia of rulers that leads to tragic consequences for others; it is their corrupt practices, their repressive tactics, or their grandiose schemes. While demented, they often can barely remember from one moment to the next what they wanted to give orders about, and, when they do manage to remember, their aides simply act out the farce of obeying, as they did with Salazar. Or their spouse may rule covertly on their behalf, as happened with Woodrow Wilson. Or a pretender for high office simply displaces them.

Then, of course, there is the special case of Ronald Reagan, who likely suffered from a mild dementia during his second term in office and who, arguably, may find a place in history as one of the great American presidents. What this suggests is that, even with an impairment in memory and concentration, a ruler may still inspire his nation and be credited with important accomplishments provided his personality, communication skills, and overall judgment remain intact (and he surrounds himself with reasonably competent and responsible people), all of which are possible during the early stages of Alzheimer's disease.

MENTAL ILLNESS OR WHAT?

Here is the fundamental question: If mental illness, by definition, is supposed to be associated with a decline in social functioning, then how do you explain the findings that those rulers who wield the most power and authority, who operate with the least governmental restraints—namely, tyrants and visionaries—show the highest rates of alcoholism, drug abuse, mania and paranoia during their lifetimes and (along with monarchs) have the highest lifetime rates for any psychiatric illness or combinations of psychiatric illnesses? If mental illness is supposed to impair social functioning, then those suffering from it should be least likely to get what most people want most—wealth, power, and fame. But with rulers the reverse seems to be true. With the exception of authoritarians, who appear to be the most mentally stable of the lot, those rulers with the least executive powers, the least opportunities to accumulate fabulous wealth, and the least prospects of exerting godlike powers—namely, democrats and transitionals—are the least likely to show any kind of emotional disturbance. This seeming paradox forces us to examine what we mean by mental illness and whether, under certain special conditions, certain mental disturbances such as alcoholism, depression, drug use, paranoia, mania or anxiety actually help certain rulers achieve their goals. If so, then perhaps these so-called psychological "disturbances" should be regarded as social "facilitators" in the case of rulers.

Special Condition #1

The situational aspects of "psychopathology":
What represents a mental disturbance under one set of circumstances may not under another. For instance, if a would-be ruler was impulsive, emotionally volatile, and grandiose before achieving absolute power, you would regard him as showing socially maladaptive behavior ("psychopathology") because it would alienate his superiors and colleagues and keep him from advancing up the political or military ladder. In a regimented or bureaucratic setting, with standard operating procedures and clear lines of authority, the successful aspirant for high office not only would have to keep these socially abrasive, undesirable behaviors in check but also would have to act the part of an exemplary officer or bureaucrat, much as many of the tyrants, caudillos, and apparatchiks managed to do before they gained ultimate power. Once the would-be ruler gained absolute authority, then the old rules no longer would apply. Those actions that were socially maladaptive before become interpreted in a new light. Impulsiveness becomes transformed into decisiveness, volatility into passion, and grandiosity into ambitiousness. Also, since the ruler now need not worry about antagonizing his superiors, he could act however he damned well pleased.

As I noted before, paranoia is a good example of a behavior that can be maladaptive under certain circumstances and adaptive under others. It may be a handicap for democratic leaders because of the necessity for forging alliances with various groups, but it may be advantageous for dictators. Once they gain power, dictators, who had previously managed to keep their suspiciousness under wraps, now need to become acutely aware of the greater likelihood of assassination attempts, coups, or subversive plots. As they should know from their own past experience, whenever subordinates get close to the seat of power, they are apt to begin having sugar-plum fantasies of sitting on it themselves. Therefore, if dictators want to impose absolute rule, they would be foolish not to become extremely suspicious not only of potential challengers but even those they hire to protect themselves against usurpers. The price of freedom may be eternal vigilance but so, too, is the price of keeping freedom under wraps.

Special Condition #2

A personal palette of "psychopathology":
Each of the different types of rulers seems to have its favorite variety of mental disturbances. Tyrants show more alcoholism and drug use than other rulers. Tyrants and visionaries show more mania. Monarchs and visionaries show more depression and anxiety. What these statistically significant findings suggest is that certain kinds of emotional disturbances seem more suitable for certain kinds of rule than others do. In a broad sense, any mental disturbances that increase personal confidence, mental acuity, and alertness—for instance, mania, drug use, alcoholism, paranoia—should be favored by dictatorial leaders who rely on the force of their personalities and armed force as the basis for their authority. Leaders who are grandiose, talkative, euphoric, extravagant, and paranoid should be better suited for the role of visionary or tyrant than for the role of democrat or authoritarian. In the former roles, these sorts of behavioral excesses can potentially increase the personal basis of the ruler's authority; in the latter roles, these same behavioral excesses may decrease it.

Conversely, depression and anxiety may be the most maladaptive kinds of emotional responses for dictators. When they are depressed and anxious, rulers are likely to relax their vigilance and let down their emotional guards. Or even if they remain wary or fearful about being deposed, depression and anxiety are apt to lessen their self-confidence and make it more difficult for them to make decisions and cope with affairs of state. When severe, depression and anxiety can be immobilizing and incapacitating. Obviously, rulers prone to prolonged bouts of serious depression usually do not fare well as tyrants, who, by virtue of their rule, need to be able to act decisively when necessary. As an aid in fending off depression, the psychological makeup of tyrants lets them blame others for any of their failings, so they never need to suffer from self-recriminations or personal doubts. Because of these factors, it makes practical sense that tyrants should be the least likely rulers to suffer from depression.

With many exceptions, the need to remain constantly vigilant seems to be less so for visionaries and monarchs, who, unlike tyrants, tend to bind their followers to them on the basis of ideology or established tradition. Seeing themselves as one with their people or the embodiment of their nation, they are less apt to rule under a siege mentality. As a result, they have the luxury of being able to withdraw into periods of depression as long as they are not too extended. In the case of leaders of emerging or established democracies, in which constitutional mechanisms exist for fixed terms in office and smooth transitions of power, they also can have lapses into depression without being at too great a political disadvantage. Also, in a strange sort of way, a dash of depression, which may cause rulers to seem more sober, reasonable, and reflective, actually may be advantageous to them within certain parliamentary or democratic forms of government in which debate, consensus, and coalition-building are more valued than autocratic rule. Certainly, one must wonder if susceptibility to depression is a requirement for becoming a British prime minister.

Special Condition #3

Political situations shape the nature of the mental disturbance:
The political condition the leader finds himself in may be responsible for the expression of certain latent tendencies within him that never might have been realized under other circumstances. When a dictator holds absolute power and has a personality cult proclaiming his greatness and his sycophants treat him with deference and his televised speeches are proclaimed to be brilliant by his own press and people do whatever he says, he may begin to show much of the grandiosity and ebullience associated with mania, even if he has masterminded all this hullabaloo himself.

Also, when you combine the natural ambitiousness of certain rulers with the job demands of ruling, you sometimes have trouble telling the difference between real mania and artificially induced mania in them. By immersing themselves in the activity of ruling a nation, rulers may manage to create an artificial "high"—a pseudomania of their own making. In undertaking grand schemes, juggling various projects, coping with assorted crises, constantly interacting with others, spending vast sums of money, working night and day, and being the center of national attention, they not only mimic on a grand scale what many manic persons do in their daily lives but those susceptible to melancholia may even manage to keep the ever-present threat of depression at bay.

Conversely, when leaders live in constant fear for their lives or of being overthrown by potential enemies, they are likely to be revved up, suspicious, anxious, irritable, and emotionally volatile because of their constant state of arousal. In that condition, they are more likely to seek out alcohol or drugs to help them wind down or to offset their dysphoria or to relax or to help them sleep. In certain ways, then, their growing dependence on alcohol and drugs may represent a form of self-medication and a way for them to cope with stress. Also, because they are not accountable to anyone, tyrants or visionaries need not fear arrest for drunken driving or public intoxication or for using contraband drugs, since they themselves determine what is or is not legal. Therefore, when these leaders use heroin, cocaine, or other potentially addicting drugs or get their physicians to give them mind-altering drugs, their drug use may not hold the same clinical significance as for leaders of countries in which these drugs are contraband.

Special Condition #4

Moderation may not be possible:
Although a temperate amount of depression, mania, paranoia, alcohol, drugs, or anxiety may not hamper job performance, rulers often lack the ability to moderate their mood and behavior. Responses that originally start out as "adaptive" may become maladaptive because certain behaviors are self-reinforcing or naturally worsen over time. While it may be essential for rulers to be self-confident and ambitious when they take on the enormous problems of governing a nation, a series of successes in predisposed individuals may cause their self-confidence and ambition to soar and become grandiose, as happens in florid mania, eventually causing them to show poor judgment, megalomania, and impulsiveness. Leaders may start out using alcohol or contraband drugs for medicinal or recreational purposes, as a way to relieve pain, relax, or sleep, but after using them to excess, they begin to suffer from all the adverse consequences of becoming psychologically and physically dependent on them. A certain amount of wariness about the intentions of others may let rulers preserve their power and their lives, but when their suspiciousness turns into frank paranoia, it can become a personal monster that eventually devours them. As I mentioned before, the problem with paranoia is that it feeds on itself and so becomes a self-fulfilling prophesy. The more leaders act to foil suspected assassination attempts or plots to overthrow them, the farther they begin casting the net of their suspiciousness until the haul includes even their most loyal followers—and sometimes, as with Bourguiba, even those closest to them. Also, the paranoid lifestyle isolates these leaders more and more from their people, widening the gulf between them and depriving them of even the simple pleasures of having cronies or fawning subjects trying to curry their favor, and even alienates them from their families.

A Mutual Interaction

These assorted findings warrant three main conclusions. One, mental illness is no bar to ruling. Rulers throughout the world show rates of mental illness comparable to estimates for the United States population at large and, with certain kinds of psychiatric syndromes, considerably higher. Two, different kinds of rulers seem more susceptible to particular kinds of mental disturbances than others. Three, with the exception of authoritarians, rulers wielding the most power tend to display the highest rates of mental illness over the course of their lives.

What the combination of these conclusions suggests is that rulers vulnerable to certain kinds of mental disturbances may be more suited for certain kinds of rule than those with other kinds. For example, would-be rulers with a tendency for mania do not seem as likely to rise to leadership positions within established democracies or governments controlled by the military as in totalitarian societies or emerging nations. Would-be rulers whose moods are predictable and stable fare better in established democracies or bureaucratic governments than in utopian-style societies or governments based on personal rule. Would-be rulers susceptible to depression are not likely to last as long in repressive dictatorships as in parliamentary forms of government. Would-be rulers who are frankly paranoid are more apt to have trouble succeeding in democratic societies than in societies run by force. In other words, would-be rulers tend to gravitate to the kinds of leadership positions and create those kinds of government that let them express their natural tendencies best. In that way, those behaviors that are socially maladaptive in one kind of government can become socially adaptive in another.

Just as would-be rulers with certain kinds of emotional tendencies tend to be drawn to certain kinds of rule, certain kinds of government tend to draw out certain kinds of emotional responses and attitudes from rulers, resulting in an ongoing interaction between these individuals and the situations they find themselves in. Most forms of dictatorial personal rule tend to foster suspiciousness and distrust in rulers and, in many instances, paranoia. Attempts at revamping society or social engineering or expanding national borders induce a sense of grandiosity and manic energy in rulers. Authoritarian types of rule, with the emphasis on discipline, law, and order, discourage the expression of wide mood swings, grandiosity, drug abuse, or excessive suspiciousness in rulers. Monarchical rule, with its emphasis on tradition and divine right, may elicit anxiety and depression in rulers who have to deal with the steady erosion of their authority and the potential extinction of their entire way of life. Democratic systems, which require leaders to work closely with colleagues and, in the case of parliamentary governments, to end their careers as losers after spending limited terms in office, may be evocative of depression. And all kinds of rule, democratic and dictatorial alike, in which the leaders are under attack by critics or their jobs are being threatened, tend to produce a certain degree of paranoia in them depending on their particular psychological dispositions, as well as a greater desire for alcohol and other mind-altering drugs to reduce their tension, insomnia, and stress.

In previous chapters, we saw that would-be rulers with certain kinds of personal attributes were drawn to certain types of rule, or, put differently, that each kind of rule tended to induce rulers to express certain attributes relatively common to it. Now we need to amend that conclusion to take these current observations about mental disturbances into account. Exactly the same situation applies to the different emotional responses in rulers. Certain kinds of emotional "disturbances" may be advantageous for certain kinds of rule and disadvantageous for others. What this shows is that even the presence of certain kinds of "psychopathology" in rulers may suit Nature's purpose well in enabling individuals to compete for ultimate power and then later to function as the heads of nations.

THE MEASURE OF POLITICAL GREATNESS

Alpha males respond aggressively to external disturbances, such as predators or other groups, but also internal circumstances, such as conflicts within the group. Smothering the latter is achieved through direct interference, often by chasing off the aggressor. There is great variation in the effectiveness of control measures. I have known alpha males who could stop a fight by raising an eyebrow or with a single step forward, whereas others only aggravated the situation by getting involved. Competent control requires special skills, such as interceding with just the right amount of force—enough to command respect, yet not so much that everyone would have been better off left alone.

—Frans de Waal, *Good Natured:*
The Origins of Right and Wrong in Humans and Other Animals

One problem in judging the political genius of rulers is knowing what they should get credit for. The situation for rulers is a lot different than for other kinds of professionals. With creative artists, scientists, military commanders, athletes, or surgeons, you have no trouble telling who should get credit for what. Creative artists paint, sculpt, build, and compose works under their own signature. Scientists conduct experiments and publish their results. Athletes compete against others in contests. Military commanders win or lose wars. And surgeons operate on patients and take responsibility for their lives. In contrast, political rulers often rely on expert advisors to help them formulate foreign, domestic, and economic policies. They also may delegate responsibility to their cabinet members, diplomats, and staff to implement these policies or even to start programs of their own. Also, unlike other professionals, they may be credited with the long-term effects of initiatives launched by their predecessors and be blamed for events beyond their control.

Even when you can identify the work products that bear the personal stamp of rulers—laws, construction projects, executive decisions, declarations of war, or even key personnel appointments—you often have no objective way to judge their merits. You can evaluate the creative works of artists, sculptors, actors, architects, or composers by their originality, compositional structure, narrative quality, usefulness, beauty, and universal appeal. You can test the validity of scientific theories in experiments. You can measure the performance of athletes by their times, distances, or scores in competitive events. You can judge the skill of surgeons by their mortality rates. But when you try to assess the accomplishments of rulers, such as the results of their social and economic policies, there are no universally agreed-upon ways to do so. People of different political persuasions often interpret the results of these policies differently. And even if they agree at one point in time, they may disagree at another.

Take the case of Amanullah Khan, ruler of Afghanistan from 1919 to 1929.[1] After he waged a successful holy war against the British, Muslims everywhere hailed him as a hero. Reveling in their adulation, he then took on the task of modernizing and secularizing his country, which was dominated by tribalism, religious orthodoxy, xenophobia, and a 90 percent illiteracy rate. Some of his most ambitious projects were liberating women from purdah and having to wear their veil, a shift from polygamy to monogamy, compulsory elementary education, the elimination of ranks and titles, and the establishment of a fairer tax structure—all those wonderful goals "enlightened" Westerners would admire. But since his people were not enlightened Westerners, he managed in one fell swoop to antagonize almost everybody: tribal leaders, the military, and the religious community. Widespread rebellion throughout his kingdom forced Amanullah, the once revered and almost all-powerful leader, to abdicate his throne and go into permanent exile. Soon afterward, the new ruler ordered Amanullah's name expunged from the history books and erased from the public memory. When he died, his name even was removed from his tomb. Officially, in the public's mind, the once-popular hero never had existed, although no one was imaginative enough to explain away the resulting ten-year calendar gap of his reign from 1919 to 1929. Years later, in a speech, King Zahir disinterred his memory from oblivion and restored the missing years. Now, instead of being ten years younger, people returned to their original age, and children born during those years officially could exist. But this time, with his resurrection, Amanullah was recast as a pitiable, misguided figure.

What Amanullah's reign shows so well is the evanescent and insubstantial nature of many political accomplishments. The products often turn out to be like certain postmodern art happenings that are created to disappear. Nations coalesce into supernations and then fragment into ethnic or regional territories. Movements like communism or naziism threaten world domination and then lose impetus and die. Countries that were once bitter enemies become staunch allies, and former allies become enemies. Great achievements at one point in time become national disasters at another. In this shifting political landscape, you often have trouble finding any objective criteria for political greatness that are immune to political ideology or nationalistic, religious, or ethnic prejudices. The only universal agreement you are apt to get about judging the greatness of rulers is that great leaders are not supposed to plunder, oppress, or murder their own people, but it is all right for them to plunder, oppress, or murder the people of other nations if they have suitable reason or cause.

Unfortunately, the political science literature offers little help on how to measure political greatness objectively across different cultures other than to convene panels of "experts" to rate rulers on ill-defined criteria. Aside from periodic magazine ratings of the fifty or one hundred all-time greatest world leaders, comparisons of the relative achievements of rulers have been few. Among the different rating schemes I have examined, the most ingenious is by D.K. Simonton, a well-known researcher in the field of creativity and greatness, who devised a weighted equation that reliably predicted the relative rankings of American presidents.[2] The variables in the equation included whether the president had been a war hero, the number of years he served in office, the length of time the nation was at war during his reign, whether he had been assassinated in office, and whether a cabinet-level scandal plagued the administration. Unfortunately, an equation of this sort was not suitable for my purposes since it applied only to American presidents in a democratic system and equated greatness with events such as a war, scandal, or assassination during a leader's rule, rather than with his actual political accomplishments.

THE POLITICAL GREATNESS SCALE

If you ever hope to establish an objective measure of political greatness, you need a reliable rating scale that can rank leaders worldwide according to relatively culture-free indicators of greatness. In the past, most attempts by scholars to measure greatness have been indirect, relying on the evaluation by "expert" raters, counting the number of words for each ruler in encyclopedia entries, counting the number of biographies written about that person, or using other oblique criteria. Supposedly, the more words, entries, biographies, or whatever, the greater the greatness. The approach I have taken to measuring political greatness is entirely different than any tried before. Instead of manufacturing my own criteria for political greatness or borrowing those manufactured by others or using indirect measures, I decided to turn to the lives and achievements of the greatest leaders ever known, such legendary figures as Julius Caesar, Napoleon, Moses, Genghis Khan, Kublai Khan, Bismarck, Augustus Caesar, Darius, Frederick the Great, George Washington, Hadrian, Abraham Lincoln, Tamerlane (Timur the Lame), Charlemagne, Simon Bolivar, Pericles, Richelieu, Cyrus the Great, Constantine, Ptolemy II, Hammurabi, Oliver Cromwell, Shih huang-ti, Louis XIV, Peter the Great, and Alexander the Great, to identify what features they had in common. Once I could identify the achievements that most of these immortals shared, I then could use them as the gold standard against which all other rulers could be compared.

After studying the lives and achievements of these political immortals, I was able to identify eleven common features, with some overlap among them. I then incorporated these features into a *Political Greatness Scale* (PGS), which turned out to be a highly "reliable" and "valid" measure. By "reliable," I mean that, when two people rate a sample of rulers from the information available on them, they come up with roughly the same total scores on the Political Greatness Scale.[3] By "valid," I mean that the total scores on the PGS corresponded highly to certain indirect measures of political greatness that others sometimes use.[4] For example, when I correlated the PGS scores for the entire sample of 377 rulers with the combined number of words allotted to them in the *Encyclopaedia Britannica* and the *Encyclopedia Americana*, I found an impressively high, statistically significant relationship between them.[5] In other words, the total PGS score of rulers appears to be highly predictive of the length of their biographical entries within either of these encyclopedias. To my knowledge, no other culture-free measure exists that can match the PGS in its ability to rank worldwide leaders in this fashion.

Let's examine each of the eleven separate components of the Political Greatness Scale now to see how the sample of rulers fared on each.

The particular items and their scoring is given in chart 8.1 below. The appendix contains instructions for raters on how to score the items.

Chart 8.1 Political Greatness Scale

I. SOMETHING FROM NOTHING
    0 no creation of a new country (**default**)
    1 active participant in the creation or liberation of a new country
    2 one of several leaders in the creation or liberation of a new country
    3 leader of a struggle to create or liberate a new country

II. MORE THAN BEFORE
    0 lost territory
    1 neither won not lost territory (**default**)
    2 added new territory during reign but then lost much of it
    3 gained new territory

III. STAYING POWER
    0 <2 years
    1 2 to <4 years
    2 4 to <8 years
    3 8 to <12 years
    4 12 to <16 years
    5 >16 years

IV. MILITARY PROWESS
    0 lost war
    1 no war (**default**)
    2 avoided defeat in war but no clear-cut victory
    3 won war

V. SOCIAL ENGINEERING
    0 none (**default**)
    1 laws with precedent
    2 selected laws with no precedent
    3 general laws with no precedent

VI. ECONOMICS
    0 worse
    1 same (**default**)
    2 improved
    3 boom economy

VII. STATESMANSHIP
    0 none (**default**)
    1 active in ethnic or religious matters

  2 active in regional affairs

  3 active in international affairs

VIII. IDEOLOGY

  0 none (**default**)

  1 distinctive but not forced on populace

  2 not original but forced on populace

  3 original and forced on populace

IX. MORAL EXEMPLAR

  0 corrupt

  1 neither corrupt nor good (**default**)

  2 good

  3 wonderful

X. POLITICAL LEGACY

  0 disgrace

  1 neither disgrace nor good (**default**)

  2 gain in reputation at end of reign

  3 legendary status

XI. POPULATION OF COUNTRY

  0 <2 million

  1 2–<10 million

  2 10–<25 million

  3 25–<50 million

  4 50–<100 million

  5 >100 million

* "Default" means rater assigns that value if information is equivocal or unclear.

I. Something from Nothing

Surely one measure of political greatness has to do with bringing something entirely new into being that never existed before. This is the essence of creative achievement. In the political realm, this corresponds to creating a new country, bringing about independence, establishing a new homeland, or redefining the boundaries of a country. This accomplishment often happens against insuperable odds, since colonial powers or occupying nations or entrenched regimes usually command more military resources than those challenging them and resist giving up their power.

At least two-thirds of the twenty-six political immortals were instrumental in creating a political entity that did not exist before. Among all these rulers, the accomplishment of Moses was perhaps the most remarkable. With the assistance of Yahweh as his secular and religious advisor, he not only led the Hebrews to freedom but established a new home-land and religion for them. Although the other legendary rulers could not conjure up Moses-like miracles to exert diplomatic pressure on their en-emies—unleashing a pestilence of frogs, gnats, mosquitoes, locusts, boils, and thick darkness on the not-so-swift-of-mind Pharaoh Ramses, who kept refusing the Lord, the God of Israel's command, articulated by Moses, to "Let my people go," or calling upon Yahweh to open a corridor across the Red Sea (Sea of Reeds?) for the Jews to cross and then drowning the pursuing Egyptians—their feats were sometimes almost as awesome (or arguably more impressive, since they did them without all the divine fan-fare). Alexander the Great founded thirty separate Alexandrias in the wake of his conquests. Charlemagne united almost all the Christian lands of Western Europe into one superstate. Constantine founded Constantinople and contributed to the Christianization of the Roman empire. Bismarck founded the German empire. Napoleon proclaimed a new French empire in 1804. Cyrus the Great founded the Achaemenian empire. George Wash-ington, as the Revolutionary Army general and later first president of the United States of America, overthrew British rule. Shih-huang-ti, who be-gan building the Great Wall to defend China against barbarians, created the first unified Chinese empire. Oliver Cromwell overthrew the Stuart monarchy and imposed a constitutional, parliamentary form of govern-ment in England. Kublai Khan became the first emperor of China's Mon-gol dynasty. Caesar Augustus established the Roman principate, which gave him absolute control over all the provinces in the Graeco-Roman world. And Simon Bolivar, alias "The Liberator," liberated what is now Colombia, Venezuela, Equador, Peru, and Bolivia from the Spaniards and later man-aged to serve as president of both Colombia and Peru.

Among the twentieth-century rulers in the sample, 14 percent accomplished feats of comparable magnitude—establishing a new empire, creating a new country, or helping their nation gain independence from a colonial power—while another 12 percent played subsidiary but major roles in this drama. Visionaries (64 percent) headed the list of those who created something from nothing, followed next by monarchs (31 percent), transitionals (26 percent), authoritarians (12 percent), and tyrants (5 percent). Except for unusual circumstances, like overthrowing a temporary dictator or occu-pying power during war, leaders of established democracies (2 percent), naturally, hardly figured in this equation, since their role was to perpetu-ate a system of government that already existed.

Because of almost equally great achievements, many of the twentieth-century rulers in my sample earned the title of Father, Founder, or Liberator of their country. This insured them a measure of immortality—at least for as long as the country continued to exist. Others wrought so much destruction in the creation of their new nation that their countrymen would just as soon forget them. There was nothing inherently good or noble about a leader creating a new nation or gaining independence for an existing one or overthrowing an entrenched regime and then installing his own kind of rule. These accomplishments were undoubtedly momentous, but they did not guarantee enlightened rule. However, regardless of whether these liberators ended up being hated or revered, they need to be credited with the awesomeness of their feats. Imagine the incredible effort, dedication, single-mindedness, courage, and self-confidence it took for Mao or Lenin to unify a vast, populous, and splintered country with many factions, such as China or the Soviet Union, and forge an entirely new form of government.

One of the first questions that arises is how so many world leaders managed to do something entirely new. The reason has to do with certain unique features of the twentieth century. In the year 1900, there were fifty-two independent countries listed in the *World Almanac and Encyclopedia*,[6] with a number of these countries having colonies. At that time, for instance, the German empire had twenty-five colonies, France had thirteen colonies (including Algeria, Senegal, Tunis, Cayenne, Cambodia, Cochin China, Tonquin, New Caledonia, Tahiti, and Madagascar), the British empire had over forty colonies and dependencies, and the United States had five colonies. Over the course of the century, colonialism gave way to nationalism, and nationalism gave way to ethnicity, tribalism, and fundamentalism as a basis for nation-building, leading to an unraveling of these empires and about a fourfold increase of independent nations by the year 2001.

Then add to the number of liberated countries and the carving out of new ones the radical transformations in governments that took place in existing countries, and you have a phenomenal amount of political upheaval throughout the world. What this means is that this past century has given certain leaders ample opportunity to become fathers of their nations by capitalizing on the desire of their people for independence and self-determination, but, for complex reasons that I shall discuss later, it confined this birthing experience to men. In no single instance were woman chiefly instrumental in the birth of their country, which says more about how certain men gain power than the ability of women to rule.

With so many rulers creating new countries or regimes or liberating existing ones from colonial powers or foreign conquerors, you have to wonder how they managed to accomplish these feats. The answer is that they did it in every way possible after capitalizing on the anger of the people toward the reigning power and their desire for ethnic, religious, racial, or political independence. Sometimes they created new nations by seceding from the mother country, as when Ojukwu unsuccessfully declared Biafra independent from Nigeria, Moise Tshombe formed the secessionist state of Katanga, Ian Smith declared Rhodesia independent from Britain, or Tito freed Yugoslavia from Soviet hegemony. Sometimes they did it by conquering more and more territory and later consolidating it into a country, as Ibn Saud did in Saudi Arabia. Sometimes they did it by negotiating independence with the occupying power after that power found that, because of the growing protests, revolts, and resistance within the country, it no longer was politically or economically feasible for it to keep control. Sometimes they did it by launching ideological revolutions to counter the growing anarchy and disaffection sweeping their countries, much as Mao did in China or Lenin did in Russia. In other instances, they brought about the collapse of the reigning power by serving as symbols of resistance during their time in jail or in exile. They sometimes became fathers of their nation almost by default after the colonial power selected them to be rulers before the granting of independence, foolishly expecting that these selected rulers would gratefully now offer their former oppressors exclusive trade agreements and de facto control of the country. They sometimes also radically transformed the nature of their countries, much as Adolph Hitler was able to do by bringing about a political union of Austria with Germany through annexation.

For information purposes, I have listed the names and countries of selected twentieth-century rulers who have been instrumental in the formation of their nations or in the introduction of entirely new forms of government in chart 8.2 below.

Chart 8.2 Selected Founders, Liberators, Fathers, or Creators of their Nation

Leader/Country	Leader/Country
Atatürk Turkey	**Mohammed Jinnah** Pakistan
Jomo Kenyatta Kenya	**Ho Chi Minh** Vietnam
Bourguiba Tunisia	**Adolph Hitler** Germany, Third Reich
Chiang Kai-shek Taiwan	**Josip Broz Tito** Yugoslavia
Faisal I Syria & Iraq	**Makarios III** Cyprus

Chart 8.2 Continued

Leader/Country	Leader/Country
Vladimir Lenin Soviet Union	**Kenneth Kaunda** Zambia
Ibn Saud Saudi Arabia	**Mao Zedong** (Modern) China
Tomas Masaryk Czechoslovakia	**Abdullah** Jordan
Cheddi Jagan Guyana	**Menelik II** Ethiopia
Muhammad V Morocco	**Mujibur Rahman** Bangladesh
Kwame Nkrumah Ghana	**Ben Gurion** Israel
Agostinho Neto Angola	**Sobhuza II** Swaziland
Ian Smith Rhodesia	**Sekou Toure** Guinea
Sukarno Indonesia	**Ayub Khan** Pakistan
Eric Williams Trinidad and Tobago	**Paul Kruger** South African Republic
Amanullah Khan Afghanistan	**Leopold Senghor** Senegal
King Ferdinand Bulgaria	**Odumegwu Ojukwu** Biafra
Moise Tshombe Katanga	**Alexander I** Yugoslavia
U Nu Burma	**Emilio Aguinaldo** Philippines

II. More Than Before (The Pangaea Complex)

One of the main ingredients of political greatness is the expansion of national boundaries or the acquisition of new territory. Almost all of the twenty-six political immortals conquered other nations, extended their nation's hegemony over other countries, or spread their nation's culture and influence far and wide. You cannot become a great leader if you mind your own business and strictly tend to your own nation's affairs. If you want fame and glory, you had best abandon your modest ambitions for peace and prosperity for your own people. Political immortality is most apt to come with leaving your country bigger and more influential than it was before you took over. Bigger is better, and more and more is best. "Expansion is everything," lamented Cecil Rhodes, and fell into despair because every night he saw above him "these stars . . . these vast worlds which we can never reach."[7] Rhodes truly would have appreciated the simple aspirations of the farmer who only wanted all of the land immediately adjoining his.

After Julius Caesar crossed the Rubicon in 49 B.C. to become dictator, he added to the glory and power of Rome by *veni-vidi-vici*-ing through all the surrounding city-states in Italy and Spain, Egypt, and Africa as well. Augustus Caesar, who proclaimed himself the son of a god, continued in the tradition of his adoptive father and launched the

Augustan Age through his acquisition of additional territories and spreading of the Roman culture. Charlemagne conquered the Lombard kingdom in Italy, annexed Bavaria, subdued the Saxons, and united all but a few of the Christian lands in Western Europe under his rule. Louis XIV extended France's borders at the expense of the Hapsburg kingdom, admitting on his deathbed, "I have loved war too much." Alexander the Great overthrew the Persian empire, conquered Asia Minor, invaded India, and spread the Hellenistic culture in his many conquests. There was no stopping him. During his siege of Tyre, Darius offered to pay him a large ransom for his family, which Alexander held captive, and also turn over to him all his lands west of the Euphrates. His second-in-command, Parmenio, advised, "I would accept were I Alexander." Alexander's famous reply, which exemplifies his uncompromising attitude so well, was, "I too were I Parmenio."[8] And that difference between Alexander and Parmenio is what often separated the great conquerors from the ordinary rulers.

Napoleon Bonaparte extended the hegemony of France throughout all of Europe and Asia Minor and, for a while, threatened to do so in Russia and England as well. Peter the Great sought to extend the boundaries of Russia by gaining access to the Black Sea, the Caspian, and the Baltic. Frederick Barbarosa fought to establish German dominance in Europe. Cyrus the Great conquered Lydia and Babylonia. Darius the Great captured Thrace and the Aegean islands of Lemnos and Imbros but failed to conquer Greece. Constantine ascribed his military triumphs over the Samaritans, Franks, and Goths to his conversion to Christianity. Kubla Khan conquered China and became the first emperor of its Mongol dynasty. Tamerlane became known for his conquests from India and Russia to the Mediterranean Sea. Victorious in three wars during extended terms as prime minister of Prussia and then chancellor of the German Empire, Bismarck redrew the map of Europe and established his country's military dominance. Essentially all of the immortal leaders extended the spheres of influence and power of their nations, sometimes consolidating their gains into a new republic or empire. In many instances, this territorial expansion was not only to gain new mineral resources, oil, spoils, and slaves or even for strategic purposes. Many of these conquerors justified all their killing, rape, and looting with the claim that they were bringing civilization and enlightenment to these subjugated people.

All these leaders had what I call the "Pangaea Complex." It was almost as though a Jungian primitive archetype existed in them of a single land mass as the natural state of affairs, and although they did not have the geological knowhow to reunite the separate continents physically, they hoped to do so governmentally under one rule, their own. Through their conquests, they wanted to extend their dominion over the entire world and create a mega-nation, one and indivisible, under them.

During the past century, there have been rulers on the political scene who were no less ambitious than these political immortals. Leaders such as Adolph Hitler, who kept a globe of the world in his office with the Nazi swastika superimposed on it; Benito Mussolini, who wanted to recapture the glory of ancient Rome; and Joseph Stalin, who sought to

8.1: Hitler in Paris after conquering France. The Eiffel Tower may convey more than political symbolism. Photograph from the National Archives.

> While almost all of the immortal rulers extended their nation's borders, gained new territory, or took control of certain areas or countries through war, colonization, or other coercive means, and gained hegemony over other nations, only 8 percent of the rulers in my sample did so. Four percent gained substantial territory during their reign but lost it later, and an additional 10 percent ended their reign with shrunken national borders and a more weakened position. The remainder neither gained nor lost territory during their time in power.

foment world revolution, would have been the match of any Napoleon, Caesar, or Alexander the Great in their desire to dominate the world either through military might or the spread of their ideologies; and many other dictators of smaller nations would have been delighted to join them in their pursuit of world conquest if they had commanded the resources, weaponry, and manpower to do so.

Other twentieth-century leaders who have gained territory during their reigns include David Ben-Gurion, Levi Eshkol, and Menachem Begin, who increased the boundaries of Israel after the 1948, Six-Day, and Yom Kippur Wars; and Yassir Arafat, who was able to gain some of this territory back from the Israelis through a policy of terrorism and diplomacy. As the victors in World War I or World War II, Georges Clemenceau, David Lloyd George, Woodrow Wilson, Franklin Delano Roosevelt, Harry S Truman, Winston Churchill, and Joseph Stalin extended the hegemony of their countries throughout much of Europe and Asia. Helmut Kohl oversaw the uniting of East and West Germany in 1990. King Abdullah, whose ambition was to create a united Arab kingdom that included Syria, Iraq, and Transjordan, eventually had to settle for becoming ruler of Transjordan after negotiating its legal separation from the Palestine mandate. William McKinley, perhaps the most expansionist of American presidents, wrested the Philippines and Cuba from Spanish control after the Spanish-American War.

King Leopold II of Belgium won't qualify for political greatness, but he illustrates well the unmitigated territorial ambitiousness of many of these rulers. Although constrained in his role as a constitutional monarch within Belgium, Leopold sought to extend his country's sphere of influence in places far afield and at the same time increase his own wealth. After gaining international support for his claim to the Congo, a colony that was seventy-six times the size of Belgium and larger than England, France, Germany, Spain, and Italy combined, Leopold became an absolute monarch there and ran the colony as a cruel despot, creating a situation much as Joseph Conrad described in his "fictional" account of the nightmarish African nation in his story, *Heart of Darkness*. Wanting to exploit the rubber boom in the latter part of the nineteenth century, which was stimulated by the invention of the inflatable bicycle tire and then adapted to the automobile, Leopold drove the inhabitants of the Congo mercilessly with his nineteen-thousand-man private army and forced most of the males to be slave laborers. As a way to make the men meet their work quotas, he held their women hostage under abysmal conditions. By the time he ended his rule, millions of people had died.[9] With Leopold showing the same expansionist ambitions that drove many of these great leaders, imagine what his stance might have been in Africa, Europe, and the world at large if he had been the ruler of a more powerful nation and commanded enough weaponry and manpower to transform his greed into action.

Though expansionism is an important component of political greatness, it is important to recognize that it is not absolutely essential. Much as happened with Napoleon, a number of infamous leaders managed to conquer other nations or occupy parts of their territory during times of war but then later had to give up what they had gained or even surrender their own country in defeat. During this past century, there even was a unique instance of a ruler who arguably will gain a measure of immortality, at least in the Western world, for peaceably giving up more territory and losing more power in the shortest period of time than any other person in history. Mikhail Gorbachev, who became known as the Communist who destroyed Communism, almost singlehandedly unleashed the forces that led to the disassembling of the Soviet Union. Although reviled by many of his countrymen for the role he played in diminishing Russia's international stature, Gorbachev himself had no doubts about the greatness of his own achievements. When asked about his place in history, he compared himself to three reformer tsars: Peter the Great, Catherine the Great, and Alexander II. But of course, he added, the one leader he felt closest to was Lenin.[10]

III. Staying Power

Another important ingredient of political greatness appears to be how long leaders rule. Given the inertia of bureaucracies and public resistance to change, it is almost impossible to revamp society, get the economy booming, put down civil wars and revolts, or conquer nations unless you have enough time and power to do so. As they say, Rome was not built in a day. Even if leaders do not accomplish anything memorable, being able to rule for many years is a remarkable achievement in itself when you consider all the people who would have liked to take their place. It is even more difficult to do in democratic societies in which constitutions explicitly limit their term in office to help them avoid the corruption that comes with wielding too much power for too long a period of time.

Among our immortals, Caesar Augustus ruled from 31 B.C. to 14 A.D., Bismarck from 1862 to 1890, Charlemagne from 768 to 814, Alexander the Great from 336 to 323 B.C., Constantine from 306 to 337, Darius from 522 to 486 B.C., Frederick Barbarosa from 1152 to 1190, Hadrian from 117 to 138, Hammurabi from 1792 to 1750 B.C., Cyrus the Great from 550 to 529 B.C., Ptolemy II from 285 to 246 B.C., Attila the Hun from 434 to 452 (?), Kublai Khan from 1260 to 1294, Genghis Khan from about 1187 (??) to 1227, Louis XIV from 1643 to 1715, Napoleon Bonaparte from 1800 to 1815, Pericles from 450 to 429 B.C., Peter the Great from 1682 to 1725, Richelieu from 1624 to 1642, Shih-huang-ti

---

For the entire group of over 1,941 rulers worldwide, the average time in office was 5.3 years, with over one-fourth spending less than one year. Among these short-timers, 2 percent were in office for one week or less, 3 percent for one week to one month, 5 percent for one to three months, 6 percent for three to six months, and 10 percent for six months to one year. The average time in office for the sample of 377 rulers was almost twice that for the entire sample, confirming the importance of time in office as a major factor for becoming renowned, that is, if you judge (as I do) having a major encyclopedia entry and biographies written about them as indicators of worldwide fame. Among the members of the sample, 10 percent ruled for less than two years, 17 percent from two to four years, 26 percent from four to eight years, 16 percent from eight to twelve years, 11 percent from twelve to sixteen years, and 20 percent over sixteen years. On average, monarchs (twenty-two years) and visionaries (twenty-one years) were in office the longest, followed next by tyrants (fourteen years) and authoritarians (eleven years). Leaders of emerging democracies (ten years) and those of established democracies (six years), understandably, spent the shortest time in office, mainly because they had no other choice. If they had decided to abrogate their constitutions and extend their terms in office, they then would change from being democrats to dictators.

from 221 to 209 B.C., Tamerlane from 1370 to 1405, Oliver Cromwell from 1653 to 1658, Bismarck from 1862 to 1890, Simon Bolivar from 1821 to 1830, and Moses from 1290 B.C.E. for an estimated forty years. *The average term in office for our collection of immortals was twenty-nine years*, considerably longer than the two-, four-, six-, or eight-year terms of modern rulers in democratic systems. But there were notable exceptions. Julius Caesar (49 to 44 B.C.) and Oliver Cromwell realized their phenomenal achievements in only five years, George Washington (1787 to 1795) in eight, and Abraham Lincoln (1860 to 1865) in less than five.

Many twentieth-century rulers have had comparably long reigns. Chart 8.3 below includes the names of the eighty-one twentieth-century rulers worldwide who have spent twenty or more years in office. When you consider that one-fourth of all world leaders over the past century spent less than one year in office, several spending even less than one day, this staying power of one generation in time or more is a momentous achievement, a testament to the survival instincts of these leaders or the self-defeatism of those who try to dethrone them or the general apathy of their subjects. Although leaders may need lengthy periods in office to accomplish their ambitious goals, being in office for lengthy periods does not guarantee that they will take full advantage of their opportunities. As you peruse the list of long-termers, you will recognize the names of many familiar rulers, but you also will note names that will be unfamiliar, not because of your political ignorance but because they have not done anything noteworthy. You also will note that many of the greatest political leaders of the past century are not included on this list, especially those who ruled within established democracies. So while remaining in office for one or two or three or more generations may still be impressive, it is not absolutely necessary for accomplishing remarkable feats. Rome was not built in one day, but Caesar accomplished an incredible amount in five years, and Alexander the Great came close to conquering the known world in thirteen.

Chart 8.3   Rulers Serving More Than Twenty Years in Office

NAME	COUNTRY	YEARS
Hirohito	Japan	20
Somoza, A., Tacho I	Nicaragua	20
Jigme Dorji Wangchuck	Bhutan	20
Boris III	Bulgaria	20
Reza Khan	Iran	20

Chart 8.3   Continued

NAME	COUNTRY	YEARS
Senghor, Leopold Sedar	Senegal	20
DeRoburt, Hammer	Nauru	20
Marcos, Ferdinand	Philippines	20
Rashid ibn Said al-Maktum, S	United Arab Emirates	21
Ulbricht, Walter	Germany, East	21
Mussolini, Benito	Italy	21
Habyarimana, Juvénal	Rwanda	21
Ibn Saud	Saudi Arabia	21
Siad Barre, Mohammed	Somalia	21
King, W.L. Mackenzie	Canada	21
de Valera, Eamon	Ireland	21
Ahidjo, Ahmadou	Cameroon	22
Estrada Cabrera, Manuel	Guatemala	22
Traoré, Moussa	Mali	22
Price, George Cadle	Belize	23
Umberto I	Italy	23
Thani, Shaykh Khalifa ibn Ha	Qatar	23
Huggins, Godfrey	Rhodesia and Nyasaland	23
Nicholas II	Russia/Soviet Union	23
Erlanger, Tage Fritiof	Sweden	23
Nyerere, Julius	Tanzania	23
Balaguer, Joaquín	Dominican Republic	23
Menelik II	Ethiopia	24
Jawara, Dawda	Gambia, The	24
Horthy, Miklós	Hungary	24
Ceausescu, Nicolae	Romania	24
Stalin, Josef	Russia/Soviet Union	24
Ho Chi Minh	Vietnam, North	24
Karamanlis, Konstantinos	Greece	24
Sihanouk, Norodom	Cambodia	24
Mara, Ratu Sir Kamisese	Fiji	25
Albert I	Belgium	25
Kekkonen, Urho	Finland	25
Touré, Sekou	Guinea	26
Mao Zedong	China	27
Tubman, William V.S.	Liberia	27
Gómez, Juan Vicente	Venezuela	27
Kaunda, Kenneth	Zambia	27
Chandra Shumshere Bahad	Nepal	28
Ne Win	Myanmar (Burma)	28

Chart 8.3   Continued

NAME	COUNTRY	YEARS
Alfonso XIII	Spain	29
Yahya Muhammad ibn Hamid	Yemen	29
William II	Germany	30
Banda, H. Kamuzu	Malawi	30
Bourguiba, Habib	Tunisia	30
Díaz, Porfirio	Mexico	30
Trujillo, Rafael	Dominican Republic	31
Suharto	Indonesia	31
Lee Kuan Yew	Singapore	31
Kádár, János	Hungary	32
Mobutu Sese Seko	Zaire	32
Houphouët-Bouigny, Félix	Côte d' Ivoire	33
Abdul–hamid II	Ottoman Empire	33
Carol I	Romania	34
Zhivkov, Todor	Bulgaria	35
Stroessner, Alfredo	Paraguay	35
Tito, Josip Broz	Yugoslavia	35
Salazar, Antonio	Portugal	36
Mohammad Pahlevi	Iran	36
Chulalongkorn	Thailand	37
Christian IX	Denmark	38
Tsedenbal, Yumzhaghiyun	Mongolia	38
Franco, Francisco	Spain	39
Haile Selassie	Ethiopia	39
Mohammad Zahir	Afghanistan	40
Hoxha, Enver	Albania	41
Baudouin I	Belgium	43
Leopold II	Belgium	44
Meiji	Japan	45
Victor Emmanuel III	Italy	46
Hussein Ibn Talal	Jordan	46
Kim Il Sung	Korea, North	46
Tz'u-hsi Dowager Empress	China	47
Chiang Kai-shek	China	47
George I	Greece	49
Franz Joseph	Austria	68

What these findings also reveal is an overlooked but obvious feature of ruling, which is that there is no place to go after reaching the top. How else do you explain rulers who have held power for so long? You have to wonder whether rulers holding the same job for that long a time—some people may feel that even ten to fifteen years is too much—can still bring the same enthusiasm to their jobs as when they first deposed their predecessors, instituted martial law, assumed power, and eliminated much of their opposition. Surely, after doing the same thing day after day, year after year, generation after generation, many of these leaders should be experiencing burnout. Or else they have to keep stirring up trouble to keep from being bored. This certainly seems to fit the bill for the Methuselah of all rulers, the emperor Franz Joseph of Austria, whose reign of sixty-eight years was longer than Moses's and also longer than the life spans of many people. The point is that ruling is not a job like other jobs or even like being the CEO of a large corporation. Once they become a ruler, unless they set out to conquer other nations, there is no more career advancement, no switching jobs, no buying up of other companies, and no long sabbaticals except for exile to rejuvenate their enthusiasm. What this means is that being in power has a momentum of its own. The longer they are in power, the more they want to be in power and the greater their desire to keep it. And as suggested by the many rulers with long, uneventful reigns, they eventually find that keeping power becomes an end in itself, independent of anything they may hope to do with it.

IV. Military Prowess

With notable exceptions, rulers are not likely to achieve political greatness without winning a war, either as the commander of the army or a guerrilla leader or the head of an armed insurrection before they gain office or as the ruler and commander-in-chief of their country during their reign. The careers of our twenty-six immortals confirm the importance of military prowess as a critical ingredient for greatness. It was through war that many legendary leaders showed their godhead. After an entranced Pythian priestess proclaimed Alexander the Great invincible, confirming what he wanted to hear (and probably ensuring that he would contribute generously to her temple), and after he cut the Gordian knot, which according to legend augured that he was destined to rule the world, Alexander set out to prove these prophesies right with an army of only thirty-five thousand men to face a Persian force of over a million. Frederick Barbarosa launched the Third Crusade to liberate the Holy Land from the heathens. Hammurabi conquered many cities in Babylon to bring them under one rule. After he invaded the Netherlands, Louis XIV, also called the Sun King, became a national hero by defeating the powerful coalition of Spain, the Holy Roman Emperor, and the Dutch. This victory then let him extend the frontiers of France in the north by annexing part of Flanders and in the east by seizing Lorraine and other territories. Shih-huang-ti conquered rival states during his quest to unify China. George Washington defeated the British in the War for Independence. Abraham Lincoln won the Civil War, which, aside from ending slavery, let him preserve the Union. Napoleon won victory after victory until his defeat and exile to Elba and then his final defeat at Waterloo. Moses waged a successful war against the Midianites after he delivered the Hebrews to the Promised Land. Simon Bolivar's legendary attack on New Granada with only a small army of about twenty-five hundred men through flood-swept plains and icy mountains over seemingly impassable routes caught the Spaniards by surprise and led to their defeat in a battle that was the turning point in the liberation of Colombia, Venezuela, and Equador.

Genghis Khan, known as a military genius, conquered Peking and defeated other great empires; and his grandson, Kublai Khan, continued the family tradition. With his battalions of nomadic warriors, Tamerlane became known for the barbarity of his many conquests ranging from India to Russia and to the Mediterranean. Then there was Attila the Hun, celebrated in the Nibelungenlied as one of the greatest barbarian rulers, who terrorized the Roman Empire, Greece, the Balkans, and Italy. The reason "civilized" countries saw the Mongols and Huns as barbarians and lacking in culture was because of their ferocity and unorthodox ways of fighting. Instead of fighting according to civilized rules of engagement, they attacked in a seemingly helter-skelter fashion, making it difficult for their enemies to know where to direct their counterattack. Instead of killing all of their prisoners after judicial proceedings, as civilized victors did, they killed them without due process. Instead of extracting treasures and booty from defeated kingdoms by official decrees, the Mongols and Huns simply took what they wanted without legal authorization. Instead of making slaves of their prisoners, which had no purpose in a nomadic culture, they killed them so that they need not worry about leaving potential enemies at their rear. Because of their savage ways, it was no wonder that all civilized people looked upon them with disgust and saw little admirable in their culture, except for Marco Polo who extolled the virtues of Kublai Khan, and Coleridge who immortalized him in his poem, but needed to take laudanum to do so.

Among the rulers of this past century are some who could put the most bloodthirsty of the immortals to shame when you take into ac-

count international wars, civil wars, revolutions, terrorist activities, bor-
der skirmishes, and disastrous social policies like forced collectivization,
the Cultural revolution, dekulakization, or forcing people to shift suddenly from an urban to a rural economy, as happened in Cambodia.
What also needs emphasis is that killing large numbers of people is not
the exclusive prerogative of dictators. Harry Truman's decisions led to
an estimated 2.8 million deaths during the Korean War and the hundred
thousand Japanese deaths caused by the two atom bombs, George Bush's
to over a hundred thousand Iraqis being killed during the Gulf War, J.F.
Kennedy's, L.B. Johnson's, and Richard Nixon's to over 4 million people
killed during the Vietnam War, and on and on. No matter how these
various leaders—dictators and democrats alike—sought to justify their
actions and no matter how noble their cause, they all seemed to be operating under Stalin's famous maxim, "One death is a tragedy. One million
is a statistic."

As the above observations suggest, twentieth-century rulers were not
to be outdone by their ancient predecessors when it came to waging wars.

8.2: To the victors go the spoils. During the Potsdam Conference of 1945, Joseph
Stalin, Harry S Truman and Winston Churchill discuss which defeated countries
they will control. Photograph courtesy of the Harry S Truman Library.

Calculation of the percentage of rulers that engaged in any kind of battle during their reign, including armed conflicts with other nations and civil wars and revolutions within their own nations, shows that over one-half of the rulers (52 percent) had a chance to show their military prowess either as aggressors or defenders. Tyrants (88 percent) and visionaries (88 percent) were among the most likely to launch wars to quench their territorial thirst or quell rebellions within their own borders or defend themselves against armed attacks, followed next by authoritarians (78 percent) and monarchs (75 percent). Transitionals (45 percent) and democrats (29 percent) were least likely to be directly or indirectly responsible for the deaths of others.

In almost all instances, aggressors justified their actions as a response to provocation by the nations or parties they attacked, as a remedy for past wrongs, or for the benefit of the nation; and those attacked claimed to have no alternative but to defend themselves. However, in many of these instances, when you learn about both sides of the debate, you cannot be sure who the aggressors or defenders were and whether many of these wars were ever truly moral and just.

Although rulers always offer moral justifications for their military interventions, you have to wonder whether lurking somewhere in their minds is the realization that if they show their toughness and resolve in battle, they will become national heroes (or get high public approval ratings) and go down in history as great leaders. This even holds for democratic leaders. Teddy Roosevelt's greatest frustration during his term in office allegedly was that he did not have a war to fight to show off his manliness. Other democratic leaders were more resourceful. Two big world wars over this past century gave a slew of leaders a chance to slay many enemies and, in the process, gain some measure of immortality, with even the losers sharing in the fame because for a while, like Napoleon before Waterloo or Louis IV before the fall of his empire, they seemed to be winning. But there were smaller operations as well that gave leaders a chance to shine. William McKinley liberated the Philippines from the Spanish colonialists and then conquered them so that they could be put under United States control. Margaret Thatcher saved Grenada from the Argentinians, who "unjustly" wanted it back after it had been taken from them by the British many years earlier. After his failure to liberate Cuba in the Bay of Pigs fiasco, John F. Kennedy risked nuclear warfare during his confrontation with Khrushchev over missile bases there.

Reagan invaded Grenada with the avowed intention of rescuing U.S. medical students attending an unaccredited medical school on the island and, in the process, succeeded in removing the nation's communist government. He also bombed Qaddafi's residence in Tripoli in retaliation for the Libyan leader's sponsorship of a terrorist bombing of a German café. After these military strikes, Reagan's approval ratings soared.

Presidents Lyndon B. Johnson and Richard M. Nixon also had golden opportunities to be heroes but failed to crush the Viet Cong, who threatened to destroy the personal freedom of the South Vietnamese people living under the rule of an American-sponsored dictatorship ("our guys"). So Johnson—still basking in the afterglow of his decisive invasion of the Dominican Republic—kept escalating the war, ostensibly to contain communism but perhaps also because he refused to lose this contest of his manhood. Nixon, after trying more of the same in Vietnam, eventually surrendered the country to the North Vietnamese, not in defeat but as having won a "Peace with honor," using the same bit of verbal legerdemain as Saddam Hussein, who later transformed his crushing defeat in the "Mother of All Wars" in Kuwait into a victory for his people over the United States and Zionism. George Bush was doubly blessed, first when he invaded Panama to bring the corrupt, drug-trafficking General Noriega to justice, and second, when he launched Operation Desert Storm, designed to teach Saddam Hussein a lesson about the impropriety of violating the territory of a sovereign nation. He then passed the mantle to his successor by sending troops to Somalia. Then Bill Clinton had his own chance to be tough by getting involved in Bosnia, launching Operation Desert Fox to punish Hussein for not complying with the United Nations resolutions, and then, supposedly under the aegis of NATO, taking on Slobodan Milosevic again for "humanitarian purposes," this time over the ethnic Albanians in Kosovo. All of these actions may have been justified, but they nevertheless fit the expectation of a strong leader to show military prowess.

V. Social Engineering

The chance to be part of a utopian society in which people live together harmoniously, never experience hunger or want, and leave troublesome decisions to their leaders holds great popular appeal. A utopia of this sort is the equivalent of a heaven on earth. By helping to create this utopia, which will continue to exist long after they die, the people ensure that some part of them will live on, too. This longing for a Shangri-la is understandable, but in most instances they would be wise to wait until they actually get to heaven to realize paradise, because, if they actually ever happen to become part of a ruler's utopian vision, they are likely to find themselves living a hell on earth.

One of the greatest attractions of ultimate power for rulers is the chance to transform their utopian vision into a reality. With enough determination and ingenuity, they can fashion the people in their vision, much as God fashioned man in His. And they can do so without any personal guilt or recrimination, since their motives are pure and selfless and untainted by personal avarice or greed. All they want to do is create an ideal society for the eventual betterment of their people (so they tell themselves), even if they have to force their people to do what is best for them. In the process of making their own utopia a reality, they may not gain actual immortality, but they will come as close to it as they can get. In the affairs of mankind, it is the ultimate act of creation.

The notion of a utopia usually stimulates a sugar-plum vision of social harmony and the satisfaction of all wants in the minds of people. That is because they have come to believe that a utopian society is the equivalent of paradise. The derivation of the word *utopia* may contribute to this belief. The word has two possible Greek roots—*ou topos*, meaning "no place," and "*eu topos*, meaning "place where all is well." A combination of these meanings comes closest to capturing the usual connotation of this term.[11] But this connotation is more appropriate to fiction than to reality.

Perhaps the best-known of all utopias is Plato's *The Republic*, which had such an effect on all later utopian writings that most of them seem poor imitations in comparison. Plato conceived of a society in which a philosopher-king ruled three classes of people: the guardian class, the warrior class, and the workers. Since the multiplication of personal wants and desires led to an unjust state, all citizens, regardless of class, would be expected to subordinate their personal interests to the common good (as defined by the philosopher-king) and invest all the responsibility for the common good with the state (naturally, run by the philosopher-king). To relieve people of the burden of decision-making, the state (again, the philosopher-king) would regulate domestic life, indoctrinate its citizens in proper forms of thought and behavior, and assign suitable ranks and professions to individuals.

Since Plato wanted to build his utopian society on a rational foundation that eliminated the sentimentality of family life and all the fuss and bother about sex, he conceived of a system of common marriage, with communal property, where the wives and children of the guardians would belong to all members of this caste and where no child would know his true parents. Although Plato never says whether the philosopher-king would be too old or too wise to be above all these carnal concerns, I suspect that if he was pressed to comment he would grant him the privilege of droit du seigneur with whomever, whenever, and wherever he wished so that his mind would be unfettered when he attended to community affairs. At least, that is the way many cult leaders of quasi-utopias and visionary rulers of actual ones seemed to interpret the notion of a utopia with reference to themselves.

Almost two thousand years elapsed between the writing of *The Republic* and the next major utopian work, *Utopia*, by Sir Thomas More. In the long expanse of time between these works, man envisioned his idyllic existence in terms of an afterlife in the Kingdom of Heaven where the rewards for earthly suffering would be forthcoming. Although this dream of a heavenly paradise captured the imagination of people for many centuries, due mainly to the profound influence of St. Augustine's inspiring but unimaginative work, *The City of God*, they eventually became dissatisfied with the uncertain promises of an afterlife and began looking for more immediate heavenly gratifications on earth. The impetus for utopias came from this need.

More's *Utopia* is remarkable not so much because of its originality but in the courage it showed by indirectly criticizing the existing social order. Undoubtedly, the publication of this book played some role in More's martyrdom at the hands of Henry VIII. In any event, *Utopia*, except for some minor variations, reiterates the sentiments and philosophies of Plato. The community of property, the communal meals, the common and simple dress, and the emphasis on a Spartan existence all hark back to similar views expressed by Plato. The state, again, is all-powerful, and all individual interests and luxuries must be abandoned for the common good. Reason (as defined by the ruler) governs behavior, and most immediate pleasures are discouraged.

Andreae's *Christianopolis*, Campanella's *City of the Sun*, Hertzka's *Freeland: A Social Anticipation*, Cabet's *Voyage to Icaria,* and Bellamy's *Looking Backward*, as well as countless other minor utopian systems, all echo, to a greater or lesser degree, the basic sentiments advocated in *The Republic*. Naturally, there have been a number of utopian systems, such as those written about by H.G. Wells that proposed a more individualistic basis for society, but none of these utopias have succeeded in capturing the imagination of man to the extent of the more communistic or socialistic utopian societies. The utopian mentality is basically a communal and anti-individualistic one and predicated on the notion that the meek shall inherit the earth—but usually under the aegis of some all-knowing, elitist, godlike ruler.

What the public expects from a utopian system is fairly stereotyped. Unless the utopian writers conform to the formulas laid down by Plato and More, the utopia won't make its mark. The utopian mentality demands a society in which people can have their basic needs for food, clothing, and shelter met for the small price of forfeiting their personal freedom to the state (or some other higher authority). Conformity and sameness and commonality of property are the hallmarks of any utopian society. This demand for the suppression of individualism is depicted so well in such supposedly anti-utopian satires as Aldous Huxley's *Brave New World*, George Orwell's *Animal Farm* and *1984,* and Ira Levin's *This Perfect Day,* which actually are realistic portrayals of utopian societies.

Among my collection of twenty-six immortals, most tried to impose their utopian vision on their people by issuing decrees or imposing laws that dictated how people were expected to act in society. Charlemagne launched a spiritual and literary movement, called the Carolingian renaissance, which restructured social institutions and tried to raise the level of religious observance, morality, and justice throughout the empire. Alexander the Great tried to fuse Macedonians and Persians into one master race as part of his broader vision for the empire. Constantine's personal vision was to spread the Christian faith throughout his kingdom. Caesar Augustus imposed the Pax Romana to spread Roman influence and culture throughout all the individual provinces. Hadrian, who assumed the title of Hadrianus Augustus to remind people of his greatness, likewise passed many laws to spread Roman culture throughout the empire. But because of his abhorrence of physical mutilation, he miscalculated on the repercussions of certain bold new laws, like his universal ban on circumcision, which led to a fierce revolt by the Jews in Judea.

The predilection of the great rulers for social engineering was enormous. Darius was a great law-giver in the Egyptian tradition, organizing the empire into satraps and fixing annual tributes, which usually concerned rulers more than individual rights. Moses strove to curb the heathen practices and excesses of the early Hebrews through the Ten Commandments and the imposition of the Mosaic Laws. With his Council of State, Oliver Cromwell passed over eighty ordinances affecting domestic policies. Hammurabi, ruler of Babylon from 1792 to 1750 B.C., supposedly was the first ruler to introduce an elaborate code of laws to establish permissible transactions among people. Although keeping the traditional ways of determining guilt and punishing the guilty, such as the trial by ordeal and the lex talionis (i.e., an eye for an eye, a tooth for a tooth), the Code added some revolutionary wrinkles, like prohibiting marriage by capture, not recognizing blood feuds as a justification for personal retribution, and the radical notion of not taking the law into your own hands.

Other immortal rulers adopted similar approaches. Kublai Khan set up a nationalities policy to administer China in which the population was divided into four categories: a privileged, military caste (the Mongols) that was exempted from taxation; merchants and higher officials (foreign auxiliaries) with special privileges; the peasants from Northern China; and southern barbarians, who provided the labor and paid the taxes to support the upper two classes. Abraham Lincoln issued the Emancipation Proclamation in 1863, which freed the slaves of the rebellious Confederate states and thereby transformed the entire structure of American society. After overthrowing the Stuart monarchy, Oliver Cromwell helped to construct a new constitution that defined the rights and responsibilities of British citizens. Napoleon Bonaparte imposed the Napoleonic Code on all subjects within the empire, the genius of which was that it created for the first time a system of law based on "sublimated common sense" rather than on ancient tradition, and it unified under one system of justice all the separate laws and codes dealing with family and marital affairs, individual rights, property matters, and contract law.

To portray the utopian mentality of my sample of rulers, I have taken a broad view on this matter. I defined a utopian society as one in which the ruler tries to regulate almost all aspects of people's lives to conform to his vision of an ideal society. Whether the people living within or outside such a society judge it to be good or bad is irrelevant. Although there are degrees to which different rulers go to implement their vision— with many going to any lengths to do so—those who fare best not only succeed in creating a new social order but also in shaping the attitudes of their people so that they embrace it with almost a religious zeal. These rulers do this by enforcing legislation that transforms the nature of society and has an impact on all aspects of peoples' lives. In some instances, they rely on precedent or existing ideologies to reconstruct their societies. In other instances, they create societies that never existed before. But although the utopian mentality expresses itself in different ways, it usu-

Within the sample of rulers, a total of 19 percent qualified as utopians—7 percent changed the entire fabric of their society, and an additional 12 percent changed only certain aspects. While the utopian mentality could be found to some degree in all classes of rulers, visionaries, by definition, were well ahead of the pack. As a group, visionaries (100 percent) were four to five times as likely as authoritarians (23 percent) and transitionals (19 percent), and about ten times as likely as monarchs (11 percent), tyrants (9 percent), and democrats (9 percent) to refashion their countries through social engineering, either according to their own or other people's notions.

ally derives from one common premise, which is that the rights of the individual are always subservient to those of the state. Or, stated differently, the good of the individual must always be subordinate to the common weal.

It is important to realize that rulers do not have to be visionary to be a utopian and that there are different degrees of utopianism. For instance, visionary utopians rely on the totalitarian state to implement their policies, whereas transitional or established democrats rely on the federal government. Naturally, because they control the reins of power, dictators usually are more effective than democrats in bringing their utopian society into being. The utopian nightmares created by such infamous visionaries as Adolph Hitler, Mao Zedong, Joseph Stalin, Pol Pot, and Benito Mussolini are well known. But many other dictators have resorted to extensive social engineering to implement their notions. Muammar Qaddafi, for example, created a conglomerate society with a unique blend of Islamic reformism and pre-capitalist socialism based on his own bedouin and tribal experience. Atatürk emancipated women from the strict Islamic tradition, implemented a modern legal civil code based on the Swiss legal code, reformed the alphabet, passed a law making the use of family names compulsory, and replaced religious dress codes with European styles. The Reza Shah, who began the Pahlavi dynasty in Iran, made Western dress mandatory for government employees, forbade women to wear the traditional veil, and even tried to westernize Persian music. All of the changes wrought by the Reza Shah and then his son were undone later by the Ayatollah Khomeini, whose own utopian vision was to transform Iran into an ultra orthodox Islamic state that controlled almost all aspects of social and political life.

Although the social ramifications of the policies adopted by democratic leaders are not nearly as drastic as those adopted by dictators, they nonetheless can have a profound impact on the underlying structure of the society by concentrating more power within the federal government to govern the lives of its citizens. For example, in an ostensibly democratic system, Daniel Malan had the dubious distinction of forming the first exclusively Afrikaner government of South Africa and being the architect and apostle for apartheid. Later, in another stroke of social engineering, F.W. de Klerk dismantled these racist policies after he began negotiating with Nelson Mandela about restructuring the government of South Africa. And Indira Gandhi, who served as prime minister of India for three consecutive terms (1966–77) and a fourth term (1980–84), tried her hand at social engineering during her declared state of emergency when she implemented several unpopular social policies, including large-scale sterilization as a form of birth control.

Other democratic utopians addressed other social issues. Lazaro Cardenas, president of Mexico (1934–40), for instance, moved his country closer to socialism by launching a major agrarian reform program that distributed nearly twice as much land to peasants as had all of his predecessors combined and making efforts to expropriate foreign-owned industries. Salvador Allende, the first democratically elected Communist leader in Chile, tried to restructure Chilean society along socialist lines by redistributing incomes, expropriating the U.S.-owned copper companies in Chile without compensating the owners, and launching other programs that smacked too much of communism to suit his critics in North America. Clement Attlee headed the cabinet that created Britain's welfare state by nationalizing its major public utilities and several industries, instituting free medical and hospital care, and establishing various relief programs for the underprivileged. Franklin Delano Roosevelt overhauled the entire social system in the United States with the passage of his New Deal Legislation. Lyndon Johnson accomplished almost as great a feat with the creation of his Great Society.

Undoubtedly, the social legislation introduced by these democratic leaders differed drastically from the practices of visionary dictators, since, instead of suppressing individual rights for the common good, in many instances it expanded them while at the same time providing greater social benefits for all. However, not all people accept the value of these social changes. Although the supporters of these forms of legislation would claim that they helped to create more equitable and just societies, their libertarian or ultraconservative opponents might look upon "big government" and the welfare state as oppressive and destructive to individualism and personal initiative, much as might happen in a totalitarian state.

VI. Ideology

As the ultimate expression of social engineering, many rulers aspire to control the minds of their subjects. Part of the utopian mentality is to create a society of like-minded individuals who not only do the ruler's bidding but affirm whatever he says to be true. When a ruler can fill the minds of others with "correct" thoughts and values, he has achieved the ultimate in interpersonal control. What greater power can he have over others than to have them spout out catechisms that he had formulated for them? The more other people mouth his ideas, the greater his own lien on truth—for, after all, what else is truth but the social consensus of opinion? And whose opinion in society is more important than his? And if he holds a lien on social truth, then that makes him omniscient. Or so he believes.

Since earliest times, rulers have espoused an ideology as a basis for their conquests or rule—for God, Allah, Rome, Christendom, the empire, or whatever. In the case of the immortal leaders, religion and nationalism have been the main forms of ideology. Without recourse to the mass media and more sophisticated methods of mind control, they had to rely on cruder but still highly effective techniques to spread the faith or to get the subjugated masses to profess allegiance to their new ruler, which was to force them to renounce their faith and convert to the new one under fear of torture and death. The reason that forced conversions often stuck was simple. If the conqueror's gods were more powerful than those of the conquered, then the conquered saw it as only sensible to begin believing in the more powerful god. As long as they had to believe in a god, they might as well believe in one who could do the most for them, and the most immediate benefit the new god could bestow on them was to keep them from being slaughtered by their conquerors once they began believing in him.

Among the immortals, Moses, of course, worked fervently at indoctrinating the Hebrews with the revealed truths of Yahweh and the contents of the Covenant. Constantine was one of the first to systematically spread the faith other than through forced conversions. Constantine imbued his ideology with divine inspiration, credited his victories to Christianity, erected churches to Christ, distributed Bibles and religious writings to the troops, and tried to unify beliefs within a coherent system. As "God's chosen instrument for the suppression of impiety," he saw it as his sworn duty to remove erroneous beliefs and spread the true religion. Charlemagne, convinced he was at one with the Divine Will, spread Christianity throughout the heathen lands. The Roman conquerors forced their gods upon the conquered people, and the Moslem conquerors did likewise for Islam. Napoleon Bonaparte disseminated his more secular ideology about proper legal conduct throughout the empire.

Many of the twentieth-century rulers have gone far beyond their earlier predecessors in spreading ideologies with a more original cast than the more orthodox religious or nationalistic ones. This past century has seen the introduction of some unique world views such as Maoism, Fascism, Naziism, Leninism, Kemalism, Mobutism, Bourguibism, and Stalinism. Rulers have been able to spread their ideologies and remove the threat of deviationism through control of the public media, censorship, elaborate informer systems, indoctrination, legislation, and a sophisticated system of rewards and punishment. All ideological and religious movements strongly police wrong-thinking—and with good cause. If even one person can espouse heretical views with impunity, then he can infect the entire ideological system like a virulent microbe. No totalitarian belief system can brook contradiction, since the existence of an alternative way of constructing reality contradicts the validity of the entire ideology. Any self-respecting ideology must be all-embracing and unassailable. There can be no other competing ideologies before it, as Yahweh, in his divine wisdom, also knew to be so for other gods.

In identifying the ideological convictions within my sample of world rulers, I put aside the usual distinctions made between rulers, such as their conservative or liberal leanings, their more populist or elitist approach, or their operating under a democratic, socialistic, or fascistic government, that colored their political decisions. The only criterion used to judge if rulers were guided by an ideology was whether they themselves espoused a coherent or even incoherent system of thought that shaped the nature of their rule. Among the twentieth-century rulers, as with the great rulers of the past, were only a handful who promulgated their own unique ideologies. However, there were substantially more who promoted their own special twists on ideologies already in existence, such as communism, fascism, Zionism, Islam, or Christianity. The political doctrine of "Francoism," for instance, was an ambiguous mixture of patriotism, nationalism, authoritarianism, and Catholicism. Josip Broz Tito advanced his special brand of communism. Ayatollah Khomeini preached a militant form of Islam based on his own interpretations of the Koran.

Within the sample of world rulers, only 2 percent of them (e.g., Adolph Hitler, Benito Mussolini, Mao Zedong) tried to indoctrinate the populace with their own unique, mostly unprecedented ideologies or held views that were such bizarre interpretations of those already in existence that they qualified as being distinctive. Another 8 percent of rulers made concerted efforts to spread ideologies they borrowed and corrupted as an important aspect of their rule. In addition, 8 percent of rulers clearly followed the tenets of a communistic, fascistic, or religious ideology but did not rely on that ideology as the defining basis for their rule. While they continued to espouse the ideology of their predecessors, they were not as fanatic in imposing it on their subjects, probably because they took no proprietary interest in it, and the mechanisms for promoting the ideology were already in place. The remaining 82 percent of rulers adopted a pragmatic approach toward running their governments and did whatever was necessary to remain in office. If they espoused any political ideology, it played only a negligible role in their political decision-making.

Chiang Kai-shek's "New Life Movement," which combined fascism with Confucianism and, at his wife's insistence, also a bit of Christianity, was designed to infuse China with a puritanical unity, resurrect ancient principles, and cast off Western influences.

Ideologies serve an important function in governing a nation, especially one composed of different ethnic, religious, and racial peoples. They serve as a unifying force for the majority of the population, binding them together under one system of thought. A good example is the attempt by Mustafa Kemal, alias Atatürk, to reduce the ethnic and religious tensions that threatened to tear his nation apart by seeking a unified theory to restore pride in his countrymen. In his sun-language theory, likely inspired when he was under the influence of alcohol, he claimed that the first sounds made by primitive man were due to awe of the sun and that pure Turkish, purged of Arabic influences, was the original language of primordial mankind. Claiming that all humans began as Turks, he concluded that all human achievement must be Turkish. To his credit, he eventually realized the preposterousness of his theory and rescinded it.[12]

Atatürk's sun-language theory was a lot more sophisticated and erudite than most of the other ideologies leaders advanced over this past century. Because of the needs of the people to find simple causes for their discontents or simplistic meaning for their seemingly meaningless existence, they tend to be drawn to political ideologies that are emotionally appealing and give the impression of being scientific. Mobutism, for instance, which a government official explained to be "the sum total of Mobutu's actions," advocated "authenticity" as an answer to the problems facing Zaire. This supposedly innovative program claimed that, if the people changed their Western names to African ones, dropped titles like Mr. and Mrs. in favor of "citizen," wore tribal dress rather than European clothes, and emphasized folk art and traditional ways, they would resolve all of their economic, health, and spiritual troubles.

Kwame Nkrumah promulgated an ideology, sometimes called "Nkrumahism," "consciencism," or "African scientific socialism," which seemed to be a peculiar mix of Marxism, socialism, African metaphysics, and mumbo jumbo. For those impressed by the precision of mathematics, Nkrumah expressed the essential notions of his ideology in the following equation: Given that S = socialism, M = materialism, C = consciencism, U = unification, GI = a liberated territory, then $S = M + C + UGI$." While most of his listeners appeared to understand most of the terms in his equation, some had trouble with the coined word, *consciencism*.[13] When asked what it meant, Nkrumah said it was "a philosophy and doctrine of decolonization and development, with particular reference to the African revolution." With that ambiguous clarification, Nkrumah supposedly gave the people of Ghana a more precise notion of the nature of their government and a convincing rationale for all their sacrifices.

Then there was Manual Noriega's formula of "M.A.N. = PAZ" for social stability throughout Panama, which supposedly had the same simplicity and brilliance as Einstein's $E=MC^2$. Translated, it meant "Manuel Antonio Noriega = Peace."

VII. Economic Prosperity

"It's the economy, stupid," the slogan invented by President Bill Clinton's campaign staff, may have helped him get elected, and the booming economy during his term in office may have kept him from being removed from office. Most pragmatic rulers know that their prospects of remaining in office are far better if their subjects benefit materially during their reign than if they suffer economic hardships.

Among the immortals are many rulers who gained renown by increasing the wealth of their nations. Caesar Augustus restructured the financial system, imposed new taxes, expanded commerce, built massive buildings and monuments, and brought prosperity to Rome. Alexander the Great added to the wealth of his empire by bringing back treasures from conquered nations and selling the women and children of his slain enemies into slavery. Julius Caesar increased the wealth of the Roman Empire through exacting tributes, taxes, and treasure from his defeated enemies. In his zeal to spread Christianity, the emperor Constantine, who saw himself as the thirteenth apostle, felt free to loot pagan temples and then use the accumulated fortune for the benefit of the empire. Ptolemy II developed a highly planned economy that advanced the agricultural and commercial practices of his country. The Mongols enjoyed a long period of prosperity under Kublai Khan. Louis IV began an economic revolution to make France self-sufficient. Industry thrived during the Napoleonic wars. Under Peter the Great, Russia experienced rapid industrial growth and an expansion in trade and commerce. The economy of France thrived during the reign of Cardinal Richelieu.

The national economies boomed or improved during the reigns of certain twentieth-century rulers and fluctuated or worsened during the reigns of others. Whether you legitimately can credit these leaders with the deterioration or improvement in their nation's economy is not the point. Although some leaders were brilliant in managing their nation's economy, many others simply floundered about while their economies seemingly ran on their own, independent of their intervention. In many instances, the competency of the leader had little bearing on the economic situation. Take the cases of three U.S. presidents. Warren Harding was undoubtedly the most incompetent of the bunch, and you can take

---

Within the sample of leaders, the economy boomed for 2 percent, improved for 13 percent, stayed relatively stable or underwent both ups and downs for 62 percent, and worsened for 23 percent while they were in power. Among the different kinds of rulers, the economy of a nation was most likely to decline under the reign of tyrants (50 percent)—understandably, since they treated the state coffers as their own—and visionaries (48 percent)—understandably, since they were more interested in immaterial than material rewards for their themselves and their people—and was least likely to decline under monarchs (19 percent)—understandably, since they did their own accounting—transitionals (16 percent)—understandably, since they would have a hard time worsening a situation that did not exist before—and leaders of established democracies (18 percent)—understandably, since they had recourse to longstanding governmental agencies that were designed to stabilize the economy.

his own words as testimony: "I can't make a damn thing out of this tax problem," he told a confidante one day. "I listen to one side and they seem right, and then—God!—I talk to the other side and they seem just as right, and here I am where I started. I know somewhere there is a book that will give me the truth, but hell! I couldn't read the book."[14] Yet despite his befuddlement about money, the economy remained much the same during his reign. Herbert Hoover was perhaps the most experienced and knowledgeable administrator, yet his reign ushered in the Great Depression. And Ronald Reagan, certainly not an expert in economics, eliminated the rising inflation, high interest rates, and high unemployment of his predecessor, Jimmy Carter, with a fiscal approach his own vice president, George Bush, had earlier referred to as "voodoo economics" and that led to the greatest budget deficit in the history of the country.

The point is that the economies often worsen, remain the same, or improve while leaders are at the helm, and the leaders either are credited or blamed for the results. The people, so to speak, want their leaders to be able to make rain in times of drought; and, when they do not, they look for another rainmaker. Inflation, depression, stagflation, unemployment, high interest rates, and devaluation of the currency all lead to riots or political unrest. Economic booms and prosperity, whether through oil revenues, the spoils of wars, or other means, can make the public complacent about many transgressions by the leader. Economic decline and financial hardship can drive people to revolt.

Although democratic leaders were more likely than dictators to fare better with the economy, many dictators likewise had achieved remarkable results. For instance, Lee Kuan Yew, who was prime minister of Singapore for thirty-one years, showed well how an authoritarian ruler, relying on dictatorial methods, could stay in power for a long time by tending to the economic welfare of his subjects.[15] Instead of buying into the conventional notion that too much power corrupted rulers, he held the reverse notion, that ordinary people could not be entrusted with power because it corrupted their judgment as voters. Being sheep, people easily could be misled, so therefore a nation had to be ruled from the top down. Governing of a nation was too important to be left to an uninformed and ignorant populace. Because he believed that economics was the major stabilizing force in society, Lee took a number of controversial steps to stimulate the ailing economy. Seeing himself as a captain in a shipwreck whose men had to obey orders without question, he effectively eliminated all opposition by using his constitutional powers to detain suspects without trial for renewable two-year terms and without the right of appeal. He recruited the top scientific and academic minds in the country to manage the economy and brought technocracy into politics. He eliminated welfare and preached the value of hard work. He crashed down on left-leaning trade unions and forbade strikes.

To implement his policies, Lee Kuan Yew artificially created social consensus by allowing only one party, one press, one trade union movement, and one language. As part of his paternalism, he encouraged people to uphold the family system, discipline their children, be more courteous to others, refrain from self-indulgence, and avoid pornography. He even urged the people to take better aim in public toilets and be more accurate when they spit in spittoons. The people seemed to tolerate these restrictions on their freedom not only because they feared losing their jobs but also because they seemed to value their economic security and benefits more than democracy. Besides, like their responses to their respected parents, many people credited Yew's remonstrances and disciplinary actions and authoritarianism toward them to be well-intended and therefore above criticism.

VIII. Statesmanship

Statesmanship is the ability of rulers to transcend their own national interests and take positions for the worldwide good and get other leaders to do so as well. Most rulers find it hard enough to get consensus on issues within their own country. They find it even harder to get other independent rulers to agree with them. But great statesmen somehow manage to do this. Along with their diplomatic skills, many of these statesmen possess a great breadth of vision as well, which lets them anticipate the unfolding of regional or international events long before they happen and often act on what they know.

Political genius, said Bismarck, consisted of hearing the distant hoofbeat of the horse of history and then leaping to catch the passing horseman by the coattails. Winston Churchill, for instance, showed an amazing prescience about world events. Before becoming prime minister, he was right about the worthlessness of the Munich Pact and the imperialistic intentions of Nazi Germany; and while prime minister, as the Third Reich crumbled, he was right about the growing menace of the Soviet Union in Eastern Europe. But being right about important events does not mean that a ruler is right about everything. In Churchill's case, because of his conservatism, he initially expressed admiration for Mussolini, Franco, and even Hitler, whom he credited with raising his country's pride. As a friend once commented with respect to Churchill's remarkable vision, "Winston was often right, but when he was wrong, well, my God."

Of course, if you have enough power or rule a vast empire, then you do not need statesmanship to get other nations to comply with your wishes. You simply intimidate them to get them to do what you want. Diplomacy is what the rulers of weaker, threatened nations resort to when they do not have the power to tell stronger nations what to do, or what leaders of more powerful democratic nations rely on when they cannot rely on military force or economic sanctions to implement their will.

Among our immortal leaders, statesmanship was not always apparent, since most were preoccupied with their narrow interests and exerted their wills by force. However, a notable handful did rely instead on the force of their personality and diplomatic skills at times to better the positions of their nations and also forge regional and international alliances. Bismarck, for instance, was very influential in foreign affairs, serving nineteen years as chancellor and all twenty-eight years he was in power as the prime minister. Cyrus the Great was able to extend his conquests through diplomacy. Tamerlane conducted sophisticated negotiations with neighboring and distant powers. Peter the Great expanded foreign trade through his diplomacy with other nations. George Washington forged an alliance with France against England during the Revolutionary War and later assumed great stature among many European nations. When Cardinal Richelieu made an alliance with a Protestant nation during the Thirty Years War, he transcended narrow religious interests and contributed to the secularization of diplomacy. By means of his statesmanship, he not only helped to establish royal absolutism in France but also the end of Spanish-Hapsburg hegemony in Europe.

Over the past century, the growing ease of travel and technological advances in mass communication have made the world a lot smaller if not a more complex place. The interests of most countries now transcend national boundaries. Because of the greater chance of conflicting interests in a shrinking world, there seems to be a greater need for skilled diplomacy. But only a minority of rulers show the ability to assume leadership within a regional or international arena. In my sample of rulers, two-thirds were concerned primarily with running their own countries, or, if they did attend regional or international meetings, they did so more as a participant than as an active leader. What leadership they showed in their dealings with other nations was mostly focused on narrower ethnic, religious, or economic interests such as Arab concerns about the existence of Israel, the control of oil prices through OPEC, resolving

> Among the different kinds of rulers, visionaries (72 percent) and leaders of established democracies (35 percent) were the most likely to take the initiative in regional and international affairs. Next came transitionals (30 percent), monarchs (28 percent), and authoritarians (20 percent). Understandably so, tyrants (9 percent) were last.

national boundary disputes, or forging pan-Islamic alliances. The remaining one-third of rulers in my sample were actively involved in regional issues such as limited free trade agreements, Latin-American concerns, the Organization of African States, NATO, or Soviet bloc concerns, or served as respected statesmen on the international scene dealing with such issues as global peace, nuclear nonproliferation, the global economy, open trade agreements, environmental protection, international fishing rights, disease prevention and control, human rights, family planning, and the elimination of hunger. A number of these rulers won Nobel Prizes for their contributions to regional or international peace.

Not surprisingly, visionaries, by far, showed the greatest tendency to become involved in regional and international affairs, presumably because this gave them more opportunity to spread their ideology and extend their influence to other countries. At the opposite end of the continuum, tyrants and authoritarians devoted their efforts mostly to domestic national concerns for a number of reasons. Aside from not having political clout with other rulers, they probably were reluctant to go to meetings outside of their own countries for fear of being overthrown in their absence. Also, their interests usually did not transcend personal greed or keeping social stability within their country.

IX. Moral Exemplar

As leader of a country, the ruler represents a unifying symbol for his people. As such, he is supposed to embody all the virtues of the culture and stand for everything that is right and good. Above all, people expect that their leader will put the welfare of the nation ahead of his personal desires. Once in office, he is supposed to serve as a moral exemplar, giving inspiration for the nation during times of national crisis and being immune to personal corruption and greed. At least, that is an idealistic conception of a ruler.

Among our pantheon of immortal leaders, moral exemplars abound, if you can discount all their conquering, slaying, and enslaving of others. Perhaps the ultimate expression of becoming a unifying symbol for the people is to be proclaimed a god, who, by definition, must be above all human failings or, if not, is allowed to have them in caricature. Moses was the prophet of his people and had a close relationship with Yahweh. Alexander the Great was deified. Julius Caesar was descended from the goddess Venus and later assumed the stature of a deity. Caesar Augustus, his adopted son, referred to himself as the Son of a God. Dedicating himself to the Christianization of the Roman Empire, Constantine saw himself as the thirteenth apostle. The antipope Paschall III canonized Charlemagne for his efforts on behalf of Christianity. Oliver Cromwell was known for his religious toleration and contributed to the evolution of constitutional government. Ptolemy II was accorded divine status. Hammurabi made special efforts to be a just ruler. Before his defeats, the people saw Napoleon as almost divine. For his dedication on behalf of his fledgling nation, the House of Representatives voted George Washington "first in war, first in peace, and first in the hearts of his countrymen." Simon Bolivar became a revered figure throughout Latin America for risking his life to liberate various countries from Spanish rule. Abraham Lincoln became the champion of human rights not only in America but throughout the world as well.

Although no leaders have been sanctified by their people during the past century, a sizable number have been touted as the fathers of their nations or won Nobel Peace Prizes or served as inspirational symbols for their countrymen during crises or wars. Teddy Roosevelt used the presidency as a bully pulpit to appeal to the higher ideals of the people. Other leaders have done likewise. Within the sample of leaders, almost one-fourth seemed to be acting selflessly according to their own lights in the best interests of their country, showing no evidence of exploiting their office for financial gain above and beyond the normal perks that go with the position. A handful of these rulers, such as Nelson Mandela, Jomo Kenyatta, Atatürk, Franklin D. Roosevelt, Charles de Gaulle, Winston Churchill, Jawaharlah Nehru, David Ben Gurion, and Mohammed Jinnah,

Transitionals (i.e., leaders of emerging democracies) (47 percent) were most likely to have gained in reputation after serving in high office or be viewed as moral exemplars. Next came visionaries (36 percent) and leaders of established democracies (24 percent). Only a small percentage of monarchs (17 percent) and authoritarians (12 percent) became more respected or qualified as moral exemplars. By definition, no tyrants fit this category.

also gained a kind of hero status throughout much of the world that was mainly reserved for many of the immortals.

Overall, what the findings reveal is that leaders espousing democracy or working toward creating a social utopia are far more likely to be seen as selfless and dedicated than those operating under dictatorial systems without the saving grace of a political ideology. Of course, there is another complicating factor that may affect whether rulers were judged to be moral exemplars. And that is whether they ended up their time in office as victors in war and reasonably successful in their social policies.

X. Political Legacy

Most people would be delighted to be remembered for several years after their deaths, or maybe even for two or three generations, until their grandchildren die off. Within the sample of legendary leaders, all achieved some measure of immortality. For a good many of these immortals, their name recognition and exploits are remembered not only for several centuries but for one or two or even over three millennia, as is the case for Moses. Only as a ruler do you have the potential for continuing name recognition, which is the only provable kind of eternity. From what I know about these immortal rulers, I suspect that, if any of them actually chanced to make it to Heaven, they would have been long gone by now, since the Almighty would have tired long ago of all their constant machinations and manipulations and banished them to some celestial Elba before they had a chance to launch a celestial coup against Him. Although most seemingly worshiped God during their lifetimes, I cannot imagine them playing second fiddle to Him after their deaths.

Unlike the collection of immortals, who are a proven quality, you would be hard-pressed to know with certainty what the reputations of the leaders in my sample will be several millennia from now or even in one century, but you can make some educated guesses. For the purposes of my study, I decided to estimate what their legacy would be by their general reputation at the time they left office, and, in the case of those still in power, by the reputations they had at the close of this past century. I based my estimate on the well-known psychological principle that the best predictor of future behavior is past behavior. Another assumption I have made (for which the data offer strong support) is that rulers who leave office as failures are not as likely as those who leave as successes to be remembered as great leaders years later, although there are some notable exceptions. But I am also aware that fame and recognition are fickle and depend on many factors, and time and circumstance can change a lot. Even in the case of the immortal leaders, several chanced being forgotten if certain events rather than others had happened.

Take Ollie Cromwell, for instance. I wonder what he was thinking when he looked back from the Great Beyond to witness what happened after his death. He probably figured that after he overthrew the Stuart monarchy and signed the death warrant for King Charles that parliamentary government was in England to stay. But he had not counted on the strong sentiment within the country to restore the monarchy. After the restoration of King Charles II in 1661, he ordered Cromwell's embalmed remains removed from his Westminster Abbey tomb and hung up at Tyburn, where criminals were executed. He eventually had Cromwell's body buried beneath the gallows but kept his head stuck on a pole on top of Westminster Hall, where it stayed until the end of Charles II's reign. On the basis of my extensive clinical experience as a psychiatrist and only after long and deep deliberation, I have reached the conclusion that the good king must have had been angry at Ollie, who by now was long beyond being upset by this act of royal vengeance, but I am open to other interpretations of his actions.

Because of changing world events, rulers often cannot be certain how history will treat them. I already have mentioned Amanullah, whose name was expunged from his nation's history books and then only years later reintroduced. Tomas Masaryk, the founder of Czechoslovakia, experienced a similar fate.[16] Before 1914, his contemporaries either praised him or condemned him. In 1918, after his return from exile and election as president, he became very popular. Then, after the Nazi invasion of Czechoslovakia, he was expunged from history, but his name reemerged after freedom was restored in 1945. After the communists took charge, they could not seem to make up their minds about him. For a couple of years, they treated his memory with respect for his prewar activities and as the liberator of the country. Then during the 1950s, the powers-that-be orchestrated a vicious campaign against him. Toward the latter part of the 1960s, the authorities partly restored him to his former greatness. He was stripped of his hero status again after 1968 and remained in a no-man's-land of fame until the liberation of Czechoslovakia in 1989, when the new authorities rehabilitated his image. At this point in time, he happened to be a great man, but given what happened before, who knows how long that would last?

What these various findings show is that the chances for posthumous fame seem greatest for those who undertake to create new nations

Among the sample of rulers, 38 percent finally left office as failures or with worse reputations than when they had first begun. This could have come about as a result of being overthrown in a civil war, coup, uprising, or war, leading to their imprisonment, execution, exile, forced resignation, or abdication. Or the leader could have lost a bid for reelection and never gained office again. While it is not necessarily a failure to have to give up being prime minister in a parliamentary government when a new government is formed, it is when you then are removed as head of your party because the members no longer have any faith in your leadership. An additional 25 percent of rulers neither gained nor lost in political stature or reputation by the time they left office. Another 26 percent gained in political stature as a result of accomplishing notable deeds during their reigns, such as winning a war, stemming inflation, or improving the economy. Only 11 percent of the rulers managed to gain an exalted status because of their extraordinary deeds, such as revamping society, initiating radical changes in government, gaining national independence, or starting a new political movement that continued long after they left office.

Visionaries (60 percent) were the most likely of the twentieth-century rulers to gain an exalted status, and, as in the case of the moral exemplars, transitionals (26 percent) were the next most likely. Only a small percentage of monarchs (8 percent), authoritarians (9 percent), and leaders of established democracies (2 percent) seemed likely to gain some measure of immortality. No tyrants (0 percent) gained a revered status, although many became infamous.

or refashion older ones or introduce new political ideologies. As in the creative arts or the sciences, political rulers are most likely to be remembered for the establishment of a recognizable and distinctive product that had never existed before. In the case of ruling, it makes little difference whether others judge that product to be morally sound or bankrupt, good or evil, or of long or short duration. A leader can gain some measure of political immortality only if he manages to change the status quo of his nation or create a new social order.

XI. Size of Constituency

As the final criterion of political greatness, I have to introduce some elementary statistics. Perhaps the most important sign of political achievement is getting to be a ruler in the first place. The greater the odds against gaining office, the greater the achievement of getting there. But how do

> For the purposes of this study, I categorized rulers according to different population ranges. Among the rulers in the sample, 9 percent came from nations with populations under 2 million, 33 percent from nations between 2 million and <10 million, 20 percent from nations between 10 million and <25 million, 13 percent from nations between 25 million and <50 million, 12 percent from nations between 50 million and <100 million, and 13 percent from nations with populations more than 100 million. Since 100 million is already so high, I arbitrarily decided to lump all countries with populations over that size in the same category. I am aware that a mathematician has shown proof that there are different-sized infinities, but, from my perspective, the infinitesimally small chances for becoming a ruler in a country of 100 million and a billion people are about the same. They both seem equally improbable.

you take these odds into account? There are so many variables that figure into this, but, for the sake of simplicity, I have assumed that people aspiring to power in densely populated countries have to overcome greater odds against gaining power than people in sparsely populated ones, and that there is a rough correspondence between the magnitude of the achievement and the odds in bringing it about. In St. Exupery's *The Little Prince*, the king who inhabited the asteroid on which he was the only subject had no trouble being the ruler. The odds were one chance in one. If there were ten, 1 million, or 100 million people on the asteroid, the odds would be one in ten, one in 1 million or one in 100 million, assuming there was not a hereditary basis for ruling and all other things were equal. When a person manages to become the leader of a country with 500 million or 800 million people, as Nehru did in India or Mao did in China, respectively, the odds against their doing so are incredibly high. So that makes the magnitude of their achievement even greater.

Given these observations, it is not surprising that judgments of political greatness tend to be weighted toward leaders from more populous countries—and with good reason, since these leaders usually wield greater power, command more people, control more land and resources, and originally beat out more people for the job. However, that is not always so. Sometimes leaders of less-populated but more strategic countries play huge roles on the world scene. But with allowances made for exceptions, you can expect that the size of the country will make a difference in the likelihood of judging a leader to be great.

From PGS Scores to the Prediction of Greatness

These, then, are the ingredients of the Political Greatness Scale (PGS). As it happened, the range of scores obtained by the 377 rulers in the sample covered the entire spectrum from political ineptness to greatness. The scores also corresponded roughly to a normal bell-shaped curve, similar to what you find for intelligence, height, or weight in the general population, and tended to be evenly distributed around the world, suggesting that cultural bias did not play much of a role in the relative rankings (see PGS scores for rulers in the appendix).

Because these rankings cover the entire gamut of political achievement, we now are in a position to discover the personal qualities that distinguish those rulers within the upper rung of greatness from those in the lower rung. This then should let us tackle an important issue with regard to the nature of ruling: namely, whether these rulers are psychologically responsible for their political actions or whether they are simply acting out of biological and historical necessity. How we resolve this issue should help us to understand better the reasons why rulers act as they do.

THE SEVEN PILLARS OF GREATNESS

We sat watching each other. The large male, more than the others, held my attention. He rose repeatedly on his short, bowed legs to his full height, about six feet, whipped his arms up to beat a rapid tattoo on his bare chest, and sat down again. He was the most magnificent animal I had ever seen. His brow ridges overhung his eyes, and the crest on his crown resembled a hairy miter; his mouth when he roared was cavernous, and the large canine teeth were covered with black tartar. He lay on the slope, propped on his huge shaggy arms, and the muscles of his broad shoulders and silver back rippled. He gave an impression of dignity and restrained power, of absolute certainty in his majestic appearance.

—George B. Schaller, *The Year of the Gorilla*

THE GREAT MAN VERSUS HISTORICAL NECESSITY CONTROVERSY

Here is the question: How can you be sure that the activities of any particular ruler really make a difference in the fate of a nation? Because you cannot run the reel of history over again, you never can know for sure if the same outcome would have happened with someone else or even nobody at all at the helm. If any ruler or no ruler can be associated with certain political events, then that suggests social and historical forces brought those events about. To be able to hold a ruler morally responsible for certain political happenings during his reign, you would have to show a connection between certain personal attributes or particular actions of the leader, not just his physical presence, and the specific happenings attributed to him. Otherwise, any leader with other personal attributes or actions might have done just as poorly or well.

Thomas Carlyle, the most notable advocate of the great-man theory of history, claimed, "History is the biography of great men."[1] Heroes and villains fill the pages of history with their deeds, define their ages, and determine the course of nations. Through their creative or destructive genius, great men have the capacity to break with the convention and orthodoxy of their times and take their nations along entirely new paths. According to supporters of this theory, great men have contributed to such momentous historical happenings as the rise of capitalism, the Industrial Revolution, the Reformation, the Bolshevik Revolution, and the great wars.

William James, the well-known psychologist, philosopher, and physiologist, elaborated on this view. While he recognized the importance of social and natural factors on political events, he nevertheless claimed, "The mutations of societies from generation to generation are in the main due directly or indirectly to the acts or examples of individuals whose genius was so adapted to the receptivities of the moment, or whose accidental position of authority was so critical that they became ferments, initiators of movement, setters of precedent or fashion, centers of corruption, or destroyers of other persons whose gifts, had they had free play, would have led society in another direction." Great men had the capacity to alter their environment much as the introduction of a new species could change the flora and fauna around it.[2]

While crediting a leader with the power to shape the course of history, advocates of the great-man theory often fall prey to a type of *post hoc ergo propter hoc* reasoning that attributes a direct causal relationship between rulers and the events unfolding during their reign. Unfortunately, aside from numerous anecdotal accounts of men who seem to have influenced their ages, no scientific proof exists to indicate that great men can change the course of history. I say "unfortunately," because it would be nice to believe that certain people do have that potential. Only the methodologically flawed study by F.A. Woods, *The Influence of Monarchs*, which deals with the reigns of 368 sovereigns in 14 western European countries from the eleventh century until the French Revolution, suggests otherwise.[3] In his study, Woods found that strong, mediocre, and weak monarchs were associated with strong, mediocre, and weak periods in history, respectively, in 70 percent of the cases. Since the characteristics of the monarchs and the state of their nation were closely connected, he concluded that sovereign rulers must be responsible for what did or did not transpire in their countries.

Taking all of these arguments into account, Sidney Hook, the social philosopher, tried to clarify the role of the great man in history by distinguishing between the "eventful man" and the "event-making man."[4] In the case of the eventful man, the events leading up to an important decision by him are at a very advanced stage, so the potential for something momentous happening is high. By engaging in a simple act, such as making a crucial decision or issuing a decree, the eventful man can transform the potential into a reality. While the actual act of the eventful man is important, it can be performed by all sorts of people who happen to be in the decision-making position at the time. In a sense, the eventful man acts like the little Dutch boy who put his thumb in the dike and saved his town. It was a heroic act, but almost any boy with a thumb who had happened to walk by and detect the leak could have done it. Arguably, by his fateful decision to drop the atom bomb on Hiroshima and Nagasaki, Harry S Truman, like the Dutch boy, likewise became an eventful man, because any United States leader could have done the same.

In contrast, the event-making man—the truly great man in history—not only brings about momentous happenings by what he does but also by what he is. The assumption is that the historical event would not have happened without him. Like the eventful man, he likewise stands at the fork of the historical road poised to act, but unlike him, by virtue of certain personal qualities, he also bears the responsibility for bringing his nation to that moment of decision. Mao Zedong, who unleashed the Hundred Flowers campaign, the Great Leap Forward, and the Cultural Revolution in China, each of which was a momentous event, is an example of such a person. Though the distinction between the eventful and the event-making man seems apt, Hook never really offers convincing proof that event-making men are more likely to possess certain characteristic personal attributes than eventful men or even than noneventful men, for that matter. Had he done so, he might have settled the great-man debate.

On the opposing side of this debate, G.W.F. Hegel, the philosopher, saw nothing contradictory in the notions of the great man and historical inevitability.[5] Using his patented dialectic of thesis-antithesis-synthesis, which thrives on the reconciliation of polar opposites, he saw the great man as the hero who "actualizes his age." The "world-historical" hero was someone who fulfilled the necessary requirements of his culture at a particular stage in history so that, in doing what was necessary, he tautologically did what had to be done. For Hegel, the great man was not necessarily a product of material conditions, as he later would be for Karl Marx, but was an expression of "the spirit" of his times or "the soul" of his culture. Herbert Spencer, the English philosopher, likewise argued that, since the great persons were themselves the products of social forces, then whatever they did must be socially determined.[6] With this view, world history would have been the same even if all the great leaders never had existed, since social-historical forces would have selected other individuals to do what had to be done.

Interestingly, the same study mentioned above that was used to support the great-man theory of history likewise reported results that strengthen the case for social determinism. In his study of monarchs, F.A. Woods admitted that no sovereign of outstanding ability sat on the English throne for over two hundred years, from 1603 to 1811, perhaps with the exception of William III (but he failed to note the shift to a more parliamentary form of government over this time period). Yet despite this long period of mediocre or uninspired leadership, England enjoyed continued prosperity. The same situation applied to Scotland. Why England and Scotland should differ from the other countries in the study is hard to say, but the very fact that they did cannot be easily dismissed. If you can accept Woods's methodology as sound, which I do not, then the lack of any relationship between the leadership capabilities of the various sovereigns and the progress of these two nations over this long time span suggests that historical forces were more important in shaping their destinies than their rulers were. It also highlights one of the practical arguments against the historical necessity position—it gives you nobody to blame and punish when things go wrong.

This notion of social determinism was developed to its fullest, perhaps even to the point of *logicum ad absurdum*, by orthodox Marxists such as Engels, Lenin, and Trotsky. Since all human values and actions were conditioned by economic necessity, these writers argued, leaders could work with it or against it. If they work against economic necessity, they are destined to fail. If they work with it, they are likely to succeed. In essence, the equivalent notions of social determinism, historical materialism, or historical necessity are all based on four assumptions. One, all rulers are limited by their times and culture, and none makes history *de nova*. Two, what great men imagine they are doing has no bearing on what they actually are doing from a historical perspective. They may believe they are acting upon their own motives, but they really may be instruments for some grander historical design. Three, the world-shattering political events that are attributed to great men are possible only when the culture is ready for them. Great men cannot give birth to something that is not ready to be delivered. Four, because of all the above, great men are simply individuals who happen to be at the right place and right time in history. What makes them great is their ability to oversee the unfolding of certain inevitable events and then be credited with what happens.[7]

These, then, are the two opposing sides of the great-man debate. Now let me illustrate how it applies to judging the relative greatness of the rulers in my study. An interview that Lee Lockwood conducted with Fidel Castro highlights how the perspective you adopt can affect how you interpret the accomplishments of various rulers.[8]

> Lee Lockwood: "Haven't you been overmodest in the assessment of yourself . . . ? In your hands are concentrated the four most potent sources of power: political, military, social, and economic. It is difficult to imagine what more legal authority one person might hold in Cuba. Beyond all of that, you have a kind of personal power which may be even more significant: that is, the ability of your own mind and personality to inspire people, to convince them, to enthuse them, even to turn them into fanatics. . . . Everyone seems to agree that without the almost magnetic force of your personality there wouldn't have been any Revolution in the first place. Without you, . . . the rebellion in the Sierra Maestra probably would have failed. Really, in January 1959, it was you who brought the Cuban people to power, not the Cuban people who carried you to power. Furthermore, it is difficult to give credence to your implication that it was the people of Cuba who decided for themselves that they wanted to be socialists, that they wanted a Communist society. Rather, it was you who concluded that this was the road they should take, and they followed you, not out of theoretical conviction about Marxism-Leninism—in fact, if anything, they had a strong prejudice against Communism— but out of love and trust in Fidel Castro, their *líder máximo*."
>
> Fidel Castro: "It seems to me . . . in your question there is a somewhat distorted conception of the role of individuals in history. I admit that individuals can play a very important role in essential things, owing to a series of circumstances, many of which are fortuitous and external to the wills of men. Your question seems to presuppose that a man can make history in a completely subjective way, or write a piece of history of his country, and that really isn't true. All men, whatever they do, have always acted within objective circumstances that determine the events. That is, no attitude is completely voluntary on the part of individuals, something that can come into being by the will or at the whim of men. I believe that the most a man can do is interpret the circumstances of a given moment correctly for a definite purpose, and if that purpose is not based on something false, on something unreal, it can be carried out."[9]

So who is right—Lee Lockwood, the interviewer who is in awe of the virtuoso achievements of Fidel Castro, or Castro, the great man who modestly credits historical forces for his singular accomplishments, even though a personality cult proclaiming his greatness thrives in Cuba? The challenge now is to figure out which view is correct, or at least to take this debate beyond polemics by considering some empirical findings bearing on it. In testing out the great-man theory of history, I assume that if "great" rulers are to be held responsible for certain momentous events, then a close relationship should exist between the presence of certain distinctive personal characteristics on their part and the occurrence of these particular events. As a corollary, great rulers should be more likely to possess these distinctive personal characteristics than mediocre or inferior rulers. If the presence of great rulers is only incidental or coincidental to the occurrence of these momentous events, then there should be no significant relationship between their distinctive personal characteristics and the sociopolitical events credited to them, since almost any leaders, even those with entirely different personal characteristics, could have brought about the same results. Or possibly, because of historical inevitability, the same results could have happened without any leader.

Up until now, it has been impossible to test the great-man theory. That is because both systematic information about the personal characteristics and backgrounds of a large sample of rulers and reliable, objective measures of political greatness were unavailable. As a result, there was no way to tell what personality characteristics if any distinguished great from not-great rulers. Without being able to identify the characteristic traits of the great and not-great rulers, you could not tell if they were connected in any way to certain political events transpiring during their reigns. Now that this personal information is available on rulers and you can measure their relative achievements in office by means of the Political Greatness Scale, it becomes possible to test the theory.

The only conceptual decision left is how to tell "great" and "not-great" leaders apart. Obviously, you cannot contrast the personal characteristics of great and not-great rulers if you do not have an objective way to tell which rulers are which. The way I chose to resolve this issue was to use a statistical ranking procedure that automatically assigned rulers to the top third or bottom third of greatness based on their total Political Greatness Scale (PGS) scores. Those with the highest scores were in the top third (= the "great" rulers), and those with the lowest scores were in the bottom third (= the "not-great" rulers).[10] When you examine the list of these great rulers in the appendix, you should find that it includes the most noteworthy names of the past century.

At this point I need to make a disclaimer, much as Janos Kadar, the apparatchik, often did before he took a stand with any superiors. The designation of rulers as "great" according to their total scores on the PGS simply reflects a social rather than personal judgment about their relative greatness. It does not mean that in my estimation they are *truly* great as people or that I necessarily admire what they did. Numbered among this ruling elite are leaders such as Franklin D. Roosevelt, Charles de Gaulle, Winston Churchill, Indira Gandhi, and Jomo Kenyatta, whom I do admire, and Adolph Hitler, Joseph Stalin, and Benito Mussolini, whom I do not. My point is that you should not mistake great political achievements with noble or admirable ones, and, conversely, you should not assume that the lack of these achievements, which would place rulers within the not-great category, necessarily means an indictment of their political accomplishments. In many instances, the only reasons certain rulers were classified in the lower third of relative greatness was because they had the "misfortune" of not fighting any wars, not expanding their country's boundaries, not forcing their own vision upon society, and not monopolizing power for long periods of time. What was bad for their political reputations may have turned out to be good for the health and welfare of their people. Had they instead truly wanted to gain posthumous fame, they would have sought success in military ventures or the restructuring of their society and perhaps shown their toughness as well by quashing some political demonstrations, which then would have increased their chances for greatness according to the usual social criteria.[11]

THE SEVEN PILLARS OF POLITICAL GREATNESS

Despite the unquestioned importance of historical events and the political climate of the time, my studies yielded strong evidence that the personal attributes of rulers could influence the extent of their political achievements. For instance, when I ran a specific statistical procedure, known as multiple regression analysis, to calculate the extent to which a selected set of certain personal attributes in rulers were related to their total scores on the Political Greatness Scale, which measured the extent of their political achievements, I found that a high statistically significant relationship existed between them.[12] This finding suggested that this particular collection of personal attributes, which I shall describe shortly, seemed capable of predicting, at least retrospectively, the relative political accomplishments of rulers during their reigns.

Using another statistical procedure known as logistic regression,[13] I then sought to learn the extent to which these same personal attributes of rulers could predict whether they belonged in the upper third or lower third of political greatness based on their total PGS scores. With this analysis, since there theoretically were only two choices for these two groups of rulers, either being regarded as great or not-great, the chances of correctly assigning any particular ruler to one or the other of these categories by this statistical procedure should be 50 percent, just as it is with predicting heads or tails during coin-flipping, if the relationship between their total PGS scores and the extent of their particular personal characteristics was due entirely to chance. As it turned out, the procedure correctly assigned 88 percent of all rulers to either the upper or lower third of political greatness based on these particular personal attributes of rulers, a much higher success rate than expected by chance.[14] This added further support to the notion that a true relationship existed between certain personal characteristics of rulers and the political events transpiring during their rule.

Rather than identifying any single personal attribute as determining political greatness, these various analyses revealed that seven distinctive but overlapping clusters of attributes separated the great from the not-great rulers. These clusters of attributes, which I refer to as the "seven pillars of greatness," appear to represent the personal underpinnings for political greatness rather than being equivalent with political greatness itself (See figure 9.1 below). Though unique in their entirety, these clusters of attributes bear a resemblance to the "template of greatness" that I previously identified in eminent twentieth-century individuals, which likewise predicted the extent of their creative achievements.[15] This resemblance suggests that individuals achieving greatness in almost any field of human endeavor are likely to share certain personal characteristics. In rulers, certain of these attributes, such as "dominance" or "contrariness," often can be detected during their childhood. Others, such as personal "presence," "vanity," and "courage," become more prominent during their rise to power. Yet others, such as being a social "change agent" or displaying a "wary unease," are more likely to be evident after they gain high office.

What the results of my studies show is that the possession of these clusters of attributes is a relative matter, with great rulers as a group showing significantly more of them than the not-great ones. For instance, 64

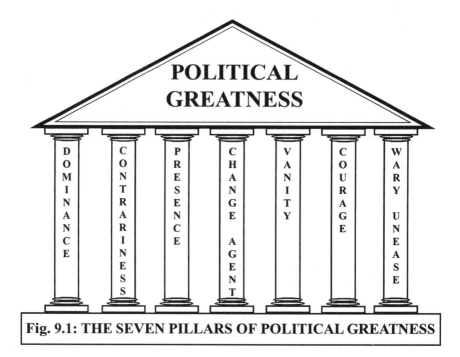

Fig. 9.1: THE SEVEN PILLARS OF POLITICAL GREATNESS

percent of rulers in the top third of political greatness compared to only 25 percent in the bottom third possess three or more of these pillars, while 75 percent of those in the lower rung compared to only 36 percent in the upper rung have two or fewer. These findings dramatically highlight that, despite certain similarities in their backgrounds, educations, and personal characteristics,[16] the great and the not-great turn out to be basically different kinds of people in certain important respects and that the actual ways they differ have a powerful bearing on what they eventually will or won't accomplish during their reigns. Simply put, those who possess more of these pillars of greatness tend to accomplish more during their reigns than those who possess fewer.

The First Pillar: Dominance

One of the most striking features of the great rulers is their tremendous drive to be the foremost person in their group, organization, political party, nation, geographic region, and sometimes even the world. Their striving to dominate others has a profound effect on most of their decisions and actions. At almost every gathering of people, they compulsively seek a chance to emerge as the leader. They can work well with others as a team as long as they assume a predominant position. Anybody who ranks above them or wields more influence represents an ob-stacle in their path.

An anecdote about Kemal Atatürk, one of the most charismatic and dynamic rulers of all time, illustrates well this imperial need for domi-nation. One evening, after engaging his guests in a rambling argument about some inconsequential matters, he called on Halide Adibe, a female politician, for her opinion. She replied that she did not get his point. His tone suddenly changed, and he shocked her with his reply:

"What I mean is this: I want everyone to do as I wish and command."

She countered, "Have they not done so already in everything that is fundamental and for the good of the Turkish cause?"

Ignoring her question, he continued, "I don't want any consider-ation, criticism, or advice. I will have only my own way. All shall do as I command."

"Me too, Pasha'm?"

"You too."

"I will obey you and do as you wish as long as I believe that you are serving the cause."

"You shall obey me and do as I wish," he answered, looking her straight in the eyes.

"Is that a threat, Pasha'm?" she quietly asked.

He hesitated for a moment, thought better of his answer, and de-cided that he had revealed too much.[17]

Although Atatürk backed off at that moment, he meant what he ini-tially told her. He did expect everyone to obey him, and in time he would get an entire nation to comply with his wishes.

Sometimes this urge to command and for others to obey flowers only after rulers gain high office, but, more often than not, those who achieve political greatness show signs of dominating others even in their youths. These youths seemed primed from an early age to dominate others during play and ordinary interactions or within the context of clubs, groups, or organizations. Because of their personalities, they got other children to defer to them, to give added weight to their opinions, or to

> As children, teenagers, or young adults, 50 percent of those who eventu-ally became great, compared to 37 percent of those who did not, already were ordering siblings, playmates, and classmates about, forming groups to lead, bossing others around, or getting others involved in assorted ac-tivities.

9.1: Male chimpanzee bowing to dominant one. From *In The Shadow of Man* by Jane Goodall. © 1971 by Hugo and Jane van Lawick-Goodall. Reprinted by permission of Houghton Mifflin Company and Weidenfeld & Nicholson. All rights reserved.

follow their lead in games, meetings, or social events. For example, even when Louis Botha was a child, others always looked to him for approval, even his older brothers and sisters. A sister admitted, "It's hard to disobey Louis."[18] Or like the proverbial story about Anatole France, the novelist, who instructed his manservant to go out onto the balcony to find out in what direction the crowd was moving on the cobbled street below so that he could run to their fore to lead them, many of these childhood leaders had an uncanny ability to sense what others wanted or where they were headed and then found ways to lead them to where they wanted to go.

Taking over and making over the organization:

As youths, those who eventually became politically prominent as rulers often served as high-ranking officers in student groups, clubs, or councils at school; formed new organizations; or led political rallies or protests. They became leaders by being so involved or outspoken that the other group members, who could not match their initiative or zeal, soon begin deferring to them. Because they took on so much more responsibility than others were willing to assume, others begin entrusting them with even more responsibilities. Leadership seemed to be an inevitable consequence of the enthusiasm, commitment, and guidance that they brought to their group. Then once they became the leader of a particular organization, they seemed compelled to run other groups as well.

Being resourceful, these youths were not likely to leave the prospects of becoming the leader of these organizations entirely to chance. When they needed an influential sponsor, they usually managed to find one. Not to be denied, when they were excluded from some desirable group that they hoped to join or if a suitable group was not available to meet their needs, they simply created their own group by actively recruiting others as members. Then after the group was formed, they automatically assumed the role as the head.

Bureaucratizing the group:

Many of those who achieved some measure of political greatness relied on their superior organizing ability as a route to leadership. Unless organizations or groups of people have defined goals, they tend to be amorphous entities, susceptible to the influence of anyone capable of giving them shape and direction. Because most people are intimidated by the task of establishing organizational procedures and regulations or getting others to carry out assigned functions, certain aspiring rulers come to prominence at a relatively early age because of their talent for structuring tasks and directing others. For instance, Deng Xiaoping showed a knack for being able to organize cadres of disaffected youths into committed fighting units long before he came into prominence. Boris Yeltsin also was adept at organizing groups for some purpose or other, and usually it made no difference which. Being in charge of the group was more important for him than worrying what the particular group would accomplish. For example, he often would turn spontaneous get-togethers into some kind of group outing or athletic contest, but mostly he preferred to foment rebellions against those in authority. As a teenager, Indira Gandhi recruited thousands of boys and girls for a monkey brigade, modeled after the monkey army of legend, then drilled them, marched them, and assigned them various duties. By the time he was ten years old, Yassir Arafat was training and drilling all the children in the neighborhood to become Arab guerrilla fighters, and, by the time he was in college, he assumed authority over all aspects of Palestinian students' lives. Although many of his fellow students became irritated with him, they still kept following his orders, simply because he expected them to obey.

Challenging authority figures:

Another common route to leadership among youths involved challenging established authorities, whether they be school administrators, occupying powers, or reigning political leaders, either by direct confrontations, protests and underground activities, or by forming organizations designed to

9.2: Dominance confrontation between two male gelada baboons (note the white eyelid flash). Irwin S. Bernstein/WRPC AV Archives.

> As youths, those who would achieve political greatness were much more likely than those who would not to be nonconforming and rebellious (51 percent versus 34 percent, respectively).

change the existing order. These would-be leaders had a knack for getting into trouble with the school authorities, not only for missing classes or for being disobedient but also for participating in forbidden political activities. Standing up to an authority figure gave the challenger instant credibility among those who were too timid to do so themselves. By challenging the right of those in authority to exert power over them—and sometimes risking their lives and liberty in doing so—the challengers gained a power of their own among their admiring friends, classmates, and colleagues.

Examples of these kinds of behaviors are plentiful. Sekou Toure, president of Guinea, was expelled from school at the age of fifteen after one year of leading a food strike against the authorities. Gamal Abdul Nasser organized underground activities against the British as a student and then later, as a military officer, formed a secret organization to overthrow the king. Willy Brandt became leader of the Karl Marx group of the Socialist Youth Movement at the age of fifteen. He was expelled temporarily from school that year for provocatively reading a poem in class while wearing his forbidden political uniform, consisting of a blue shirt and a bright red insignia tie. And Mao was one of the first students to cut off his pigtail to signify his independence. At about age fourteen, after his father's death, he began shocking his schoolmates by wearing eccentric, outlandish outfits; interrupting boring teachers with nasty remarks; revolting against all forms of discipline; and reveling in his rebelliousness. As a consequence of these and other activities, his fellow students voted him "student of the year" and elected him secretary to the Student Society.

Passion and intimidation:

In other instances, youths were able to dominate fellow students and others by the forcefulness of their personalities and the strength of their convictions and, when that did not work, through bullying and intimidating tactics, much as Mussolini and Hitler did. Fidel Castro, too, bossed his peers, but he also had been able to win their admiration because of his bravado and athletic prowess. As adolescents and young men, these youths often tended to be rabble-rousers who gave voice to the frustrations and anger of their listeners. They had the capacity to sway followers by their ideological swagger and the simplistic solutions they proposed.

Because they were so opinionated, they automatically dominated most groups, probably because nobody could match their passion in order to counter what they said or, even if they could have, would have been too scared to try.

Plain, old-fashioned popularity:

Perhaps the most common route to leadership for youths during their school years was through personal popularity, especially within democracies. Being popular meant being liked and admired by others. Many of those youths destined for greatness were able to do this by making others feel good about themselves, displaying what is known as "the common touch." They had the capacity to give others the impression that they mattered, that their problems and aspirations were important, and that they personally understood their needs and wants. As a result, others came to believe that these aspiring rulers would represent them and look out for their interests. Aside from being liked, many of these rulers also gained popularity because of their talents or achievements, such as athletic prowess, musical talent, acting ability, editing the student newspaper, debating skill, or heading the student body. Once they were in the limelight, they managed to capitalize on their special status to further their careers and obtain positions of increasing prominence.

The Second Pillar: Contrariness

Although many of the great leaders expected obedience from underlings, they themselves rebelled against any superiors who expected obedience from them. Throughout their lives, they tended to be defiant toward those in positions of authority and kept pushing their limits. Nor was their contrariness limited toward those who ranked above them or had any power over them. They also reflexively resisted any unsolicited advice or criticism by comrades and colleagues even when they fully agreed with it. Nobody could tell them what to think, feel, or do—or, at least, without upsetting them.

Rebelliousness against parents:

One of the initial ways these potential greats showed their contrariness was in rebelling against the authority of their parents. Fidel Castro, for

---

While the majority of the great rulers were not oppositional, a much higher percentage of them (34 percent) than of the not-great rulers (24 percent) were contrary during their youths toward various forms of authority and restrictive traditions.

example, organized a group of workers against his father, who owned a sugar plantation, because he felt his father was exploiting them. Mao also openly challenged his father's authority. Identifying his father as an oppressor, he gave an apt description of the discontent and revolutionary forces at work in his own household. "There were two 'parties' in the family," he said. "One was my father, the Ruling Power. The Opposition was made up of myself, my mother, my brother, and sometimes even the laborer. In the 'United Front' of the Opposition, however, there was a difference of opinion. My mother advocated a policy of indirect attack. She criticized my overt display of emotion and attempts at open rebellion against the Ruling Power. She said it was not the Chinese way."[19]

Challenging school authorities:

Once in school, a far greater percentage of the great than of the not-great had trouble with the school authorities. They got in conflicts with their teachers. They missed classes. They organized unauthorized political protests. They got expelled or suspended. And they dressed in unconventional ways. Stalin, for example, vehemently resisted the Jesuitical attempts to control him in college, and he was punished fifteen times in school for reading prohibited books. After Vladimir Lenin enrolled in law school, he was expelled for joining a student demonstration against the university's inspector. Mujibur Rahman, the Bengali leader and first prime minister and later president of Bangladesh, started taking part in demonstrations at the age of seven. He organized strikes and continued to be active in politics after enrolling as a law student in Dacca University. He was arrested and released. The university expelled him, stating that it would readmit him only if he signed a bond for good behavior. He refused and left law school.

Defiance against traditional religious beliefs:

You would expect that, because they wanted to win the backing of their people, great rulers would espouse traditional religious beliefs and present themselves as defenders of the faith. That was not necessarily so. The great were more likely to be atheists or agnostics than the non-great. Though many of these nonbelievers were confirmed communists or socialists, some espoused their own idiosyncratic ideologies, which sometimes were a conglomerate of their political, spiritual, and philosophical views or bastardized versions of existing ideologies. Stalin, Mao, Tito, Pot Pol, Ho Chi Minh, and Castro, for example, each espoused his own brand of Marxism-Leninism, which formed the political underpinnings for their radically different forms of government.

> While about two-thirds of the sample of rulers continued to affirm the religious beliefs of their parents, over twice as many of the great than of the not-great became agnostics or atheists (32 percent versus 15 percent, respectively). Again, consistent with their antipathy to all forms of authority and their greater lack of religious beliefs, the great rulers (43 percent) were less apt to attend church or follow prescribed religious practices than the not-great ones (36 percent).

Another sign of their defiant attitudes toward religion had to do with church attendance or compliance with important religious rituals. Although many nonbelieving rulers hypocritically attended church, prayed in temples, or visited religious shrines simply for practical political reasons—as did Indira Gandhi, who was an atheist, and Kemal Atatürk, who was an agnostic—many did not, even in countries where it would have been politically expedient to do so.

Challenging the authority of the party:

This same friction with authority also showed up when those destined for greatness began their political careers. They simply did not like to be beholden to anyone. Or if they were disposed to remain loyal to past mentors, they no longer sought advice or assistance from them once they themselves were in charge. Their frictions were not only with the former superiors who had appointed them to key positions or helped them in their careers but often with anyone in a leadership role. Theodore Roosevelt was constantly at odds with the party leadership. Churchill antagonized many of his colleagues and administrative superiors over the years. Charles de Gaulle got his instructors at the military academy so angry at him that they lowered his grades in order to block his advancement. De Gaulle also got Franklin Delano Roosevelt furious at him during World War II because he was not as deferential as Roosevelt expected someone to be who was totally dependent on the Allied nations to rescue his country and whose only real authority was in what he granted himself.

Discarding social customs:

This same tendency by the great to challenge authority and buck tradition showed up in their married lives as well. Great rulers were less likely than the not-great ones to abide by their vows of marital fidelity. Again, this seemed to be yet another example of the resistance by the great rulers against any kinds of restrictive social customs that potentially kept them from doing what they wanted to do.

About two-thirds of the great rulers had extramarital affairs or practiced polygamy, compared to one-half of the not-great ones. With this the case, it was not surprising to find that a greater percentage of the great than the not-great rulers separated from or divorced their mates (27 percent versus 15 percent) and, on average, remarried more often (1.4 versus 1.1).

Sometimes this tendency of rulers for not wanting to be bound by social conventions takes the preposterous form of not even wanting to be restrained by themselves. Again, Kemal Atatürk, as in so many other areas, illustrates this well. True to his convictions about wanting to improve the lot of women in Turkish society, he married a modern, sophisticated, and liberated woman, Latife, who had studied law and was conversant in English. After his Western-style marriage, he then pushed for the emancipation of all Turkish women. But because his wife was also headstrong and outspoken and refused to accept the lot of an uncomplaining wife, they inevitably came to loggerheads over his frequent sexual affairs. Finally tiring of his wife's efforts to curb his sexual desires, Atatürk banished her from his house, which, in the Muslim tradition, was the equivalent of divorce. Later, once he was free of her, he switched back to his Western outlook and instituted a new legal code that granted men and women equal rights and made divorce by repudiation illegal.

The Third Pillar: Personal Presence

According to Max Weber, the great German sociologist, the charismatic leader demands obedience on the basis of the mission he feels called upon to perform. He dominates other men by virtue of mysterious qualities inaccessible to others and incompatible with the rules of thought and action that govern everyday life. People surrender themselves to him because they are carried away by a belief in his authenticity and powers.[20] Charisma, of course, is not an objective personal quality, like height or weight. Someone you perceive to be compelling, others may perceive to be repelling. But despite the subjectivity involved in judgments about charisma, it is hard to deny that certain people possess a magnetic presence that binds your attention and makes you want to defer to them.

Although Weber claimed that this charisma was natural, you can find many instances of democratic leaders, such as Charles de Gaulle, who deliberately cultivated it. Henry Kissinger, who met most of the world leaders during his time as secretary of state, wrote that de Gaulle "domi-

9.3: Note the gorilla's powerful presence and air of authority. SteveBloom.com

nated a room with an almost physical force of his authority." Aided by his height and ramrod military bearing, de Gaulle had an electric air about him as he walked down a street wearing his white gloves and his beret tipped to the right or stood before a crowd with his fists clenched or his arms raised or when he simply sat behind a desk and imperiously deigned to answer questions at a news conference. More than monarchs, he conveyed a sense of majesty in his very bearing, manner, and being. And his vanity was enormous. Long before he appeared on the political scene, a young fellow officer once approached him on maneuvers and

While this charisma was not confined only to the great rulers, a substantially greater percentage of them than the not-great possessed it (53 percent versus 30 percent). With great rulers being only slightly more likely than not-great ones to be excellent orators (47 percent versus 43 percent, respectively), it was apparent that this charisma applied more to their bearing and manner than to verbal eloquence.

said, "I am going to say something that will probably make you smile, but I have a curious feeling that you are heading for a very great destiny." De Gaulle gave a slight nod as he gazed out into the distance and then answered matter-of-factly, "Yes, I do too."[21]

In many instances, the personal magnetism shown by the great rulers appeared long before they gained high office and was often an important factor in their rapid rise to power. What needs emphasis is that personal magnetism or charisma is primarily nonverbal and need not be associated with great oratory. Certain individuals can have both, others one or the other, and yet others neither. For instance, certain charismatic rulers, such as Sekoe Toure of Guinea, could be soft-spoken or even inarticulate at times and still have every word uttered become instant law.

Loneliness at the top:

Unlike those who possessed a natural presence, de Gaulle intentionally set out to create and to heighten his own mystique. He had written, "There can be no prestige without mystery," and he deliberately tried to make himself as mysterious as possible. One of the ways he did this was to isolate himself from others and discourage intimacies. He even had a distant relationship with his own son. He preferred to be in the presence of the person he most admired and respected, which happened to be himself. He took long walks alone and on occasion with his wife, whom he saw as an extension of himself. Solitude became his solace. "Solitude was my temptation," he wrote. "It became my friend. What else could satisfy anyone who has been face to face with history!"[22]

As it happens, rulers have a sound reason for embracing the burden of solitude and avoiding close relationships. Observed up close, they may be forced to give up their cherished mystique. Just as Gulliver

---

Great rulers (29 percent) are less likely to be trusting of others than are not-great ones (38 percent) and, consequently, are less apt to have close friends (23 percent versus 30 percent). As with de Gaulle, a higher percentage of great (25 percent) than not-great rulers (20 percent), but far from a majority of them, prefer to spend their time alone rather than in the company of others. They tell themselves that remaining apart is the necessary burden they bear for being a leader. Still, that does not stop them from complaining about their isolation. In a letter, Nkrumah confessed to an "intense loneliness which makes me sometimes burst into tears,"[23] but, like most other rulers, he did nothing to change his lot.

noted all the pimples, moles, warts, pores, crooked teeth, peculiar smells, and the hairs sprouting from the nostrils of the giant Brobdingnagians, others who got too close to rulers likewise would be able to observe all of their imperfections and flaws. And perhaps also become aware of their personal worries and anxieties . . . and their often less-than-brilliant reflections and responses. How, then, were these rulers supposed to inspire awe and reverence in their subjects who discover that they are all too human?

It may be lonely at the top, as the popular notion goes, but what many observers often overlook is that, for many of these rulers, it also was lonely on the way up, and it was lonely for them as children, long before they ever became interested in politics. These were not people who easily formed friendships on the basis of equality. They could be friendly and cordial but not intimate or chummy despite being a leader among their peers. Other than voicing their views on politics, they usually were not adept as conversationalists and did not feel comfortable in social settings. Many could work well with others but only when they were in charge. While giving the impression of openness and sincerity, they did so more as a tactic to enlist political support than as a way to share personal intimacies. Despite their outer veneer of sociability, they remained very private people, taking few others into their confidence. Ultimate power may have made it harder for these rulers to share intimacies with others, but, despite their pro forma protestations, they only ended up doing what they were naturally inclined to do.

The Fourth Pillar: Change Agent

It is simply the nature of political greatness that history looks most favorably on strong leaders who act decisively in times of crises, take bold initiatives, change the ideological underpinnings of society, or introduce new programs designed to improve the prosperity or power of the nation.

Great rulers were more likely than the not-great ones to assume dictatorial powers at some point in their rule (52 percent versus 36 percent), and, conversely, not-great rulers were more likely than great ones to be indecisive, cautious, and collaborative in their administrative styles (46 percent versus 34 percent).

An autocratic style:

During the past century, dictators were not the only kinds of leaders to assume dictatorial powers. In many instances, leaders of emerging or established democracies declared states of emergency or martial law or changed the nature of the constitution to grant themselves more power. Mostly this happened in times of war or national crises, but it could happen at other times as well. Within the dominant one-party systems of Latin America, for instance, the caudillo tradition favored strong, decisive leadership, which sometimes became hard to distinguish from autocratic or dictatorial rule. Indira Gandhi's actions in 1972 also illustrate the arbitrariness often found in the strong leader. Shortly after Gandhi led her New Congress Party to a landslide victory in national elections after India's victory over Pakistan, her defeated Socialist opponent charged that she had violated the election laws. In June 1975 the high court ruled against her, which meant that she would be deprived of her seat in Parliament and would have to stay out of politics for six years. In response, she declared a state of emergency throughout India, imprisoned her political opponents, and assumed emergency powers, passing many laws limiting personal freedoms. During this period she implemented several unpopular policies, including large-scale sterilization as a form of birth control. Eventually, when she finally allowed national elections in 1977, she and her party were defeated, but, during some of the time she was in power, she ruled as a virtual dictator.[24]

> Almost twice as many of the great rulers (60 percent) as the not-great ones (31 percent) were responsible for changing the basic nature of the government and, in some instances, the entire fabric of their society.

According to my criteria, social change agents are those who bring about greater democracy, greater freedom, or greater independence in their nation or, conversely, transform it into a totalitarian state according to some utopian ideal. Those who simply establish a strict, repressive dictatorship, mainly for personal gain or to keep law and order, do not qualify as being social change agents, largely because they are implementing a regressive, stereotypical form of government. Social change agents are those who liberate their country from colonial rule, oversee the transition from dictatorship to democracy, make sweeping constitutional changes, switch from an absolute to a constitutional monarchy, or transform their society according to some political or religious ideology.

Great causes require great sacrifices:
With most of these bold initiatives, the great rulers make decisions that usually lead to the loss of many lives, both within and outside their own nations. Whether or not these leaders acted for just or moral reasons is beside the point from the standpoint of history. What mattered was the moment of these events. Mao's Cultural Revolution, Stalin's dekulakization program, Pol Pot's forced rural relocation of city dwellers, or Hitler's genocidal programs that have led to countless deaths and incalculable suffering have won them far more posthumous fame or infamy throughout the entire world than Arias Sanchez's Nobel Prize–winning peace plan in 1987 that helped resolve the Nicaraguan civil war.

> The large majority of those rulers who qualified as being great (67 percent) compared to a minority of the not-great ones (40 percent) declared wars on other nations or defended their countries against aggressors or responded to civil uprisings or violent disturbances within their own countries with force and so were responsible for the pain, death, and suffering of others.

The point is that the odds of leaders becoming immortalized are low if they do not sacrifice people for some great cause. History ennobles leaders, as it did Napoleon and Caesar, who offer selfless or patriotic or ennobling reasons for their military actions or adventures— thwarting aggression, ensuring peace for all time, fighting a war to end all wars, preserving democracy, honoring a covenant with God, establishing a homeland, ridding the world of infidels, gaining independence, keeping the empire intact, defending the country's honor, or creating a better society. Tyrants such as Macias Nguema, Idi Amin, or Bokassa, who killed people without just or worthy reasons, end up on the slag heap of history.

The Fifth Pillar: Vanity

In ancient Rome, the true measure of a nobleman lay in his *dignitas.* "His auctoritas was his clout, his measure of public influence, his ability to sway public opinion and public bodies from Senate to priests to the Treasury. Dignitas was different. It was personal and private, yet it extended into all parameters of a man's public life. Dignitas was . . . a man's personal degree of impressiveness . . . of glory? Dignitas summed up what a man was, as a man and as a leader of his society. It was his pride, his integrity, his word, his intelligence, his deeds, his ability, his knowledge, his standing, his worth as a man. Dignitas survived a man's death, it was the only way he could triumph over death."[25] Dignitas also gave a man ascendancy over all those who did not possess it.

This distinction between auctoritas and dignitas helps to clarify the difference between two basic qualities that many great rulers possess. Their auctoritas has to do with their authority or sense of presence. It involves all those natural or acquired personal qualities that are capable of commanding the attention of others and getting them to obey. In its most dramatic expression, it takes the form of personal charisma. Dignitas is different. It mostly pertains to how individuals regard themselves—how comfortable they feel about who they are and what they want to do in life. Persons who possess dignitas usually seem to have great composure, self-confidence, and poise. Because there may be considerable overlap between the qualities of auctoritas and dignitas, individuals who seem very self-assured also may appear to be charismatic, and the converse also is so.

Composure, self-confidence, and poise:

What applied to the leading citizens of ancient Rome also applies to rulers of more modern nations. If I can substitute terms such as composure, self-confidence, and poise for the outmoded notion of dignitas, then it becomes apparent that the great rulers are far more apt to show this trait than the not-great ones. They expressed this personal confidence by seeming certain in their judgments, seeming at ease around others, forcefully stating their opinions when necessary, stubbornly persisting on a course of action, not becoming ruffled by challenges or confrontations, seeming secure in their abilities, and rarely second-guessing themselves. Sometimes, though, when accentuated, this self-confidence may appear as narcissism, egotism, conceit, or arrogance—qualities that tend to be associated with vanity. And sometimes the dividing line between supreme self-confidence and megalomania becomes hard to define. However, in whatever degree this self-confidence expressed itself, whether it appears as simple composure or as vanity or as seeming megalomania, the great rulers were much more likely to show it than the not-great ones.

For many of these rulers, their supreme self-confidence seemed fueled by a sense of destiny or mission. Sometimes this conviction in their destiny began in childhood, and sometimes it struck them much later. Sometimes it came to them as gradually unfolding, crystallizing experiences. And sometimes it struck them during sudden epiphanies or rev-

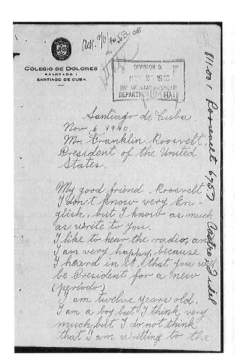

9.4: Letter from Fidel Castro, age twelve, to President Franklin D. Roosevelt. See next page for text of letter. Imagine the self-confidence and brazenness of someone so young (or anyone) to write this letter. Photograph from the National Archives.

Text of letter from Castro to Roosevelt

Santiago de Cuba
Nov. 6, 1940
Mr. Franklin Roosevelt
President of the United States

My good friend Roosevelt. I don't know very English, but I know as much as write to you. I like to hear the radio, and I am very happy, because I heard in it that you will be President for a new (periodo). I am twelve years old. I am a boy but I think very much but I do not think that I am writing to the President of the United States. If you like, give me a ten dollars bill green american, in the letter, because never have I not seen a ten dollars bill green american and I would like to have one of them. My address is:

Sr. Fidel Castro
Coledio de Dolores
Santiago de Cuba
Oriente. Cuba

I don't know very English but I know very much Spanish and I suppose you don't know very Spanish but you know very English because you are American but I am not American.

Thank you very much. Good by.
Your friend,
Fidel Castro

If you want iron to make ~~sheaps~~ ships I will show to you the bigest (minas) of iron in the land. They are in Mayari. Oriente Cuba.

---

elations. David Ben Gurion, for instance, had this sense of destiny from an early age. As a student at religious school, he announced to his classmates, "One day, I will be the leader of Israel."[26] After first being appointed prime minister, Winston Churchill wrote in the first volume of his history of the war, "At last I had the authority to give directions over the whole scene. I felt as if I were walking with Destiny, and that all my past life had been but a preparation for this hour and for this trial."[27] McKenzie King, a Canadian prime minister for twenty-one years, wrote

> Within the sample of rulers, 75 percent of the great rulers seemed very
> poised, possessed, and self-confident compared to only 63 percent of the
> not-great ones. For a portion of them, this great self-assurance could be
> attributed to an epiphany or crystallizing experience. About four times as
> many great rulers (28 percent) as not-great ones (7 percent) had unusual
> experiences that heightened their feelings of specialness or their sense of
> mission.

in his diary after being elected, "I feel I am being guided from above
(and) that dear Mother & Max & Father & Bell, the whole family in
Heaven, are guiding and directing me."[28] After undergoing a spiritual
conversion at the age of thirty-three, Paul Kruger, president of the
Transvaal, or South African Republic, from 1883 to 1900, believed he
was ordained by God to save the Boer people from themselves.[29] Ibn
Saud became convinced that God had entrusted him with the mission
of uniting the kingdom of Arabia and making it a great power again.
Hitler became absolutely convinced that Providence was looking out
for him. Franco perhaps was more modest than Hitler in his belief that
God had chosen him not to conquer the entire world but simply to restore Christianity to Spain and combat the atheism and materialism of
the modern world.

Tooting your own horn and touting yourself:
One expression of the narcissism or vanity of many great rulers is their
belief in their own importance, that they hold a special perspective of
reality, and that their deeds and ideas need to be recorded for posterity.
Most great rulers know that if they want to be remembered posthumously,
they cannot entrust something as important as their political legacy to
others, many of whom will be biased, and so, to "keep the record straight,"
they need to make sure their accomplishments are duly noted and their
failures are excused. Humility and modesty may be admirable traits in
ordinary persons, but those qualities do not suit those who want to be
seen as heroes and leave their mark on history.

Some rulers, such as Mao Zedong or Muammar al- Qaddafi, recorded
their overly simplistic, Rorschach-like guides for revolution and living
life in general in Red, Green, Black, or Blue books, fondly referred to by
their color. Other rulers produced monumental works that elevated their
political standing and helped to shape the opinions of scholars about the
historic role they played during certain important happenings. Mikhail

> Far more great rulers (55 percent) than not-great ones (38 percent) published books containing their political views, their own interpretation of certain critical national or world events, or justifications for their actions.

Gorbachev's *Perestroika and the New Thinking*; Winston Churchill's six-volume work, *The Second World War*, and his four-volume *A History of the English-Speaking Peoples*; Chiang Kai-shek's *China's Destiny* and *Chinese Economic Theory*; Anwar Sadat's autobiography, *In Search of Identity*; Jawaharlal Nehru's *The Discovery of India*; Vladimir Lenin's *The State and Revolution*, which became communism's handbook of revolution; Joseph Stalin's *The Foundations of Leninism*; Nelson Mandela's *I Am Prepared to Die* and his later autobiography, *Long Walk to Freedom*; and Ho Chi Minh's *French Colonization on Trial* are examples of highly influential books written by great rulers that documented their views and helped to define their mythic place in history.

Whether or not rulers actually wrote their own books or got speechwriters, public relations firms, or ghostwriters to do it for them really did not matter. What mattered was that they were committed to getting the word out about themselves and letting the world know how brilliant and important they were. This even held for writing their own autobiographies. Ronald Reagan, for instance, collaborated with a writer to compile his autobiography, *An American Life,* during the time that his Alzheimer's disease was probably advancing. As Reagan was leaving a press gathering called to announce the publication of the book, he told the reporters, "It's really a great book." And then he added, "I'm looking forward someday to reading it myself."[30]

Making sure the message gets across:
For those rulers who did not have the luxury of a prison sabbatical to write about themselves or who had no noteworthy views to offer or who did not want to commission biographers to concoct stories about their lives or who lived in countries where most of the population could not read, they were able to bypass writing entirely by using the state-controlled television, radio, or newspaper media to laud their accomplishments and the specialness of their being. That way, they did not have to worry about political opponents misrepresenting or criticizing their works or casting aspersions on them. By establishing a personality cult, they could create their own legends about themselves, monitor the effectiveness of their propaganda, and ensure their own living and posthumous fame.

About three times as many of the great rulers (45 percent) as the not-great ones (15 percent) depended on state-operated propaganda machines or personality cults or party-sponsored public relations firms to attest to their greatness.

These cults sometimes elevated these leaders to semi-divine status, converting their former homes or the jails where they were imprisoned or the places where they fought into national shrines. In addition, they built museums to house their memorabilia; built monuments to them around the countryside; named mountains, rivers, cities, and streets after them; speckled the landscape with their statues; ordered their pictures hung in governmental buildings and public places; and commissioned official "hagiographies" about them. Not leaving anything to chance, they also insisted that schoolchildren learn catechisms, sayings, or slogans attributed to them and organized parades and public spectacles in their honor.

What is so intriguing about many of these personality cults is that their sponsors—namely, the rulers themselves—often become their most

9.5: The cult of "Der Fuhrer." Hitler accepts the ovation of the Reichstag after announcing the "peaceful" acquisition of Austria. Photograph from the National Archives.

avid devotees. Since no one was allowed to contradict the propaganda, these rulers had little difficulty in becoming convinced that it must be true. Not unlike authors who take pride in the glowing inside-the-cover, book-jacket blurbs about their brilliance and the originality of their book, often forgetting that they themselves had written them at the request of their publishers, rulers likewise had good reason for being so easily duped by themselves. No matter how exaggerated the personal hype or praise, it merely reflected what these rulers believed or preferred to believe about themselves.

The Sixth Pillar: Courage

It seems only fair to expect that people who are willing to sacrifice others for a worthy cause also should serve as role models for their followers by being willing to risk their own lives when the occasion demands. As it happens, this expectation is fulfilled by those who go on to become great rulers. Somewhere along the way in their quest for high office and some-times even afterwards, they show their courage, bravery, and seeming selfless dedication to their cause. This wins them the respect and admiration of their countrymen and establishes their credentials as great leaders. Whether their heroism comes from courage, foolhardiness, patriotism, or ignorance of the consequences of their acts, this distinction makes little difference to the public. In many countries throughout the world, people willing to risk their lives for a grand cause automatically assume the mantle of political greatness even if they do not know anything about running the complex machinery of government, have not the foggiest idea about how to cure the nation's social and economic ills, and have no other personally redeeming features.

Risk-taking:

The great rulers were far more likely to expose themselves to personal danger than the not-great ones on every indicator of courage or bravery available and to show their ferociousness as warriors. Battle was not the only arena where potential leaders could show their valor. They also had a chance to become heroes by risking their lives confronting those in power during political demonstrations or antigovernmental activities. As a result, they were far more likely to be imprisoned for a gamut of political reasons, from being involved in protests to inciting violence to organizing coups. They also were more likely to be exiled and undergo other privations.

The message of these various findings is clear. Prometheus was not the only mythological figure who had to endure daily suffering for defy-

Within the sample of rulers, the great were much more likely than the not-great to have fought in battles (48 percent versus 35 percent)—involving struggles for national liberation, civil wars, or wars with other nations—or participated in coup attempts (34 percent versus 24 percent) either as a way of gaining ultimate power for themselves or while under the command of others. During the fighting, twice as many of the great as the not-great were wounded (14 percent versus 7 percent). Even more telling, because of their bravery, valor, or resourcefulness under fire, or their leadership during war, the great were more likely to receive medals, decorations, and honors for their military prowess or to be rapidly promoted for their performance (39 percent versus 27 percent). On their climb toward ultimate power, the great were more likely than the not-great to have been arrested and incarcerated for their political activities (44 percent versus 38 percent) and also to have spent much more time in jail (an average of thirteen months versus two months). Also, twice the percentage of great leaders (22 percent) as not-great ones (11 percent) spent time in exile before they came to power.

ing the gods. Greater percentages of the great than the not-great also paid the penalty for challenging the existing political order or the regime then in power. But unlike Prometheus, they somehow found ways to throw off their shackles and capitalize on their sufferings to establish their credentials as heroes, and then use their newfound popularity as a stepping stone toward ultimate power.

The chance for the great to impress others with their daring and courage was not over once they finally got to be in power. Other dangers awaited them. Assassination attempts were more likely to be made on their lives. But despite taking great risks and being exposed to all these dangers, these great rulers—who almost fit the legendary mold of the great hero or warrior—still managed to live an average of one year longer than the not-great rulers, seventy-one versus seventy. It appears that they must have been truly favored by the gods.

Perhaps because the great rulers managed to rankle so many people with their grand schemes for social change, substantially higher percentages of them not only endured assassination attempts than the not-great rulers (49 percent versus 30 percent) but they had almost three times as many attempts made on their lives (an average of 1.1 versus 0.4 attempts per ruler).

The Seventh Pillar: A Wary Unease

In my past study of over a thousand eminent persons of the twentieth century, I was able to identify a sense of psychological "unease" as a crucial ingredient for great creative achievement.[31] The greatest achievers were more inclined than those among the lower elite to be restless, discontent, impatient, and driven people whose successes did not satisfy them for long. Those who suffered from mental illnesses capitalized on their emotional conflicts as a source of creative tension and inspiration, while those who were emotionally stable had the natural ability to generate their own psychological "unease" by seeking out large problems or challenges that demanded their complete attention.

Like these great writers, artists, scientists, academicians, and other eminent persons, great rulers likewise seem to experience a state of chronic psychological unease, which may serve as a motivational fuel for their tremendous productivity, ambitiousness, and drive. Like Vladimir Lenin, who seemed totally absorbed by the revolution twenty-four hours a day, even dreaming of it in his sleep, they are restless, energetic, indefatigable people who often seek out ambitious projects and grand schemes as a way of dissipating their energies and coping with their general unease. Mostly, these are not manic individuals whose projects reflect their grandiosity. If anything, their drive is often fueled by emotional or physical discomfort. Great rulers, such as Winston Churchill, Atatürk, Mao Zedong, Teddy Roosevelt, and Lyndon Johnson all suffered from depression. And other great rulers such as Franklin D. Roosevelt, George Clemenceau, Deng Xiaoping, Anthony Eden, Jomo

Almost twice as many of the great rulers (42 percent) as the not-great ones (24 percent) had extended periods of moroseness, social withdrawal, sleep difficulties, morbid thinking, problems concentrating, or even suicidal thoughts during their lifetimes—all the hallmarks of depression—but these symptoms occurred in different contexts and in different forms. Moreover, although the large majority of these great rulers showed no signs of being pathologically suspicious, a sizable minority, 20 percent, twice the percentage for not-great rulers (10 percent), did. Furthermore, 42 percent of the great rulers, compared to 27 percent of the not-great ones, suffered from life-threatening chronic medical conditions during their tenure in office.

Kenyatta, Vladimir Lenin, Nelson Mandela, Sukarno, and Boris Yeltsin had to contend with various life-threatening chronic medical illnesses while in office.

However, what often seems distinctive about the unease of the great rulers, whether induced by mental or physical causes or simply present for no apparent cause, is that it tends to be tinged by wariness. With certain of these great rulers, like Adolph Hitler or Joseph Stalin, this wariness takes the form of overt paranoia; but with other rulers, such as Charles de Gaulle, Josip Tito, Sukarno, Chiang Kai-shek, or Benito Mussolini, it tends to reflect a pervasive suspiciousness and distrustfulness of others. With this mind-set, best described as a "wary unease," the great rulers not only have difficulty ever resting on their laurels but also remain constantly on guard against the potential machinations of others and so seem less likely to be thwarted in their plans.

The Great Man as a Political Catalyst

On the basis of all of these findings, I believe it is now possible to take a more informed stand in the great-man versus historical necessity debate. The empirical evidence unequivocally shows that a close relationship exists between certain distinctive personal characteristics of great rulers and the extent of their political achievements. While it is possible to interpret this relationship in different ways, one obvious way to do so, which does not go beyond the empirical findings, is simply to acknowledge that rulers who display more of certain distinctive characteristics, which I have called "the seven pillars of greatness," are more likely than those who display fewer of these characteristics to be credited with certain important political achievements. As you examine the lives and careers of many of these great rulers, you cannot help but be impressed by the ways many of their decisions and actions *seemed* to have had tremendous repercussions for their nations and even for the world at large. Please note that I said *seemed*, because you need to temper that observation with certain qualifications. In almost all instances, these great rulers came to power at times and in places that were most opportune for them, so it becomes an almost futile exercise to determine whether they would have been judged as great at other times and in other places. Also, a strong association between the personal characteristics of these rulers and the major political events happening during their reign does not mean that these rulers *caused* these events. It only means that a strong linkage between them exists.

Now how can there be a strong linkage between certain personality attributes of rulers and certain political events occurring during their reign without there being a direct causal relationship between them? As I interpret the situation, one of the main reasons that the great-man versus historical necessity controversy continues to exist (aside from the previous lack of empirical evidence to support one position or another) is that the notion of causality underlying this debate has served as a kind of logical strawman. This implicit notion of causality underlying the great man theory has been that, if a ruler initiates certain political actions, then he must be responsible for all the subsequent events that unfold. In other words, a linear causal relationship must exist between the actions of that particular ruler (A) and the appearance of these political events (X), so that A → X. Or alternatively, if you want to temper the influence of the ruler somewhat, a multilinear causal relationship must exist between the ruler (A), along with other important factors at a particular time, such as the state of the economy (B), a war (C), or a natural catastrophe (D), and subsequent political events, so that A (plus B, C, and D) → X. With this strictly linear view of causality, supporters and critics of the great-man theory then debate whether the ruler represents a necessary, a sufficient, or both a necessary and sufficient condition for certain political events to take place or whether he is irrelevant to their realization. What this simplistic notion of causality fails to take into account is the complex nature of most societies, the powerful historical forces operating on them, and the potential for many different political outcomes, depending on which particular constellations of problems rulers choose to address and how they deal with them.

Instead of seeking a strict causal relationship between the decisions and actions of rulers and certain ensuing political happenings, which forces you into a conceptual corner, I have come to the conclusion that a more appropriate model for interpreting the role of great rulers is to look upon them as *political catalysts* rather than causal agents who facilitate or inhibit the expression of certain social reactions that have the historical potential for happening. Since the role of the great man remains essential for the realization or prevention of certain events, but not in a strictly causal way, the debate over whether these rulers were personally responsible for causing these outcomes or merely served as stewards for their inevitable occurrence becomes moot.

Now let me explain what I mean by a political catalyst. But first, I have to define the term *catalyst*. In chemistry, a catalyst is any substance that can increase (promote) or decrease (inhibit) the rate of a reaction without itself being consumed. The common way the catalyst makes a chemical reaction go faster is to increase the chances of molecules colliding, either through adsorption (getting molecules to stick on its surface to bring them closer together) or through the formation of unstable intermediary compounds, which then release new compounds along with the original catalyst. Examples of catalysts in industry include compounds that facilitate oxidation or more efficient burning of gasoline or those that inhibit the formation of rust.

A catalyst ordinarily reacts with a reactant to alter the rate of one specific kind of reaction, but "polyfunctional catalysts" exist that have more than one kind of interaction with the reactants. Theoretically, since catalysts are not consumed in chemical reactions, they should be able to be used repeatedly for an indefinite period of time. However, in reality, after multiple reactions, "poisons," which come from the products of these reactions, may accumulate on the surface of solid catalysts and progressively destroy their effectiveness. Other factors that affect the rate of a catalytic reaction involve the nature of the reactant itself and the actual conditions under which the reaction takes place.

Now let's extrapolate from a chemical reaction to a political development. Picture a country such as Yugoslavia, Russia, or Afghanistan during a time of economic chaos in which many divisive ethnic and religious tensions exist. In such a country, many political outcomes are possible, depending upon which issues leaders choose to address and how they choose to address them. In adopting the chemical reaction metaphor, you can imagine the country as consisting of multiple reactants (e.g., ethnic conflicts, religious tensions, economic difficulties) that offer the potential for many kinds of chemical products (e.g., civil war or peaceful coexistence), depending upon what kind of political catalysts (e.g., demagogues, ideologues, authoritarians, or democrats) come upon the scene. Certain kinds of political catalysts, responding primarily to certain kinds of reactants, would have the capacity to unleash certain kinds of reactions, whereas other kinds of political catalysts, responding primarily to other kinds of reactants such as foreign pressures or religious influences might produce other kinds of reactions. Also, certain kinds of political catalysts whose properties might not be suitable for interacting with any of the existing reactants would be completely ineffective, while others, whose properties were capable of only a narrow action, would only give rise to more limited results without addressing the more pervasive problems.

The great man, in distinction to those catalytic rulers with a more narrow action, would have the properties of a polyfunctional catalyst, showing a broad spectrum of activity by responding to multiple social reactants such as ethnic tensions, the economy, religious differences, pressing social needs, and foreign influences. In contrast to those rulers with more limited capabilities, the ruler with these polyfunctional capabilities would have an impact on all aspects of society. Under certain conditions, because of the broadness of his decisions or policies, the ruler may unleash chain reactions such as an escalating war or runaway inflation or the unraveling of the empire, which he no longer can regulate or control. Under other conditions, the accumulation of noxious products arising from the ruler's decisions and actions may slowly poison his *modus operandi* and render him completely ineffective to bring about any further change.

Now what about the matter of causality? By conceptualizing the role of the ruler in this way, you avoid the knotty issue of whether certain kinds of political events were due to deliberate actions on his part. The entire controversy over free will or necessity, which is tied into the greatman debate, ceases to exist. Just as it is logically imprecise to say that a specific catalyst "causes" a particular chemical reaction, since the potential for that reaction already exists or the reaction is already happening but at a very slow or negligible speed, it is not valid to look upon the great ruler as being causally responsible for the unfolding of certain major political events. As with the chemical catalyst, the great ruler becomes a facilitator or inhibitor of historical events, whose antecedents lay dormant, awaiting the proper catalyst, or already were in the process of unfolding but in a barely noticeable way. In a sense, the great man gives these potential political happenings a nudge, sometimes a shove, and occasionally a violent shake, but he does not "cause" them in a strictly logical sense. By definition, he cannot cause what does not have the potential for being what it becomes. However, because he is not the direct causal agent for those momentous events attributed to him does not mean that he is not a critical factor in their eventual emergence. Had the great ruler not appeared on the scene at an opportune time, the potential for those momentous events may not have been realized when they were. By being yoked together, the great ruler and his political legacy give each other meaning.

For emphasis, let me state this somewhat differently. When you examine what makes certain leaders "great," you cannot validly do so without taking into account what happens to be brewing on the public stove at the time. The social situation, with its potpourri of potential "reactants," offers the leader with the appropriate personal characteristics the chance to season the political stew to his liking while adding his own blend of condiments as he stirs. And the leader with the appropriate characteristics, by being able to flavor the political mix to his liking, gives the social situation the opportunity to realize its historical necessity but only in a modified way. With so many potential substrates existing in society upon which different political catalysts can act, the notion of historical necessity now takes on a different connotation than neo-Marxian theory or social determinism would imply. Just as the great man can act only within the parameters of social possibility, certain potentially inevitable social outcomes are not likely to be realized unless suitable kinds of rulers initiate them.

Mikhail Gorbachev is a case in point. While many people hold him directly responsible for the collapse of the Soviet Union, the more likely scenario, according to the political catalyst model, was that his politics of perestroika and glasnost only accelerated the pace of certain unfolding events. The Soviet Union was rife with ethnic tensions and nationalistic fervor and, along with the growing economic crisis, likely would have fallen apart in time, much in the manner of Yugoslavia and Czechoslovakia, with or without Gorbachev's presence. Gorbachev did not "cause" the dissolution of the Soviet Union (nor did Ronald Reagan, whom certain political analysts likewise credit for pushing the Soviet Union to the brink of economic collapse by forcing it to keep pace with the U.S. military buildup). As a political catalyst, he simply made it easier for what probably was going to happen take place. Then, once he began the process, the floodgates burst open, unleashing the surge of independence movements that had been building for years.

Once we realize that rulers and their achievements are yoked together in much the same way that specific chemical catalysts and their particular reactants are, we begin to grasp what makes certain political leaders great. Great rulers do not create the historical climate of their times before they come to power or even the potential range of options realistically available to them, but they do have the ability to capitalize on certain opportunities that other potential rulers may not fully apprehend and, by virtue of their particular personal characteristics, exercise options that other potential rulers might not choose or ever see. The more "polyfunctional" their potential actions are, the greater their political impact and achievements are likely to be. Typically, the great visionary or great democratic leader operates in a polyfunctional way, initiating policies that affect almost every aspect of social functioning. By interpreting the role of the great ruler in this way, you then become able to reconcile the notion of historical necessity with that of individual initiative and achievement. Once you can do that, you render the great-man versus historical necessity debate moot.

WARMONGERS OR PEACEMAKERS?

The chimpanzee, as a result of a unique combination of strong
affiliative bonds between adult males on the one hand and an
unusually hostile and violently aggressive attitude toward nongroup
individuals on the other, has clearly reached a stage where he stands at
the very threshold of human achievement in destruction, cruelty, and
planned intergroup conflict. If ever he develops the power of language—and, as we have seen, he stands close to that threshold, too—
might he not push open the door and wage war with the best of us?
—Jane Goodall, *The Chimpanzees of Gombe*

RECAPITULATION

Now it is time to take stock of where we are. In the beginning of the
book, I laid out my thesis that the reason men seek to rule and cling to
power as long as they can is because they are biologically programmed
to do so. Humans may contemplate the heavens and be creatures of God,
but they are still primates to the core, albeit extraordinary ones, and remain grounded by their primate heritage. Just like their monkey, chimpanzee, and gorilla kin, they are disposed to compete among themselves
to become the reigning member of their society and, once they realize
that rank, to beat back all challengers who threaten to displace them. Of
course, humans, being human, seem ashamed of their primate roots and
go to great lengths to hide them in their political practices. But, as the
popular saying goes, "breeding always shows through." As nouveau riche
social climbers up the evolutionary ladder, humans may put on a gaudy
display of being high-minded in their political actions—and, in fact, many
do succeed in rising above their nature—but they often have trouble,
metaphorically speaking, keeping their tails tucked in their pants.

The fact that the sequences of DNA within human and chimpanzee chromosomes are virtually identical represents something more than a Ripley's believe-it-or-not oddity. It shapes how humans engage in politics, choose their leaders, run their societies, and conduct their international affairs. In particular, as my findings suggest, it accounts for the many striking resemblances, summarized in chart 10.1 below, between humans and *one or another but not necessarily all* of the other higher primates in how they ascend to ultimate power, how they exercise power, and how they try to keep power as long as possible.

Chart 10.1 Characteristic Features in the Struggle for Social Dominance

Comparisons between Simian Leaders and Human Rulers

	Simians	Humans
GAINING POWER		
Males Dominant	Yes	Yes
No Special Experience or Skills Needed	Yes	Yes
Danger of Physical Harm	Yes	Yes
Vie with Competitors for Power	Yes	Yes
Form Alliances to Topple Leader	Yes	Yes
Repetitive Attempts to Depose Leader	Yes	Yes
Physical Prowess and Courage	Yes	Yes
Cunning and Deviousness Useful	Yes	Yes
THE EXERCISE OF POWER		
Greater Access to Females	Yes	Yes
Breeding Advantage	Yes	Yes
Material Rewards	Yes	Yes
Deference by Subordinates	Yes	Yes
KEEPING POWER		
Keeping Peace among Subjects	Yes	Yes
Risking Harm during Challenges	Yes	Yes
Repeat Mistakes of Past Leaders	Yes	Yes
Resist Giving Up Power	Yes	Yes
Posturings and Displays	Yes	Yes
Change in Demeanor and Manner	Yes	Yes
Fending Off Challengers	Yes	Yes

These many resemblances hold more than theoretical interest. It is not as if we are watching ourselves engaged at political play on some "human island" at a zoo and chuckling over how quaint or amusing we are. Aside from affecting almost all aspects of our daily lives, the primate model of ruling has important ramifications for our very survival. The predilection of rulers to wage war potentially threatens all societies. At first, it may not seem that a close connection exists between the aggressiveness of certain species of monkeys and apes and the violence displayed by humans, mainly because nobody has witnessed one community of monkeys or apes using weapons to wage full-scale war against another community. But a growing body of scientific evidence suggests there is a close connection.[1] Although instances of intraspecies murder are uncommon among nonhuman primates, this is not because they lack the temperament to respond like humans. As with humans, chimpanzees from one community display xenophobia toward chimpanzees from other communities. Bands of raiding chimpanzees have been known to exterminate other chimpanzees from neighboring regions, usurp their territory, and carry out planned killings. With a backhanded compliment to the intelligence of chimpanzees, Jane Goodall suggested that, with the acquisition of language, they soon would be able to match the destructive potential of man.[2]

In his book, *On Aggression*,[3] Konrad Lorenz, the well-known ethologist, argued that large predators living together in a society must possess reliable and effective inhibitory mechanisms that keep them from killing each other during aggressive encounters. In the case of wolves, these mechanisms involve exposing the neck, and in the case of chimpanzees or baboons, they involve a variety of ceremonial submissive behaviors. In early humans, these same inhibitory mechanisms likely existed, but, once they acquired weapons of destruction that let them kill fellow humans more efficiently and at a distance and thereby avoid face-to-face encounters with their victims, they became able to override more easily their instinctive inhibitions about slaying members of the same species, even those metaphorically waving the white flags of defeat.[4] From what we now know about the natural combativeness of chimpanzees, it seems likely that, had they been smart enough to develop such lethal weapons, then they, too, like humans, would have been able to engage in genocide and kill others without compunction. The fact that they were too ill-equipped to wipe themselves out, along with the evolving apemen as well, gave humans by default a marvelous potential opportunity to eradicate themselves. That way, humans, at the top of the evolutionary chain, could ensure that no more advanced primates would ever surpass them.

Why Rulers Wage War

As I stated in my thesis, rulers serve a vital role for society. As head of the social body, they mold, guide, and direct their nation in all activities that are essential for its existence. Responsible for fostering a cohesiveness among their people, they set economic, educational, health care, and moral policies and oversee most aspects of social life. They are supposed to ensure that their people have enough food to eat, sufficient shelter to shield them from the elements, and adequate ways to defend themselves against attack. They also bear the responsibility for preserving law and order within their society. Of all the functions of rulers, perhaps the most puzzling one, which seems to countermand all the positive things they do, is their propensity to lead their people into war or to adopt disastrous social policies that result in the wholesale killing of others. It is this particular propensity that I now want to address mainly because it sheds more light on the nature of rulers and ruling.

After producing a ten-volume monumental work, *The Story of Civilization*, Will and Ariel Durant published a little-known slim book called *The Lessons of History* in which they sought to reveal what their lifetime studies of history had taught them about humans.[5] Their sobering message was that since the beginnings of recorded history there has been little alteration in the conduct of man. The means and instrumentalities change over time, but the motives and ends are the same. For instance, in 3,241 years of recorded history, only 268 years have been free of wars. Put differently, somewhere in the world humans have been killing each other in wars more than 92 percent of the time. My guess is that, during the remaining 8 percent, people in some nation or another probably were planning revolutions, civil uprisings, wars of conquest, or retaliations for past defeats—or fights were taking place where nobody noted. The reason the Durants give for their discouraging observation about the immutability of human conduct is that humans are subject to inexorable biological laws (a remarkable observation for historians to make!) that keep them responding in the same way to similar circumstances. These biological laws involve the struggle for existence, the selection of the fittest, and the perpetuation of the species.

In the famous exchange of letters between Albert Einstein and Sigmund Freud about why men are drawn to war, Freud came to almost the same conclusion as the Durants, but he held out a ray of hope.[6] Although he blamed war on man's aggressive instincts, he considered several possibilities for preventing it. After first endorsing the creation of a superagency, such as the League of Nations, as a supreme authority that might be able to intervene when leaders threatened war, he then went on to discount its potential effectiveness because it would not command sufficient power of its own to back up its stands. Then, noting that men tended to fall into one of two classes, leaders and followers, he proposed that those in the upper stratum should be trained to subordinate their instinctual life to "the dictatorship of reason" so that they could better lead the masses. Aside from his simplistic classification of men, Freud should have been ashamed of himself for making this naive suggestion, since he himself already had established how much instinctual forces shaped the mental activity of people and the incredible capacity of humans to deceive themselves, often most convincingly when they believed they were being reasonable. Perhaps that is why as an afterthought Freud backed off from this notion because, as he said, it probably was "too utopian."

Freud then ended his discourse about war with his most serious proposal. After observing that the cultural process had the capacity to modify instinctual impulses such as the sexual urge, he felt it likewise could strengthen the intellect so that it could better govern the instinctual life and also internalize aggressive urges. He concluded that a highly developed "culture" should be the best prophylaxis against war. Without close

---

Since it is virtually impossible to get accurate body counts from confrontations all around the globe, the best you can do is to make estimates. Reliable sources reveal that the world leaders during the twentieth century have been collectively responsible for well over 200 million deaths due to wars or to disastrous social policies—about 170 million civilian deaths and about 35 million combatants killed[7]—and at least another 1 billion casualties if you figure five wounded for every person killed, not to say anything about the incalculable suffering experienced by their loved ones or families.[8] Among the recordholders in mass murder are Stalin with about 40 to 50 million deaths, Mao with about 38 to 40 million, Hitler with about 20 million, Chiang Kai-shek with over 10 million, and King Leopold II with roughly 10 million (if you count all those who indirectly died because of his policies). Among the runners-up with deaths in the "measly" 1- to 5-million range are Pol Pot with over 2 million, Tojo Hideki with almost 4 million, Vladimir Lenin with about 4 million, Yahya Khan with over 1 million, and Josip Tito with almost 2 million. Then there are the large number of trailers with deaths in the several-hundred-thousand range.[9]

examination, this was a reasonable assumption. Freud wrote his famous letter in 1932, seven years before his beloved Germany—which likely represented his notion of the most civilized and advanced culture at the time—marched on Poland, unleashed the most devastating war on mankind ever known, and dramatically rendered his argument moot about the beneficial impact of a culture upon the intellect.

But as naive as they may seem, Freud's speculations about how to prevent wars need to be lauded. At least he was trying to be creative about one of the most serious problems threatening mankind's survival. If there is any behavior in humans that needs to be changed, it is their ability to find reasons for killing each other. Unfortunately, during the past century, all of the main approaches that concerned leaders have tried to prevent war so far have been flops.

The first approach involved the creation of a superordinate international agency, such as the League of Nations after World War I and the United Nations after World War II, with limited powers to intervene militarily in regional disputes to prevent the outbreak or further spread of war. In simplistic terms, the fundamental idea of such an organization was to promote dialogue and diplomacy among nations to ward off conflicts and, if this did not work, then to intervene with military force. It is not my intention to critique this concept in an informed way. I simply want to note the obvious facts that the League of Nations did not prevent World War II, the most destructive war ever fought, and the United Nations did not stop Mao Zedong's, Joseph Stalin's, or Pol Pot's disastrous social policies or the India-Pakistan Wars, the Korean War, the Vietnam War, or other major regional and civil wars, all of which resulted in countless deaths and casualties. No doubt the United Nations serves many important functions and has many good deeds to its credit, but the reality is that it has not been able to achieve the grand goals of ensuring international peace, and that is not only because it lacks the military clout to do so. Much of the problem is that the participating nations often cannot agree on a united course of action in response to potentially dangerous situations, and the more powerful nations do whatever they want to do.

The second approach follows the ancient Pax Romana model of maintaining law and order within the confines of an empire. Supposedly, the conquering nation would be responsible for quelling rebellions and preserving peace throughout its far-flung empire. During this past century, the British empire, the Ottoman empire, the French empire, the Austro-Hungarian empire, the German empire, and the Soviet Union, among others, all tried to impose law and order within their colonies, territories, and conquered countries. But the Pax Romana approach proved a failure in modern times, just as it had in early Roman times when periodic outbreaks of violence occurred within the empire and battles with German hordes occurred on the borders. The creation of these separate empires did not keep the rulers of one empire from fighting with the rulers of another empire to settle grievances or simply to gain more territory and power. Nor could it prevent the many civil wars, rebellions, and uprisings because of nationalistic, ethnic, religious, racial, tribal, and cultural forces, which always threatened to tear these conglomerate empires apart.

A third approach had to do with the successful efforts of several ambitious leaders—Gustav Stresemann of Germany, Austen Chamberlain of Britain, and Aristide Briand of France—to get sixty-three nations to sign an agreement after World War I, known as the Kellogg-Briand Pact of 1928, that outlawed war as an instrument of national policy. This was a noble exercise in futility, since the signatory nations granted themselves so many qualifications and exceptions that still would let them fight wars in self-defense, honor ongoing military obligations, uphold the Monroe Doctrine, or abide by postwar treaties with allies. The upshot of this pact was that the participating nations still could wage war whenever they wanted to as long as they could come up with a suitable rationale for doing so. But even if a leader did not want to take the trouble to concoct a rationale for his naked aggression, these signatory nations never could agree on how to enforce the pact.

Aside from these efforts to preserve peace, other developments occurred during the past century that seemed promising as potential safeguards against war. With the world divided up in mid-century between the Soviet sphere of influence and the American sphere, this "balance of powers," especially because of the nuclear deterrent, was supposed to prevent war since, if hostilities ever broke out, there would be no real winners. Although these two major powers never actually fought head-on (but came close to doing so during the Cuban missile crisis), they continued to vie for power in many small-scale wars by proxy in various parts of the globe while nations outside their direct orbit of influence went merrily on their way finding various causes to fight about.

After the collapse of the Soviet Union near the latter part of this past century, some political pundits, seeking something hopeful to tell their audiences, held out the prospects of a lasting peace because the United States, as the only real superpower, now could exert the necessary leadership to decrease the prospects of war. With its military, economic, and political clout, it would be able to do what an often divided and relatively impotent United Nations could not do in policing the world. Aided by the globalization of the world economy, the greater ease of travel, the information explosion, the growing power of the media, the spread of democracy, and the advances of modern technology, this modern pax Americana supposedly would be able to impose peace on a much more shrunken and presumably more responsive world. At last, though "the mountains divide and the oceans are wide," peace would descend on a global Disneyland, because humans would finally realize, as the song goes, "There's so much that we share that it's time we're aware, it's a small world after all."

As seductive as the idea of one world order under the aegis of the United States may seem for Americans, I simply cannot picture non-Americans embracing it for any extended length of time. Loving your neighbor as you love yourself may be "the Christian way," but it is not the way of primates and, therefore, not the way of the world. As history repeatedly shows, most humans, like most primates, tend to be xenophobic and harbor a natural suspicion and hostility toward others who belong to groups different than theirs: ethnic, religious, racial, or otherwise. Pluralism and cultural diversity may be wonderful notions in the abstract and even may be intellectually, physically, and aesthetically broadening experiences during annual food bazaars, athletic contests, or theatrical events, but, unfortunately, they often have been constant sources of friction for people in day-to-day living.

Although past experience should lead us to predict that wars both within and between nations during the new century are inevitable, these prospects become even scarier now than before because of the greater availability of weapons of mass destruction. Optimists prefer to believe that nuclear bombs and the prospects of chemical or biological warfare will serve as deterrents to keep nations from fighting with each other, because any battles will be zero-sum games with no clear winner. Pessimists worry about the destructive urges of zealous leaders seeking martyrdom, who seem willing to risk everything for "principle" or for the "glory of God" or for some other, equally intoxicating reason.

War As an Ultimate Expression of Alpha Male-ism

The reasons for war are complex, and no single theory can do them justice. In the past, there have been four main approaches to the understanding of war. Biological theories sought the roots of human violence in the aggressive tendencies of many species of animals, especially over sexual access to females, the defense of territory, or dominance struggles. Psychological theories emphasized an innate destructive urge, unresolved anger toward authority, or drive for power in humans that was best expressed in war. Religious theories viewed many wars as symbolizing the struggle between good and evil or the divinely commissioned obligation to convert heathens and infidels to the true cause. Social theories, which are by far the most common, usually attributed the causes of war to economic and social inequities within nations or competing ideologies or nationalistic ambitions or the exploitative designs of certain groups such as industrialists or the military establishment.

But no matter what theory we adopt to explain war, one constant exists. War still boils down to one leader of a nation wanting to impose his will on another leader and his followers. It serves the broader political function of extending the struggle for social dominance beyond the artificial confines of a single ethnic group, culture, or country to other groups, cultures, or countries. As such, it represents a natural expression of the primate model of ruling. Without a leader, individuals can engage in violent rioting, random looting, and even brutal killings, but they cannot make a concerted effort to defeat another nation, confiscate its land, and subjugate its people. The leader insures that his people won't run amok headless. He gives his people reasons for fighting—for the glory of God, for Allah, for the Fatherland, for the People, for Democracy, for *lebensraum*, for Freedom, Peace, or for Whatever—and then, through his generals, mobilizes them to act, heedless of the danger to themselves.

The practical value of war for rulers:

Aside from whatever social and political functions war serves for a country, it often holds certain practical "survival" value for the victorious rulers with regard to their tenure in office and their potential place in history. Perhaps more than anyone before him, Machiavelli was more keenly aware of the personal and political advantages of war for rulers. In *The Prince*, he advised that a ruler "ought to have no other aim or thought, nor select anything else for his study, than war and its rules and discipline; for this is the sole art that belongs to him who rules, and it is of such force that it not only upholds those who are born princes, but it often enables men to rise from a private station to that rank. And, on the contrary, it is seen that when princes have thought more of ease than of arms they have lost their states. And the first cause of your losing it

> Within the sample of rulers, 52 percent waged full-scale wars, fought civil wars, put down rebellions, or made decisions resulting in the deaths of others. When you disregard the actual type of rule, you find that those who engaged in the art of war, as Machiavelli might put it, or implemented disastrous social policies that resulted in the deaths of many civilians, averaged fourteen years in office and those who did not averaged six years, a greater than two-fold advantage for those who were willing to sacrifice their own people and kill others. This difference reflects something far more than the kind of rule. Among the four groups of dictators, the same general relationship applies, with those responsible for killing others averaging seventeen years in office and those not, twelve years. Comparably, among the democratic leaders, those responsible for killing others in wars averaged nine years in office, and those not, five years.

is to neglect this art; and what enables you to acquire a state is to be master of the art."

From Machiavelli's perspective, the stated intentions of rulers for war are irrelevant. If rulers want to perpetuate their rule, they should find any excuse to wage war, he says. War itself is what matters. This is a daring and reckless claim. Fortunately, I had a chance to test its validity with information gathered on my twentieth-century rulers. To my dismay, I discovered that what Machiavelli advised was true. Despite numerous reasons given for their wars, rulers who engaged in military pursuits or killed their own countrymen to enforce their social agendas remained in office far longer than those who did not.

Other writers offer a somewhat different perspective than Machiavelli about the expediency of war for rulers. Karl von Clausewitz, whose book, *On War*,[10] has served as a Bible on military strategy for countless admirers for almost two centuries, claimed war was nothing but a continuation of political policy and maneuvering with the introduction of different means over the years. It was a rational instrument of foreign policy designed to compel an adversary to fulfill a ruler's will. As an integral part of human political activity, war was not the result of incomprehensible social forces; it was an extreme expression of normal ways to bring about certain favorable political ends. Mao Zedong seemed to appreciate this reality. "War is politics," he wrote. "Politics is war by other means." Since the ultimate goal of most political activity by individuals is to gain power and influence by striving to become the alpha male and to preserve that status, war is derivative of this instinctive urge. It represents the ultimate form of competition among men and the ultimate form of domination by the victors—whether it be to establish military might, to spread ideological beliefs, or to gain territory.[11]

When we look upon war as a natural elaboration of the dominance struggle—an attempt to gain and maintain ultimate power as long as possible—we become better able to understand why wars have been an integral part of the human condition. Because humans are primates, they are biologically primed to seek dominion over others within their own community and then, once their positions are secure, over leaders of other communities whom they perceive as threats or as obstacles to their interests. Despite these ostensible reasons for seeking supremacy over others, rulers seem to be responding unwittingly to the biological imperative to test themselves against other contenders for ultimate power. Nature exploits this urge for dominance as a surefire way to ensure leadership within a community and, in the case of humans, sometimes over other communities as well.

War and social stability:

Though not immediately obvious, a natural consequence of war is peace. Once a leader establishes his supremacy over another leader and his people, he becomes obliged to maintain peace and order over these defeated people. Fighting and peacemaking—or social instability and social order—seem to represent opposite sides of the same coin. Just as the function of a strong leader is to eliminate unrest and friction and provide social stability within his nation, he likewise may seek to conquer other nations to impose his will on them, too. As a victor, he has a strong investment in establishing social stability within a conquered nation; otherwise it constitutes a direct threat to his sense of dominance. Subjugated people are supposed to heed the dictates of their masters. With this the case, I am forced to wonder whether Nature, in a streak of perversity, allowed humans to wage war as an instrument of political policy not for population control, as some Malthusian theorists have speculated, but to reduce friction between nations so that, once dominance was settled, a greater measure of social stability could be achieved. In a bizarre way, as Clausewitz suggests, wars between nations then could be construed as attempts to resolve the differences and grievances that could not be settled by ordinary political means. The victor would then dictate the terms.

The dual role of leaders to serve both as warmongers and peacemakers is exemplified by all of the Nobel Peace Prize winners who had been involved as terrorists, militant activists, freedom fighters, guerril-

Former Nobel Peace Prize winners who previously engaged in war include Menachem Begin of Israel (commander of the terrorist organization, Irgun, from 1945 to 1948 and, as prime minister, responsible for invading Lebanon in 1982 to oust the PLO), Anwar Sadat of Egypt (invaded Israel and launched the Yom Kippur War in 1973), Yassir Arafat of the Palestine Liberation Organization (organized guerrilla and terrorist actions against Israel for many years), Yitzak Rabin of Israel (chief of staff during the Six-Day War), Shimon Peres of Israel (a former member of the Haganah movement, a Zionist military organization), Jose Ramos-Horta of East Timor (involved in the militant independence movement), David Trimble of Northern Ireland (Protestant leader of the Ulster Unionist Party (UUP), which was involved in thirty years of violence), Mikhail Gorbachev of the Soviet Union (sent Soviet troops to Afghanistan for several years before he withdrew them), Woodrow Wilson of the United States (involved the country in World War I), and Theodore Roosevelt (organized the First Volunteer Cavalry, known as the Rough Riders, and took them to Cuba to fight in the Spanish-American War).

las, insurgents, or revolutionaries or had supported violence or had made ruthless policy decisions during wartime before being honored as esteemed peacemakers. It is ironic that these particular exemplars for peacemaking often were hailed for their efforts to settle the very conflicts that they once supported, were party to, perpetuated, or actually started. It is also pertinent to the primate model of ruling that, of the nine women who received the Nobel Peace Prize during this past century, not a single one, in contrast to many of the male winners, had taken up arms or advocated violent activity beforehand or participated in major policy decisions that had led to the death of others—which points up an important difference in gender roles.

These observations have certain practical implications. Instead of war being interpreted as a social aberration that works contrary to the intentions of Nature, we now can view it as an integral part of the human condition that derives from our primate heritage. Whether we like it or not, aggression is part of our primate nature. We may condemn wars, but we cannot escape them. They are part of the worldwide social matrix. But because wars seem inevitable does not mean that we cannot lessen their likelihood or curb their destructive potential. However, if we have any hope of doing so, we first would need to address two root causes of war that we potentially have some power to control: *our leaders and ourselves!*

10.1: Leaders aid social stability. Dominant male chimpanzee calms subordinate male by touching him. Photograph by Hugo van Lawick, courtesy of the Jane Goodall Institute.

Diagnosing the Social Pathogens

Since leaders play such a vital role in starting and perpetuating wars (even though they may merely serve as conduits for powerful historical forces), any reasonable approach to keeping wars from happening would first have to decrease the prospects of potential warmongers gaining ultimate power. For that to happen, certain kinds of leaders would have to be kept out of power. Whether that is possible depends on whether you believe in the capacity of humans to modify their basic instinctual nature and alter ingrained social practices.

Although democratic leaders have been known to launch wars to "preserve the peace," "to deter aggression," to defend their nation's honor, and to prevent the spread of seemingly dangerous ideologies, most wars and disastrous social policies tend to be initiated by dictators.[12] As my results reveal, dictators are twice as likely to wage war as democratic leaders.

> Seventy-four percent of all of the dictators within the sample of twentieth-century rulers were involved in civil wars, wars with other nations, or international wars at some point in their reigns compared to *only* 37 percent of the democratic leaders.

Since not all dictators are warmongers and not all democratic leaders are peace-loving, any attempt to detect those leaders, dictators and democrats alike, who are most likely to resort to war as a way of achieving their aims requires more precise criteria than simply the kind of rule. As it happens, the task of identifying these "social pathogens" should not be too difficult. First of all, according to the primate model of ruling, which is essentially autocratic in nature, those leaders most apt to resort to war to settle disputes and impose their will on others should be those who were most ruthless, authoritarian, and belligerent before coming to power. This naturally follows from the psychological principle that the best predictor of future behavior is past behavior. From the information I have been able to gather on a large number of twentieth-century rulers, I have been able to identify certain personal characteristics of those leaders that, I believe, make them more likely to be attracted to war because of their unbridled ambition and their willingness to sacrifice others to achieve their ends. Although leaders with these characteristics do not always spell disaster for their people (and some, in fact, actually may increase social stability and improve the general lot of their countrymen), the *likelihood* of violent oppression, civil uprisings, and war seems much greater the longer these kinds of leaders hold power because sooner or later opportunities are bound to appear for them to do what they are emotionally disposed to do.

- Ideologues who want to foist a comprehensive belief system on others—political, religious, economic, or otherwise—with the aim of controlling their actions and thoughts;
- Demagogues who foment hatred against certain ethnic, religious, or national groups;
- Revanchist would-be rulers who whip up nationalistic fervor to reclaim disputed territories or to recapture the glorious days of the past;
- Candidates who identify with a past national hero or great ruler whose feats involved great military conquests,
- Aspiring rulers with a history of personal violence in the form of duels or other tests of manhood;
- Leaders who overthrow democratically elected rulers through military coups or who have a past history of trying to do so;
- Would-be rulers who oppose the freedom of expression or who advocate oppressive measures to suppress dissent; and
- Leaders who seek to concentrate or extend their powers beyond

what the existing constitution allows, or who find ways to subvert the constitutions for their purpose, or who circumvent their constitutions.

Of course, from a predictive standpoint, *all of the above criteria have to be regarded as speculative*, since they have yet to be tested out prospectively over the course of the current century. Also, no criteria for warmongering are foolproof. There always would be the possibility that using these criteria to judge the suitability of rulers might cause us to indict certain potentially great leaders with the qualifications of a Charles de Gaulle, a Josip Tito, a Winston Churchill, a Kemal Atatürk, or a Franklin Delano Roosevelt as likely to be noxious to the health and welfare of their citizens, or by exclusion to endorse a Neville Chamberlain, a Herbert Hoover, or a Warren G. Harding as being politically sanitized and safe. But the identification of a large number of "false positives" among the would-be rulers is the necessary risk we would need to take if we held to the goal of keeping any potential warmongers out of high office. If we did want to decrease the prospects of war, we would have to apply our criteria ruthlessly, even at the cost of missing out on some potentially great leaders. Anybody with the disposition of a warmonger simply would be disqualified as a potential ruler—a restriction that sometimes runs counter to the desire for decisive and strong leaders. Naturally, most people would be reluctant to do this, especially when they perceive their nation to be under threat.

Since we do have the capacity to identify the kinds of leaders we need to be wary of, we next have to consider why we let them lead us during times that a nation is in no obvious danger. If we do not elect them, revere them, support them, believe them, and obey them, then they would be unable to lead us to war. By definition, rulers cannot be warmongers if they have no power, no constituency, and no troops to lead.

As it happens, humans, as primates, are very susceptible to the charisma, oratory, charm, self-assurance, and other influencing techniques used by those aspiring to be rulers, and so can be manipulated to respond uncritically to their exhortations. Most natural leaders seem to know this intuitively, but others, like Vice President Al Gore, a United States candidate who ran for high office in 2000 A.D., deliberately took lessons on how to upgrade his image from a beta to an alpha male.[13] In any event, despite reason and prior experience, when under stress or duress, humans seem to revert to type in their affinity for autocratic rulers who are most likely to deprive them of their hard-won freedoms and meet the profile of a *potential* warmonger.

To illustrate, we need look no further than the rise to power by many military strongmen happening around the turn of the current century in such countries as Venezuela, Turkmenistan, Israel, Guatemala, Niger, the Congo, and Sudan to get a notion about what potentially may lie in store for the world in the new millennium.[14] To illustrate what I mean, let me cite the situation in Pakistan. Shortly after Gen. Pervez Musharraf launched a coup that overthrew Prime Minister Nawaz Sharif, he suspended parliamentary government and instituted martial law, claiming that his country's troubled democracy needed to be demolished so that it could be built on a surer foundation. Although the people had heard similar promises before from Field Marshal M. Ayub Khan in 1958 ("Our ultimate aim is to restore democracy but of the type that people can understand"), from Gen. A.M. Yahya Khan in 1969 ("I have no ambition other than the creation of conditions conducive to the establishment of constitutional government"), and from Gen. Zia-ul-Haq in 1977 ("The survival of this country lies in democracy and democracy alone"), all of whom subsequently ruled as dictators, they cheered Musharraf after he overthrew their democratically elected leader and established his own brand of dictatorship.[15] It is as if the people in the nations involved had learned nothing from all their past miseries with repressive governments and military leaders or else felt helpless to do anything about them even when these new leaders were metaphorically carrying large *caveat emptor* signs around their necks.

These ominous political happenings occurring during so relatively short a time period, which are only a sampling from a larger pool, do not bode well for the current millennium. What we can do about it is another matter. Short of requiring all potentially dangerous rulers to wear skull-and-crossbones warning labels across their chests before they come to power, with captions beneath reading "Dangerous to Your Health" or "Possibly Fatal" (which possibly would increase their popular appeal), or stiffly fining potential rulers for preaching hatred and stirring up the martial passions of their audiences, or, failing to be able to adopt any of these measures, putting any potential social pathogens in quarantine indefinitely until their testosterone levels dropped to senescent levels, I do not see many realistic options available.

Some misanthropes may respond to the public's toleration of autocratic leaders with the well-known saying that people get the kinds of leaders they deserve. This judgment misses the point. It is not so much that people get the kinds of leaders they deserve as that they get the kinds of leaders they are socially primed and biologically programmed as primates to accept. When they vote for leaders who have little regard for human rights or enthusiastically embrace a new coup leader or tolerate rulers who curtail their political rights, they are not necessarily favoring a dictatorship or hungering for war as much as they often are believing that those particular persons, by virtue of their personal stature and heroic actions, have a solution for their country's woes and will make life better for them. This may be gullible on their parts, but that is how their minds are prone to respond to a strong leader in the position of an alpha male. It is not only ignorant, poorly educated, impoverished, backward, or desperate people who respond this way. As the experience during World War I and World War II so vividly reveals, many individuals within the most advanced nations in the world also fall prey to the appeal of demagogic, warmongering leaders.

Humans Are People, Too

Do these observations mean that the future prospects for world peace are bleak? Not necessarily. We need to remind ourselves that, although we belong to the order of primates, we likewise represent a distinct species, homo sapiens, the most highly evolved of all our simian kin. As such, we possess certain unique capabilities that have let us develop advanced cultures, construct philosophical systems, display creativity, and discover the laws of nature. And in the political realm, unlike our primate ancestors, we have evolved democratic forms of government that potentially shield us from the autocratic leadership implicit in the primate model of ruling. We may have inherited our belligerency, competitiveness, and urge for domination from our primate progenitors, but as humans we have evolved unique political systems that diffuse executive power, establish checks and balances in government, and limit a ruler's term in office, to protect us against our own natural tendencies.

At the outset of this new millennium, we find that a dynamic tension exists between those primitive forces that draw us toward rulers who seek domination over their people and over other nations and those higher human urges that favor leaders committed to individual liberty, freedom, and world peace. So far, my discussion has focused mainly on all those political trends that affirm our primate heritage. But despite the widespread selection or seeming popular support of certain political leaders who fit the profile for warmongers, other encouraging developments that may serve as countervailing influences also are taking place.

Over the past century, there has been a steady decline in the number of absolute monarchies. By the end of the current century, it seems likely that monarchies, even constitutional ones, will be outmoded institutions except perhaps in a few Arab nations in which sheikhs and kings rule by divine right or because the blood of the Prophet supposedly runs in their veins. As early as 1948, King Farouk of Egypt commented, "The whole world is in revolt. Soon there will be only five kings left: the King of England, the King of Spades, the King of Clubs, the King of Hearts, and the King of Diamonds."[16] Four years later he was overthrown in a coup.

Along with the likely demise of the monarchy, dictatorships also seem to be on the decline. In his inaugural speech marking his second term in office, President Clinton declared, "For the first time in history, more people on this planet live under democracy than dictatorship."[17] According to the United Nations population data in 1996, about 3.1 billion people lived in democracies and 2.7 billion did not. By the year 2000, with Indonesia at least for the moment in the democratic camp, the percentage of people living under democratic rule is even greater. Naturally, any estimates about democracy need to be tempered by how we define that form of government. Granting people the right to vote may not be a suitable criterion for democracy if the country has a one-party form of government, does not provide for a separation of church and state, makes accommodations with the military to prevent takeovers, or lets ill-informed and illiterate people cast ballots. It also may not safeguard the country against sham elections, voting irregularities, and rampant corruption in government. But even with these qualifications, the trend away from more autocratic forms of rule—or, more accurately, toward creating the impression that people have a say in picking their leaders—cannot be ignored.

Moreover, despite the recent spate of nations in which dictators, demagogues, or potential warmongers have come to power with the seeming blessing of the people, other recent developments tend to offset this regression to more autocratic forms of rule. For example, on the African continent, which has spawned many dictatorships, the decade after the end of the Cold War led to the dramatic rise of multiparty political systems, with more than two-thirds of its rulers being chosen in "free elections." That contrasted sharply with the situation a quarter of a century ago when less than ten percent of its rulers were democratically elected.[18] More immediately, at the turn of the new century, we find instance after instance of democracies that have emerged after a period of autocratic rule. In mid-1999, after a long period of military dictatorship, the people of Nigeria elected Olusegun Obasanjo to office. In Indonesia, after the dictator, Suharto, was forced out of office and his vice president, B.J. Habibie, took over until elections could be held, the people voted Abdurraham Wahid into office in October 1999. In Croatia, after the autocratic rule of Franjo Tudjman, Stipe Mesic, a more moderate leader who promised democratic reform and more cooperation with the West, was elected president in February 2000. Months after the former president was ousted from office, Kumba Yala was sworn in as president of Guinea-Bissau after winning a runoff election in February 2000. In Zimbabwe, when President Robert Mugabe allowed a public referendum during February 2000 on a draft constitution that granted him more powers, his resounding defeat opened the way for a more democratic election in 2002 and perhaps his removal from office. In Iran, the growing strength of the moderates in parliament after the elections in February 2000, under the leadership of President Mohammad Khatami, may pave the way for more sweeping democratic reforms. In Mexico, Vincente Fox broke the longtime stranglehold the PRI held on political power when he won the presidential election in July 2000. And the popular uprising in October 2000 against Slobodan Milosevic after his unwillingness to concede defeat in the election and the subsequent installation of Vojislav Kostunica as president represented a major shift toward a more democratic government in Yugoslavia.

Despite these encouraging trends, it is hard to remain confident about their permanence. The problem is that autocratic rule seems to represent the more natural state of affairs among all higher-order primates. The overthrow of fledgling democracies by fascist, authoritarian, and other totalitarian regimes during the past century suggests that representative democracy, a relative parvenu on the historical scene, tends to thrive during stable political times and economic prosperity. When social crises that threaten the livelihood or lives of people arise, they become more prone to lapse to more primitive modes of responding in their selection of leaders and the kinds of government they will tolerate, much as those who learn a second language later in life tend to revert to their native tongue during times of confusion or stress. More forceful leaders, empowered to rely on more drastic means, are expected to rectify the social problems. Because there is no evolutionary precedent or biological basis for democratic rule in lower forms of animal life as there is for autocratic rule, in which dissent can be forcibly suppressed, democracy appears to possess an inherent fragility that presumably makes it vulnerable to attack. As such, if it is to survive and thrive, it must be safeguarded and never taken for granted. In Turkey, for instance, and other countries, we have the bizarre but perfectly understandable situation whereby the military, entrusted with the responsibility for preserving freedom, periodically launches coups to overthrow elected leaders and then declares martial law whenever it believes democracy is threatened. As the saying goes, the price of freedom is eternal vigilance–and, it seems, sometimes authoritarian rule as well.

By documenting the trends of an increase in more democratic forms of rule worldwide and an associated decline in dictatorships, I need to make certain points clear. This is not a case of "good" winning out against "evil," as many politicians are wont to portray it. Democratic leaders, who also happen to be primates, are not necessarily devoid of an alpha male mentality that seeks to impose its will on others. During the earlier part of this past century, leaders of "civilized," democratic nations showed imperialistic tendencies, exploiting their colonial possessions and governing by force. Although they engaged in far fewer wars than dictators, many democratic leaders found suitable pretexts to do battle, and once hostilities began, they were just as ruthless in killing their enemy or doing whatever it took to win. It should be remembered that the United States, which many regard as the bastion of democracy, has developed the most powerful weapons of destruction available today and was the first and only nation so far to unleash the atom bomb against an adversary.

Aside from democratic leaders possessing certain kinds of personality traits that ease their functioning within a democratic system, what distinguishes them the most from dictators is the greater number of constitutional constraints imposed on them. The reason they have these constraints is because those who framed the constitutions of their countries recognized how easy it was for leaders with unrestrained power to abuse it. As a result, leaders operating within a political system of checks and balances may be less efficient than dictators in handling crises decisively, but ideally they also should be less likely to harm others by acting in the heat of passion.

Nothing I have said so far should be taken as criticism of the primate model of ruling or the role of the alpha male within it. Although an appreciation for how this model shapes the behavior of rulers and their constituencies is essential for understanding the nature of political leadership throughout the world, the model itself is morally neither commendable nor condemnable. It is simply a useful construct to account for the way things are. From an evolutionary standpoint, alpha males played a crucial part in the survival of early humans, allowing them to mobilize their clans against outside dangers, organize hunting parties, and impose social stability. In more advanced times, many military strongmen or caudillos, who usually represent the prototype of the alpha male, have provided needed leadership in underdeveloped nations and elsewhere for mostly poor, uneducated people who either were not yet prepared for more democratic forms of rule or actually preferred an autocratic leadership style. For better or worse, this primate model of ruling, operating with different degrees of political constraints on leaders, has helped to get us where we are. As long as humans remain primates—and I see no way for that to change unless they somehow can undergo species transformation operations—our primate nature will continue to play a major role in all political affairs.

The problem, however, is that this is a another day and age. With our present weapons of mass destruction, we have far outstripped any inherent limitations Nature may have imposed on us to ensure survival of the species and soon may be able through chemical and nuclear warfare to annihilate the entire human race as well as other forms of life. In this new world, the tried-and-true alpha male response of wielding military might to achieve strategic ends and settle conflicts has the potential now to destroy mankind rather than protect the troops.

Obviously, the issue cannot be settled by any simplistic answers. However, the results of my study of twentieth-century rulers suggest a general course of action for the future that takes three incontrovertible facts into account: humans are primates, democratic rulers are less likely to engage in wars than dictators, and almost all rulers worldwide are males. These may seem to be ho-hum, so-what's-new? observations, but their potential ramifications are enormous.

Many opinions exist about the nature of our primate heritage. Some cynics say we are apes with an attitude or, as certain wishful persons believe, angels in overcoats. Whether we are one or the other or a combination of both or even figments of our own imagination, which is not as absurd a notion as it may seem,[19] one thing is certain. While chimpanzees likewise have a capacity to transmit culture, humans as a species have been remarkably more resourceful than any other primates at creating different cultures that adapt to the particular demands of climate and geography. By culture, I mean the system of shared values, assumptions, and beliefs transmitted from one generation to the next that lets people within particular societies cope with their world and each other. With the advent of multinational corporations, international cartels, a global economy, vast telecommunication networks, the worldwide web, and other advances of modern technology, humans now face an entirely new kind of world. Now humans not only will have to modify their cultures to adapt to their rapidly changing physical universe; they also will have to adapt to the increasing overpopulation of a shrinking world that faces a steady depletion of its natural resources. As Western values and products continue to infiltrate the entire globe via industrial development and the communication media, the risk of culture clash grows, with leaders in many undemocratic countries responding with an instinctive hostility to these foreign influences. And with good cause, because the threat to their particular cultures is real. Under these circumstances, the new challenge for humanity, which somehow must deal with these new realities, seems to be how to construct an overarching culture that can subsume all existing cultures within it—one that de-emphasizes national boundaries, tries to reduce the economic disparities between impoverished and wealthy nations, and accommodates the existence of different religions and political ideologies—all for the purpose of reducing the risk of war.

Earlier, I showed surprise at Freud's naivete in his answer to Einstein when he proposed that culture, presumably German culture in particular, could be a remedy for preventing war. Obviously, his failure to recognize that Germany was steeped in a long militaristic tradition, and, even more important, despite its civilized veneer, relied heavily on the primate model of leadership, undermined the value of his proposal. Any proposal for reducing aggression among the leaders of nations that does not make provision for altering man's constant striving for dominance along with his willingness to gain his ends in battle seems doomed to failure. But despite Freud's apparent blind spot, his invoking culture as a potential moderating force for the expression of instinctive urges was appropriate. After all, if a culture can ritualize a powerful, natural urge like sex in people, which many are willing to kill or die for, by crippling them with guilt if they deviate from expressing it in certain socially sanctioned ways, then it potentially should be able to curb the natural potential for aggressiveness by leaders, too.

As I noted before, the difference between democratic leaders and dictators as participants in wars during this past century—37 percent versus 74 percent—is dramatic. What this should tell us is that if we ever hope to reduce the risks of war, we need to develop a more global culture that takes into account the potential dangers of letting alpha male leaders reign without any reins on their power. Certainly, the increasing trend globally toward democracy is encouraging, not because the "good guys" are triumphing but because more people are using their sapient capacities as humans to put restraints on their instinctive responses as primates. But not all nations will choose to follow the democratic path. For those recalcitrant nations that do not, we need to find some way to get them to impose limits on the power of their leaders to wage wars. So far, economic sanctions or levers levied by a consortium of powerful nations to prevent the proliferation of nuclear weapons throughout the world have met with limited success. More foolproof methods of control are needed. What they are is up for grabs. Perhaps an effective way to prevent the outbreak of hostilities would be to bureaucratize the governmental system somehow within "rogue nations" so that the cumbersomeness of the procedures for gaining approval to kill others would be so great that the leader would give up in frustration and instead vent his anger against those who were creating all the red tape or against maybe even himself. Others more imaginative than I can devise more realistic scenarios.

Along these lines, we may need to make some major adjustments in the primate model of ruling to acknowledge an unfortunate reality. Although women constitute about half of the world population, they are woefully under-represented as world leaders, and, for that matter, as key political advisors and military commanders as well. This meager number of women rulers worldwide in positions of high authority is understandable in more fundamentalistic nations that, like their great ape forebears, exclude women from political affairs, but it is less acceptable in democratic nations whose constitutions are supposed to ensure equal rights for all people. Should the percentages of female and male rulers ever approach parity, thereby diluting out the traditional alpha male ways for dealing with conflicts, leaders of nations may begin handling disputes among themselves differently. Since men have held center stage as leaders of nations for so long, perhaps it now is time to have more women rulers to see if they can do a better job of keeping nations from destroying each other. An estrogenic approach to world peace may be substantially different than an androgenic one. Then again, when we recognize that actual physiological changes can take place in certain primates once they become dominant, Nature already may have decided to forestall the possibility of a more feminine outlook by placing a hidden gland in the brains of women that releases a testosterone-like substance if substantial numbers of them ever gain high office. Or once in power, the female leaders themselves may begin taking male hormones or anabolic steroids, much like many women athletes do to help them compete. So it really may not make a difference. But it is worth a try.

What next? With all of the formidable challenges ahead, we can look toward the future with despair or hope, depending upon which political trends we choose to emphasize. *Despair*, if we emphasize that in the past century more human lives were lost in wars and as a result of disastrous social policies than ever before during any comparable period in history. Also, despite the collapse of certain totalitarian movements (e.g., communism and fascism), other ideological movements (e.g., ultranationalism and fundamentalism), which foster the emergence of fanatic leaders who place more value in their cause than on human life, are on the increase in many parts of the world. *Hope*, if we emphasize the growing appeal of democracy throughout the world, which, depending upon our interpretation, either tends to foster the emergence of less bellicose leaders or, perhaps more accurately, forces them to act that way. It is difficult to know which of these trends will eventually win out.

10.2: "Life will be much safer, folks, if, like us, the most dangerous weapons you allow are dropped banana peels for the enemy to slip on." © Corbis/Hulton-Deutsch Collection.

Appendix A

Sample of Rulers (N = 377)

(Type of Ruler: 0 = Monarch, 1 = Tyrant, 2 = Visionary, 3 = Authoritarian,
4 = Transitional, 5 = Democrat.)
(Third: 1= Bottom Third, 2= Middle Third, 3 = Top Third of Political Greatness as
determined by the total PGS score.)

Leader	Country	Began Rule	Type Ruler	PGS Score	Third
Abdul Rahman	Malaysia	1957	4	12	2
Abdul-hamid II	Ottoman Empire	1876	0	12	2
Abdullah	Jordan	1946	0	15	3
Adenauer, Konrad	Germany	1949	4	19	3
Aguinaldo, Emilio	Philippines	1899	4	7	1
Albert I	Belgium	1909	0	14	3
Alessandri, Arturo	Chile	1920	5	13	2
Alexander	Serbia	1889	0	11	2
Alexander I	Yugoslavia	1921	0	15	3
Alfonsín, Raúl	Argentina	1983	5	12	2
Alfonso XIII	Spain	1902	0	9	1
Allende, Salvador	Chile	1970	5	12	2
Amanullah Khan	Afghanistan	1919	0	16	3
Amin, Idi	Uganda	1971	1	7	1
Andropov, Yuri	Russia/Soviet Union	1982	3	10	2
Antonescu, Ion	Romania	1940	3	6	1
Aquino, Corazon	Philippines	1986	5	9	1
Arafat, Yassir	Palestine Authority	1996	4	17	3
Arbenz, Jacobo	Guatemala	1951	5	10	2
Arias Sánchez, Oscar	Costa Rica	1986	5	13	2
Arias, Arnulfo	Panama	1940	1	3	1
Asquith, Herbert	United Kingdom	1908	5	12	2
Assad, Hafiz al-	Syria	1971	3	16	3
Atatürk	Turkey	1923	2	31	3
Attlee, Clement	United Kingdom	1945	5	16	3

Leader	Country	Began Rule	Type Ruler	PGS Score	Third
Ayub Khan, Mohammad	Pakistan	1958	3	17	3
Azana, Manuel	Spain	1936	5	7	1
Baldwin, Stanley	United Kingdom	1923	5	8	1
Balewa, Abubakar Tafawa	Nigeria	1960	4	14	3
Balfour, Arthur James	United Kingdom	1902	5	11	2
Banda, H. Kamuzu	Malawi	1964	3	11	2
Bandaranaike, S.W. R.D.	Sri Lanka	1956	5	7	1
Bandaranaike, Sirimavo	Sri Lanka	1959	5	8	1
Barthou, Louis	France	1913	5	8	1
Batista, Fulgencio	Cuba	1933	1	11	2
Batlle, Jose	Uruguay	1903	5	12	2
Begin, Menachem	Israel	1977	5	13	2
Bell, Francis	New Zealand	1925	5	5	1
Ben Bella, Mohammed Ahmed	Algeria	1962	4	14	3
Benes, Edvard	Czechoslovakia	1935	5	9	1
Ben-Gurion, David	Israel	1948	4	21	3
Bennett, R.B.	Canada	1930	5	7	1
Betancourt, Romulo	Venezuela	1945	4	13	2
Bhutto, Benazir	Pakistan	1988	5	9	1
Bhutto, Zulfikar	Pakistan	1971	3	20	3
Blair, Tony	United Kingdom	1997	5	13	2
Blum, Leon	France	1936	5	10	2
Bokassa, Jean-Bédel	Central African Rep.	1966	1	9	1
Borden, Robert L.	Canada	1911	5	15	3
Boris III	Bulgaria	1923	0	10	2
Bosch, Juan	Dominican Republic	1962	5	6	1
Botha, Louis	South Africa	1907	4	14	3
Bourguiba, Habib	Tunisia	1957	2	24	3
Brandt, Willy	Germany, West	1969	5	16	3
Brezhnev, Leonid	Russia/Soviet Union	1964	3	19	3
Briand, Aristide	France	1906	5	15	3
Bruce, Stanley Melbourne	Australia	1923	5	9	1
Bush, George	United States	1989	5	15	3
Bustamante, Alexander	Jamaica	1962	4	7	1
Cabral, Amílcar	Guinea	1964	4	11	2
Caillaux, Joseph	France	1911	5	7	1
Callaghan, James	United Kingdom	1976	5	9	1
Calles, Plutarco Elías	Mexico	1924	5	8	1
Campbell, Kim	Canada	1993	5	6	1

Leader	Country	Began Rule	Type Ruler	PGS Score	Third
Campbell-Bannerman, Henry	United Kingdom	1905	5	10	2
Cardenas, Lázaro	Mexico	1934	5	16	3
Carol II	Romania	1930	0	6	1
Carranza, Venustiano	Mexico	1914	4	9	1
Carter, Jimmy	United States	1977	5	14	3
Castelo Branco, H.	Brazil	1963	3	11	2
Castillo Armas, C.	Guatemala	1954	3	9	1
Castro, Cipriano	Venezuela	1899	1	7	1
Castro, Fidel	Cuba	1959	2	23	3
Ceausescu, Nicolae	Romania	1965	2	14	3
Chamberlain, Neville	United Kingdom	1937	5	11	2
Chamorro, Violeta Barrio	Nicaragua	1990	5	9	1
Chernenko, Konstantin	Russia/Soviet Union	1984	3	10	2
Chiang Ching-kuo	Taiwan	1978	3	10	2
Chiang Kai-shek	China	1928	2	21	3
Chifley, Ben	Australia	1945	5	11	2
Chrétien, Jean	Canada	1993	5	15	3
Chulalongkorn	Thailand	1873	0	16	3
Chun Doo Hwan	Korea, South	1980	3	9	1
Churchill, Winston	United Kingdom	1938	5	22	3
Clark, Joe	Canada	1979	5	7	1
Clemenceau, Georges	France	1906	5	20	3
Clinton, Bill	United States	1993	5	15	3
Collins, Michael	Ireland	1922	4	9	1
Combes, Émile	France	1902	5	9	1
Constantine I	Greece	1913	0	6	1
Cook, Joseph	Australia	1913	5	5	1
Coolidge, Calvin	United States	1923	5	14	3
Curtin, John	Australia	1941	5	13	2
Daladier, Edouard	France	1933	5	9	1
De Gasperi, Alcide	Italy	1945	5	17	3
de Gaulle, Charles	France	1944	5	27	3
de Klerk, Frederik	South Africa	1990	5	16	3
de Valera, Eamon	Ireland	1932	4	16	3
Deakin, Alfred	Australia	1903	5	10	2
Deng Xiaoping	China	1979	3	27	3
Desai, Morarji	India	1977	5	12	2
Díaz, Porfirio	Mexico	1876	3	16	3
Diefenbaker, J.G.	Canada	1957	5	10	2

Leader	Country	Began Rule	Type Ruler	PGS Score	Third
Dimitrov, Georgy	Bulgaria	1946	3	9	1
Doe, Samuel	Liberia	1980	1	5	1
Dollfuss, Englebert	Austria	1932	3	10	2
Dönitz, Karl	Germany	1945	3	6	1
Douglas-Home, Alec	United Kingdom	1963	5	9	1
Duvalier, François	Haiti	1957	1	7	1
Duvalier, Jean-Claude	Haiti	1971	1	7	1
Eden, Anthony	United Kingdom	1955	5	10	2
Eisenhower, D.D.	United States	1953	5	18	3
Eshkol, Levi	Israel	1963	5	13	2
Fahd	Saudi Arabia	1982	0	11	2
Farouk	Egypt	1936	0	10	2
Faysal I (Faisal)	Iraq	1921	0	17	3
Ferdinand	Bulgaria	1908	0	12	2
Figueres, Jose	Costa Rica	1948	5	18	3
FitzGerald, Garrett	Ireland	1981	5	8	1
Ford, Gerald	United States	1974	5	11	2
Franco, Francisco	Spain	1936	2	21	3
Franz Joseph	Austria	1848	0	21	3
Fraser, Malcolm	Australia	1975	5	8	1
Fraser, Peter	New Zealand	1940	5	13	2
Frei, Eduardo	Chile	1964	5	7	1
Fuad	Egypt	1922	0	11	2
Gandhi, Indira	India	1966	5	19	3
Gandhi, Rajiv	India	1984	5	12	2
Giscard d'Estaing	France	1974	5	10	2
Gómez, Juan Vicente	Venezuela	1908	1	13	2
Gomulka, Wladyslaw	Poland	1945	3	13	2
Gorbachev, Mikhail S.	Russia/Soviet Union	1985	2	24	3
Gorton, John	Australia	1968	5	7	1
Gottwald, Klement	Czechoslovakia	1946	3	9	1
Gowon, Yakubu	Nigeria	1966	3	10	2
Griffith, Arthur	Ireland	1922	5	8	1
Haile Selassie	Ethiopia	1928	0	13	2
Hara Takashi	Japan	1918	5	9	1
Harding, Warren G.	United States	1921	5	9	1
Hassan II	Morocco	1961	0	18	3
Haughey, Charles	Ireland	1979	5	8	1
Havel, Václav	Czechoslovakia	1989	4	15	3

Leader	Country	Began Rule	Type Ruler	PGS Score	Third
Hawke, Robert	Australia	1983	5	12	2
Heath, Edward	United Kingdom	1970	5	9	1
Hernández Martínez	El Salvador	1931	3	11	2
Hertzog, James	South Africa	1924	5	11	2
Hindenburg, Paul von	Germany	1924	5	12	2
Hirohito	Japan	1926	0	12	2
Hitler, Adolph	Germany	1933	2	25	3
Ho Chi Minh	Vietnam, North	1945	2	27	3
Holt, Harold	Australia	1966	5	8	1
Holyoake, Keith	New Zealand	1957	5	13	2
Honecker, Erich	Germany, East	1971	3	15	3
Hoover, Herbert	United States	1929	5	10	2
Horthy, Miklós	Hungary	1920	3	15	3
Huerta, Victoriano	Mexico	1913	1	6	1
Huggins, Godfrey	Rhodesia	1933	4	9	1
Hughes, William Morris	Australia	1915	5	14	3
Hussein Ibn Talal	Jordan	1953	0	11	2
Hussein, Saddam	Iraq	1979	1	12	2
Ibn Saud	Saudi Arabia	1932	0	25	3
Inonu, Ismet	Turkey	1938	4	13	2
Inukai Tsuyoshi	Japan	1931	5	8	1
Ito Hirobumi	Japan	1885	5	17	3
Jagan, Cheddi	Guyana	1992	5	12	2
Jinnah, Mohammed Ali	Pakistan	1947	4	18	3
Johnson, Lyndon B.	United States	1963	5	18	3
Juan Carlos I	Spain	1975	4	14	3
Kadar, Janos	Hungary	1956	3	12	2
Karamanlis, Konstantinos	Greece	1955	5	13	2
Karolyi, Mihaly	Hungary	1918	4	6	1
Kato Takaaki	Japan	1924	5	10	2
Kaunda, Kenneth	Zambia	1964	4	13	2
Keating, Paul	Australia	1991	5	8	1
Kennedy, John F.	United States	1961	5	15	3
Kenyatta, Jomo	Kenya	1963	4	22	3
Kerensky, Aleksandr	Russia/Soviet Union	1917	3	11	2
Khama, Seretse	Botswana	1966	4	15	3
Khomeini	Iran	1979	2	23	3
Khrushchev, Nikita	Russia/Soviet Union	1955	3	19	3
Kim Dae Jung	Korea, South	1997	5	11	2

Leader	Country	Began Rule	Type Ruler	PGS Score	Third
Kim Il Sung	Korea, North	1948	2	20	3
King, W.L. Mackenzie	Canada	1921	5	19	3
Kirk, Norman	New Zealand	1972	5	7	1
Kishi Nobusuke	Japan	1957	5	9	1
Kohl, Helmut	Germany	1982	5	23	3
Konoe Fumimaro	Japan	1937	5	12	2
Kreisky, Bruno	Austria	1970	5	14	3
Kruger, Paul	Transvaal	1883	4	12	2
Kuang-hsü	China	1898	0	11	2
Kubitschek, Juscelino	Brazil	1955	5	10	2
Kun, Béla	Hungary	1919	3	14	3
Kuyper, Abraham	Netherlands	1901	5	8	1
Lange, David	New Zealand	1984	5	9	1
Laurel, José Paciano	Philippines	1943	3	7	1
Laurier, Wilfrid	Canada	1896	5	12	2
Laval, Pierre	France	1931	3	8	1
Law, Andrew Bonar	United Kingdom	1922	5	9	1
Lee Kuan Yew	Singapore	1959	3	19	3
Leguía, Augusto	Peru	1908	3	8	1
Lemass, Seán Francis	Ireland	1959	5	9	1
Lenin, Vladimir	Russia/Soviet Union	1917	2	28	3
Leopold II	Belgium	1865	0	17	3
Leopold III	Belgium	1934	0	9	1
Liaquat Ali Khan	Pakistan	1948	4	21	3
Lloyd George, David	United Kingdom	1916	5	22	3
Lumumba, Patrice	Zaire	1960	4	14	3
Lynch, John	Ireland	1966	5	10	2
Lyons, Joseph	Australia	1932	5	10	2
Macapagal, Diosdado	Philippines	1961	5	9	1
Macdonald, Ramsay	United Kingdom	1924	5	10	2
Machado y Morales, G.	Cuba	1924	1	7	1
Machel, Samora	Mozambique	1975	4	15	3
Macmillan, Harold	United Kingdom	1957	5	15	3
Madero, Francisco	Mexico	1911	4	15	3
Magsaysay, Ramon	Philippines	1953	5	11	2
Major, John	United Kingdom	1990	5	12	2
Makarios III	Cyprus	1960	4	14	3
Malan, Daniel	South Africa	1948	2	13	2
Malenkov, Georgy M	Russia/Soviet Union	1953	3	10	2

Leader	Country	Began Rule	Type Ruler	PGS Score	Third
Mandela, Nelson	South Africa	1994	4	20	3
Mannerheim, Carl Gustaf	Finland	1944	5	10	2
Manuel II, King	Portugal	1908	0	7	1
Mao Zedong	China	1949	2	30	3
Marcos, Ferdinand	Philippines	1965	1	10	2
Masaryk, Tomas	Czechoslovakia	1918	4	20	3
McEwen, John	Australia	1967	5	7	1
McKinley, William	United States	1897	5	20	3
Meighen, Arthur	Canada	1920	5	5	1
Meir, Golda	Israel	1969	5	12	2
Mendès-France, Pierre	France	1954	5	7	1
Menelik II	Ethiopia	1889	0	20	3
Menzies, Robert	Australia	1939	5	12	2
Merriman, John X.	South Africa	1908	5	7	1
Metaxas, Ioannis	Greece	1936	3	8	1
Millerand, Alexandre	France	1920	5	9	1
Milosevic, Slobodan	Yugoslavia	1989	1	6	1
Mitterrand, Francois	France	1981	5	17	3
Mobutu Sese Seko	Zaire	1965	1	13	2
Mohammad Pahlevi	Iran	1941	0	15	3
Mossadegh	Iran	1951	4	12	2
Mugabe, Robert	Zimbabwe (Rhodesia)	1980	4	11	2
Muhammad V	Morocco	1957	0	11	2
Mujibur Rahman	Bangladesh	1972	4	16	3
Muldoon, Robert	New Zealand	1975	5	8	1
Mulroney, Brian	Canada	1984	5	12	2
Mussolini, Benito	Italy	1922	2	26	3
Nagy, Imre	Hungary	1953	3	10	2
Nash, Walter	New Zealand	1957	5	7	1
Nasser, Gamal	Egypt	1952	2	22	3
Nehru, Jawaharlal	India	1947	4	25	3
Neto, Agostinho	Angola	1975	3	18	3
Ngo Dinh Diem	Vietnam, South	1954	3	9	1
Nicholas II	Russia/Soviet Union	1894	0	13	2
Nixon, Richard	United States	1969	5	11	2
Nkrumah, Kwame	Ghana	1957	2	16	3
Noriega, Manuel	Panama	1983	1	7	1
Nu, U	Myanmar (Burma)	1948	4	12	2
Nyerere, Julius	Tanzania	1962	2	21	3

Leader	Country	Began Rule	Type Ruler	PGS Score	Third
Obote, Milton	Uganda	1962	4	9	1
Obregón, Álvaro	Mexico	1920	4	13	2
Odría, Manuel A.	Peru	1948	3	8	1
Ohira Masayoshi	Japan	1978	5	9	1
Ojukwu, Odumegwu	Biafra	1967	3	6	1
Okuma Shigenobu	Japan	1898	5	11	2
Osmeña, Sergio	Philippines	1944	5	6	1
Paasikivi, Juho Kusti	Finland	1946	5	12	2
Palme, Olof	Sweden	1969	5	11	2
Park Chung Hee	Korea, South	1961	3	17	3
Pasic, Nikola	Serbia	1891	5	18	3
Pearson, L.B.	Canada	1963	5	12	2
Peres, Shimon	Israel	1977	5	8	1
Pérez Jiménez, Marcos	Venezuela	1952	1	7	1
Perón, Juan	Argentina	1946	3	18	3
Pétain, Philippe	France	1940	3	7	1
Phibunsongkhram, Luang	Thailand	1938	3	11	2
Pilsudski, Josef	Poland	1918	3	17	3
Pinochet, Augusto	Chile	1973	3	12	2
Poincaré, Raymond	France	1912	5	17	3
Pol Pot	Cambodia	1975	2	15	3
Primo de Rivera, M.	Spain	1923	3	9	1
Qaddafi	Libya	1970	2	17	3
Qassem	Iraq	1958	3	8	1
Quirino, Elpidio	Philippines	1948	5	8	1
Quisling, Vidkun	Norway	1940	3	5	1
Rabin, Yitzhak	Israel	1974	5	14	3
Ramos, Fidel V.	Philippines	1992	5	13	2
Rao, P. V.N.	India	1991	5	10	2
Reagan, Ronald	United States	1981	5	22	3
Reid, George	Australia	1904	5	6	1
Renner, Karl	Austria	1918	5	9	1
Reynaud, Paul	France	1940	5	6	1
Reynolds, Albert	Ireland	1992	5	7	1
Reza Khan	Iran	1921	2	19	3
Rhee, Syngman	Korea, South	1948	3	13	2
Ribot, Alexandre	France	1882	5	8	1
Roosevelt, Franklin D.	United States	1933	5	30	3
Roosevelt, Theodore	United States	1901	5	23	3

Leader	Country	Began Rule	Type Ruler	PGS Score	Third
Rowling, Wallace	New Zealand	1974	5	6	1
Roxas, Manuel	Philippines	1946	5	8	1
Sadat, Anwar	Egypt	1970	3	21	3
Saionji Kimmochi	Japan	1901	5	11	2
Salazar, Antonio	Portugal	1932	3	19	3
Salisbury, Robert Arthur	United Kingdom	1885	5	20	3
Sarit Thanarat	Thailand	1958	3	13	2
Saud, Ibn	Saudi Arabia	1953	0	6	1
Savage, Michael	New Zealand	1935	5	7	1
Schmidt, Helmut	Germany, West	1974	5	15	3
Schuschnigg, Kurt	Austria	1934	3	6	1
Scullin, James H.	Australia	1929	5	8	1
Senanayake, Don Stephen	Sri Lanka	1948	4	14	3
Senghor, Leopold Sedar	Senegal	1960	4	20	3
Shagari, Alhaji Shehu	Nigeria	1979	5	9	1
Shastri, Lal Bahadur	India	1964	5	12	2
Shekhar, Chandra	India	1990	5	9	1
Shevardnadze, Eduard	Georgia	1992	5	12	2
Sihanouk, Norodom	Cambodia	1954	0	14	3
Singh, Charan	India	1979	5	9	1
Smith, Ian	Rhodesia	1965	4	10	2
Smuts, Jan Christian	South Africa	1919	4	15	3
Soares, Mário	Portugal	1976	4	11	2
Sobhuza II	Swaziland	1968	0	14	3
Somoza, A., Tachito	Nicaragua	1967	1	5	1
Somoza, A., Tacho I	Nicaragua	1937	1	11	2
St. Laurent, L.S.	Canada	1948	5	14	3
Stalin, Josef	Russia/Soviet Union	1929	2	29	3
Steyn, Marthinus Theunis	Orange Free State	1899	5	2	1
Stolypin, Petr	Russia/Soviet Union	1906	3	13	2
Stresemann, Gustav	Germany	1923	5	13	2
Stroessner, Alfredo	Paraguay	1954	3	10	2
Suharto	Indonesia	1967	3	25	3
Sukarno	Indonesia	1949	2	21	3
Sun Yat-sen	China	1912	3	21	3
Suzuki Zenko	Japan	1980	5	11	2
Taft, William H.	United States	1909	5	12	2
Tanaka Giichi	Japan	1927	5	9	1
Tanaka Kakuei	Japan	1972	5	9	1

Leader	Country	Began Rule	Type Ruler	PGS Score	Third
Tardieu, André	France	1929	5	7	1
Thatcher, Margaret	United Kingdom	1979	5	21	3
Tiso, Jozef	Slovakia	1939	3	7	1
Tito, Josip Broz	Yugoslavia	1945	3	25	3
Tojo Hideki	Japan	1940	3	7	1
Torrijos Herrera, O.	Panama	1969	3	10	2
Touré, Sekou	Guinea	1958	2	21	3
Trudeau, Pierre	Canada	1969	5	16	3
Trujillo, R.	Dominican Republic	1930	1	9	1
Truman, Harry	United States	1945	5	23	3
Tshombe, Moise	Katanga	1960	3	8	1
Tubman, William V.S.	Liberia	1943	1	13	2
Turner, John	Canada	1984	5	6	1
Tz'u-hsi Dowager Empress	China	1861	0	13	2
Ubico, Jorge	Guatemala	1931	3	13	2
Ulbricht, Walter	Germany, East	1950	3	12	2
Vajiravudh (Rama VI)	Thailand	1910	0	10	2
Vargas, Getúlio	Brazil	1930	2	21	3
Velasco Alvarado, Juan	Peru	1968	3	15	3
Venizelos, Eleutherios	Greece	1910	4	18	3
Verwoerd, Hendrik	South Africa	1958	5	14	3
Vorster, John	South Africa	1966	5	14	3
Waldeck-Rousseau, René	France	1899	5	9	1
Walesa, Lech	Poland	1990	4	12	2
Ward, Joseph	New Zealand	1906	5	8	1
Welensky, Roy	Rhodesia	1956	5	9	1
Whitlam, Gough	Australia	1972	5	6	1
Wilhelm II	Germany	1888	0	12	2
Williams, Eric	Trinidad and Tobago	1962	4	17	3
Wilson, Harold	United Kingdom	1964	5	13	2
Wilson, Woodrow	United States	1913	5	24	3
Yahya Khan, Agha	Pakistan	1969	3	7	1
Yamagata Aritomo,	Japan	1889	4	13	2
Yeltsin, Boris	Russia/Soviet Union	1991	5	21	3
Yoshida Shigeru	Japan	1946	5	15	3
Yüan Shih-K'ai	China	1912	1	10	2
Zelaya, José Santos	Nicaragua	1893	3	9	1
Zhivkov, Todor	Bulgaria	1954	3	14	3
Zia ul Haq	Pakistan	1977	3	15	3
Zog	Albania	1925	3	8	1

APPENDIX B

Methodology

CRITERIA FOR INCLUSION WITHIN THE STUDY:*

All political leaders of all independent nations (plus the Palestine Authority) who held chief executive power for *any* length of time during the "baker's century" (1/1/1900–12/31/2000) were included in the study. De facto leaders (those with the most political authority or clout), with or without formal titles or positions, took precedence over any constitutionally appointed or elected officials who had only nominal authority or ceremonial positions. For inclusion in the database, the executive heads might or might not share power with other governmental branches (i.e., legislature, council, etc.), but they could not share power equally with other individuals, such as in a junta. They had to be "in charge."

Ideally, the guiding principle for the selection of rulers was that there could be *only one ruler for one country at any given period of time* during the past century. Practically, this guiding principle was sometimes difficult to implement, since there were instances when it was hard to tell who really was in charge or when the balance of power shifted between individuals.

Three primary sources were consulted in establishing the list of actual leaders: Harris M. Lentz's encyclopedia of *Heads of States and Governments*, E.K. Ambrose's *Chronology of World Leaders: 1996* (Merrifield, VA: Historical Enterprises, 1996), and the "Rulers" database downloaded from the Internet (url: http://www. geocities.com/Athens/1058/rulers.html). At times it was hard to establish whether the real executive power was vested in the monarch, the president, or the prime minister,

---

*Much of the above discussion documenting the methodological approach was prepared under my direction for inclusion in this section by Gregory Guenthner, my research assistant.

regardless of the specific provisions of the constitution and sometimes because of constitutional ambiguities. To clear up such matters, *Britannica Online* (the online version of the *Encyclopædia Britannica*), the Library of Congress Country Studies, and any number of topical studies specific to a country were consulted. Also, the *Europa World Year Book* for 1997, 1998, and 1999 and the Lexus-Nexus® Academic Universe were consulted for information on many of the late-century leaders, relatively neglected by Lentz and Britannica.

Once selected, leaders were then categorized into two groups: those who had separate encyclopedia entries in either the *Encyclopædia Britannica* (online version) or *Encyclopedia Americana* (published hardcopy) and those who did not. A ruler did *not* meet the criterion of having a separate entry if he or she was simply mentioned in the body of a country's entry or was written up in Britannica's *Book-of-the-Year*.

FirstSearch, an online bibliographic database, then was used to identify all the biographical and political information available on each leader who had a separate encyclopedia entry. FirstSearch contains over 35 million records to books and other materials cataloged by Online Computer Library Catalog, Inc., linking over thirty thousand libraries, including the Library of Congress. Potential information sources included dictionaries, encyclopedias, topical studies, theses, dissertations, and biographies. These sources then were examined to determine if they contained adequate reliable information on those rulers with encyclopedia entries to provide the necessary data. Those rulers who had adequate data available about their personal lives and professional careers were selected as the sample for special, in-depth study and analysis.

Ultimately, leaders were categorized into two groups: the entire group of all the rulers of all the countries in the world, both alive and dead, regardless of whether they had encyclopedia entries, and the special sample of rulers mentioned above, both alive and dead, who not only had at least one encyclopedia entry but also had sufficient additional biographical information about their personal lives and professional careers to meet the requirements of the Data Form.

At the termination of the project on December 31, 2000, the entire database included 1,941 individuals from 199 countries. The special sample contained 377 rulers. Of these rulers, 9.5 percent were monarchs, 5.8 percent were tyrants, 6.6 percent were visionaries, 18.3 percent were authoritarians, 12.5 percent were leaders of emerging democracies, and 47.2 percent were leaders of established democracies. (See chapter 2 for a description of this classification of rulers.) The justification for performing a more probing study only on this special sample of rulers with separate encyclopedia entries has to do with the impracticality of locating adequate biographical materials on those rulers without entries. For example, of those rulers who had encyclopedia entries, 53 percent had adequate biographical materials, whereas among a large random sample (N=100) of those who did not have encyclopedia entries, only 4 percent had adequate materials.

Birth Order

To determine if the firstborn child was more likely to be the ruler of a country than later-born children, we used a method similar to that used by N. Mantel and M. Halperin ("Analyses of Birth Rank Data," *Biometrics* 19 [1963]: 324–40) when analyzing birth-rank data. In this method, a table is formed with rows indexed by R, the total number of children in a family. Other entries in the Rth row include N, the total number of families having R children; O, the number of firstborn rulers among these families; and the mean and variance of the expected number of firstborn rulers under the null hypothesis of randomness. Randomness states that O is a binomial variate with mean N/R and variance $NR(1 - 1/R)$. Hence, given R children in a family the firstborn has a probability of $1/R$ to be a ruler; that is, the firstborn is no more likely to be famous than any of the other $R - 1$ children. A test of this hypothesis is obtained by squaring the difference between the total observed firstborn rulers and total expected divided by the total variance. This yields a chi-square statistic having one degree of freedom. Statistical significance is determined at the .05 level. Notice in Table 1, which was formed by using the procedure outlined above, that, except for single-children families and for the few very large families, in every row the observed number of families with firstborn rulers is larger than the hypothesized mean. Since this excess is highly significant ($P < 0.0001$), there is evidence that the firstborn is more likely to be a ruler even after adjusting for the number of children in a family.

NOTE ABOUT COUNTRIES

The 199 countries represented included Palestine, a nation yet to be born, and nations no longer in existence such as Biafra, Hejaz, Orange Free State, the Ottoman Empire, the Federation of Rhodesia and Nyasaland, and the Transvaal. The total count of 199 nations may be somewhat misleading because of various political changes. For instance, Germany, Vietnam, and Yemen were represented as three distinct political entities during

Table 1: Birth Order Analysis for Both Genders Combined

R	N	O	M	V
1	33	33	33.000	0.0000
2	56	33	28.000	14.0000
3	48	24	16.000	10.6667
4	60	24	15.000	11.2500
5	26	8	5.200	4.1600
6	17	5	2.833	2.3608
7	28	5	4.000	3.4286
8	19	3	2.375	2.0781
9	5	0	0.556	0.4942
10	6	0	0.600	0.5400
11	7	2	0.636	0.5782
12	3	1	0.250	0.2292
13	2	0	0.154	0.1422
14	1	0	0.071	0.0659
15	3	1	0.200	0.1867
18	2	0	0.111	0.1048
19	1	0	0.053	0.0502
TOTAL	317	139	109.039	50.3356

CHI-SQUARE = $(139 - 109.039)^2/50.3356 = 17.83$ (p < 0.0001)

Table: *R, the number of children in a family; N, the number of families with R children; O, the observed number of firstborn rulers among the N families; M, the mean; and V, the variance of the number of firstborn rulers under randomness.* (Analyses done by R.J. Kryscio)

the past century (i.e., Germany, West Germany, East Germany; Vietnam, North Vietnam, South Vietnam; Yemen, North Yemen, South Yemen). Russia and the former Soviet Union have been counted together as one entity. The Kingdom of Serbs, Croats, and Slovenes, formed in 1908, was later called Yugoslavia, the country designated in the study. Meanwhile, Serbia, Croatia, and Slovenia each has its own entry for periods when they were independent and not part of the larger federation. Notably, two independent countries were excluded from the study because of their collective presidencies, with no single individual having clear executive authority over the entire country. In Switzerland, a council of presidents representing the twenty-six independent cantons selects a president each year, who functions mostly in a ceremonial role. Also, Bosnia's collective presidency consists of three members representing each of the three communities living in the country—Muslims, Croats, and Serbs, with each president rotating as chairman every eight months.

Gaps in Reign

Because of political circumstances, several countries had gaps in time when no single leader was in charge. This usually occurred under one of the following circumstances:

A junta ruled with no single leader in charge.

A collective presidency existed, such as Yugoslavia's constitutional collective between Tito's death and the breakup of the Federation.

A triumvirate or foursome ruled, such as existed for a few years in Vietnam following Le Duan's death in 1986 or after Mao's death in China.

A caretaker regency ruled while child monarchs held the title or adult monarchs were incapacitated by sickness. As an exception, the Empress Tz'u-hsi, a former regent and later the adoptive mother of the emperor Kuang-hsü (reigned 1875–1908), was included in the study because she wielded so much power and dominated the Chinese empire for almost half a century. Political chaos or upheaval existed, especially during civil or international wars, when no single leader was clearly in control. During these times, interim or acting leaders sometimes were appointed to lead a caretaker government for relatively brief periods of times, but their powers often were seriously curbed by the military or a revolutionary council or the party in power, and so they sometimes did not qualify as being suitable for inclusion in the study.

The leader of a government in exile, even if the government was constitutionally "legitimate," was not acknowledged as the chief executive of that nation if other leaders or groups were governing the nation at those times. Many countries, such as Greece, which was occupied by the Axis powers during World War II, had leadership gaps; but others, such as France or Norway, did not. In these latter instances, a leader held executive power of a working government despite ruling under the shadow of the occupying armies. As a result, rulers such as Petain and Quisling qualified for inclusion in the study.

Overlaps in Reigns

The exception to the principle of one ruler for one country at one time exists when power shifts occurred between two leaders or a leader and a governing group, such as between a monarch and prime minister or a president and prime minister or a ruler and a ruling council, as happened in Cambodia, China, France, Italy, Japan, or the Soviet Union in the past. When ambiguities existed as to which ruler was in power or there were indications that one person held the upper hand at one time and the other at another time, both individuals were included in the study, but this was determined on a case-by-case basis. Generally, overlapping reigns of this sort were rare, and attempts were made to weigh all the evidence and choose one leader or the other. Nevertheless, a few exceptions still existed. The emperor Kuang-hsü was included in the study even though his adoptive mother, the empress Tz'u-hsi, held considerable power at the time, because he ruled absolutely for about a hundred days prior to 1900 and afterward nominally continued to have absolute power even though he did not wield it. A similar situation also applied to the emperor Hirohito and his prime minister, Hideki Tojo. Also, the two Turkish leaders, Bayar and Menderes, likewise held the upper political hand at different periods in time.

Chronological Gaps and Leadership Overlaps

Over the course of the twentieth century, many gaps in leadership existed during times of political chaos or uncertainty. A selected list of the countries and the time periods involved follows: Greece around the time of World War II; Hungary during the roughly one-year gap between Bela Kun and Horthy; Italy during the power shifts between Umberto and the early twentieth-century prime ministers, as well as during the forty-six-year overlap (1900–46) between Vittorio Emmanuel and certain prime ministers, notably Benito Mussolini; Iran during the unstable years from 1909 to 1921 when the British and other outsiders ruled or exerted political influence; Iraq between 1937 and 1953, during the reign of Faysal II when he was a child and living in England and his uncle, Abdul-Ilah, ruled; Japan during several overlaps between the prime minister and emperor; Russia under Stolypin and Tsar Nicholas and during the gap between Lenin and Stalin when Stalin formed alliances to wrestle control from Trotsky; Somalia since 1991 when warlords controlled the country; Spain during the overlap between the monarchy (i.e., Alfonso XIII, Juan Carlos) and certain prime ministers; The Sudan during the rule by the Sovereignty Council or Committee of Sovereignty; Thailand during the overlap between the king and first prime minister for two years; Turkey during the overlap between Bayar, serving as president, under the prime ministership of Menderes; and Vietnam during the six-year gap in leadership from 1986 after General Secretary Le Duan's death and before the presidency of Le Duc Anh in 1992, when power was delegated to the presidency and the Communist Party's role was considerably reduced.

POTENTIAL DATABASE DISCREPANCIES

At times, the various authoritative sources (i.e., Lentz, the "Rulers" database from the Internet [url: http://www. geocities.com/Athens/1058/rulers.html], encyclopedia entries, Europa, and actual biographies) did not agree on dates of key events, spellings, or other information. In these instances, a judgment was made about which source of information appeared to be most accurate.

Unfortunately, the dates of reign do not always match the dates listed in Lentz, "Rulers," or Britannica, because these sources include legal and ceremonial dates regardless of the political reality. As noted above, the dates for a constitutionally elected or appointed executive officeholder are inconsequential to the rule of a de facto ruler. In the database used for this study, the chronological lists include a start date and an end date marking the time that leader held "real" power, not for when a political leader entered and "left" a legal office. This is not a minor distinction. Several de facto leaders held authoritarian power while intermittently holding office. For example, Nicolae Ceausescu, the Romanian dictator, held authoritarian power from 1965 to 1989, while being listed as "president" only for the years 1974–89. His presidential span of fifteen years is inconsequential to his twenty-four-year dictatorship. In contrast, some leaders held office longer than they held real power, when a coup relieved them of their duties but retained them as figureheads. Again, except for certain instances of overlapping of shifting power, leaders are included in the study only for the days they held "real" power. Portugal and Salazar illustrate this scenario. Portugal had a presidency when the military removed all power from the position and granted authority to Salazar. The individual who relinquished the executive powers of the presidency continued in office. His *legal* dates of rule were lengthy, running concurrently with Salazar's. In the database, he was credited only for his initial ruling days, a considerably shorter span of time than the dates listed in Lentz or the *Encyclopedia Britannica*. So when such discrepancies existed about when rulers were in power or how they lost power, decisions were made on a case-by-case basis in which all the facts were taken into account. For instance, a determination was made that

Mexico's president Álvaro Obregón lost political power in 1928 because of assassination even though his actual last year in office was 1924. The reason for this decision was because he won the presidency again in 1928 but was killed before he could be inaugurated.

Missing Names

Several names appear in one database only to be neglected by another. Lentz generally listed fewer names than were found in the "Rulers" database, often neglecting presidents and prime ministers who served as interim head-of-state for days or even mere hours. Still, he did mention a few names that were not in the "Rulers" database. Latin America seemed to be the region with the most discrepancies between the sources.

The decision whether to include certain questionable rulers was further complicated because there was no "final authority" database that superseded all others. Generally, the database of rulers used in this study included only those individuals who appeared in Lentz, but this broke down for the last five years of the century because Lentz's publication rarely listed anyone after 1995, and sometimes stopped earlier. So the "Rulers" database, Europa, and the Lexus-Nexus® Academic Universe became the main authorities for rulers throughout the 1990s. For many countries, the *New York Times* or *Britannica Book-of-the-Year* also were used as aids to resolve conflicts or fill in missing information about rulers. Perhaps the best way of describing the complete database of rulers for this study is that it represents a conglomerate of names gathered from Lentz, the "Rulers" database, *Encyclopedia Britannica*, the *New York Times*, and *Europa World Year*.

Some examples in which conflicts and discrepancies were encountered between these different sources for information are described below.

Ecuador, Guatemala, Haiti, Honduras, Kiribati, Lebanon, Nicaragua, Mexico (several leaders), New Zealand, Panama, Peru, Poland, Portugal, Sierra Leone, The Sudan, Syria, Thailand, Turkey, Uganda, Uruguay, and Venezuela had at least one leader, sometimes several, listed in the "Rulers" database but missing from Lentz. Often the missing leader served only days. Many were listed as "acting," so their absence in Lentz was likely intentional; however, Lentz did include some "acting" presidents and prime ministers.

Figureheads and de facto leaders popped up anywhere. Unfortunately, when they did, the constitutional leader often became a figurehead whose title was now ceremonial. Both Lentz and the "Rulers" database listed these powerless leaders. In my complete database of rulers, no figure-head leaders were included.

Several leaders in Mexico who were listed in the "Rulers" database were not listed in Lentz's. Mexico was also a good example of these authoritative sources listing powerless leaders at times with ceremonial titles without regard for who really ruled. As a result, some "interim" presidents were listed, such as Lascurain Paredes, who held title as president for a few hours in February 1913 between Madero's assassination and Huerta's assumption of the presidency. Huerta deposed Madero, and he was clearly the de facto leader. However, Lentz did not always neglect these interims leaders, including, for example, Panama's Ernesto Jaen Guardia, who was in power for only hours in 1941.

Variables That Were Likely Under-reported for the Total Group of Rulers

Leaders who had gained and lost power in the last ten years, especially of the lesser countries, either were not listed in Lentz or, if listed, their entries were terse, providing only cursory information. Also, Britannica's *Book of the Year* usually gave these individuals only a passing notice. This relative sparsity of information about many rulers in the total group brings up certain methodological issues regarding the interpretation of certain results. For example, the relative inconsistency of reporting certain events about rulers, such as "assassination attempts" or "coup attempts," meant that all results needed to be qualified by the statement "*at least (blank) percent.*" This meant that the results obtained for certain variables should be considered as underestimates. In no instances were they less than the figures reported. However, despite these figures, comparable results obtained on the special sample of 377 rulers on similar variables with more reliable and extensive information likely provide a more accurate estimate.

APPENDIX C

Data Collection and Statistics

GENERAL OVERVIEW OF DATA COLLECTION AND STATISTICAL METHODS

Information forms were used to record all appropriate biographical data about subjects and, when available, their immediate relatives as well. Appropriate materials were mainly "hard data," behavioral observations and judgments based on scientific evidence or expert sources. Opinions and interpretations by the biographers or others for which there was no documented evidence were ignored.

Based on the extensive material contained in the information forms, a data form (with definitions for all variables and explicit criteria for coding and recording of information) consisting of 182 items was filled out for each subject. Since the methodological approach and key personnel were similar to that adopted in my prior study on eminent individuals (See A.M. Ludwig, *The Price of Greatness*, Guilford Press, New York, 1995), there was no need to repeat inter-rater reliability with the data forms. In those studies, in order to determine the adequacy of information transferred from a standard biographical source to the initial Information Form, four raters independently read the same biographies on six different individuals and filled out separate information forms consisting of 116 categories of information. Each form was then independently coded on a categorical basis as to whether it had the designated information. Cohen's kappa statistic, which ranged from .69 to .75 (mean = .71), indicated high levels of agreement (see D.G. Altman, *Practical Statistics for Medical Research*, Chapman and Hall, London, 1991). The percentage of agreement among pairs of four raters ranged from 82 to 88 percent (average = 86 percent). In addition, to learn the extent to which error or bias potentially influenced the coding of material from the information form to the data form used for computer entry, four raters independently filled out data forms on eight different subjects using the same information forms on each. Because the items on the data form were a mixture of nominal, ordinal, and fixed interval data, inter-rater reliability was established on the basis of the percentage of complete agreement between pairs of raters on the items, with the values ranging from 84 to 87 percent (average = 86 percent).

In the current study, the Political Greatness Scale (PGS) (see appendix D) was used to measure the relative political achievements of rulers in the selected sample. Inter-rater reliability on the total PGS scores was exceptionally high. One analysis of thirty randomly selected subjects yielded an r value of +0.95 (p<.000). Another analysis of eighteen United States presidents resulted in an r value of +0.93 (p<.001). Other methodological details about this scale are described in chapter 9 and the appropriate chapter notes.

STATISTICAL PROCEDURES

Since the total group included all the rulers of all the countries in the world during the entire "baker's century," the usual kinds of statistical analyses that attempt to assess whether the results obtained on a *representative* sample of subjects can be generalized to the group as a whole or were due mainly to chance did not seem appropriate for most of the recorded events. Instead, the actual rates of occurrence for these events (e.g., the percentages of suicide, the length of time in office, the percentages of rulers deposed) were, by definition, reportable facts. When relatively complete and reliable information is available on an entire group of subjects, it makes no logical sense to use statistical tests on results that already applied to all of the rulers in the world over a long time period such as a century. Whatever the rates, averages, or distributions were, they simply were! The results spoke for themselves. While the results obtained on all the rulers of the twentieth century may not reflect the situation for all rulers throughout all of recorded history, they do apply to a large enough group to permit certain generalities to be made with reasonable confidence about the relative frequencies or percentages of certain characteristics or happenings in rulers. Nonetheless, bowing to convention, I routinely did run the requisite statistical tests as well simply for interest to determine the levels of significance of the various results. Naturally, because of the extremely large number of rulers in the database, even small differences in frequency or percentages in comparisons of the different variables turned out to be statistically significant beyond the p<.05 level for two-tailed tests of probability.

With the exception of the regression analyses, I utilized simple, straightforward statistical procedures such as cross-tabulations for categorical variables (e.g., comparing the percentage of the different ruler types who did or did not engage in war) or analyses of variance for continuous data (e.g., the average longevity or years served in office by the different ruler types) to determine the likelihood that the differences were due to chance, or correlation analyses to determine the extent to which two different continuous variables were related to one another (e.g., the extent to which the grades obtained in school by rulers were related to their relative political achievement) mainly for descriptive purposes. Descriptions of these standard procedures can be found in any elementary statistical text.

Although statistical comparisons among ruler types and other categorical variables also were carried out routinely for the sample of 377 rulers, certain methodological problems had to be taken into account. The sample, while representing over one-fifth of the group of all rulers, by definition, could not be considered strictly representative of the entire group of rulers since it included only those rulers with entries in either the *Encyclopedia Americana* or *Encyclopaedia Britannica* who had adequate additional biographical materials available about them in English to answer the various items on the Data Form. Despite this qualification, the objective method for selecting the rulers to be included and the large size of this sample suggests that any significant results obtained may be reasonably representative of twentieth-century rulers as a whole and, as I argue in places, perhaps all rulers and in all times. Moreover, regardless of the issue of the potential representativeness of the sample, the findings speak for themselves as being descriptive of the largest group of twentieth-century rulers ever assembled and studied in depth.

The SPSS for Windows, Versions 6.1. 8.0, and 9.0, were the main statistical software packages employed for data analyses. Aside from the specific product-moment correlation analyses described above for evaluating inter-rater reliability, other statistical procedures used to compare groups and to test the general hypotheses under investigation were as follows:

Differences among the ruler groups for categorical variables were analyzed largely by means of cross-tabulation analyses, using chi-square statistics on the raw data or actual frequencies. Post hoc tests for significant chi square values between individual pairs or groups were undertaken only if the overall chi square proved statistically significant. Between-group comparisons were interpreted as "meaningful" only if one group differed significantly from at least two others. For instances in which the proportion of responders was too small for chi-square analysis, Fisher's exact test was used.

One-way analyses of variance were used to compare mean responses among professions for interval level variables. Post hoc tests for significant F ratios were based on Scheffe's multiple comparison procedure, which was undertaken only if the omnibus ANOVA proved statistically significant.

Multiple and logistic regression models were employed only for the purpose of theory construction to assess whether the results supported my general impressions about the importance of certain variables as potential predictors of political greatness. Multiple regression techniques tend to be useful when more than one independent variable are likely related to one outcome (dependent) variable. These techniques allow not only an analysis of the extent to which the different independent variables are related to each other but also a determination of the relative extent to which they are related to a predicted outcome. With a logistic regression model, the approach is comparable to a multiple regression model, which uses linear, continuous variables, except that the variables are categorical and the outcome variable is dichotomous. Since multiple regression analyses rely on complete data sets for all the variables used in the equation, methodological and conceptual difficulties often differ with regard to how missing data is treated (See discussion in F.J. Sulloway, *Born to Rebel: Birth Order, Family Dynamics, and Creative Lives,* Pantheon Books, New York, 1996). Although missing values can reduce the sample size substantially, I made it a point to select only those independent variables with relatively complete data for my analyses so that the final sample of rulers still remained sufficiently large to judge the extent to which these multiple variables correlated with the Political Greatness Scale total scores in the multiple regression analysis or the Top Third versus Bottom Third classification of political greatness in the logistic regression analysis. That way, I could avoid making the assumptions necessary to compensate for missing data (e.g., using average scores) for these regression analyses.

Although I am mainly reporting descriptive statistics, it is of incidental interest that, unless otherwise specified, essentially all comparative results reported in the text were statistically significant (i.e., $p < .05$, two-tailed test of probability). The actual values for these statistical comparisons are included in the corresponding Method and Statistics section for each chapter. In order to simplify most data tables, I included only summary percentages or mean scores (plus standard deviations). In many instances, the numbers of subjects in groups varied because of missing information. This naturally was taken into account in all statistical analyses.

APPENDIX D

Political Greatness Scale (PGS)

All ratings apply to the recognized works, products, performances, accomplishments, and creations (or lack thereof) of a single individual (as the primary leader of a country) that have an impact on the lives of others. The ratings should represent a composite judgment of the leader for the entire time in power and also take into account trends over time toward the end of rule. Except where indicated, the ratings should not incorporate actions before the leader's rule or after having relinquished power. For persons still alive, the rater should make the best estimate on the basis of available evidence and time frame. All ratings should be as value-free as possible with respect to moral judgments about "good" and "evil" or what type of government is best. The rater should rate each item independently of others. When in doubt about the level of rating for a particular item, the rater should select the lower of the two levels. (N.B.: For leaders still in office at year 2000, the rater should make a best estimate of their performance up until that time and the likely consequences of the performance.)

A. SOMETHING FROM NOTHING

0. Did not participate actively in the creation of a new nation or the establishment of independence or the formation of a new form of government. *(This is the default rating if no evidence exists to the contrary.)*

1. An active participant (but not the leader) in the struggle to create a new nation or the establishment of independence, but not one of the main leaders. *(This is the default rating for leaders of coups or civil wars who overthrow existing regimes and form new ones.)*

2. A leader (one of several) in the struggle to create a new nation or the establishment of independence.

3. The leader in the struggle to create a new nation or the establishment of independence (i.e., Father of the nation).

B. MORE THAN BEFORE

0. The leader lost existing territory or reduced the country's hegemony over other nations during rule.

1. The leader did not add new territory to existing country or extend its hegemony. Or the leader had some gains and some loses. Or the leader granted independence or greater autonomy to countries it ruled but retained major influence over them by keeping them in an alliance or commonwealth. Or the leader deliberately extricated his/her own country from an "impossible" situation by granting independence or autonomy to another nation over which it formerly held dominion, thereby quelling unrest within his/her own country or strengthening its resources (e.g., France vs. Algeria, Russia vs. Georgia, France vs. Indochina, U.S. vs. Vietnam). On balance, the territorial situation was essentially the same (or not appreciably different) at beginning and end of reign. *(This is the default rating if no evidence exists to the contrary.)*

2. The leader extended his/her nation's hegemony over other countries through control of strategic resources and industries (e.g., operating Panama Canal), operating military bases, (e.g., protectorship, unilateral defense treaty), etc., *without* actual territorial gains.

3. The leader extended his/her nation's borders or gained new territory or took control of certain areas or countries through war, colonization, or other coercive means.

C. STAYING POWER

0. Exerted leadership for <2 years.
1. Exerted leadership for 2 to <4 years.
2. Exerted leadership for 4 to <8 years.
3. Exerted leadership for 8 to <12 years.
4. Exerted leadership for 12 to <16 years.
5. Exerted leadership for >16 years.

D. MILITARY PROWESS DURING REIGN

(If several wars had been fought, the rating should pertain to the most important war or the overall situation in general.)

0. Lost war or military conflict/confrontation. On balance, the leader was a loser.

1. No war or military conflict/confrontation during reign (i.e., or deliberately kept country from getting involved in a war). Preserved military status quo with potential adversaries while avoiding conflict. *(This is default rating if no evidence is available to the contrary.)*

2. Leader avoided defeat in war or military conflict/confrontation

but no clear-cut victory. Or military victories and losses roughly balanced out. Or leader established an equitable peace.

3. Leader won war or major military conflict/confrontation during reign. Leader gained influence over other country or gained territory by fiat or fomenting revolutions or coups or coercion. On balance, leader was a winner. *(Rate item above if leader lost election or died in office before final victory).*

E. SOCIAL ENGINEERING

("Social Engineering" refers to the utopian restructuring of the social order with ideological underpinnings.)

0. No substantial change (or only minor change) of status quo in basic social structure, whether or not leader continued in same form of government, overthrew a prior government, or introduced a new constitution or laws. *(This is the default rating if no information is available to the contrary.)*

1. The leader issued decrees or enacted laws that expanded established social precedents (e.g., extending civil rights, expanding health benefits) built on social policies of predecessors.

2. The leader issued *limited* decrees or enacted laws with little or no social precedent, which led to some restructuring of society (e.g., social security, medicaid, Prohibition, civil rights).

3. The leader introduced *broad* legislation with little or no social precedent that changed the basic structure of society for better or worse (e.g., apartheid, cultural revolution, universal enfranchisement, forced collectivization, New Deal, nationalization of industries, privatization of industries, establishment of a free market economy).

F. ECONOMIC PROSPERITY

0. Economy became substantially worse by end of reign (i.e., serious unemployment, depression, or inflation resulting in widespread strikes, riots, or demonstrations).

1. No (or minor) overall improvement or worsening of economy noted. Fluctuations in the economy with no clear trends. Essential continuation of economic situation that existed prior to assuming power. *(This is the default rating if no contrary information is available.)*

2. Major improvement of economy over the course of reign in the absence of a pre-existing crisis (such as serious unemployment or inflation associated with widespread strikes, riots, or demonstrations).

3. Economic boom after leader instituted measures to deal with prior or existing crisis such as serious unemployment, depression, poverty, or inflation (e.g., New Deal, Nazis cranking up the war machine).

G. STATESMANSHIP

(N.B. Participation in meetings and conferences does not constitute active leadership even if leader is head of a large nation!)

0. *No* evidence of *active* leadership role or *taking the initiative* in multinational (i.e., blocs of nations) concerns, regional interests, or international affairs. *(This is default rating without information to the contrary.)*

1. *Active* leadership or *taking the initiative* with respect to certain *ethnic, religious, or emotional* concerns that do not directly bear on the economic survival or social welfare of the leader's nation (e.g., apartheid, Palestinian statehood, united Ireland).

2. *Active* leadership or *taking the initiative* with respect to issues or alliances that directly bear on the economic survival or social welfare of the involved countries (e.g., OPEC, NAFTA, United Arab Republic, Pan-Arabism, Potsdam agreement, SALT) rather than mankind as a whole. These alliances are formed primarily to address more regional or intracontinental concerns than global ones and have more limited than international repercussions.

3. *Active* leadership role in *worldwide* political or economic issues that potentially affect large segments of humanity or human values (e.g., nuclear nonproliferation treaty, creating the United Nations, solving the problem of hunger, offering solutions to the environment, protecting human rights). Winning the Nobel Peace Prize for brokering peace agreements between other nations and advancing the cause of peace.

H. IDEOLOGY

0. No special ideological underpinnings for leadership. No overall vision for society. Leader had own agenda for rule rather than some greater purpose. Leader held power for the sake of power. Leader compromised goals to gain consensus or to remain in office. Leader espoused an existing ideology (not original to the ruler) as the basis for leadership (e.g., communism, nationalism, democracy, pan-Arabism, royalist) and appeared to operate within that framework. *(This is default rating without information to the contrary.)*

1. Leader's approach to governing appeared distinctive (e.g., New Deal, Fair Deal, Great Society, Brezhnev doctrine, Perestroika) even though it may not have been articulated as an ideology. Leader communicated a personal or distinctive ideology through speeches, writings, or the media (e.g., fireside chats, bully pulpit) but did not systematically indoctrinate the public or impose it on society.

2. Leader adopted or modified an existing ideology (not original to

the ruler) as the basis for leadership (e.g., Qaddafi's Green Book, Stalinism), with systematic attempt to indoctrinate or impose this ideology on the populace through schools, media, forced conversion, legislation, or other means.

3. Leader formulated a relatively original ideology as the basis for leadership (e.g., Maoism, Mein Kampf, Leninism) with systematic attempt to indoctrinate or impose this ideology on the populace through schools, media, forced conversion, legislation, or other means.

I. MORAL EXEMPLAR

0. Leader exploited high office for personal financial gain. Leader showed evidence of illegally expropriating state funds for personal use (e.g., unauthorized foreign bank accounts, squandering public funds for unnecessary palaces or residences or grandiose schemes that benefited leader). Leader engaged in highly questionable business practices or was involved in graft during term in office. Leader appointed family members (nepotism) or friends to positions of power that permitted financial gain. Leader showed evidence that his/her actions were directed more toward personal gain than the welfare of the populace or the good of the country. Widespread corruption or scandal within administration.

1. No evidence that leader exploited high office for financial gain or tolerated graft by family or key members of administration. *(This is the default rating on all leaders on whom insufficient information is available to make another rating.)*

2. Leader seemed to be acting in the best interests of the country by his/her own lights (with no evidence of exploiting high office for financial gain above the normal perks that go with the position). Actions of leader appeared to be selfless and in service to a higher cause. The leader used his/her high office as a moral platform to promote honesty and self-sacrifice.

3. Leader showed self-sacrifice on behalf of the nation or some greater cause as manifested by prior or present deeds that involved pursuit of some noble end such as nationhood, overthrowing a corrupt government, or promulgating some ideology. Examples of personal sacrifice include risking one's life in a civil war or coup, guerrilla warfare, imprisonment, torture, and exile. Leader provided inspiration and served as a unifying force at a time of national crisis. As a consequence of these "credentials," the leader assumed a hero status for the nation. *(This rating can be given only if leader showed no personal evidence of graft or corruption.)*

J. POLITICAL LEGACY

0. The leader left office in disgrace or with a worse reputation than

when he began. The leader was overthrown by a civil war, coup, uprising, war, etc., resulting in imprisonment, execution, exile, forced resignation, or abdication. Leader lost bid for reelection and never gained
office again. The leader ended term in office as a failure despite prior
victories or achievements. In a parliamentary government, the leader
was removed from office when new government formed and then lost
leadership of party.

1. The leader neither gained nor lost political stature as a result of
term in office. The leader died in office before completion of term or
resigned for reasons of health. In a parliamentary government, the leader
retained leadership of party after a new government was formed. (*This is
the default rating for all leaders who completed term in office or died in
office or resigned voluntarily or left office because of the formation of a new
government without evidence that leader substantially lost or gained in
political reputation.*)

2. The leader gained in political stature as a result of notable deeds
or accomplishments during term(s) in office (e.g., won war, overcame
inflation, won confrontation with another nation). In the case of parliamentary government, the prime minister was credited with notable deeds
during at least one term in office, and reputation was not discredited
appreciably after any subsequent terms in office. The reputation of the
leader became greater rather than lessened over the course of time.

3. The leader gained almost legendary status as a result of national
symbolism (e.g., Father of the nation) or extraordinary deeds (e.g., revamping society, initiating radical changes in government, gaining national independence) during term in office. Even though the leader may
have fallen from grace, his/her movement continued after he/she left office or remained an object of veneration for a large number of people or
created a political system that endured or assumed posthumous heroic
stature for many.

K. SIZE OF CONSTITUENCY (excluding colonies or protectorates)
(At time assumes power)

0. Ruler of country <2 million population
1. Ruler of country with 2 million to <10 million population
2. Ruler of country with 10 million to <25 million population
3. Ruler of country with 25 million to <50 million population
4. Ruler of country with 50 million to <100 million population
5. Ruler of country with >100 million population

NOTES

INTRODUCTION

1. I first began collecting information on political leaders in about 1982 when I launched my studies on the relationship between mental disturbances and creative achievement in eminent twentieth-century figures. See A.M. Ludwig, *The Price of Greatness: Resolving the Creativity and Madness Controversy* (New York: Guilford, 1995).

2. See appendix B for a detailed description of how the sample was collected.

3. Most past studies of rulers have been anecdotal in nature, usually limited to certain geographical regions or handfuls of better-known leaders or dictators. As a result, comparative studies on the different kinds of rulers have been rare. Prior to my own study, Dean Simonton published a study designed to predict the relative greatness of American presidents. See D.K. Simonton, *Why Presidents Succeed: A Political Psychology of Leadership* (New Haven: Yale Univ. Press, 1987). And Mostafa Rejai and Kay Phillips published the results of their studies dealing with the differences between revolutionary leaders and loyalists who partook in various political revolutions (*Loyalists and Revolutionaries: Political Leaders Compared* [New York: Praeger, 1988]). Unfortunately, their results have only a limited bearing on my present study, because their samples of revolutionaries and loyalists included both rulers and nonrulers, were confined to discrete political revolutions, and spanned several centuries. As a result, while there are some parallels, it is not legitimate to extrapolate from their findings to mine. See also M. Rejai and K. Phillips, *Leaders of Revolution* (Beverly Hills: Sage, 1979); idem, *World Revolutionary Leaders* (New Brunswick, N.J.: Rutgers Univ. Press, 1983); and idem, *Demythologizing an Elite: American Presidents in Empirical, Comparative, and Historical Perspective* (Westport, Conn.: Praeger, 1993).

4. See H.M. Lentz, *Heads of States and Governments: A Worldwide Encyclopedia of Over 2,300 Leaders, 1945–1992* (Jefferson, N.C.: McFarland, 1994); idem, *Encyclopedia of Heads of States and Governments, 1900 through 1945* (Jefferson, N.C.: McFarland, 1999); *The Europa World Yearbook* (London: Europa Publications); and *Political Handbook of the World: 1998* (Binghamton, N.Y.: CSA Publications).

An incomplete listing of the various historical dictionaries of different countries and regions includes: R.J. Alexander, ed., *Biographical Dictionary of Latin American and Caribbean Political Leaders* (New York: Greenwood Press, 1988); H. Boylan, *A Dictionary of Irish Biography* (New York: St. Martin's Press, 1988); D.C. Briggs and M. Alisky, *Historical Dictionary of Mexico* (Metuchen, N.J.: Scarecrow Press, 1981); A.F. Clark and L.C. Phillips, *Historical Dictionary of Senegal* (Metuchen, N.J.: Scarecrow Press, 1994); D. Commins, *Historical Dictionary of Syria* (Lanham, Md.: Scarecrow Press, 1996); F.J. Coppa, ed., *Dictionary of Modern Italian History* (Westport, Conn.: Greenwood Press, 1985); J.F. Copper, *Historical Dictionary of Taiwan* (Metuchen, N.J.: Scarecrow Press, 1993); J.W. Cortada, ed., *Historical Dictionary of the Spanish Civil War, 1936–1939* (Westport, Conn.: Greenwood Press, 1982); C. Fluehr-Lobban and R.A. Lobban Jr., eds., *Historical Dictionary of the Sudan* (Metuchen, N.J.: Scarecrow Press, 1992); H. Glickman, ed., *Political Leaders of Contemporary Africa South of the Sahara: A Biographical Dictionary* (Westport, Conn.: Greenwood Press, 1992); P. Gunson, and G. Chamberlain, *The Dictionary of Contempo-*

rary Politics of Central America and the Caribbean (New York: Simon and Schuster, 1991); R. Hutchings, *Historical Dictionary of Albania* (Lanham, Md.: Scarecrow Press, 1996); P.H. Hutton, ed., *Historical Dictionary of the Third French Republic, 1870–1940* (Westport, Conn.: Greenwood Press, 1986); S. Iwao, *Biographical Dictionary of Japanese History,* trans. B. Watson (Tokyo : International Society for Educational Information, 1978); R. Kern, ed., *Historical Dictionary of Modern Spain, 1700–1988* (New York: Greenwood Press, 1990); M. Liniger-Goumaz, *Historical Dictionary of Equatorial Guinea* (Metuchen, N.J.: Scarecrow Press, 1988); M.R. Lipschutz and R.K. Rasmussen, *Dictionary of African Historical Biography* (Chicago: Aldine Publishing, 1978); S. Mansingh, *Historical Dictionary of India* (Lanham, Md.: Scarecrow Press, 1996); R.A. Nickson, *Historical Dictionary of Paraguay* (Metuchen, N.J.: Scarecrow Press, 1993); B.J. Nordstrom, ed., *Dictionary of Scandinavian History* (Westport, Conn.: Greenwood Press, 1986); W. Northcutt, *Historical Dictionary of the French Fourth and Fifth Republics, 1946–1991* (Westport, Conn.: Greenwood Press, 1992); J.S. Olson, *Dictionary of the Vietnam War* (New York: Greenwood Press, 1988); D. Owusu-Ansah and D.M. McFarland, *Historical Dictionary of Ghana* (Metuchen, N.J.: Scarecrow Press, 1995); E. Pak-Wah Leung, *Historical Dictionary of Revolutionary China, 1839–1976* (New York: Greenwood Press, 1992); A. Plakans, *Historical Dictionary of Latvia* (Lanham, Md.: Scarecrow Press, 1997); B. Reich, *Political Leaders of the Contemporary Middle East and North Africa: A Biographical Dictionary* (New York: Greenwood Press, 1990); G.H. Scholefield, ed., *A Dictionary of New Zealand Biography* vols. 1 and 2 (Wellington: Department of Internal Affairs, 1940); Y. Shimoni, *Biographical Dictionary of the Middle East* (New York: Facts on File, 1991); H.E. Smith, *Historical and Cultural Dictionary of Thailand* (Metuchen, N.J.: Scarecrow Press, 1976); J. Suchlicki, *Historical Dictionary of Cuba* (Metuchen, N.J.: Scarecrow Press, 1988); F.W. Thackeray and J.E. Findling, eds., *Statesmen Who Changed the World: A Bio-Bibliographical Dictionary of Diplomacy* (Westport, Conn.: Greenwood Press, 1993); S.B. Várdy, *Historical Dictionary of Hungary* (Lanham, Md.: Scarecrow Press, 1997); D.J. Whitfield, *Historical and Cultural Dictionary of Vietnam* (Metuchen, N.J.: Scarecrow Press, 1976); and J.L. Willis, *Historical Dictionary of Uruguay* (Metuchen, N.J.: Scarecrow Press, 1974).

CHAPTER 1

1. In the Swiss form of government, the president is regarded as the head of the nation during the rotating one-year term in office, although the role is largely symbolic.

2. D. Fossey, *Gorillas in the Mist* (Boston: Houghton Mifflin, 1983), and J. Goodall, *The Chimpanzees of Gombe: Patterns of Behavior* (Cambridge: Harvard Univ. Press, 1986), and R.M. Sapolsky, *A Primate's Memoir* (New York: Scribner, 2001).

3. See F. de Waal, *Chimpanzee Politics: Power and Sex among Apes* (Baltimore: Johns Hopkins Univ. Press, 1998), idem, *Peacemaking among Primates* (Cambridge: Harvard Univ. Press, 1990). and idem, "Bonobo Sex and Society: The Behavior of a Close Relative Challenges Assumptions about Male Supremacy in Human Evolution," *Scientific American*, March 1995, pp. 82–88.

4. G.B. Schaller, *The Mountain Gorilla: Ecology and Behavior* (Chicago, Univ. of Chicago Press, 1976).

5. In his book, *Bonobo: The Forgotten Ape* (Berkeley: Univ. of California Press, 1997), Frans de Waal describes a more female-dominated and polymorphous sexual society among these greater apes than noted in other simian species.

6. From C. McCullough, *The First Man in Rome* (New York: Avon, 1990), pp. 219–20.

7. E.B. Keverne, R.R. Meller, and A.M. Martinez-Arias, "Dominance, Aggression and Sexual Behavior in Social Groups of Talapoin Monkeys," in D.J. Chivers and J. Herbert, eds., *Recent Advances in Primatology* vol. 1 (New York: Academic Press, 1978), pp. 533–48. Also see R.M. Rose, I.S. Bernstein, T.P. Gordon, and S.F. Catlin, "Androgens and Ag-

gression: A Review and Recent Findings in Primates," in R.L. Holloway, ed., *Primate Aggression, Territoriality, and Xenophobia* (New York: Academic Press, 1974), pp. 275–304.

8. In response to my request, Richard Lederer (richard.lederer@pobox.com) kindly provided me with many of the military terms used in political contexts.

9. C.D. Ameringer, *Don Pepe: A Political Biography of José Figueres of Costa Rica* (Albuquerque: Univ. of New Mexico Press, 1978), pp. 262–63.

10. R.M. Sapolsky, "Endocrine Aspects of Social Instability in the Olive Baboon," *American Journal of Primatology* 5, pp. 365–76.

11. See discussion of state-dependent learning in alcoholics in my book, *Understanding the Alcoholic's Mind: The Nature of Craving and How to Control It* (New York: Oxford Univ. Press, 1988).

12. T. Clark, *A Right Honourable Gentleman: Abdubakar from the Black Rock* (London: Edward Arnold, 1991), pp. 304–5.

13. A. Dornbach, *The Secret Trial of Imre Nagy* (Westport, Conn.: Praeger, 1994); G. Stokes, *From Stalinism to Pluralism: A Documentary History of Eastern Europe since 1945* (New York: Oxford Univ. Press, 1991), and P. Unwin, *Voice in the Wilderness: Imre Nagy and the Hungarian Revolution* (London: Macdonald, 1991).

14. See de Waal, *Peacemaking among Primates.*

15. See idem, *Good Natured: The Origins of Right and Wrong in Humans and Other Animals* (Cambridge, Mass.: Harvard Univ. Press, 1996).

16. J. Diamond, *The Third Chimpanzee: The Evolution and Future of the Human Animal* (New York: HarperCollins, 1992).

CHAPTER 2

1. As with male leaders in the study, the list of female leaders includes only those who hold chief executive power in their countries and who are not serving in primarily ceremonial roles. Prime Minister Sylvie Kinigi of Burundi, for instance, never exerted full presidential powers during the period of political chaos when she took refuge in the embassy. As president of the council of presidents in which presidents are rotated on a yearly basis, Ruth Dreifuss of Switzerland held mostly a ceremonial position. Most of the true executive authority in Switzerland resides within each of the twenty-six independent cantons. The same situation applies to Tarja Halonen of Finland, who was appointed president on March 1, 2000, because of passage of a new constitution that now makes the role of president largely ceremonial. Other prominent female leaders without chief executive authority include Elisabeth Domitien, Milka Planinc, Kazimiera Prunskiene, Edith Cresson, Hanna Suchocka, Agathe Uwilingiyimana, Claudette Werleigh, Irena Degutienë, and Nyam-Osoriyn Tuyaa.

2. M. Navarro, "The Widow of Ex-Leader Wins Race in Panama," *New York Times*, May 3, 1999; and idem, "Mireya Elisa Moscoso: Earnest Icon for Panama," *New York Times*, May 4, 1999.

3. From *Encyclopædia Britannica Online*, "Elizabeth I." <http://members.eb.com/bol/topic? eu=108513&sctn=5> [Accessed Dec. 22, 1999].

4. R.J. Rummel, *Death by Government* (New Brunswick, N.J.: Transaction, 1994), and *Statistics of Democide: Genocide and Mass Murder since 1900* (Charlottesville: Center for National Security Law, University of Virginia, 1997) provide the most detailed mortality statistics available.

5. No actual figures are available worldwide on the numbers of wounded to killed persons as a result of wars. From my analyses of many statistical reports listing the numbers of persons killed or wounded in various wars or civilians killed or wounded during bombings, my overall estimate is that somewhere between three and ten persons were

wounded for every one killed. Therefore, for descriptive purposes, I conservatively estimated a five-to-one ratio of wounded to killed persons.

6. Numerous classifications of ruler types exist, but to date none has been universally accepted. The distinction between dictators and democratic leaders, and among dictators, the distinction between tyrants and fair rulers, extends back to antiquity. In his *Republic*, for instance, Plato claimed that the enlightened statesman must be absolute, but he disapproved of the tyrant. Rousseau's *The Social Contract* and Thomas Hobbes's *Leviathan* described the characteristics of the ideal ruler. In the sixteenth century, Machiavelli, in his *Discourses*, discussed the strengths and weakness of three different kinds of rule. In more modern times, most classifications of ruler types start with discussions of Max Weber's classification of "traditional," "legal," and "charismatic" kinds of authority. (Also see H. Arendt, *The Origins of Totalitarianism* [New York: Peter Smith, 1983].) Although the various classifications of ruler types have different emphases, most seem to agree about several points: They distinguish between democratic rulers and dictators. They also tend to subtype dictators into tyrants, totalitarians, or authoritarians. However, few of the classifications are comprehensive, covering the full range of all kinds of rulers. P.C. Sondrol ("Totalitarian and Authoritarian Dictators: A Comparison of Fidel Castro and Alfredo Stroessner," *Journal of Latin American Studies* 23 [1991], pp. 599–620), for instance, compares only totalitarian and authoritarian kinds of rulers. Totalitarian leaders have high charisma, function in a symbolic fashion, use public ends of power, show low corruption, promote an official ideology, do not allow pluralism, and have high legitimacy. Authoritarian leaders, in contrast, have low charisma, serve as individuals, use private ends of power, show high corruption, have no official ideology, allow limited pluralism, and have low legitimacy. Another classification divides leaders into (1) dynasts who assume extended dictatorial power as representatives of inherited authority, (2) revolutionaries who assume dictatorial power as representatives of discontented elements of the population, and (3) crisis-men who gain power in times of crisis but with the aid of the ruling economic class. Among the various typologies, I found the one contrasting the prince, autocrat, tyrant, and prophet (R.H. Jackson and C.G. Rosberg, *Personal Rule in Black Africa* [Berkeley: Univ. of California Press, 1982]) to be the most useful, although it dealt only with the kinds of leadership found in Black Africa. While I have relied on the observations of past authors for the typology of rulers used in this book, I am not aware of any prior classifications that likewise describe six general ruler types and then later rely on empirical data to distinguish among them.

7. E. Abbott, *Haiti: The Duvaliers and Their Legacy* (New York: Touchstone, 1991); B. Diederich and A. Burt, *Papa Doc: Haiti and Its Dictator* (Maplewood, N.J.: Waterfront Press, 1991); J. Ferguson, *Papa Doc, Baby Doc: Haiti and the Duvaliers* (Oxford: Basil Blackwell, 1987); B. Weinstein and A. Segal, *Haiti: The Failure of Politics* (New York: Praeger, 1992).

8. D. Chirot, *Modern Tyrants: The Power and Prevalence of Evil in Our Age* (New York: Free Press, 1994), p. 355.

9. See C. Stern, *Ulbricht: A Political Biography* (New York: Praeger, 1965), pp. 41–47, for an excellent description of the apparatchik.

10. See W. Shawcross, *Crime and Compromise* (New York: Dutton, 1974).

11. See accounts on Mussolini in R. Collier, *Duce! Biography of Benito Mussolini* (New York: Viking, 1971), and D. Mack Smith, *Mussolini* (New York: Knopf, 1982).

12. H. Glickman, ed., *Political Leaders of Contemporary Africa South of the Sahara* (Westport, Conn.: Greenwood Press, 1992); Jackson and Rosberg, *Personal Rule in Black Africa*; V. Malhorta, *Kenya under Kenyatta* (Delhi: Kalinga Publications, 1990), and J. Murray-Brown, *Kenyatta* (London: George Allen, 1972).

13. K.I. Boodhoo, ed., *Eric Williams: The Man and the Leader* (Lanham, Md.: Univ. Press of America, 1986), pp. 66–67.

14. S.E. Ambrose, *Eisenhower: The President* vol. 2 (New York: Simon and Schuster, 1984), pp. 17–18.

15. P. Seale, *Assad of Syria: The Struggle for the Middle East* (Berkeley: Univ. of California Press, 1988), p. 494.

16. The 110 percent figure I made up is probably no more fanciful that the 99.9 percent approval rating that actually was reported. As a way of making my point, I could not resist the temptation to be playful here.

17. H. Kummer, *In Quest of the Sacred Baboon* (Princeton: Princeton Univ. Press, 1995).

18. See R.A. Dahl, *On Democracy* (New Haven: Yale Univ. Press), 1998.

19. See F.A.K. Yasamee, *Ottoman Diplomacy: Abdülhamid II and the Great Powers, 1878–1888* (Istanbul: Isis Press, 1996), and J. Haslip, *The Sultan: The Life of Abdul Hamid II* (New York: Holt, Rinehart and Winston, 1958).

20. For instance, in Switzerland, the presidency, which is largely ceremonial, rotates among the seven ministers (equals among equals) on the Federal Council on a yearly basis, with succession determined by seniority. The parliamentary vote is little more than a seal of approval for the country's highest representative by protocol. The real executive power for running the country resides within each of the twenty-six relatively independent cantons. Because of this unique form of government and the absence of a ruler with clear executive authority for the entire country, I did not include the rotating presidents from this country in my sample.

CHAPTER 3

1. J.M. Reinisch, *The Kinsey Institute New Report on Sex* (New York: St. Martin's Press, 1990). Also see J.L. McCary, *Human Sexuality: Physiological, Psychological, and Sociological Factors* (New York: Van Nostrand Reinhold, 1973), and S. Hite, *The Hite Report on Male Sexuality* (New York: Ballantine Books, 1982), for other estimates. An overview of the major sex surveys can be found in L. Stanley, *Sex Surveyed, 1949–1994: From Mass-Observation's "Little Kinsey" to the National Survey and Hite Reports* (London: Taylor & Francis, 1995).

2. See M. Smith, *A Physician at the Court of Siam* (Oxford: Oxford Univ. Press, 1982), for an excellent description of polygamy.

3. B. Titley, *Dark Age: The Political Odyssey of Emperor Bokassa* (Montreal: McGill-Queen's Univ. Press, 1997), p. 51.

4. H. Kuper, *Sobhuza II: Ngwenyama and King of Swaziland: The Story of an Hereditary Ruler and His Country* (New York: Africana Publishing, 1978).

5. M. Osborne, *Sihanouk: Prince of Light. Prince of Darkness.* (Honolulu: Univ. of Hawaii Press, 1994), p. 35.

6. D.B. Adams, "Monarchy and Political Change: Thailand under Chulalongkorn (1868–1885)" (doctoral dissertation, University of Chicago, 1977); W.G. Barry, "Rama V of Siam" (master's thesis, Washington University, 1930); W.S. Bristowe, *Louis and the King of Siam* (New York: Thai-American Publishing, 1976); Smith, *Physician at the Court of Siam*; and D.K. Wyatt, *The Politics of Reform in Thailand: Education in the Reign of King Chulalongkorn* (New Haven: Yale Univ. Press, 1969).

7. For an excellent description of life in a harem, see Joan Haslip in *The Sultan: The Life of Abdul Hamid II* (New York: Holt, Rinehart and Winston, 1958).

8. R.D. Crassweller, *Trujillo: The Life and Times of a Caribbean Dictator* (New York: Macmillan, 1966), pp. 79–80, 434.

9. H.E. Salisbury, *The New Emperors: China in the Era of Mao and Deng* (Boston: Little, Brown, 1992), p. 218.

10. T. Szulc, *Twilight of the Tyrants* (New York: Henry Holt, 1959), p. 256.

11. M. Peyser, "The Sultan of Smut?" *Newsweek*, March, 31, 1997, p. 47.

12. H. Kyemba, *A State of Blood: The Inside Story of Idi Amin* (New York: Grosset and Dunlap, 1977), pp. 145–50.

13. L. Kinross, *Atatürk: A Biography of Mustafa Kemal, Father of Modern Turkey* (New York: William Morrow, 1965), p. 297.

14. E. Berenson, *The Trial of Madame Caillaux* (Berkeley: Univ. of California Press, 1992), p. 51.

15. S. Baumann-Reynolds, *François Mitterrand: The Making of a Socialist Prince in Republican France* (Westport, Conn.: Praeger, 1995), pp. 16, 164; A. Cole, *François Mitterrand: A Study in Political Leadership* (London: Routledge, 1994), p. 107; A. Gopnik, "Elvis of the Élysée: How François Mitterrand Orchestrated His Own Afterlife," *New Yorker*, June 3, 1996, pp. 40–45; D. MacShane, *François Mitterrand: A Political Odyssey* (New York: Universe Books, 1982), p. 42; and C. Nay, *The Black and the Red François Mitterrand, the Story of an Ambition*, trans. A. Sheridan (New York: Harcourt Brace, Jovanovich, 1987), p. 56.

16. R.M. Koster and G. Sanchez, *In the Time of The Tyrants: Panama: 1968–1990* (New York: W.W. Norton, 1990), p. 53.

17. C.L. Mee Jr., *The Ohio Gang: The World of Warren G. Harding* (New York: M. Evans, 1981); H. L'Etang, *The Pathology of Leadership* (New York: Hawthorn Books, 1970); and F. Russell, *The Shadow of Blooming Grove: Warren G. Harding in His Times* (New York: McGraw-Hill, 1968).

18. See A. Heckster, *Woodrow Wilson* (New York: Charles Scribner's Sons, 1991).

19. S.E. Ambrose, *Eisenhower, Volume I: Soldier, General of the Army, President Elect, 1890–1950* (New York: Simon and Schuster, 1983), p. 285.

20. P. Collier and D. Horowitz, *The Kennedys: An American Drama* (New York: Summit Books, 1984), pp. 174–75, 297; R. Reeves, *President Kennedy: Profile of Power* (New York: Simon and Schuster, 1993); and idem, *A Question of Character: A Life of John F. Kennedy* (New York: Free Press, 1991).

21. K.S. Davis, *FDR: The Beckoning of Destiny, 1882–1928, A History* (New York: Random House, 1972), pp. 488–90, and F.S. Davis, *FDR: The New Deal Years, 1933–1937, A History* (New York: Random House, 1986), pp. 166–67.

22. For Prime Minister Wilfrid Laurier, see B. Robertson, *Wilfrid Laurier: The Great Conciliator* (Toronto: Oxford Univ. Press, 1971). For Brian Mulroney, see M. Gratton, *Still the Boss: A Candid Look at Brian Mulroney* (Scarborough, Ontario: Prentice-Hall, 1990), and J. Sawatsky, *Mulroney: The Politics of Ambition* (Toronto: Macfarlane Walter and Ross, 1991). For Prime Minister Pearson, see J. English, *Shadow of Heaven: The Life of Lester Pearson, 1897–1948* vol. 1 (Toronto: Lester and Orpen Dennys, 1989), and idem, *The Worldly Years: The Life of Lester Pearson, 1949–1972* vol. 2 (Toronto: Alfred A. Knopf, 1992). And for Pierre Trudeau, see K.J. Christiano, *Pierre Elliott Trudeau: Reason before Passion* (Toronto: ECW Press, 1994); S. Clarkson, *Trudeau and Our Times: The Magnificent Obsession* vol. 1 (Toronto: McClelland and Stewart, 1990); idem, *Trudeau and Our Times: The Heroic Delusion* vol. 2 (Toronto: McClelland and Stewart, 1994); M. Vastel, *The Outsider: The Life of Pierre Elliott Trudeau*, trans. H. Bauch (Toronto: Macmillan of Canada, 1990); and G. Weston, *Reign of Error: The Inside Story of John Turner's Troubled Leadership* (Scarborough, Ontario: McGraw-Hill Ryerson, 1988).

23. J. Campbell, *Edward Heath: A Biography* (London: Jonathan Cape, 1993), p. 55, and C.P. Stacey, *A Very Double Life: The Private World of Mackenzie King* (Toronto: Macmillan of Canada, 1976).

24. P.B. Waite, *The Loner: Three Sketches of the Personal Life and Ideas of R.B. Bennett, 1870–1947* (Toronto: Univ. of Toronto Press, 1992), p. 69.

25. F. Redlich, *Hitler: Diagnosis of a Destructive Prophet* (New York: Oxford, 1999).

26. Titley, *Dark Age*, p. 57.

27. Sometimes, though, these good intentions of monarchs in producing many heirs can backfire. For example, before his death in 1953, King Abdelaziz al-Saud of Saudi Arabia, to avoid violence among his forty-four sons over succession to the throne, introduced the notion of fraternal succession. See D. Jehl, "The Wisdom of a Saudi King: Choosing an Heir to the Realm of Abdel Aziz," *New York Times*, May, 24, 1999. To date, Kings Saud, Faisal, Khalid, and now Faud have taken their turns in order of age. Now with King Faud continuing to rule at age seventy-eight after several strokes, the next in line are well into their seventies. If this same policy continues, the gerontocracy should produce octogenarians and heptaseptuagenarians and perhaps even centenarians among the surviving successors to provide continuing fresh leadership for that nation during the twenty-first century.

28. S. Decalo, *Psychoses of Power: African Personal Dictatorships* (Boulder, Colo.: Westview Press, 1989); A. Shoumatoff, *African Madness* (New York: Knopf, 1988); Titley, *Dark Age*; and "Jean-Bedel Bokassa, African Dictator, Dies," *Lexington Herald-Leader*, April 5, 1996.

29. R. Bonner, *Waltzing with a Dictator: The Marcoses and the Making of American Policy* (New York: Times Books, 1987), p. 310.

30. P. Brooker, *Twentieth-Century Dictatorships: The Ideological One-Party States* (Washington Square, N.Y.: New York Univ. Press, 1995); D. Jenkins, *Suharto and His Generals: Indonesian Military Politics, 1975–1983* (Ithaca, N.Y.: Cornell University, 1984); W. Lidsker, *Suharto Finds the Divine Vision: An Interpretive Biography* (Honolulu: Semangat Press, 1992); N.B. Mody, *Indonesia under Suharto* (New York: APT Books, 1987); and M.R. Vatikiotis, *Indonesian Politics under Suharto: Order, Development and Pressure for Change* (London: Routledge, 1993).

31. P. Gupte, *Mother India: A Political Biography of Indira Gandhi* (New York: Charles Scribner's Sons, 1992), p. 441.

32. Crassweller, *Trujillo*; B. Diederich, *Trujillo: The Death of the Goat* (Boston: Little, Brown, 1978); J. De Galíndez, "Inside a Dictatorship," in H.M. Hamill, ed., *Caudillos: Dictators in Spanish America* (Norman: Univ. of Oklahoma Press, 1992), pp. 234–45; R.L. Trujillo Molina, "A Dictator Extols Democracy," in ibid., pp. 218–33; and H.J. Wiarda and M. Kryzanek, "J. Trujillo and the Caudillo Tradition," in ibid., pp. 246–56.

33. Szulc, *Twilight of the Tyrants*, p. 257.

34. "Three Brutal Decades under Lord of Misrule," *London Times*, May 17, 1997.

35. W. Shawcross, *The Shah's Last Ride* (New York: Simon and Schuster, 1988), and M. Zonis, *Majestic Failure: The Fall of the Shah* (Chicago: Univ. of Chicago Press, 1991).

36. It seems that embedded within the popular notion of the great leader is the stereotype of a Lawrence of Arabia, a Mahatma Gandhi, a Joan of Arc—self-abnegating and self-immolating individuals infused with an almost holy calling who devote their lives to the pursuit of some higher ideal. Unfortunately, this stereotype may have misrepresented the real situation among political leaders in much the same way that the stereotype of the mad artist, as exemplified by Vincent Van Gogh and his mutilated ear, has distorted any real understanding of the nature of the relationship between mental illness and creativity. Even without any convincing evidence as support, the characterization of revolutionary leaders as ascetics seems to have found its way into political science and social psychology and the popular media. While there may be some merit to this characterization, the only question I have about it is Where are these self-abnegating rulers?!

Drawing on Sigmund Freud's notion of the leader being the primal father who has few libidinal ties, Bruce Mazlish, for example, claimed that the revolutionary leader displaces his libido onto such abstractions as revolution, humanity, or virtue (B. Mazlish, *The Revolutionary Ascetic: Evolution of a Political Type* [New York: Basic Books, 1976], p. 30). This then lets him embrace asceticism, as defined by the following cluster of traits: the suppression or denial of "base" impulses such as the appetite for sex, rich foods, and a comfortable life; the exercise of self-control, stoicism, or mind over matter when dealing with any irrational desires or instinctive impulses; and dedication and hard work.

In their study of leaders, Rejai and Kay Phillips, using Mazlich's criteria, describe asceticism as perhaps the most important personal attribute of revolutionaries. Of their thirty-two revolutionary leaders, twenty-three (=72 percent!) showed self-discipline, self-reliance, self-denial of luxury and comfort, a relentless emphasis on hard work, and a commitment to a rugged spartan life (M. Rejai and K. Phillips, *Leaders of Revolution* [Beverly Hills: Sage, 1979], p. 181). That is a remarkable finding that, if true, challenges the basic assumption underlying the primate model of ruling that most rulers should be highly receptive to the sexual and material rewards that go with being an alpha male within a dominance hierarchy.

Actually, when you examine the Rejai and Phillips information closely, it appears that much of the discrepancy between their figures and mine may be due to different conceptions of asceticism. As I interpret asceticism, it represents a willing commitment to certain values and a certain style of life, not a choice forced upon individuals by circumstance. Rejai and Phillips do not seem to be making this distinction. When revolutionaries engage in a spartan existence during their struggles, they apparently identify them as ascetics. However, from my perspective, the incommodious surroundings and many deprivations revolutionaries experience during extended periods of battle or their quest for independence are no more indicative of asceticism than the hardships anybody would endure under harsh and dangerous circumstances. The temporary lack of creature comforts does not make you an ascetic; it only means you are trying to survive as best you can under the trying conditions. So before we turn these revolutionaries into holy men because of their seeming willingness to experience privations during their struggles, we need to know if they would turn down these comforts and pleasures if they had access to them. If they did not, we could not call them ascetic. For example, when Sukarno was sentenced to prison because of his struggles to overthrow Dutch rule in Indonesia, he was forced to adopt an "ascetic" lifestyle although he had no personal inclinations to do so. Listen to his own words as he reflected on the discomforts of his prison stay. "It was a shattering experience. I am a sybarite. I am a man who gratifies his senses. I enjoy fine clothes, exciting foods, love-making" (J.D. Legge, *Sukarno: A Political Biography* [London: Allen and Unwin, 1972], p. 109). What this means is that it is possible for people to lead the life of an ascetic during times of duress even if they are not one.

As examples of revolutionary ascetics, Rejai and Phillips list three persons—Vladimir Lenin, Mao Zedong, and Fidel Castro—who also happen to be included within my sample of rulers (M. Rejai and K. Phillips, *Leaders of Revolution*, p. 166). Lenin qualified as being an ascetic because he was "spartan, self-denying, self-disciplined and self-demanding," and because he ate at times "in almost biblical simplicity" and declared that revolutions "cannot be made with gloves and manicured fingernails." Mao qualified as an ascetic because he grew his own tobacco, "lived a life of utter austerity, and put the revolution above personal interests." And Castro qualified as an ascetic because after many years in power, "he continues to wear combat boots and battle fatigues, as symbols of the continuing struggle."

Lenin, Castro, and Mao ascetics???? No way! Granted, each of these great leaders risked his life, experienced all kinds of privations and hardships, and showed great dedication to his cause, but none comes close to qualifying as an ascetic according to my criterion of deliberate self-denial.

Though totally committed to the revolution, Lenin hardly suppressed his sensual and aesthetic life. He enjoyed boating and hiking in the mountains and took a special delight in literature and classical music. Always meticulous about his clothes and demeanor, he was the antithesis of the hair-shirted mystic who totally neglected his appearance. After the revolution, he likewise showed no aversion to the simple pleasures of life. Aside from enjoying an active sexual life with his wife, he began a long affair with a fellow revolutionary when he was forty.

Castro was an unadulterated sensualist who had no compunctions about satisfying his creature comforts. He loved Cuban cigars, enjoyed his rum, had a passion for baseball, and used foul language with abandon. As for his continued love of wearing fatigues and combat boots after he became the Maximum Leader, I suspect he ordered them from the equivalent of Saks Fifth Avenue in Havana. Then, in a non-ascetic and unrevolutionary fashion, he not only had many affairs during his married and later divorced life but had seven children as well, six of whom were illegitimate.

As for Mao, we should not be taken in by superficial appearances. Mao reveled in his peasant image and the hardships he endured as a revolutionary and exploited them to the hilt, sleeping on a wooden bed without a mattress, eating simple foods, wearing patched clothes, not bathing, and lecturing on the virtues of frugality. But this was the same person who in less-publicized activities had four wives, consorted with many mistresses, had ten children, owned one of the finest collections of erotica in the world, and enjoyed "water sports" with young nubile women. If this old lecher was an ascetic who denied his bodily pleasures, then Elvis Presley was another Mother Theresa.

Since the notion of asceticism looms so large in the public mind as an important attribute of dedicated leaders, I decided to estimate its frequency within my own sample of 377 rulers. I did so by searching all the biographical materials available on each ruler for descriptive adjectives like ascetic, abstemious, self-denying, abstinent, spartan, austere, monk-like, puritanical, priggish, straightlaced, pious, self-disciplined, and non-indulgent. These are my findings.

Including those who led active sexual lives, only 9 percent of rulers within my entire sample could be characterized by any of these descriptive adjectives. However, when you examine the percentages of ascetics among the different ruler types, you find that only two types, visionaries (25 percent) and transitionals (20 percent), which bear the closest resemblance to revolutionaries, seem to hold a relative monopoly on this sexually tainted form of asceticism. While these findings offer partial support for the contention by Rejai and Phillips about the importance of asceticism in revolutionaries, these rates are substantially less than their 72 percent figure. Then, if you take the results one step further to see who among the rulers was willing to forgo their sexual pleasures as well, a matter that is central to my theory, you find that only 2 percent of the sample qualify as bonafide grade-A ascetics, and I suspect that at least half of them avoided heterosexual affairs because they probably were having discreet homosexual encounters. I have no way of knowing what the rate of true asceticism is in the population at large, but, given all the chronic schizophrenics and homeless people who roam the streets, I suspect it is much higher than that. Therefore, despite the popular stereotype of self-denying rulers, my findings show that true asceticism—a puritanical lifestyle along with the denial of carnal pleasures—is a rarity among rulers. And its very rarity among rulers is consistent with their role as alpha males.

37. J. de Galíndez, "Inside a Dictatorship," in Hamill, *Caudillos,* pp. 234–45.

38. Crassweller, *Trujillo,* and Diederich, *Trujillo: The Death of the Goat.*

39. One of the advantages of absolute power is that a ruler has the godlike power to indulge his every whim. Gods have the ability to create and destroy. So, too, do godlike rulers. Nicolae Ceausescu, for example, not only undertook to restructure Romanian society but razed cities as well. Possessing a latent intelligence that seldom manifested itself, a near illiteracy that made even his simple reports unreadable, a stutter that he tried to overcome by moving his head backwards while drawing his lips sideways, and an unjustifiable self-confidence that let him boast, "A man like me comes along once every five hundred years," he tried to modernize the countryside through his system of "systemization," a planned attempt to collectivize and industrialize the agricultural and ru-

ral life by urbanizing the Romanian population and homogenizing them into a single worker people. This required that he simultaneously demolish the capitalist architecture of Bucharest and replace it with the architecture of socialism to house his transplanted workers. To accomplish this, he razed the homes of thousands of Romanians in the old city center and forcibly relocated them, sometimes giving them only six hours' notice to pack. Ceausescu's method for deciding what areas of the city to destroy was ingenious in its simplicity. After being driven through a neighborhood, he simply made a sweeping motion with his hand in his limousine, after which the block would be demolished. A running joke in Bucharest told of a wasp being trapped in the back of Ceausescu's limousine as he kept trying to shoo it away. His aides, unaware of the wasp, took note of his gestures and then tore the entire city down (E. Behr, *Kiss the Hand You Cannot Bite: The Rise and Fall of the Ceausescus* [New York: Villard, 1991], and J. Sweeney, *The Life and Evil Times of Nicolae Ceausescu* [London: Hutchinson, 1991]).

40. "A God in an Atheistic State," *Globe and Mail*, July 11, 1994; B. Martin, "Remaking Kim's Image: Octogenarian Dictator Jettisons Some Flagrant Fabrications," *Far Eastern Economic Review* 156, July 11, 1994), pp. 36–40; B. Powell, "Headless Beast: North Korea after Kim," *Time*, July 18, 1994, pp. 19–26; "Radio: Kim Jong Il to Assume Power," *Lexington Herald-Leader*, July 14, 1994; S.A. Seiler, *Kim Il-sung, 1941–1948: The Creation of a Legend, the Building of a Regime* (New York: Univ. Press of America, 1994); M. Shapiro, "Kim's Ransom," *New Yorker*, Jan. 31, 1994, pp. 32–41; and D. Suh, *Kim Il Sung: The North Korean Leader* (New York: Columbia Univ. Press, 1988).

41. The personality cult of Adolph Hitler is another example of how rulers can become transformed into gods. Over time, Hitler evolved from being the Führer, or leader, of Germany to being an agent of God to becoming God's equal. The leader of the Nazi Party in the Saar region declared, "Hitler is a new, a greater, and more powerful Jesus Christ." Prayers were directed to Hitler. "Adolf Hitler, you are our great Leader. Thy name makes the earth tremble. Thy Third Reich comes, thy will alone is law upon earth. Let us hear daily thy voice and order us by thy leadership, for we will obey to the end even with our lives." With such adulation, it is no wonder that Hitler should have come to view himself as "more godlike than human" and in true Nietzschean fashion, feel "bound by none of the conventions of human morality" (D.J. Hershman and J. Lieb, *A Brotherhood of Tyrants: Manic Depression and Absolute Power* [New York: Prometheus Books, 1994]).

CHAPTER 4

1. A. Sampson, *Nelson Mandela* (New York: Knopf, 1999).

2. A. Sadat, *In Search of Identity: Anwar-el-Sadat* (New York: Harper and Row, 1978), pp. 73–80, 88–89.

3. E. Silver, *Begin: The Haunted Prophet* (New York: Random House, 1984), pp. 26–32.

4. R. Merle, *Ahmed Ben Bella*, trans. C. Sykes (New York: Walker, 1967, pp. 116–17.

5. M. Ahmed, *Bangladesh: Era of Sheikh Mujibur Rahman* (Dhaka: Univ. Press, 1983); Y. Bhatnagar, *Mujib: The Architect of Bangla Desh* (Delhi: Indian School Supply Depot, 1971); S.R. Chakravarty, *Bangladesh under Mujib, Zia and Ershad* (New Delhi: Har-Anand, 1995); O. Huq, *Bangabandhu Sheikh Mujib: Leader with a Difference* (London: Radical Asia Publications, 1996); K. Kamal, *Sheik Mujibur Rahman* (Dacca: Kazi Giasuddin Ahmed, 1970); and L. Ziring, *Bangladesh: From Mujib to Ershad, An Interpretive Study* (New York: Oxford Univ. Press, 1992).

6. The percentage was a bit higher for the more notable leaders. Within the smaller sample of rulers, 25 percent either spent time in prison or in exile, and 9 percent spent time in both.

7. From R. Fegley, *Equatorial Guinea: An African Tragedy* (New York: Peter Lang, 1989), pp. 143–47.

8. D. Hirst and I. Beeson, *Sadat* (London: Faber and Faber, 1981), pp. 77–79.

9. P.G. Bourne, *Fidel: A Biography of Fidel Castro* (New York: Dodd, Mead, 1986); T. Szulc, *Fidel: A Critical Portrait* (New York: William Morrow, 1986); G.A. Geyer, *Guerrilla Prince: The Untold Story of Fidel Castro* (Boston: Little, Brown, 1991); and R.E. Quirk, *Fidel Castro* (New York: W.W. Norton, 1993).

10. See G. Arriagada, *Pinochet: The Politics of Power*, trans. N. Morris with V. Ercolano and K.A. Whitney (Boston: Unwin Hyman, 1988), for an excellent description of the sequence of events after a coup.

11. See B. Diederich, *Trujillo: The Death of the Goat* (Boston: Little, Brown, 1978), pp. 165–69.

12. See a detailed account of these events in W. Shawcross, *The Shah's Last Ride* (New York: Simon and Schuster, 1988).

13. Had the Shah been a student of history, he perhaps could have benefitted from the example of Tzar Peter I of Russia, who in the early part of the eighteenth century likewise set out to westernize his country. Attacking what he thought to be a symbol of his country's backwardness, the Tzar decreed that all men had to shave their beards. This was a politically courageous, if not foolhardy, decision on his part. For most Orthodox Russians, the beard was a symbol of religious belief and self-respect. It was a God-given gift, worn by the prophets, the apostles, and Jesus himself. As a result, many clergy regarded shaving as a mortal sin, and a direct affront to God. Peter, nonetheless, was so adamant in his resolve that whenever he attended a banquet or ceremony, he set a noble example for his people by personally cutting off the beards of his nobles. This proved to be a messy and painful ordeal for those who showed up unshorn. Hastily shaving long, thick beards with a dry razor left many deep gouges among the remaining rubble and tufts on their faces. Sometimes, in his merriment and enthusiasm, Peter pulled out their beards by the roots or yanked them off so roughly with a razor that some of the skin went with them. No wonder, then, that so many nobles began seeking excuses to avoid accepting the Tzar's formerly coveted invitations.

Knowing that he single-handedly could not tend to the tonsorial needs of the entire nation, Peter soon gave government officials the authority to cut off the beards of any men they encountered, no matter their rank or wealth. But, being a practical ruler, he was not so inflexible that he could pass up a chance to add to his own coffers by imposing a special tax on the Raskolniki (Old Believers) and the merchants who persisted in their backward ways and insisted on keeping their beards. By paying a graduated annual tax—two kopeks a year for peasants, and up to one hundred roubles for the wealthy—these individuals could wear a bronze medallion on a chain around their necks, with a picture of a beard and the words "Tax Paid," which attested to the legality of their beards. But where Peter showed his true genius—in stark contrast to the political short-sightedness of the Shah of Iran—was in exempting the orthodox clergy from all of these obligations. Bearded and untaxed, they could continue to make fools of themselves, as far as he was concerned. Even though Machiavelli had nothing to say on this matter, the Tzar instinctively knew that if he let the clergy alone, the clergy would let him alone, too. It was wisdom of this sort that contributed to his becoming immortalized and earning the title of "Peter the Great."

See R.K. Massie, *Peter the Great: His Life and World* (New York: Knopf, 1986) for a detailed account of the above events.

14. R.H. Erlich, *United States-Venezuelan Relations, 1948 to 1958: A Study of the Regime of Marcos Perez Jimenez* (Unpublished master's thesis, Florida Atlantic University, 1974); and J. Ewell, *The Indictment of a Dictator: The Extradition and Trial of Marcos Perez Jimenez* (College Station: Texas A&M University Press, 1981). See T. Szulc, *Twilight of the Tyrants.* (New York: Henry Holt, 1959) for what happened during the later election.

15. The delightful escapades of the Arumburu regime and the adventures of Eva's coffin are documented at length in Joseph A. Page's *Perón: a Biography* (New York: Random House, 1983). Although I have borrowed heavily from this account, I have taken a bit of literary license in the interpretation of certain events.

16. A.C.W. Aung, *Burma and the Last Days of General Ne Win* (Indianapolis, Ind.: Yoma, 1996); D. Chirot, *Modern Tyrants: The Power and Prevalence of Evil in Our Age* (New York: Free Press, Macmillan, 1994); M. Maung, *Burma and General Ne Win* (Bombay: Asia Publishing House, 1969), p. 337; and U. Thaung, *A Journalist, a General and an Army in Burma* (Bangkok: White Lotus, 1995).

17. V.B. Ibanez, *Alfonso XIII Unmasked: The Military Terror in Spain,* trans. L. Ongley (New York: Dutton, 1924); C. Petrie, *King Alfonso XIII and His Age* (London: Chapman and Hall, 1963); R. Sencourt, *King Alfonso: A Biography* (London: Faber and Faber, 1942); and W.B. Wells, *The Last King: Don Alfonso XIII of Spain* (London: Frederick Muller, 1934).

18. G. Arriagada, *Pinochet*; P. Constable and A. Valenzuela, *A Nation of Enemies: Chile under Pinochet* (New York: W.W. Norton, 1991), M.H. Spooner, *Soldiers in A Narrow Land: The Pinochet Regime in Chile* (Berkeley: Univ. of California Press, 1994); and J. Timerman, *Chile: Death in the South,* trans. R. Cox (New York: Alfred A. Knopf, 1987).

19. S. Chan, *Kaunda and Southern Africa: Image and Reality in Foreign Policy* (London: British Academic Press, 1992); B.S. Chisala, *The Downfall of President Kaunda* (Lusaka, Zambia: Co-op Printing, 1994); R. Hall, *Kaunda: Founder of Zambia* (Lusaka, Zambia: Longmans of Zambia, 1967); F. MacPherson, *Kenneth Kaunda of Zambia: The Times and the Man* (London: Oxford Univ. Press, 1974); J.M. Mwanakatwe, *End of Kaunda Era* (Lusaka, Zambia: Multimedia, 1994).

20. This account comes from J. de Galíndez, "Inside a Dictatorship," in H.M. Hamill, ed., *Caudillos: Dictators in Spanish America* (Norman: Univ. of Oklahoma Press, 1992), pp. 234–45.

21. *CIA Targets Fidel: Secret CIA Inspector General's Reports on Plots to Assassinate Fidel Castro* (Melbourne: Ocean Press, 1966), p. 77.

22. N. Miller, *Theodore Roosevelt: A Life* (New York: William Morrow, 1992), p. 531.

23. P.J. Vatikiotis, *Nasser and His Generation* (New York: St. Martin's Press, 1978), p. 144.

24. D.R. Watson, *Georges Clemenceau: A Political Biography* (New York: David McKay, 1974), p. 343.

25. E. Karsh and I. Rautsi, *Saddam Hussein: A Political Biography* (New York: Free Press, 1991), p. 2.

26. B. Berkeley, *Liberia: A Promise Betrayed* (New York: Lawyers Committee for Human Rights, 1986); M. Omonijo, *Doe: The Liberian Tragedy* (Ikeja, Nigeria: Sahel Publishing, 1990); A. Sawyer, *Effective Immediately: Dictatorship in Liberia, 1980–1986: A Personal Perspective* (The Hague: Africa Center, 1988).

27. W.A. Hanna, *Eight Nation Makers: Southeast Asia's Charismatic Statesmen* (New York: St. Martin's Press, 1964), pp. 77–78.

28. Personal interview with Alan Bullock, Dec. 16, 1992.

29. R.J.C. Butow, *Tojo and the Coming of the War* (Princeton: Princeton Univ. Press, 1961), p. 47.

30. T. Weiner, "U.S. Aides Say Nigerian Leader Might Have Been Poisoned," *New York Times,* July 11, 1998.

31. R.M. Sapolsky, *A Primate's Memoir* (New York: Scribner, 2001), p. 169.

CHAPTER 5

1. R.D. Crassweller, *Trujillo: The Life and Times of a Caribbean Dictator* (New York: Macmillan, 1966), pp. 77–78, and B. Diederich, *Trujillo: The Death of the Goat* (Boston: Little, Brown, 1978), p. 12.

2. J. Lacouture, *Ho Chi Minh: A Political Biography,* trans. P. Wiles (New York: Random House, 1968).

3. D. Reische, *Arafat and the Palestine Liberation Organization* (New York: Franklin Watts, 1991), p. 20.

4. R.A. Caro, *The Years of Lyndon Johnson: The Path to Power* (New York: Alfred A. Knopf, 1982), pp. 159–60, 189–98.

5. I am indebted to William Stadiem for his excellent biography on King Farouk, *Too Rich: The High Life and Tragic Death of King Farouk* (New York: Carroll and Graf Publishers, 1991). Most of the materials mentioned were taken from this work. In many instances, I have taken the liberty of offering my own slant on his behaviors, and, if any of it should seem disrespectful, I take full blame for the interpretation. The following biographies also have been helpful in letting me construct a portrait of the king: H. McLeave, *The Last Pharaoh: The Ten Faces of Farouk* (London: Michael Joseph, 1969); B. McBride, *Farouk of Egypt* (London: Robert Hale, 1967); and A.M. Sabit, *A King Betrayed: The Ill-Fated Reign of Farouk of Egypt* (London: Quartet Books, 1989).

6. P.D. Quinlan, *The Playboy King* (Westport, Conn.: Greenwood Press, 1995), p. 12.

7. S. Constant, *Foxy Ferdinand, 1861–1948: Tsar of Bulgaria* (London: Sidgwick and Jackson, 1979); Author unknown, *Ferdinand of Bulgaria: The Amazing Career of a Shoddy Czar* (London: Andrew Melrose, 1916); H.R. Madol, *Ferdinand of Bulgaria: The Dream of Byzantium,* trans. K. Kirkness (London: Hurst and Blackett, 1933); and J. Macdonald, *Czar Ferdinand and His People* (New York: Frederick A. Stokes, 1913).

8. Quinlan, *Playboy King,* p. 85.

9. B. Emerson, *Leopold II of the Belgians: King of Colonialism* (New York: St. Martin's Press, 1979), and J. MacDonnell, *King Leopold II* (New York: Argosy-Antiquarian, 1970).

10. Although I have not had any firsthand auditory accounts from eyewitnesses (or should the informants be called earwitnesses?), I would bet from my study of Farouk's personality that he would take a perverse delight in his royal eructions, especially in the presence of those who might be shocked.

11. See G. Arriagada, *Pinochet: The Politics of Power,* trans. N. Morris with V. Ercolano and K.A. Whitney (Boston: Unwin Hyman, 1988); P. Constable and A. Valenzuela, *A Nation of Enemies: Chile under Pinochet* (New York: W.W. Norton, 1991); M.H. Spooner, *Soldiers in A Narrow Land: The Pinochet Regime in Chile* (Berkeley: Univ. of California Press, 1994); and J. Timerman, *Chile: Death in the South,* trans. R. Cox (New York: Alfred A. Knopf, 1987).

12. L.L. Moline, "The Ulbricht Regime: A Political Analysis of Individuals, Ideas, and Events Which Have Shaped the Destiny of East Germany" (master's thesis, American University, 1970); Gregory W. Sandford, *From Hitler to Ulbricht: The Communist Reconstruction of East Germany, 1945–46* (Princeton: Princeton Univ. Press, 1983); and C. Stern, *Ulbricht: A Political Biography* (New York: Praeger, 1965).

13. S. Decalo, *Psychoses of Power: African Personal Dictatorships* (Boulder, Colo.: Westview Press, 1989); "Jean-Bedel Bokassa, African Dictator, Dies," *Lexington Herald-Leader,* April 5, 1996; A. Shoumatoff, *African Madness* (New York: Knopf, 1988); B. Titley, *Dark Age: The Political Odyssey of Emperor Bokassa* (Montreal: McGill-Queen's Univ. Press, 1997).

14. S. Albert, *The Case against the General: Manuel Noriega and the Politics of American Justice* (New York: Scribner, 1993); J. Dinges, *Our Man in Panama: How General Noriega Used the United States–and Made Millions in Drugs and Arms* (New York: Random House, 1990); R.M. Koster and G. Sánchez, *In the Time of Tyrants: Panama, 1968–1990* (New York: W.W. Norton, 1990); and M.E. Scranton, *The Noriega Years: U.S.-Panamanian Relations, 1981–1990* (Boulder, Colo.: Lynne Rienner, 1991).

15. E. Karsh and I. Rautsi, *Saddam Hussein: A Political Biography* (New York: Free Press, 1991), p. 9. Also see A.C. Elms, *Uncovering Lives: The Uneasy Alliance of Biography*

and Psychology (New York: Oxford Univ. Press, 1994); S. Henderson, *Instant Empire: Saddam Hussein's Ambition for Iraq* (San Francisco: Mercury House, 1991); F. Matar, *Saddam Hussein: The Man, the Cause and the Future* (London: Third World Centre, 1981); J. Miller and L. Mylore, *Saddam Hussein and the Crisis in the Gulf* (New York: Times Books, 1990); E. Sciolino, *The Outlaw State: Saddam Hussein's Quest for Power and the Gulf Crisis* (New York: John Wiley, 1991); E. Wakin, *Contemporary Political Leaders of the Middle East* (New York: Facts on File, 1996).

16. E. Abbott, *Haiti: The Duvaliers and Their Legacy* (New York: Touchstone, 1991); J. Ferguson, *Papa Doc, Baby Doc: Haiti and the Duvaliers* (Oxford: Basil Blackwell, 1987); and M. Westerman, "Before and After Baby Doc," *Art and Antiques* 88 (1986), pp. 56–61.

17. R.D. Crassweller, *Trujillo,* pp. 301–8, 364–69.

18. W.A. Hanna, *Eight Nation Makers: Southeast Asia's Charismatic Statesmen* (New York: St. Martin's Press, 1964); J.D. Legge, *Sukarno: A Political Biography* (Sydney: Allen and Unwin, 1972); B. May, *The Indonesian Tragedy* (London: Routledge and Kegan Paul, 1978); C.L.M. Penders, *The Life and Times of Sukarno* (London: Sidgwick and Jackson, 1974); and M.R. Vatikiotis, *Indonesian Politics under Suharto: Order, Development and Pressure for Change* (London: Routledge, 1993).

19. P.G. Bourne, *Fidel: A Biography of Fidel Castro* (New York: Dodd, Mead, 1986), pp. 17, 33; G.A. Geyer, *Guerrilla Prince: The Untold Story of Fidel Castro* (Boston: Little, Brown, 1991), pp. 40–41; and T. Szulc, *Fidel: A Critical Portrait* (New York: William Morrow, 1986), pp. 108–15.

20. L. Trotsky, *Stalin: An Appraisal of the Man and His Influence* (New York: Stein and Day, 1967), pp. 7–8.

21. D.P. Chandler, *Brother Number One: A Political Biography of Pol Pot* (Boulder, Colo.: Westview, 1992), p. 9.

22. See T.P. Coogan, *De Valera: Long Fellow, Long Shallow* (London: Hutchison, 1993), O.D. Edwards, *Éamon de Valera* (Washington, D.C.: Catholic Univ. of America Press, 1987), and C. Younger, *A State of Disunion* (London: Frederick Muller, 1972).

23. T. Sealy, *Sealy's Caribbean Leaders* (Kingston: Eagel Merchant Bank of Jamaica, 1991).

24. R. Gill, *Of Political Bondage: An Authorised Biography of Tunku Abdul Rahman, Malaysia's First Prime Minister, and His Continuing Participation in Contemporary Politics* (Singapore: Sterling Corporate Services, 1990); A.M. Healy, *Tunku Abdul Rahman* (St. Lucia: Univ. of Queensland Press, 1982); J.A. Lim, "A Study of Lee Kuan Yew, Prime Minister of Singapore, and Tengku Abdul Rahman, Former Prime Minister of Malaysia, Utilizing a Personality Theory Approach" (master's thesis, Western Michigan University, 1982); M. Sheppard, *Tunku: His Life and Times: The Authorized Biography of Tunku Abdul Rahman Putra Al-Haj* (Malyasia: Pelanduk, 1995), and A. Surattee, *Bapa Keamanan: Father of Peace* (Kuala Lumpar: Malaysian Enterprises, 1969).

25. C.D. Ameringer, *Don Pepe: A Political Biography of José Figueres of Costa Rica* (Albuquerque: Univ. of New Mexico Press, 1978); L. Bird, *Costa Rica: The Unarmed Democracy* (London: Sheppard Press, 1984); H.H. Bonilla, *Figueres and Costa Rica: An Unauthorized Political Biography* (San José: Editorial Texto Limitada, 1975); and R.K. Longley, "Resistance and Accommodation: Costa Rica and the United States during the Rise of José Figueres" (doctoral dissertation, University of Kentucky, 1993).

26. S.B. Winters, ed., *T.G. Masaryk (1850–1937): Thinker and Politician* vol. 1 (London: Macmillan, 1989); R.B. Pynsent, ed., *T.G. Masaryk (1850–1937): Thinker and Critic* vol. 2 (London: Macmillan, 1989); H. Hanak, ed., *T.G. Masaryk (1850–1937): Statesman and Cultural Force* vol. 3 (New York: St. Martin's Press, 1989); H.G. Skilling, *T.G. Masaryk: Against the Current, 1882–1914* (University Park, Pa.: Pennsylvania State Univ. Press, 1994); and Z. Zeman, *The Masaryks: The Making of Czechoslovakia* (New York: Barnes and Noble, 1976).

27. T.P. Coogan, *Michael Collins: A Biography* (London: Hutchinson, 1990), and F. O'Connor, *The Big Fellow* (New York: Picador, 1998).

28. S.E. Ambrose, *Nixon: The Education of a Politician, 1913–1962* (New York: Simon and Schuster, 1987); J. Hoff, *Nixon Reconsidered* (New York: Basic Books, 1994); R. Morris, *Richard Milhous Nixon: The Rise of an American Politician* (New York: Henry Holt, 1990); and H.S. Parmet, *Richard Nixon and His America* (Boston: Little, Brown, 1990).

29. S.E. Ambrose, *Nixon: Education of a Politician,* p. 618.

30. D. Cook, *Charles de Gaulle: A Biography* (New York: Putnam, 1983), p. 28.

31. C. Ponting, *Churchill* (London: Sinclair-Stevenson, 1994), p. 21.

32. D. McCullough, *Mornings on Horseback* (New York: Simon and Schuster, 1981); N. Miller, *Theodore Roosevelt: A Life* (New York: William Morrow, 1992); and H. Pringle, *Theodore Roosevelt: A Biography* (New York: Harcourt, Brace, 1931).

33. J. Campbell, *The Hero with a Thousand Faces* (Princeton: Princeton Univ. Press, 1968), and N.L. Goodrich, *Myths of the Hero* (New York, Orion Press, 1962).

Chapter 6

1. G.A. Geyer, *Guerrilla Prince: The Untold Story of Fidel Castro* (Boston: Little, Brown, 1991), pp. 223–24.

2. D. Hopwood, *Habib Bourguiba of Tunisia: The Tragedy of Longevity* (New York: St. Martin's Press, 1992), p. 116.

3. J. Ferguson, *Papa Doc, Baby Doc: Haiti and the Duvaliers* (Oxford: Basil Blackwell, 1987), p. 52.

4. Personal communication with Sir Alan Bullock, Dec. 16, 1992.

5. Personal communication with William Manchester, Oct. 16, 1992.

6. See A.M. Ludwig, *How Do We Know Who We Are? A Biography of the Self* (New York: Oxford Univ. Press, 1997).

7. S. Beller, *Francis Joseph* (London: Longman, 1996), and J. Bled, *Franz Joseph,* trans. T. Bridgeman (Oxford: Blackwell, 1992), served as the main sources for information.

8. For an account of Abdul–Hamid's life, see S. Erskine, *King Faisal of Iraq: An Authorized and Authentic Study* (London: Hutchinson, 1933); J. Haslip, *The Sultan: The Life of Abdul Hamid II* (New York: Holt, Rinehart and Winston, 1958); A. Wittlin, *Abdul Hamid: The Shadow of God,* trans. N. Denny (London: John Lane The Bodley Head, 1946); and F.A.K. Yasamee, *Ottoman Diplomacy: Abdülhamid II and the Great Powers, 1878–1888* (Istanbul: Isis Press, 1996). I have taken some artistic license in describing Hamid's daily activities.

9. S. Constant, *Foxy Ferdinand: Tsar of Bulgaria* (London: Sidgwick and Jackson, 1979); S. Groueff, *Crown of Thorns* (New York: Madison Books, 1987); and P. Dimitroff, *King of Mercy: Boris III of Bulgaria, 1894–1943* (London: Wexford and Barrow, 1987).

10. M. Ferro, *Nicholas II: The Last of the Tzars,* trans. B. Pearce (London: Viking, 1991); P. Kurth, *The Lost World of Nicholas and Alexandra: Tsar* (Boston: Little, Brown, 1995); D. Lieven, *Nicholas II: Twilight of the Empire* (New York: St. Martin's Press, 1994); and E. Radzinsky, *The Last Tsar: The Life and Death of Nicholas II* (New York: Doubleday, 1992).

11. Bled, *Franz Joseph,* p. 195.

12. A. Artucio, *The Trial of Macias in Equatorial Guinea: The Story of a Dictatorship* (International Commission of Jurists and International University Exchange Fund, 1979); R. Fegley, *Equatorial Guinea: An African Tragedy* (New York: Peter Lang, 1989); M. Liniger-Goumaz, *Historical Dictionary of Equatorial Guinea* (Metuchen, N.J.: Scarecrow Press, 1989); and A.A. Nwanko, *African Dictators: The Logic of Tyranny and Lessons from History* (Enugu, Nigeria: Fourth Dimension Publishing, 1990).

13. F. Forsyth, *The Dogs of War* (New York: Viking, 1974).

14. Fegley, *Equatorial Guinea.*

15. Ibid., p. 52.

16. T. Melady and M. Melady, *Idi Amin Dada: Hitler in Africa* (Kansas City, Mo.: Sheed Andrews and McMeel, 1977), p. 19.

17. M. Zonis, *Majestic Failure: The Fall of the Shah* (Chicago: Univ. of Chicago Press, 1991), pp. 39, 150.

18. R.J. Rummel, *Death by Government* (New Brunswick, N.J.: Transaction, 1994), p. 8.

19. See Li Zhisui, *The Private Life of Chairman Mao,* trans. Tao Hung-chao (New York Random House, 1994); H.E. Salisbury, *The New Emperors: China in the Era of Mao and Deng* (Boston: Little, Brown and Co., 1992); R. Terrill, *Mao: A Biography* (New York: Harper and Row, 1980); and D. Wilson, *The People's Emperor: Mao, a Biography of Mao Tse-tung* (Garden City, N.Y.: Doubleday, 1980).

20. Salisbury, *New Emperors,* pp. 19–20.

21. Ibid.

22. Hopwood, *Habib Bourguiba,* p. 138.

23. Salisbury, *New Emperors,* p. 156.

24. Ibid., pp. 156–57.

25. Wilson, *People's Emperor,* p. 307.

26. Ibid.

27. Salisbury, *New Emperors,* p. 146.

28. J.D. Legge, *Sukarno: A Political Biography* (Sydney: Allen and Unwin, 1972), pp.346–47.

29. Salisbury, *New Emperors,* p. 195.

30. See accounts of Horthy in P. Bödy, ed., *Hungarian Statesmen of Destiny, 1860–1960* (Boulder, Colo.: Social Sciences Monograph, 1989); M. Horthy, *Memoirs* (New York: Robert Speller and Sons, 1957); and T. Sakmyster, *Hungary's Admiral on Horseback: Miklós Horthy, 1918–1944* (Boulder, Colo.: East European Monographs, 1994).

31. T. Adorno, *The Authoritarian Personality* (New York: Wiley, 1964).

32. Sakmyster, *Hungary's Admiral on Horseback,* pp. 320–21.

33. P. Gleijeses, *Shattered Hope: The Guatemalan Revolution and the United States, 1944–1954* (Princeton: Princeton Univ. Press, 1991), p. 18.

34. K.J. Grieb, *Guatemalan Caudillo: The Regime of Jorge Ubico, 1931–1944* (Athens, Ohio: Ohio Univ. Press, 1979), pp. 17–18.

35. L.L. Moline, "The Ulbricht Regime: A Political Analysis of Individuals, Ideas, and Events Which Have Shaped the Destiny of East Germany" (master's thesis, American University, 1970); Gregory W. Sandford, *From Hitler to Ulbricht: The Communist Reconstruction of East Germany, 1945–46* (Princeton: Princeton Univ. Press, 1983); and C. Stern, *Ulbricht: A Political Biography.* New York: Praeger, 1965.

36. For CIA involvement in the Castillo Armas's rise to power see Gleijeses, *Shattered Hope,* and S. Schlesinger and S. Kinzer, *Bitter Fruit: The Untold Story of the American Coup in Guatemala* (Garden City, N.Y.: Doubleday, 1982).

37. R. Miranda and W. Ratliff, *The Civil War in Nicaragua: Inside the Sandinistas.* (New Brunswick, N.J.): Transaction Publishers, 1993), p. 37.

38. J.A. Page, *Perón: A Biography* (New York: Random House, 1983), p. 221. For a delightful account of the escapades and adventures of Eva's coffin, see pp. 343–44.

39. H. Glickman, ed., *Political Leaders of Contemporary Africa South of the Sahara* (Westport, Conn.: Greenwood Press, 1992); R.H. Jackson and C.G. Rosberg, *Personal Rule in Black Africa* (Berkeley: Univ. of California Press, 1982); V. Malhorta, *Kenya under Kenyatta* (Delhi: Kalinga Publications, 1990), and J. Murray-Brown, *Kenyatta* (London: George Allen, 1972).

40. M. Dönhoff, *Foe into Friend: The Makers of the New Germany from Konrad Adenauer to Helmut Schmidt,* trans. G. Annan (New York: St. Martin's Press, 1982); H. Klein, ed.,

The German Chancellors, trans. E. McCown (Chicago: Edition Q, 1996); G. McGhee, *At the Creation of a New Germany: From Adenauer to Brandt, An Ambassador's Account* (New Haven: Yale Univ. Press, 1989); T. Prittie, *Konrad Adenauer, 1876–1967* (Chicago: Cowles, 1971); F.W. Thackeray and J.K. Findling, eds., *Statesmen Who Changed the World: A Bio-Bibliographical Dictionary of Diplomacy* (Westport, Conn.: Greenwood Press, 1993); P. Weymar, *Konrad Adenauer: The Authorized Biography,* trans. P. de Mendelssohn (London: Andre Deutsch, 1957).

41. Dönhoff, *Foe into Friend,* pp. 30–31.

42. Prittie, *Konrad Adenauer,* p. 314.

43. Weymar, *Konrad Adenauer: Authorized Biography,* p. 69.

44. From P.C. Newman, *Renegade in Power: The Diefenbaker Years* (Toronto: McClelland and Stewart, 1963); H.B. Robinson, *Diefenbaker's World: A Populist in Foreign Affairs* (Toronto: Univ. of Toronto Press, 1989); D. Smith, *Rogue Tory: The Life and Legend of John G. Diefenbaker* (Toronto: Macfarlene Walter and Ross, 1995); and D. Spencer, *Trumpets and Drums: John Diefenbaker on the Campaign Trail* (Vancouver: Greystone Books, 1994).

45. P. Collier and D. Horowitz, *The Kennedys: An American Drama* (New York: Summit Books, 1984), p. 133, and R. Reeves, *A Question of Character: A Life of John F. Kennedy* (New York: Free Press, 1991), p. 67.

46. R.A. Caro, *The Years of Lyndon Johnson: Means of Ascent* (New York: Alfred A. Knopf, 1990), pp. 46–52.

47. Newman, *Renegade in Power,* p. 72.

48. A. Gelb, A.M. Rosenthal, and M. Siegel, eds., *New York Times Great Lives of the Twentieth Century* (New York: Times Books, 1988), p. 108.

49. B.B. Gilbert, *David Lloyd George: A Political Life, The Architect of Change, 1863–1912* (Columbus: Ohio State Univ. Press, 1987), and P. Rowland, *David Lloyd George: A Biography* (New York: Macmillan, 1975).

50. R. Dallek, *Lone Star Rising: Lyndon Johnson and His Times, 1908–1960* (New York: Oxford Univ. Press, 1991), p. 474.

51. D. Kearns, *Lyndon Johnson and the American Dream* (New York: New American Library, 1976), pp. 236–37.

52. R. Jenkins, *Baldwin* (London: Collins, 1987), p. 143.

53. E. Berenson, *The Trial of Madame Caillaux* (Berkeley: Univ. of California Press, 1992), and L. Laurance, *The Pomp of Power* (New York: George H. Doran, 1922).

CHAPTER 7

1. In my past study on the relationship between "madness" and creative achievement (A.M. Ludwig, *The Price of Greatness: Resolving the Creativity and Madness Controversy* [New York: Guilford, 1995]), several trained independent raters showed high agreement in their judgments about the "absence," "probable" presence, or "definite" presence of specific mental disturbances in eminent individuals after they reviewed the biographical materials available on a random sample of them. In my present study, I use similar methods and criteria for making these judgments about the emotional stability of rulers.

2. See my book, A.M. Ludwig, *How Do We Know Who We Are?: A Biography of the Self* (New York: Oxford Univ. Press, 1997).

3. See Ludwig, *Price of Greatness,* for more details about general methodology.

4. World Health Organization, *Mental Disorders: Glossary and Guide to Their Classification in Accordance with the Ninth Revision of the International Classification of Disease* (Geneva, 1978).

5. Li Zhisui, *The Private Life of Chairman Mao,* trans. Tao Hung-chao (New York: Random House, 1994).

6. C. Ponting, *Churchill* (London: Sinclair-Stevenson, 1994), pp. 287–88, 388–89, 803–14, and W. Manchester, *The Last Lion: Winston Churchill, Visions of Glory, 1874–1932* (Boston: Little, Brown, 1983), p. 23.

7. Ponting, *Churchill*, p. 783.

8. L.N. Robins and D.A. Regier, eds., *Psychiatric Disorders in America: The Epidemiological Catchment Area Study* (New York: Free Press, 1991).

9. D.C. Leighton, J.S. Harding, D.B. Macklin, A.M. MacMillan, and A.H. Leighton, *The Character of Danger: Psychiatric Symptoms in Selected Communities* (New York: Basic Books, 1963).

10. L. Srole, T.S. Langer, S.T. Michael, M. Opler, and T. Rennie, *Mental Health in the Metropolis: The Midtown Manhattan Study* (New York: McGraw-Hill, 1962).

11. T. Hundley, "Strongman of the Balkans: Milosevic Finds Strength Amid Defeat, Disaster," *Lexington Herald-Leader*, March 25, 1999, and "The Man behind the Agony," *Newsweek,* April 19, 1999, p. 26.

12. Quoted by Hundley in "Strongman of the Balkans."

13. R. West, *Tito and the Rise and Fall of Yugoslavia* (London: Sinclair Stevenson, 1994), p. 330.

14. P. Ziegler, *Wilson: The Authorized Life of Lord Wilson of Rievaulx* (London: Weidenfeld and Nicolson, 1993), pp. 167, 470–71, and B. Pimlott, *Harold Wilson* (London: Harper Collins, 1992), p. 675.

15. A. Shoumatoff, *African Madness* (New York: Knopf, 1988), p. 107.

16. L. Kinross, *Atatürk: A Biography of Mustafa Kemal, Father of Modern Turkey* (New York: William Morrow, 1965), p. 298.

17. D. Blundy and A. Lycett, *Qaddafi and the Libyan Revolution* (Boston: Little, Brown, 1987), p. 21.

18. R. Reeves, *President Kennedy: Profile of Power* (New York: Simon and Schuster, 1993), pp. 295–98).

19. F. Redlich, *Hitler: Diagnosis of a Destructive Prophet* (New York: Oxford, 1999).

20. J. Dinges, *Our Man in Panama: How General Noriega Used the United States—and Made Millions in Drugs and Arms* (New York: Random House, 1990), p. 158.

21. J.G. Vaillant, *Black, French, and African: A Life of Leopold Sedar Senghor* (Cambridge: Harvard Univ. Press, 1990), p. 104.

22. P.G. Bourne, *Fidel: A Biography of Fidel Castro* (New York: Dodd, Mead, 1986), pp. 294–95.

23. R. Payne, *The Life and Death of Hitler* (New York: Praeger, 1973), pp. 226–29.

24. R. Stephens, *Nasser: A Political Biography* (London: Penguin, 1971), p. 510.

25. P. Gupte, *Mother India: A Political Biography of Indira Gandhi* (New York: Charles Scribner's Sons, 1992), p. 232.

26. A. Horne, *Macmillan: 1894–1956: Volume I of the Official Biography* (London: Macmillan, 1988), p. 13.

27. R. Jenkins, *Asquith* (London: Collins, 1978), p. 62.

28. D. Marquand, *Ramsay MacDonald* (London: Jonathan Cape, 1977).

29. A. Gauhar, *Ayub Khan: Pakistan's First Military Leader* (Oxford: Oxford Univ. Press, 1996), pp. 298–99, 314, 336.

30. D. McCullough, *Mornings on Horseback* (New York: Simon and Schuster, 1981).

31. E. Berenson, *The Trial of Madame Caillaux* (Berkeley: Univ. of California Press, 1992).

32. R.K. Sheridon, *Kurt von Schuschnigg: A Tribute* (London: English Universities Press, 1942), pp. 205, 231–35, 282.

33. K. Middlemas and J. Barnes, *Baldwin: A Biography* (London: Macmillan, 1969), pp. 500, 960–65.

34. See discussion in D.W. Swanson, P.J. Bohnert, and J.A. Smith, *The Paranoid* (Boston: Little, Brown, 1970).

35. R.C. Kessler et al., "Lifetime and Twelve-Month Prevalence of DSM-III-R Psychiatric Disorders in the United States," *Archives of General Psychiatry 51* (1994): pp. 8–19.

36. M. Almond, *The Rise and Fall of Nicolae and Elena Ceausescu* (London: Chapmans, 1992); E. Behr, *Kiss the Hand You Cannot Bite: The Rise and Fall of the Ceausescus* (New York: Villard, 1991); R. Cullen, "Report from Romania," *New Yorker,* April 2, 1990, pp. 94–112; M.E. Fischer, *Nicolae Ceausescu: A Study in Political Leadership* (London: Lynne Reiner Publishers, 1989); G. Galloway and B. Wylie, *Downfall: The Ceausescus and the Romanian Revolution* (London: Futura, 1991); E. Salholz, T. Waldrop, and R. Marshall, "Watching the Babies Die: Romanian Aids Scandal," *Newsweek,* Feb. 19, 1990; J. Sweeney, *The Life and Evil Times of Nicolae Ceausescu* (London: Hutchinson, 1991); and R. Watson, M. Meyer, K. Breslau, and R. Nordland, "Special Report: The Last Days," *Newsweek,* Jan. 8, 1990: pp. 16–23.

37. E. Karsh and I. Rautsi, *Saddam Hussein: A Political Biography* (New York: Free Press, 1991), p. 125.

38. D.P. Chandler, *Brother Number One: A Political Biography of Pol Pot* (Boulder, Colo.: Westview Press, 1992), p. 136.

39. L. Adamolekun, *Sékou Touré's Guinea: An Experiment in Nation Building* (London: Methuen, 1976); P. Brooker, *Twentieth-Century Dictatorships: The Ideological One-Party States* (New York: New York Univ. Press, 1995); G.C. Coats, "Pre-independence Conceptions of the State in French West Africa: The Political Philosophy of Ahmed Sékou Touré and Léopold Sedar Senghor" (master's thesis, James Madison University, 1994); H.W. Fuller, *Journey to Africa* (Chicago: Third World Press, 1971); R.H. Jackson and C.G. Rosberg, *Personal Rule in Black Africa: Prince, Autocrat, Prophet, Tyrant* (Berkeley: Univ. of California Press, 1982); L. Kaba, "A New Era Dawns in Guinea," *Current History 84* (1984), pp. 94–112; W.J. Le Melle, *A Concept of the Modern African State: A Critique of the Political Philosophy of Sekou Toure* (doctoral dissertation, Univ. of Denver, 1963); *Maclean's,* April, 9, 1984, p. 4.

40. W. Mahabir, *In and Out of Politics: Tales of the Government of Dr. Eric Williams from the Notebooks of a Former Minister* (Trinidad: Inprint Caribbean, 1978), pp. 72–75.

41. A. Artucio, *The Trial of Macias in Equatorial Guinea: The Story of a Dictatorship* (International Commission of Jurists and International University Exchange Fund, 1979); R. Fegley, *Equatorial Guinea: An African Tragedy* (New York: Peter Lang, 1989); M. Liniger-Goumaz, *Historical Dictionary of Equatorial Guinea* (Metuchen, N.J.: Scarecrow Press, 1989); and A.A. Nwanko, *African Dictators: The Logic of Tyranny and Lessons from History* (Enugu, Nigeria: Fourth Dimension Publishing, 1990).

42. C.A. Dako, *Zogu the First: King of the Albanians* (Tirana, Albania: Kristo Luarasi, 1937); B.J. Fischer, *King Zog and the Struggle for Stability in Albania* (Boulder, Colo.: East European Monographs, 1984); and J. Swire, *King Zog's Albania* (New York: Liveright Publishing, 1937).

43. V.M. Berezhkov, *At Stalin's Side,* trans. S.V. Mikheyev (New York: Birch Lane Press, 1994); A. Bullock, *Hitler and Stalin: Parallel Lives* (New York: Alfred A. Knopf, 1992); A. De Jonge, *Stalin* (New York: William Morrow, 1986); R. Hingley, *Joseph Stalin: Man and Legend* (New York: McGraw-Hill, 1974); R.H. McNeal, *Stalin: Man and Ruler* (New York: New York Univ. Press, 1988); R. Richardson, *Stalin's Shadow: Inside the Family of One of the World's Greatest Tyrants* (New York: St. Martin's Press, 1994); R.C. Tucker, *Stalin in Power: The Revolution from Above, 1928–1941* (New York: W.W. Norton, 1990); idem, *Stalin as Revolutionary, 1879–1929* (New York: W.W. Norton, 1973); idem, ed., *Stalinism: Essays in Historical Interpretation* (New York: W.W. Norton, 1977); and idem, "A Stalin Biographer's Memoir" in S.H. Brown & C. Pletsch, eds., *Introspection in Biography: The Biographer's Quest for Self-Awareness* (Hillsdale, N.J.: Analytic Press, 1985).

44. Bullock, *Parallel Lives,* p. 362.

45. D. Cook, *Charles de Gaulle: A Biography* (New York: Putnam, 1983), pp. 233–34.

46. D. Kearns, *Lyndon Johnson and the American Dream* (New York: New American Library, 1976), p. 331.

47. Kessler, "DSM-III-R Psychiatric Disorders," pp. 8–19.

48. J.A. La Nauze, *Alfred Deakin: A Biography* (London: Melbourne Univ. Press, 1965), pp. 630, 634–37, and A. Gabay, *The Mystic Life of Alfred Deakin* (Cambridge: Cambridge Univ. Press, 1992), pp. 177, 189–90, 191.

49. H. Kay, *Salazar and Modern Portugal* (London: Eyre & Spottiswoode, 1970), pp. 13–15.

50. "Mao Tse-Tung," *Encyclopedia Americana,* (Danbury, Conn.: Grolier, 1990).

51. Ziegler, *Wilson,* p. 487.

52. D. Jehl, "The Wisdom of a Saudi King: Choosing an Heir to the Realm of Abdel Aziz," *New York Times,* May, 24, 1999.

53. "Reagan Failed to Recover from Shot," *London Times,* March, 3, 1998. Also see L. Cannon, *President Reagan: The Role of a Lifetime.* New York: Simon and Schuster, 1991.

54. Cannon, *President Reagan,* p. 229. Also see D. D'Souza, *Ronald Reagan: How an Ordinary Man Became an Extraordinary Leader* (New York: Free Press, 1997), p. 8–9.

55. E. Morris, *Dutch: A Memoir of Ronald Reagan* (New York: Random House, 1999), p. 318. Also see Cannon, *President Reagan,* p. 229.

56. G. Trudeau, *In Search of Reagan's Brain: A Doonesbury Book* (New York: Simon and Schuster, 1981). Also see http://www.doonesbury.com/controversial/dbcon10.html and http://www.doonesbury.com/controversial/dbcon09.html for later cartoons. Accessed 1999.

CHAPTER 8

1. L.B. Poullada, *Reform and Rebellion in Afghanistan, 1919–1929: King Amanullah's Failure to Modernize a Tribal Society* (Ithaca: Cornell Univ. Press, 1973); I.A.S. Shah, *The Tragedy of Amanullah* (London: Alexander-Ouseley, 1933); and R.H. Stewart, *Fire in Afghanistan, 1914–1929: Faith, Hope and the British Empire* (Garden City, N.Y.: Doubleday, 1973).

2. D.K. Simonton, *Why Presidents Succeed: A Political Psychology of Leadership* (New Haven: Yale Univ. Press, 1987).

3. In two separate reliability studies, high reliability between two independent raters was achieved. In rating the eighteen U.S. presidents, the two raters got over 95 percent agreement. In rating a random selection of twenty-four leaders in the study, the two raters got roughly a 94 percent agreement on their total scores.

4. For example, the PGS scores for the American presidents showed an exceptionally high correspondence ($r = +.95$) with their relative rankings by the well-known Murray-Blessing ratings (R.K. Murray and T.H. Blessing, *Greatness in the White House: Rating Presidents, Washington through Carter* [University Park: Pennsylvania State Univ. Press, 1989]). The PGS scores for forty rulers also showed a high correlation with their scores on the Creative Achievement Scale ($r = +.64$), which is an established measure for exceptional achievement in all fields of endeavor.

5. The Total PGS scores for all leaders in the sample ($N=377$) correlated $+.46$ ($p<.000$) and $+.64$ ($p<.000$) with the words allotted to them in the *Encyclopedia Americana* (Danbury, Conn.: Grolier, 1990) and *Encyclopædia Britannica Online*, respectively, as well as $+.60$ ($p<.000$) for the combined words from both of these encyclopedias.

6. *World Almanac and Encyclopedia* (New York: World Publishing, 1900).

7. H. Arendt, *The Origins of Totalitarianism* (New York: Peter Smith, 1983), p. 124.

8. "Alexander the Great" *Encyclopædia Britannica Online.* <http://www.eb.com:195/bol/topic?artcl=106078&seq_nbr=1&page=n&isctn=3> [Accessed October 5 2001].

9. A. Hochschild, *King Leopold's Ghost: A Story of Greed, Terror and Heroism in Colonial Africa* (New York: Houghton Mifflin, 1998).

10. R.G. Kaiser, *Why Gorbachev Happened* (New York: Simon and Schuster, 1991), p. 422.

11. I have taken the liberty of reproducing certain material about utopias from my book, *The Importance of Lying* (Springfield, Ill.: Charles C. Thomas, 1965).

12. V.D. Volkan and N. Itzkowitz, *The Immortal Atatürk: A Psychobiography* (Chicago: Univ. of Chicago Press, 1984), pp. 295–97.

13. J. Lacouture, *The Demigods: Charismatic Leadership in the Third World*, trans. P. Wolf (New York: Alfred A. Knopf, 1970), pp. 253–525.

14. C.L. Mee Jr., *The Ohio Gang: The World of Warren G. Harding* (New York: M. Evans, 1981), p. 15.

15. See discussions of Yew in A. Josey, *Lee Kuan Yew: The Crucial Years* (Singapore: Times Books International, 1995); J.A. Lim, "A Study of Lee Kuan Yew, Prime Minister of Singapore, and Tengku Abdul Rahman, Former Prime Minister of Malaysia, Utilizing a Personality Theory Approach" (master's thesis, Western Michigan University, 1982); J. Minchin, *No Man Is an Island: A Portrait of Singapore's Lee Kuan Yew* (North Sydney, Australia: Allen & Unwin), 1990; T.S. Selvan, *Singapore: The Ultimate Island (Lee Kuan Yew's Untold Story)* (Melbourne, Australia: Freeway Books, 1990); and J.C. Taylor, "Lee Kuan Yew: His Rise to Power: 1950–1968" (master's thesis, San Diego State University, 1976).

16. See discussion of Masaryk in H.G. Skilling, *T.G. Masaryk: Against the Current, 1882–1914* (University Park, Pa.: Pennsylvania State Univ. Press, 1994), p. 17.

Chapter 9

1. T. Carlyle, *On Heroes, Hero Worship, and the Heroic in History* (Lincoln: Univ. of Nebraska Press, 1966).

2. W. James, "Great Men and Their Environments," in *The Will to Believe and Other Essays in Popular Philosophy* (Cambridge: Harvard Univ. Press, 1979).

3. F.A. Woods, *The Influence of Monarchs: Steps in a New Science of History* (New York: Macmillan, 1913).

4. S. Hooks, *The Hero in History* (Boston: Beaon Press, 1967).

5. G.W.F. Hegel, *The Philosophy of History*, trans. J. Sibree (New York: Dover, 1956).

6. H. Spencer, *The Study of Sociology* (London: Kegan Paul, Trench, and Trubner, 1908).

7. Hooks, *Hero in History*, pp. 65–66. Also see I. Berlin, "Historical Inevitability," in *The Proper Study of Mankind* (New York: Farrar, Straus and Giroux, 1998), for a general philosophical overview of this issue.

8. L. Lockwood, "Fidel Castro Speaks on Personal Power," in H.M. Hamill, ed., *Caudillos: Dictators in Spanish America* (Norman: Univ. of Oklahoma Press, 1992), pp. 292–315.

9. Ibid, pp. 305–6.

10. Designating certain rulers as great and others as not requires you to make a judgment. If you use the average score on the Political Greatness Scale (PGS) to separate the rulers into an upper half and a lower half, with those having above-average scores being "great" and those having below-average scores being "not-great," then the relative similarities in the political achievements of the large number of those rulers who cluster on either side of the average score, the mediocre rulers, are likely to dilute any important personality differences between those rulers with very impressive or very unimpressive achievements. If you try to avoid this problem by comparing only those with the most impressive achievements (i.e., those "truly great" rulers with PGS scores in the upper 10 percent) to those with the least impressive achievements (i.e., those "far-from-great" rulers with PGS scores in the lower 10 percent), you will likely find major differences in personality between these rulers but there won't be enough of them in either group to

let you generalize from the results. The practical solution is to choose a dividing line somewhere between the average score and these upper/lower 10 percent extremes. My decision, therefore, was to use a statistical ranking procedure to assign rulers automatically to either the top third or bottom third of greatness based on their total Political Greatness Scale scores. This let me have large enough ruler groups to contrast and to minimize the problem of mediocre rulers diluting any differences between them. I then designated those in the top third as the "great" rulers and those in the bottom third as the "not-great" ones.

How Opposites May Not Differ

With the great and the not-so-great rulers inhabiting opposite ends of the spectrum of political greatness, my first task was to discover how these rulers were alike and how they were different. I did this by comparing them on over a hundred separate items dealing with their family upbringing, their education, their attributes as youths, their health, important landmarks in their lives, and their temperament and character as adults.

What became immediately apparent was how much the great and the not-so-great rulers had in common. They shared similar social, economic, and religious backgrounds. (On average, 26 percent came from lower-class, 43 percent from middle-class, and 27 percent from upper-class socioeconomic backgrounds. About equal proportions had parents who were poor, moderately wealthy, or very wealthy. Also, roughly one-third were raised Catholic, one-third Protestant, and one-third a variety of other religions.)

They came from similar-sized families, with neither group being more likely than the other to be firstborns. (Roughly, 56 percent were firstborn children.)

They got similar grades in school, received about the same amount of education, and made similar career choices. (About 65 percent of the combined groups graduated from college, and 54 percent got average or above-average grades at school.)

The above collection of findings suggests that any differences in the ultimate political stature of the great and not-so-great rulers had little to do with their family backgrounds and upbringing.

Then, as youths, members of the upper rung or bottom rung of political greatness likewise showed no major differences on a number of parameters.

They were comparable in their physical fitness or athletic prowess. (An average of 18 percent were skilled athletes.)

One group was just as likely as the other to enjoy reading, possess a special talent, or engage in some form of creative activity. (An average of 42 percent were avid readers as youths, about 11 percent showed signs of being gifted, and 22 percent played instruments, wrote poetry, painted, or had other artistic outlets.)

Roughly similar proportions of each group seemed emotionally stable, got along well with others, and enjoyed normal relationships with their parents. (An average of 32 percent were described as even-tempered and 32 percent as outgoing. About 10 percent had hostile relations with their mothers, and about 22 percent had hostile relations with their fathers.)

Likewise, the timing of certain landmark events during their adult lives was roughly the same. (They married at about age twenty-eight, entered politics at age thirty-four, and gained high office at about age fifty-one. Their health status before becoming rulers was similar, and their average life span was about seventy-one years.)

Though the list of similarities between these two groups of rulers is impressive, it does not mean that the members of these two groups are similar kinds of people. All human beings share common attributes; it is the qualities they do not share that let you distinguish one group from another. Aside from serving in office almost three times as long (14.4 years versus 5.4 years), great rulers are much more likely than not-so-great ones to possess a set of distinctive attitudes, traits, and behaviors, which I have labeled the "seven pillars of political greatness."

The Kinds of Rulers Most Apt to Achieve Greatness

As the table below shows, marked differences exist in the percentages of the different kinds of rulers composing the bottom-, middle-, and top-third groups for political achievement, based on their total PGS scores. Although leaders of established democracies are overrepresented within the entire sample, the most dramatic findings are that visionaries and transitionals are overrepresented as the great rulers (top third) while tyrants are dramatically underrepresented. All other ruler types tend to be distributed relatively evenly among the three groups. Since the PGS scores of rulers correlate so highly with the length of their encyclopedia entries, the tendency for visionaries and transitionals to get higher PGS scores and for tyrants to get lower ones than other kinds of rulers serves as a rough indicator of how society tends to value or devalue certain kinds of political achievements.

Types of Rulers within the Bottom, Middle, and Top Third of PGS Scores
Monarch Tyrants Visionaries Authoritarians Transitionals Democrats

	Monarch	Tyrants	Visionaries	Authoritarians	Transitionals	Democrats
Bottom Third	17%	64%	0%	35%	15%	41%
Middle Third	44%	36%	4%	32%	30%	33%
Top Third	39%	0%	96%	33%	55%	26%

Chi Square =77.8, DF = 10, p <.000

11. See chapter 8 for criteria of greatness.

12. See Statistics and Methods section for discussion of multiple regression analyses. Results for multiple regression analyses are in the Statistical Analyses section in the appendices for chapter 9.

13. See Statistics and Methods section for discussion of logistic regression analyses.

14. Results for logistical regression analysis are in Statistical Analyses section in the appendices for chapter 9.

15. A.M. Ludwig, *The Price of Greatness: Resolving the Creativity and Madness Controversy* (New York: Guilford, 1995).

16. See reference 10 above.

17. L. Kinross, *Atatürk: A Biography of Mustafa Kemal, Father of Modern Turkey* (New York: William Morrow, 1965), p. 272.

18. J. Meintjes, *General Louis Botha: A Biography* (London: Cassell, 1970).

19. Cited by M. Rejai and K. Phillips in *Leaders of Revolution* (Beverly Hills: Sage, 1979).

20. M. Weber, *The Protestant Ethic and the Spirit of Capitalism*, trans. T. Parsons (London: Allen and Unwin, 1976).

21. B. Ledwidge, *De Gaulle* (New York: St. Martin's Press, 1982), p. 30, and D. Cook, *Charles de Gaulle: A Biography* (New York: Putnam, 1983), p. 17.

22. Cook, *Charles de Gaulle*, p. 19.

23. D. Rooney, *Kwame Nkrumah: The Political Kingdom in the Third World* (New York: St. Martin's Press, 1989), p. 145.

24. P. Addy, *Indira Gandhi: India's Woman of Destiny* (Calcutta: Sangam Books, 1986); T. Ali, *The Nehrus and the Gandhis: An Indian Dynasty* (London: Pan Books, 1985); P. Gupte, *Mother India: A Political Biography of Indira Gandhi* (New York: Charles Scribner's Sons, 1992); P. Jayakar, *Indira Gandhi: An Intimate Biography* (New York: Pantheon Books, 1992); I. Malhotra, *Indira Gandhi: A Personal and Political Biography* (London: Hodder & Stoughton, 1989); and N. Sahgal, *Indira Gandhi: Her Road to Power* (New York: Frederick Ungar, 1978).

25. Kinross, *Atatürk*, p. 53.

26. Ibid., p. 472.

27. C. McCullough, *The First Man in Rome* (New York: Avon, 1990), pp. 219–20.

28. R. St. John, *Ben-Gurion* (Garden City, N.Y.: Doubleday, 1971), p. 17.

29. Cited by C. Ponting, *Churchill* (London: Sinclair-Stevenson, 1994), p. 26.

30. H.B. Neatby, *William Lyon Mackenzie King: 1924–1932, The Lonely Heights* (Toronto: Univ. of Toronto Press, 1963), p. 208, and C.P. Stacey, *A Very Double Life: The Private World of Mackenzie King* (Toronto: Macmillan of Canada, 1976), p. 163.

31. S. Cloete, *Against These Three: A Biography of Paul Kruger, Cecil Rhodes, and Lobengula, Last King of the Matabele* (Garden City, N.Y.: Garden City Publishing, 1947); J. Fisher, *Paul Kruger: His Life and Times* (London: Secker and Warburg, 1974); and J. Meintjes, *President Paul Kruger: A Biography* (London: Cassell, 1974).

33. M. Korda, "Prompting the President," *New Yorker*, Oct. 6, 1997, pp. 88–95.

34. A.M. Ludwig, *Price of Greatness*.

CHAPTER 10

1. R. Wrangham and D. Peterson, *Demonic Males: Apes and the Origins of Human Violence* (Boston: Houghton Mifflin, 1996).

2. J. Goodall, *The Chimpanzees of Gombe: Patterns of Primate Behavior* (Cambridge: Harvard Univ. Press, 1986).

3. K. Lorenz, *On Aggression,* trans. M.K. Wilson (New York: Harcourt Brace, 1974).

4. See J. Diamond, *The Third Chimpanzee: The Evolution and Future of the Human Animal* (New York: Harper Perennial, 1993).

5. W. Durant and A. Durant, *The Lessons of History* (Simon and Schuster, New York, 1968).

6. S. Freud, "Why War?" in *Collected Papers* vol. 5, ed. J. Strachey (New York: Basic Books, 1959).

7. R.J. Rummel, *Statistics of Democide: Genocide and Mass Murder since 1900* (Charlottesville: Center for National Security Law, University of Virginia, 1997).

8. I have based this estimate of this ratio on the examination of numerous casualty reports listing the number of dead and wounded. Considerable variation in this ratio may exist depending upon the time period, the type of weapons, and the conditions (e.g., battle versus government-sponsored extermination programs).

9. Rummel, *Statistics of Democide*.

10. K. von Clausewitz, *On War* (New York: Viking Press, 1983).

11. Will and Ariel Durant, *Lessons of History*, take a similar view.

12. R.J. Rummel, *Death by Government* (New Brunswick, N.J.: Transaction, 1994).

13. "Adviser Pushes Gore to Be Leader of the Pack," *New York Times*, Nov. 1, 1999.

14. H. See Chavez, "My Struggle," *Harper's Magazine*, Oct. 1999, p. 32; B. Bearak, "Democracy in Pakistan: Can a General Be Trusted," *New York Times*, Nov. 21, 1999; S. Erlanger, "Croatia Mourns Founder of the Nation," *New York Times*, Dec. 12, 1999; "Turkmenistan's Leader Is Given Lifetime in Office by Parliament," *New York Times*, Dec. 29, 1999; "A Guatemala at Peace Casts Ballots for President," *New York Times*, Nov. 8, 1999; "Populist Favored in Runoff," *Cincinnati Enquirer*, Dec. 26, 1999; "Former Coup Plotter in Niger Looks Set to Become Next President," AFP, reported in Yahoo! News: Asia, Nov. 26, 1999; "Chechen War Makes Hero Out of a Political Nobody," *London Times*, Nov. 23, 1999; "Sudan Leader Declares Emergency to Foil Foe," *Reuters*, Dec. 13, 1999.

15. See Bearak, "Democracy in Pakistan."

16. "Long Live the Kings in Arab Countries," *Vancouver Sun*, Aug. 13, 1999.

17. D.W. Chen, "The Numbers Favor Those Living in Democracies," *New York Times*, Jan. 21, 1997.

18. "With Africa Watching, Senegal Casts Votes That Count," *New York Times*, Feb. 27, 2000.

19. See discussion in A.M. Ludwig, *How Do We Know Who We Are*.

STATISTICAL RESULTS

INTRODUCTION

SAMPLE CHARACTERISTICS (RULERS = 377)

Type of Ruler:

Monarchs	9.5%
Tyrants	5.8%
Visionaries	6.6%
Authoritarians	18.3%
Transitionals	12.5%
Democrats	47.2%

Geographical Region:

Latin America/Caribbean	12.7%
North Africa	2.4%
Sub-Saharan Africa	7.4%
Australia/New Zealand	7.2%
Euro-Africa	3.4%
Anglo-America	8.5%
Europe	24.9%
Eurasia	4.5%
Balkans	4.5%
Central Asia	7.2%
East Asia	5.8%
Southeast Asia	6.1%
Middle East	5.3%

Gender:

Females	2.4%
Males	97.6%

Parents' Socioeconomic Status:

Under-Stratum	5.9%
Lower-Stratum	21.0%
Middle-Stratum	44.1%
Upper-Stratum	29.0%

Parents' Income Level:

Poor	30.0%
Moderate	35.9%
Wealthy	34.0%

Early Background:

Urban	43.6%
Small Town	47.7%
Rural	8.2%
Mixed	0.5%

Religious Upbringing:

None	1.3%
Catholic	39.3%
Protestant	26.0%
Islamic	10.9%
Hindu	2.4%
Shinto	1.6%
Jewish	2.7%
Buddhist	6.6%
African Tribal	1.3%
Other	0.5%
Unknown	7.4%

Education Level Completed:

None: Illiterate	1%
None: Literate	2%
Elementary School/Tutors	18%
High or Trade School	14%
Technical or Special School	3%
College	33%
Post-Graduate/Professional	21%
Doctorate	8%

Married:

Married	93%

Cause of Death/Current Status:

Natural Death	62%
Accidental/Incidental Death	2%

Suicide	1%
Assassination/Execution	14%
Still Alive	21%

Profession Prior to Entering Politics:

Business	5%
Scientist/Engineer	3%
Government Worker	5%
Royalty	10%
Skilled Laborer	1%
Rancher/Large Farmer	1%
Accountant/Banker	2%
Relative of Deceased Leader	3%
Minister/Priest	1%
Lawyer	21%
Political Journalist	9%
Creative Artist	1%
Teacher/Professor	6%
Soldier/Revolutionary	20%
Physician/Dentist	3%
Labor Leader	4%
Unskilled Laborer/Peasant	3%
Other	2%

TOTAL GROUP CHARACTERISTICS (RULERS = 1,941)

Gender:

Females	1.4%
Males	98.6%

Method By Which Rose to Power:

Presidential Election	22%
Parliamentary Election/Appt.	34%
Selected by Committee	7%
Selected by Junta	6%
Appointed by Colonial Power	4%
Constitutional Succession	6%
Hereditary Succession	4%
Coup Leader/Self-Appointed	11%
Other/Unknown	6%

Profession Prior to Entering Politics:

Business	4%
Scientist/Engineer	2%
Government Worker	2%
Royalty	6%
Skilled Laborer	1%
Rancher/Large Farmer	1%
Accountant/Banker	1%
Relative of Deceased Leader	3%
Minister/Priest	1%
Lawyer	20%
Political Journalist	3%
Creative Artist	0%
Teacher/Professor	6%
Soldier/Revolutionary	20%
Physician/Dentist	2%
Labor Leader	1%
Unskilled Laborer/Peasant	1%
Other	1%
Not known	25%

How Rule Ended:

Elected Out of Office	29%
Forced Removal	2%
Deposed	17%
Abdicated	1%
Impeached	0%
Lost War and Ousted	2%
Non-Forced Resignation	15%
Died Natural Death in Office	9%
Suicide	1%
Assassinated	4%
Completed Term	20%
Other	0%

CHAPTER 3

All results below are for the Select Sample of Rulers (N=377).

	Monarchs	Tyrants	Vision-aries	Author-itarians	Transi-tionals	Demo-crats	TOTAL N=377
Average Age Began Rule	34.3	42.6	46.6	50.8	51.4	55.5	50.8***
Average # Kids (Male Rulers)	30	28	4	3	4	3	7***
* p ≤ .05; ** p ≤ .01; *** p ≤ .001							

	Monarchs	Tyrants	Vision-aries	Author-itarians	Transi-tionals	Demo-crats	TOTAL N=377
% Married	100	95	96	93	96	96	95
% "Faithful" (Males)	87	95	72	54	64	40	57***
% Harems (Males)	32	14	8	3	4	2	6***
% Corrupt (Males)	26	100	32	19	4	4	16***
% Ascetic Males							
No Sex	0	0	4	3	2	2	2
With Sex	0	0	20	7	15	5	7*
% Personality Cult (Males)	83	52	88	38	21	6	29***
* p ≤ .05; ** p ≤ .01; *** p ≤ .001							

Average Number of Years Ruled with or without Personality Cult (s.d.)			
	All Rulers	Dictators Only	Democrats / Transitionals Only
Personality Cult	18.1 (12.2)	20.0 (12.5)	10.6 (7.0)
No Personality Cult	6.9 (6.4)	9.6 (9.5)	6.0 (4.8)
TOTALS	10.1 (9.9)***	15.5 (12.4)***	6.5 (5.2)***
* p ≤ .05; ** p ≤ .01; *** p ≤ .001			

CHAPTER 4

All the results below are for the Select Sample of Rulers (N = 377)

Before Came to Power							
	Monarchs	Tyrants	Vision-aries	Author-itarians	Transi-tionals	Demo-crats	TOTAL
% Military Service	64	77	64	75	55	39	54***
% Fought in Battle	39	55	56	61	40	23	37***
% Involved in Coup, Uprising	31	73	68	55	30	6	28***
% War Medals/ Decorations	14	50	48	58	30	20	31***
% Wounded in Battle	3	9	20	13	11	7	9
% Political Arrests	19	36	68	65	55	24	39***
Average # Months in Jail	.0	2	15	12	23	4	8***
Average # of Arrests	0.1	0.5	1.8	3.9	1.8	1.0	1.6
% Exiled	17	14	36	22	26	6	15***
% Jailed or Exiled	17	41	60	48	65	21	35***
* p ≤ .05; ** p ≤ .01; *** p ≤ .001							

After Came to Power

	Monarchs	Tyrants	Vision-aries	Author-itarians	Transi-tionals	Demo-crats	TOTAL
% Jailed	14	24	12	26	15	6	13**
Average # Months in Jail	8	11	1	8	7	1	4**
% Exiled	33	57	12	26	19	6	17***
% Coup Attempt Against	50	82	44	39	36	10	29***
% Assassination Attempt	61	77	56	46	51	19	38***
Average # Assassination Attempts	1.1	1.5	1.0	0.7	1.7	0.3	0.7**

* p ≤ .05; ** p ≤ .01; *** p ≤ .001

Cause of Death (percentages)

	Monarchs	Tyrants	Vision-aries	Author-itarians	Transi-tionals	Demo-crats	TOTAL
Disease/Natural	77	75	81	69	66	88	79
Accidental/Incidental	3	0	0	3	6	2	3
Suicide	0	0	10	0	0	2	1
Assassination	21	25	0	13	26	9	13
Execution	0	0	10	15	3	0	4

Chi Square = 56.2, DF = 20, p < .0000

End of Rule after Last Term (percentages)							
	Monarchs	Tyrants	Vision-aries	Author-itarians	Transi-tionals	Demo-crats	TOTAL
Natural Death in Office	41	15	48	21	16	9	18
Assassination in Office	12	15	4	13	18	6	10
Lost Election	0	10	5	13	23	45	28
Removal by Junta/Council	0	0	0	16	0	0	3
Deposed by Coup	23	50	17	15	16	2	12
Lost War and Removed	3	10	4	12	4	1	5
Abdication	21	0	4	3	0	0	3
Suicide	0	0	9	0	0	1	1
Non-Forced Resignation	0	0	4	3	18	25	15
Completed Term	0	0	5	4	5	11	7
Chi Square = 285.5, DF = 45, p ≤ .000							

Political Mentors or Sponsors							
	Monarchs	Tyrants	Vision-aries	Author-itarians	Transi-tionals	Demo-crats	TOTAL
Mentors (%)	19	55	44	39	26	38	36*
Betray Mentors (%)	86	100	27	52	46	25	42***
* p ≤ .05; ** p ≤ .01; *** p ≤ .001							

Average Number of Years Ruled (s.d.)			
	All Rulers	Dictators Only	Democrats / Transitionals Only
Betrayed Mentor/Sponsor	13.5 (11.3)	17.9 (11.3)	6.4 (7.0)
Loyal to Mentor/Sponsor	7.6 (7.9)	12.4 (11.6)	5.7 (4.6)
TOTALS	10.0 (9.8)***	15.7 (11.6)	5.9 (5.3)
* p ≤ .05; ** p ≤ .01; *** p ≤ .001			

Percentages of Rulers Engaging in Designated Activities							
	Monarchs	Tyrants	Vision-aries	Author-itarians	Transi-tionals	Demo-crats	TOTAL
Dictatorial Powers during Rule at Some Time (%)	89	100	92	94	26	6	44***
Adopted Government Policy Responsible for Deaths (%)	75	100	88	78	45	29	52***
Involvement in Civil, Regional, National War (%)	19	14	24	38	43	67	48***
Changed Form of Government (%)	53	73	96	67	87	7	42***
* p ≤ .05; ** p ≤ .01; *** p ≤ .001							

Average Number of Years Ruled (s.d.)	
	Democrats / Transitionals Only
Asssumed Dictatorial Powers	9.7 (6.1)
Not Assumed Dictatorial Powert	6.1 (5.0)
TOTALS	6.4 (5.3)**
* p ≤ .05; ** p ≤ .01; *** p ≤ .001	

All the results below are for the **Total Group of Rulers** (N = 1,941)

Relationship of How Rulers Gained Power to the Risks Involved Beforehand			
	Fought in Coup (%)	Arrested (%)	Exiled (%)
Presidential Election	15	18	12
Parliamentary Election/Appointment	4	16	4
Selected by Committee	27	30	15
Selected by Junta	51	32	7
Appointed by Colonial Power	6	38	16
Constitutional Succession	7	13	4
Hereditary Succession	11	7	6
Coup Leader/Self-Appointed	100	32	13
Other/Unknown	15	14	6
TOTALS	23***	20***	8***
* $p \leq .05$; ** $p \leq .01$; *** $p \leq .001$			

Relationship of How Rulers Gained Power to the Risks Involved Afterwards				
	Coup Attemps Against (%)	Exiled (%)	Assassination Attempts (%)	Deposed (%)
Presidential	26	15	13	19
Parliamentary Election/Appointment	6	5	8	3
Selected by Committee	21	12	10	15
Selected by Junta	41	21	17	36
Appointed by Colonial Power	29	18	21	24
Constitutional Succession	26	13	10	18
Hereditary Succession	35	25	29	22
Coup Leader/Self-Appointed	52	25	35	33
Other/Unknown	24	19	7	21
TOTALS	23***	14***	14***	16***
* $p \leq .05$; ** $p \leq .01$; *** $p \leq .001$				

Causes of Death					
	Natural Causes (%)	Accidental/ Incidental (%)	Suicide (%)	Assassina- tion (%)	Executed (%)
Presidential	89	2	2	5	2
Parliamentary Election/Appointment	91	2	1	5	2
Selected by Committee	93	3	0	5	0
Selected by Junta	75	5	1	8	11
Appointed by Colonial Power	86	2	0	10	2
Constitutional Succession	94	0	0	3	3
Hereditary Succession	81	3	0	11	5
Coup Leader/Self- Appointed	65	2	1	20	12
Other/Unknown	91	0	0	4	5
TOTALS	86	2	1	7	4
Chi Square = 122.9, DF = 32, p < .000, N = 1,277					

The Kind of Government under which the Leader Ruled (percentages)							
	Represen- tative Democracy	Strong Constitu- tional Monarch	Limited Represen- tative/Au- tocratic but Constitu- tional	Autocratic Leader but Under Junta, Committee	Dictator- ship Sanction- ed by Colonial Power	Frank Dictator- ship	Absolute Monarchy
Elected by the People	66	1	15	0	0	18	0
Appointed in Parliamentary Government	89	1	2	0	3	5	0
Appointed by a Committee or Oligarchy	4	0	9	44	4	30	9
Appointed by a Junta or Council	0	0	12	0	13	75	0
Appointed by a Colonial Power	22	0	7	0	21	21	29
Constitutional Succession	64	0	0	9	0	27	0
Hereditary Succession	4	24	0	0	0	0	72
Self-Appointed Ruler or Coup Leader	5	0	3	1	2	76	13
TOTALS	54	2	6	3	3	23	9
Chi Square = 586.0, DF = 42, p < .000, N = 377							

CHAPTER 5

All the results below apply to the Sample of Rulers (N = 377)

Background (percentages)							
	Monarchs	Tyrants	Vision-aries	Author-itarians	Transi-tionals	Demo-crats	TOTAL N = 377
Socio-economic Status							
Under-Stratum	0	27	4	5	13	3	6
Lower-Stratum	0	14	50	38	17	17	21
Middle-Stratum	0	46	38	36	40	57	44
Upper-Stratum	100	14	8	21	30	23	29
Parents' Income Level							
Poor	8	50	56	44	26	24	30
Moderate	0	41	28	35	34	45	36
Wealthy	92	9	16	21	40	31	34
Parents' Marrige Intact	78	64	92	64	83	89	81***
Grew Up During Childhood							
Urban	89	21	32	30	28	48	44
Small Town	11	63	60	62	57	44	48
Rural	0	16	4	6	15	8	8
Mixed	0	0	4	2	0	0	0
First-born	65	53	48	35	32	44	44
Loss of Mom or Dad before Age 14	31	27	36	12	34	18	22**
* p ≤ .05; ** p ≤ .01; *** p ≤ .001							

Information About Mothers (percentages)							
	Monarchs	Tyrants	Vision-aries	Author-itarians	Transi-tionals	Demo-crats	TOTAL N = 377
Homemakers/ Unskilled	5	56	87	73	89	79	72*
Major Political Job or Ruler	83	0	0	6	5	1	12***
Loss of Mother before Age 14	24	17	17	5	18	10	12
* p ≤ .05; ** p ≤ .01; *** p ≤ .001							

Information About Fathers (percentages)							
	Monarchs	Tyrants	Vision-aries	Author-itarians	Transi-tionals	Demo-crats	TOTAL N = 377
Unemployed/ Unskilled	0	33	23	16	14	9	12***
Major Political Office/Ruler	93	28	5	7	13	10	21***
Loss of Father before Age 14	8	26	25	9	23	11	14
Little Formal Education	0	38	77	25	50	19	28***
* p ≤ .05; ** p ≤ .01; *** p ≤ .001							

Educational Experience (percentages)							
	Monarchs	Tyrants	Visiona-ries	Authori-tarians	Transi-tionals	Demo-crats	TOTAL N = 377
Educational Level Completed ***							
No Education Beyond Primary School	63	27	28	16	19	12	20
College, Graduate or Post-Graduate Education	8	45	52	59	64	77	62
Academic Performance ***							
Below Average	38	47	45	14	24	7	
Average	31	24	20	35	30	25	
Above Average	31	29	35	51	46	68	
* p ≤ .05; ** p ≤ .01; *** p ≤ .001							

Personal Characteristics as Youths (percentages)							
	Monarchs	Tyrants	Vision-aries	Author-itarians	Transi-tionals	Demo-crats	TOTAL N = 377
Artistic Activity	24	9	36	21	19	22	22
Skilled Athlete	13	18	9	6	19	18	15
Confident/Insecure	40/17	18/18	71/0	39/7	37/6	48/20	45/15**
Conforming/ Nonconforming	70/9	50/25	22/48	58/16	54/21	68/11	61/16**
Genius/Precocity (<Age 13)	6	6	25	7	13	11	11
Exceptional Leadership	9	0	41	13	18	26	22*
Even-Tempered/ Moody	52/26	18/46	24/38	45/7	33/11	41/12	40/16**
Outgoing/Solitary	18/36	10/30	23/27	24/22	34/40	39/28	32/29
Avid Reader	17	13	58	32	37	46	39**
Politicized at School (< Age 21)	0	5	28	10	11	4	7***
Physical Handicap	6	0	17	2	6	8	7
Sickly or Frail	19	0	9	3	17	11	11*
Life-Threatening Illness	6	5	17	8	13	10	10
Either Handicap, Sickly, or Life-Threatening Illness	19	5	36	10	26	21	20*
Very Close/ Hostile Relationship with Mother	21/21	0/36	9/32	7/7	10/2	11/6	11/10***
Very Close/ Hostile Relationship with Father	0/41	0/40	0/50	0/11	3/15	3/17	2/21**
* p ≤ .05; ** p ≤ .01; *** p ≤ .001							

CHAPTER 6

All the results below are for the Sample of Rulers (N=377).

Political Activity -- Averages (s.d.)							
	Monarchs	Tyrants	Vision-aries	Author-itarians	Transi-tionals	Demo-crats	TOTAL
Age at Initial Political Activity	25.5 (9)	36.0 (9)	30.3 (10)	37.1 (13)	32.0 (9)	34.7 (10)	33.7 (11)***
Total # Years Ruled	21.5 (15)	14.2 (9)	20.7 (12)	11.2 (10)	9.7 (7)	5.6 (4)	10.1 (10)***
Longevity in Years	63 (16)	66 (11)	71 (11)	69 (13)	71 (18)	75 (11)	71 (14)***
* p ≤ .05; ** p ≤ .01; *** p ≤ .001							

Profession before Entering Politics (percentages)

	Monarchs	Tyrants	Vision- aries	Author- itarians	Transi- tionals	Demo- crats	TOTAL N = 377
Business	0	9	0	2	0	8	5
Scientist/ Engineer	0	0	4	7	4	3	3
Government Worker	0	0	0	4	7	7	5
Royalty	97	0	0	2	2	0	10
Skilled Laborer	0	0	0	3	2	1	1
Rancher/Large Farmer	0	0	0	0	9	1	1
Accountant/Banker	0	0	0	2	0	3	2
Spouse/Relative of Ruler	3	9	0	1	0	3	3
Minister/Priest	0	0	8	2	2	1	1
Lawyer	0	9	16	10	20	33	21
Political Journalist	0	0	8	3	9	14	9
Creative Artist	0	0	0	0	2	1	1
Teacher/Professor	0	0	16	2	17	6	6
Soldier/ Revolutionary	0	59	32	52	11	7	20
Physician/Dentist	0	9	0	4	2	2	3
Unskilled Laborer	0	5	12	2	2	3	3
Labor Leader	0	0	4	3	7	5	4
Other	0	0	0	2	4	3	2

Chi Square = 530.7, DF = 85, p < .000

Marital Status							
	Monarchs	Tyrants	Vision-aries	Author-itarians	Transi-tionals	Demo-crats	TOTAL N = 377
Married	100%	95%	96%	92%	96%	95%	95%
Average Age Married (s.d.)	24.4 (7)	28.3 (5)	30.0 (12)	27.7 (7)	28.7 (8)	28.6 (7)	28.2 (7)
Divorced or Separated From 1st Spouse	36%	56%	38%	23%	19%	14%	22%***
Average # of Divorces (s.d.)	.31 (.6)	.50 (.9)	.48 (.7)	.15 (.4)	.32 (1.0)	.08	(.3)***
First Spouse Died	21%	9%	18%	21%	38%	22%	23%

* p ≤ .05; ** p ≤ .01; *** p ≤ .001

Adult Personal Attributes (percentages)							
	Monarchs	Tyrants	Visionar-ies	Authorit-arians	Transi-tionals	Demo-crats	TOTAL N = 377
Antagonism to Authority	19s	59	60	26	28	19	26***
Religious Nonbeliever	0	9	60	28	23	23	23***
Church Attendance							
Regular	94	27	24	50	60	53	54
No Attendance	3	40	72	42	38	36	37
Great Self-Confidence	56	77	92	70	77	58	66**
Creative Activities	38	10	33	21	35	28	28
Even-Tempered/ Moody	29/27	5/59	24/40	31/16	45/23	40/17	35/23***
Exceptional Memory	25	9	24	10	15	24	20
Publish Books or Memoirs	17	18	60	41	40	56	46***
Trusting/ Suspicious	18/27	0/64	4/52	17/20	38/6	47/3	32/16***

(continued on next page)

Adult Personal Attributes (percentages) (continued)							
	Monarchs	Tyrants	Visionar-ies	Authorit-arians	Transi-tionals	Demo-crats	TOTAL N = 377
Administrative Style							
Autocratic	86	100	84	91	43	8	45
Collaborative	3	0	0	1	32	75	40
Conforming/ Nonconforming	70/8	50/25	22/48	58/16	54/21	68/11	61/16**
Outgoing/ Solitary	14/22	41/14	20/36	16/28	36/17	35/18	29/21*
Risks Life Before Rules	17	77	64	52	49	11	32***
Participates in Sports	27	10	13	16	26	28	24
Close/No Close Friends	6/56	5/73	4/68	12/32	38/17	41/16	28/29***
Cautious/ Impulsive	40/17	5/62	12/20	33/6	30/9	56/7	41/12***
Charismatic: Yes/Maybe	11/31	27/18	32/40	10/19	28/23	18/19	18/22*
Gifted Orator: Yes/Maybe	6/14	0/41	28/24	6/20	13/40	14/38	12/32***
Epiphany	22	23	56	15	17	11	17***
Close/Hostile to Mother	22/35	13/38	11/11	18/9	7/4	13/11	14/13*
Close/Hostile to Father	4/64	0/60	0/53	0/11	0/21	5/24	3/29***
Chronic Medical Illness Prior to Ruling	11	29	12	18	13	13	14
Chronic Medical Illness While in Office	40	43	60	42	28	24	33**
* p ≤ .05; ** p ≤ .01; *** p ≤ .001							

CHAPTER 7

Lifetime Rates of Mental Syndromes (percentages)							
	Monarchs	Tyrants	Vision-aries	Author-itarians	Transi-tionals	Demo-crats	TOTAL N = 377
Alcoholism	11	41	8	16	13	15	15*
Pathological Anxiety	19	5	20	3	6	7	8*
Depression (Melancholia)							
Definite	17	0	24	9	15	15	14*
Probable	25	14	24	12	21	18	18
Drug Abuse (or Dependence)	6	23	16	3	4	2	5***
Mania (or "Highs")	11	23	20	4	6	3	7**
Paranoia (or Paranoid Episodes)	11	55	68	10	11	3	13***
Suicide Attempts	0	0	12	3	2	2	3
Assorted Other Disorder	8	14	20	7	6	12	11
Any Psychiatric Syndrome	64	91	76	48	51	49	55**
* $p \leq .05$; ** $p \leq .01$; *** $p \leq .001$							
Average Total # of Psychiatric Syndromes (s.d.)	1.1 (1)	1.7 (1)	2.1 (2)	0.7 (1)	0.8 (1)	0.8 (1)	0.9 (1)***
% with Cognitive Impairment In Office	6	0	20	7	0	3	5**
* $p \leq .05$; ** $p \leq .01$; *** $p \leq .001$							

CHAPTER 8

Percentage of Rulers (N = 377) for Ratings on Political Greatness Scale (PGS) Ratings go from Lowest to Highest (See Description of Ratings for PGS in Appendix)						
	Ratings					
	0	1	2	3	4	5
Something From Nothing	61	13	12	14		
More Than Before	10	78	4	8		
Staying Power in Office	10	17	26	16	11	20
Military Prowess	12	68	10	10		
Social Engineering	70	11	12	7		
Economic Prosperity	23	62	13	2		
Statesmanship	60	8	27	5		
Foster Ideology	81	8	9	2		
Moral Exemplar	16	60	22	2		
Population of Country	8	33	20	13	13	13

CHAPTER 9

Averages (and Standard Deviations)							
	Monarchs	Tyrants	Vision-aries	Author-itarians	Transi-tionals	Demo-crats	TOTAL N = 377
Total PGS Scores	13 (4)	8 (3)	22 (5)	12 (5)	14 (4)	11 (5)	13 (5)***
Words in *Ency. Americana*	358	248	976	308	387	674	536**
Words in *Ency. Britannica*	553	337	1990	501	672	612	669***
* p ≤ .05; ** p ≤ .01; *** p ≤ .001							

Correlations Between Total # Words in Encyclopedia Entries and Total PGS Scores for Rulers			
	Encyclopedia Americana	*Encyclopedia Britannica*	Combined Words of *Americana* and *Britannica*
PGS Total Scores	+.46***	+.64***	+.60***
* p ≤ .05; ** p ≤ .01; *** p ≤ .001			

Professions Prior to Entering Politics for Not-So-Great and Great Rulers (percentages)			
	Lower Third PGS (N = 123)	Upper Third PGS (N = 133)	TOTALS
Business	8	3	5
Scientist/Engineer	0	5	3
Government Worker	5	4	4
Royalty	5	11	9
Skilled Laborer	0	1	0
Rancher/Large Farmer	2	1	1
Accountant/Banker	3	0	2
Spouse or Relative of Prior Ruler	5	1	3
Minister/Priest	2	1	2
Lawyer	23	22	22
Political Journalist	9	12	11
Creative Artist	0	2	1
Teacher/Professor	3	9	6
Soldier/Revolutionary	20	20	20
Physician/Dentist	3	2	2
Unskilled Laborer	4	3	3
Labor Leader	5	2	3
Other	2	2	2
Chi Square = 30.9, DF = 17, $p < .05$			

Percentages of Not-So-Great Rulers and Great Rulers by Geographical Region			
	Lower Third PGS (N = 123)	Upper Third PGS (N = 133)	TOTALS
Latin America/Caribbean	16	7	11
North Africa	0	5	2
Sub-Sahara Africa	6	10	8
Australia/New Zealand	14	1	7
Euro-Africa	3	4	4
Anglo-America	5	13	9
Europe	30	24	27
Eurasia	0	6	3
Balkans	6	5	5
Central Asia	5	10	8
East Asia	6	3	5
Southeast Asia	7	5	6
Middle East	2	7	5
Chi Square = 49.8, DF = 12, $p \leq .000$			

Percentages for Variables Used in Multiple Regression and Logistic Regression Equations Percentages of Not-So-Great and Great Rulers			
	Lower Third PGS (N = 123)	Upper Third PGS (N = 133)	TOTALS
Rebelliousness Against Authority Figures	24	34	29
Exceptional Memory	13	21	17
Published Memoirs or Political Books	38	55	47**
Trusting/Suspicious	38/12	29/19	33/16
Won Medals or Rapid Promotions in Battle	27	39	33*
Policies as Ruler Responsible for Deaths	40	67	54***
Changed Form of Government as Ruler	31	60	46***
Close Friends/No Close Friends	30/27	23/32	26/30
Marital Infidelity	49	65	58*
Political Exile After Serving in Office	22	12	17*
Epiphany	7	28	18***
Assumed Dictatorial Powers at Some Point in Rule	36	52	44**
Personality Cult	15	45	31***
Divorced or Separated in Marriage	15	27	21*
Charismatic	30	53	42***
Cautious/Impulsive	46/15	34/12	39/14*
Fought in Battle Before Becoming Ruler	35	48	42*
Assassination Attempt	30	49	40**
Civil, Regional or International War During Rule	53	41	47*
Agnostic or Atheist (Non-Believer)	15	32	24**
Self-Confidence or Self-Assurance	63	75	69*

(table continued next page)

Percentages for Variables Used in Multiple Regression and Logistic Regression Equations Percentages of Not-So-Great and Great Rulers (continued)			
	Lower Third PGS (N = 123)	Upper Third PGS (N = 133)	TOTALS
Risk-Taking	43	68	56***
Avid Reader	38	44	41
Urban/Rural Background	41/10	43/8	42/9
Even-Tempered/Moody	34/24	32/26	33/25
Gifted Orator	43	47	46
Paranoia	10	20	15*
Depression (Definite plus Probable)	24	42	33**
Any Psychiatric Syndrome	48	56	52
Handicap, Sickly or Serious Illness as Child	16	24	20
Chronic Mental Illness in Office	27	42	35**
Not Attend Church	36	43	37*
Loner as Adult	20	25	21
Leadership as a Youngster @	37	50	44*
Politicized Before Age 21 @	2	14	8**
Hostile Toward Father @	17	27	22
Hostile Toward Mother @	6	12	9*
Exile or Imprisonment Before Came to Power @	25	47	37***
Nonconformity to Many Social Demands @	34	51	44**
* p ≤ .05; ** p ≤ .01; *** p ≤ .001 @ = Added Variables			

Results of Multiple Regression Analysis (33 Independent Variables Entered) *			
Multiple R	.734		
R Square	.539		
Adjusted R Square	.402		
Analysis of Variance			
DF	Sum of Squares	Mean Squares	
Regression	33	3387.57	102.65
Residual	111	2894.26	26.07
F = 3.94	Significance of F = .0000		

* Analysis includes only those subjects on whom complete information was available. No estimates were made for missing values.

Results of Logistic Regression Analysis (34 Independent Variables Entered) *
Classification Table for Prediction of PGS Total Scores

		Predicted		
		Bottom Third	Top Third	% Correct
	Bottom Third	48	10	82.8
	Top Third	8	79	90.8
				Overall 87.6

* Analysis includes only those subjects on whom complete information was available. No estimates were made for missing values.

CHAPTER 10

<table>
<tr><td colspan="8">Percentage of Rulers who Engaged in Civil, Regional, or International War during Reign</td></tr>
<tr><td></td><td>Monarchs</td><td>Tyrants</td><td>Vision-aries</td><td>Author-itarians</td><td>Transi-tionals</td><td>Demo-crats</td><td>TOTAL N = 377</td></tr>
<tr><td>Engaged in War</td><td>81</td><td>86</td><td>76</td><td>62</td><td>57</td><td>33</td><td>52***</td></tr>
<tr><td colspan="8">* p ≤ .05; ** p ≤ .01; *** p ≤ .001</td></tr>
</table>

<table>
<tr><td colspan="4">Percentage of Dictators Versus Democratic Rulers Who Engaged in War</td></tr>
<tr><td></td><td>Dictators</td><td>Democratic Rulers</td><td>Total N = 377</td></tr>
<tr><td>Engaged in War</td><td>74</td><td>37</td><td>52</td></tr>
<tr><td colspan="4">* p ≤ .05; ** p ≤ .01; *** p ≤ .001</td></tr>
</table>

<table>
<tr><td colspan="4">Average Number of Years Ruled (s.d.)</td></tr>
<tr><td></td><td>All Rulers</td><td>Dictators Only</td><td>Democrats/ Transitionals Only</td></tr>
<tr><td>Policies Contribute to Death</td><td>13.6 (11.3)</td><td>16.6 (12.7)</td><td>8.5 (5.9)</td></tr>
<tr><td>Policies Did Not Contribute to Death</td><td>6.4 (6.1)</td><td>11.5 (10.0)</td><td>5.4 (4.6)</td></tr>
<tr><td>TOTALS</td><td>10.1 (9.9)***</td><td>15.7 (12.4)*</td><td>6.4 (5.3)***</td></tr>
<tr><td colspan="4">* p ≤ .05; ** p ≤ .01; *** p ≤ .001</td></tr>
</table>

Average Number of Years Ruled (s.d.)			
	All Rulers	Dictators Only	Democrats/ Transitionals Only
Involved in a Civil or International War	12.4 (11.1)	16.0 (12.7)	7.8 (6.1)
Not Involved in Any War	7.6 (7.7)	14.5 (11.5)	5.6 (4.5)
TOTALS	10.1 (9.9)***	15.5 (12.4)	6.4 (5.3)**
* p ≤ .05; ** p ≤ .01; *** p ≤ .001			

ACKNOWLEDGMENTS

Many people contributed directly and indirectly to this project and the preparation of this book. First and foremost, I want to thank Gregory Guenthner, my former research assistant, who did a superb job organizing the materials, managing the database, and tracking down information. Without Greg's able help, I fear it might have taken me several more years to complete this project. But more than anything, I owe him a special debt of gratitude for his perceptiveness, insightfulness, and humor over the years, which has made working with him a sheer delight.

I also want to single out Harris M. Lentz III for special thanks for his early generosity in providing me with a prepublication list of rulers, which facilitated my work considerably. E.K. Ambrose also was of enormous help in supplying me with a copy of her chronology of world leaders. In addition, I want to note the generosity of the Jane Goodall Institute, George B. Schaller, Frans de Waal, Irwin S. Bernstein, and Robert Kraus for making certain photos available to me without cost.

Because of the enormity and complexity of the information, I have written more drafts of this book than I wish to be known. In the earlier versions of the book, I benefited from the comments and suggestions of David B. Thayer, Robert Straus, and Clyde Taylor, who read portions or the entirety of the manuscript. In addition, some of the fun part of writing and rewriting my book involved my many individual meetings with Michael Nichols and Ernest Yanarella when we discussed the manuscript chapter by chapter and argued over many points. Mike helped me to loosen up on my writing, and Ernie drew my attention to important information and issues I otherwise would have ignored.

My wife, Aline, has been a valued sounding board over the years and a continuing source of support. I also thank her for putting up with me during all those times when I was physically present but my mind was absorbed with the book.

INDEX

\|